D1578975

AMERICAN FOREIGN POLICY IN THE MAKING

AMERICAN
FOREIGN POLICY
IN THE MAKING

ELEANOR LANSING DULLES

THE HOOVER INSTITUTION
STANFORD UNIVERSITY

HARPER & ROW, PUBLISHERS
NEW YORK · EVANSTON · LONDON

AMERICAN FOREIGN POLICY IN THE MAKING

COPYRIGHT © 1968 by Eleanor Lansing Dulles

Printed in the United States of America. All rights reserved. No part of this book may be used or reproduced in any manner whatsoever without written permission except in the case of brief quotations embodied in critical articles and reviews. For information address Harper & Row, Publishers, Incorporated, 49 East 33rd Street, New York, N.Y. 10016.

Library of Congress Catalog Card Number: 68-16208

CONTENTS

PREFACE

THIS ACCOUNT of foreign policy formation is based more on practical experience and personal interviews than it is on theoretical analysis and published sources. It was developed in this manner deliberately because both crisis management and the gradual evolution of programs are frequently abstracted to a point where they bear little relation to reality. This study is intended to shift the emphasis. I hope that it will aid the student in his understanding of the *workings* of the American system—of what actually happens, and why.

While I have worked on this manuscript, my friends have been indulgent and helpful. My associates at the Center for Strategic Studies have assisted me on various occasions. Several of my former colleagues have read and criticized portions of the text. I shall thank them as I can; at this time, however, I think it best not to place on them any burden of responsibility for interpretations or conclusions, since these are basically my own.

• • •

The tasks of foreign policy formation are varied and sometimes mysterious. The responsibilities are heavy. In June, 1958, Secretary of State John Foster Dulles reviewed some of the aspects of the "challenge of change"—outer space, the polar areas, peace efforts,

NATO, international trade, food needs, relations with the Soviet Union, and others. He concluded:

> If, indeed, there is to be a new birth of freedom in the world . . . it will have to be through the efforts of the individuals who . . . make it a dynamic force throughout the world.

Secretary of State Dean Rusk, testifying before a Congressional committee, said in 1963:

> In foreign affairs we are dealing with a world which we can influence, but not control, and it is a world of rapid change. We do business now with more than 112 governments. During the present calendar year, there will have been elections or changes in government in more than 50 of them, including 10 of the 15 NATO countries.

These were the demands five or ten years ago. They are even more exacting now.

The year 1967 has had its quota of important events. Again de Gaulle, holding desperately to his predominate role in France, has obstructed the entrance of Britain into the Common Market. In a herculean effort in Geneva, the negotiators arrived at a constructive solution of long trade negotiations, which promises great things for the expansion of international trade. Some progress toward accelerating development in Latin American countries was made at Punta del Este in April of 1967. In many parts of the world, the fight for freedom, and against tyranny, continued.

The unsung heroes of foreign policy continue the struggle to promote the aims of cooperation and conciliation. Whatever the criticism of policy-makers and operating programs in foreign affairs, an awareness of the enormous complexity of the task can help the serious student to gain an understanding of the awesome responsibilities of developing foreign policy. The drama of international relations has continuing fascination—it can arouse our fears as well as our hopes. Only a brief survey and a selective sampling of these many problems can be presented here, a survey prepared in the interests of urging a greater comprehension of foreign policy among a larger number of people. The unending work goes on.

ELEANOR LANSING DULLES

November, 1967

AMERICAN FOREIGN POLICY IN THE MAKING

I

FOREIGN POLICY IN
THE MAKING

PUBLIC INTEREST IN FOREIGN POLICY

A deeply concerned public and a host of inquiring students urgently ask today whether our institutions or our leaders in the conduct of foreign relations are adequate to carry the burdens now being placed upon them. It is natural that so many people should have a growing interest in the conduct of foreign relations, for both the opportunities for cooperation and the dangers of discord among the nations of the world have increased enormously over the past 20 years.

Our involvement in the affairs of other countries is the inevitable result of the demands placed upon us as a major economic and military power. As such a power, we tax our resources heavily by the extension of our involvement in the affairs of other nations. While some men hold a mystical belief that "right will triumph" with experience, others look with a more critical eye on past mistakes and wonder what can be done to assure us of foreign policies that will give us and the other nations of the world greater security. What seems to be called for is a close scrutiny of our foreign policy organizations, personnel, aims, and capabilities. An increasing understanding of the apparatus of the making of foreign policy and a review of a few recent representative cases should throw light on the process of our policy formation. We may then be able to see more clearly the problems we must cope with in order to fulfill our many objectives in the conduct of foreign policy.

THE DILEMMA OF POLICY FORMATION

Over the years from August 6, 1945, to the present, there have been crises when the nuclear weapons of this country or of a hostile power might have been used. In 1948 and 1949, in view of our commitments in Europe, we had neither the strength nor, it now seems, the foresight to prevent a communist take-over in China. At the time of the Korean invasion our armed forces were woefully inadequate. At the time of the Guatemalan subversion, our early information was not evaluated in a clear manner. In various cases—Berlin, Suez, Cuba, the Congo, Vietnam, and the Dominican Republic—our policy has resulted in a mixture of success and failure. Never in the past have such events been so closely related to the question of our ultimate survival. In such situations, the major weakness of the United States is not a matter of materiel, but of judgment as to when and how to use the enormous resources and capabilities at our command. This judgment is compounded of personal and individual, as well as institutional, insight, which is responsive in some measure to the articulated public will.

As the machinery of diplomacy increases in size and efficiency, the character and foresight of the men who direct these enormous resources are called on to meet new demands. The vast flow of information from more than 130 nations and territories* brings new problems which, in the modern state of technology and communication, call for almost instantaneous decision. Men have become not less, but more, important. This is true not only of men "at the top" in Washington, but also of the American policy-makers in more than 296 posts abroad—embassies and consulates and special missions. It is evidenced by the decisions made in a score of the more important international organizations. It is understood by the principal collec-

---

*Mozambique, Angola, Hong Kong, and other areas and special missions have to be taken into account.

tive security arrangements that are part of our new responsibilities for maintaining the peace.† At every critical position in the apparatus there are men who evaluate information, officers who recommend a certain course of action to the President and the Secretary of State. Advance planning can be outlined, but it is seldom adequate to meet the precise contingencies that occur.

Why, then, is it sometimes said that we have no policy? The criticism and the allegation arise because in some cases particular actions are not to the liking of the critic. It is an expression of frustration on the part of those who know of our resources but who do not understand the conditions under which they have to be withheld or used. Some critics know the way in which our principles limit as well as facilitate our behavior. Clearly, it is not easy for the general observer to appreciate the manner in which a policy position taken in one part of the world affects our standing in every other part. Global interaction and the willingness of others to use violence and subversion to multiply our difficulties make the formation of balanced policies difficult. The call for "a policy" is usually a demand for a change in what some consider to be incomplete or inept policy.

Our national aims and objectives should be considered at the beginning of any study of foreign policy. These are the recognized expressions of our values: the preservation of the nation, the belief in peaceful change and the rule of law, the effort to assist in the development of weaker nations, the striving for new forms of economic cooperation, the belief in the freedom and rights of individual men; these five tenets are fundamental to our foreign policy. Those at the heart of the process insist that we have an enduring, well-articulated, and well-understood foreign policy. Their articulation of our policy plans refers to every region of the world, to treaties, alliances, and a host of functional responsibilities, as well as to hopes for the future. The making of these plans is the major work of the Depart-

---

†The major alliances, with approximately 42 international commitments, are the North Atlantic Treaty Organization (NATO), Inter-American Treaty of Reciprocal Assistance (Rio Pact), Australia-New Zealand-United States Treaty (ANZUS), Philippine Treaty, Japanese Treaty, Republic of Korea Treaty, Republic of China (Formosa) Treaty, Central Treaty Organization (CENTO), and the Southeast Asia Treaty Organization (SEATO).

ment of State. It is the main preoccupation of the Secretary of State, who must advise the President.

There are many levels of policy formation. The word is used to refer not only to basic *principles* and comprehensive *programs*, but to *contingency plans* and *position papers* and specific *decisions* as well. Many aspects of the process of policy formation are visible and familiar, others hidden from view. This is not caused by secrecy or the suppression of facts, but by the part that instinct and qualities of the characters of statesmen play in the resolution of policy problems.

Policy that is outlined for the future has to be based on a limited number of assumptions as to the ability and intentions of other nations. It is precisely because the average person cannot adequately anticipate the clash of objectives and the changing aims of other governments that he often underestimates the problem. The expert or the professional is closer to the sources of information about political shifts and new local conditions. He knows that it is the continuing conflict of interest and the attacks on our position from outside that thwart our action and at times paralyze us in spite of our resources. The diplomat usually cannot reveal publicly the extent to which a change in attitude in a foreign capital or an increase of aggressive intent in an unfriendly nation makes him throw away one plan and reshape a new one. So we look not only to the aims and principles but also to the methods and mechanisms of policy formation in seeking answers to our questions about how the system operates.

The analysis here is focused on the roles of the President, the Secretary of State, the Department of State and the Ambassador, and on the outer limits to action set by Congress, the press, and the United Nations. In reviewing the allocation of responsibilities and the operations of these mechanisms and institutions, in Chapter I of this volume, emphasis is more on method than on substance. In Chapter II, in contrast, the changing nature of foreign affairs and the evolution of values and objectives over time, as they bear on many nations, are placed in a running narrative to give an idea of how we have exerted our influence and used our resources abroad.

Chapter III, taking up the same theme, endeavors to carry further a review of the decisions made and actions taken in six selected cases. The study of these crises manifests in varying degrees the "narrowing triangle of choice."* It is clear that many aspects of policy toward a country are, in an emergency, disregarded and that the options placed before the Secretary and the President become few and sharply focused. The President usually faces one major recommendation on which he can act swiftly. Policy is subsequently reviewed and sometimes reshaped.

The approach to policy is influenced by the conclusion that, now more than in previous decades, the timing of action is more important than the number of weapons or the wealth of economic resources used to carry out that action. This may influence a verdict on Vietnam, as the decisions of 1954 are reviewed. In an era when the concept of limited war is widely accepted, with its shading into the communist "wars of liberation," announced in such a way as to confuse and weaken the will to resist, the crucial importance of the man and his choice are obvious. The recognition of opportunities to act and the strength of determination by national leaders in acting can mean the difference between disaster and survival. Thus, a threefold approach to the understanding of foreign affairs (the analysis of the levels of policy formation, the offices and operations necessary to its implementation, and the timing of its implementation) can help in the search for answers to the current dilemma.

Clearly, it is almost impossible to write a completely neutral or inclusive treatment; some inadvertent bias or misinterpretation is probably inevitable. Furthermore, the process of making foreign policy cannot be explained without considering the various meanings of the term as they emerge differently in different contexts; policy seems different to those with different parts to play. Nevertheless, the continuity of the meaning is, in historical development, reasonably clear. In a concert, if one can use the analogy here, the

---

*The concept of the narrowing triangle of choice can be illustrated by the following diagram:
(1) Before emergency or crisis—several normal programs and policies
      (2) After event or crisis—some programs de-emphasized
         (3) Selected options or choices

```
o
o    o
o    o    o
o    o    o    o>  (4) Decision to act
o    o    o
o    o
o
```

orchestra leader is spectacular, but the performance of the individual musician is not without significance. Within the practical limits of the exposition, each will have his place in the account given here.

THE POWER OF THE PRESIDENT

The President, with his extraordinary powers, "makes" foreign policy. Even though he may seem to delegate much of his authority, in fact, he alone makes those crucial policy decisions that may change the course of history. As elected leader of the people, as Commander-in-Chief of the armed forces, and as head of the executive departments, he has a responsibility that he cannot shift. Advisers, experts, and legislators in this country and from abroad bring to the President problems for which he must seek solutions. This is a responsibility without parallel in the leadership of other nations.

On taking office he finds *an overall policy* that governs our foreign relations. If he intends to modify, extend, and improve it, he usually discovers that the possibility of changing it is limited in scope. For the most part, he carries on existing programs. He thus inherits a continuity in foreign policy which he may, at times, consider unfruitful.

Though continuity in policy should properly be stressed, because it is frequently underestimated and its intent misunderstood, it is the differences in the *articulation* of such consistent policies that reveal the most significant elements in the President's conduct of foreign affairs. In 1910, Woodrow Wilson said in an address at Columbia University, "The President is at liberty both in law and conscience, to be as big a man as he can. . . . His office is anything he has sagacity and force to make it. . . . His capacity will set the limit."[1] This statement, valid then, is equally true today. The President is faced with difficulties in the use of his power, but these are not in any significant degree because of the system or the organization which are his to mold and to perfect during his tenure in the Presidency. Thus, the nature of the man determines the extent of his accomplishment in foreign as well as domestic affairs.

If history is the "biography of great men,"[2] the history of the United States has been to an extraordinary extent the story of our Presidents. The power they command, the four- to eight-year tenure,* and the control over the executive branch in performing manifold functions and expending billions of dollars—as well as the traditional prestige of the office—place them in a unique position in the world. Even the dictators of a police state are more subject to sudden loss of power, in comparison with our Presidents—as the deposition of Premier Khrushchev in 1964 illustrated in a dramatic fashion.

There are those who take the philosophic position that men are shaped by events. It is true that circumstances limit the power even of a President. But insofar as any human being has free will, the President, in his determination to exercise restraint or to command a show of force, is exerting his will within a wide area. He cannot unleash the forces of the nation except to protect our vital interest, but his appreciation of where and when the vital interests are at stake is crucial for our survival. In the use of his authority he must weld together all the main issues and programs of our domestic life, as well. The interaction of these responsibilities both enhances and limits his role in foreign affairs. These many facets of decision-making add so largely to his burdens that the effectiveness of the apparatus under him, and the ability of the Secretary of State in particular, is of great importance to him. The President requires, and usually has, a smoothly functioning mechanism. He commands men selected for their ability to help him. He looks forward to the use of all the resources of the nation to attain his goals.

In dealing with the Cabinet, more than in other relations, Presidents have expressed their special ways of performing their jobs. There has been an increasing tendency to look outside the State Department for guidance and to rely less on the joint action of the heads of the executive departments. There are now more members in the Cabinet than at any other time. There are, as well, many issues of foreign policy that do not lie within the competence of all of them. Consequently, there is a preference, perhaps, for using smaller groups in the discussion of policy problems. President Kennedy went further than others in dealing with many policy issues with a few White House advisers, rather than with those officers in the State Department who normally acted in these matters. (He had,

---

*Franklin D. Roosevelt was elected to four terms before the Constitutional amendment limiting service to two terms.

as has President Johnson, an average of only one Cabinet meeting a month.)

The National Security Council, composed of the President, the Vice-President, the Secretary of State, the Secretary of Defense, the Director of Civil and Defense Mobilization, and the Director of the Office of Emergency Planning, has served some of the essential functions in advising the President.[3] This organization, established in 1947, is on a level with the Central Intelligence Agency, the Director of which, by invitation though not by legal requirement, usually attends NSC meetings. For a time, this new instrument was of great importance in bringing before the President a balanced and coordinated view of most problems affecting our security; in recent years, the NSC has been used with less frequency. President Kennedy abolished the Operations Coordination Board, an interagency body that prepared material for the National Security Council, because he thought it slowed down the flow of information and recommendations. A schedule of the several days required for the preparation, circulation, consideration, and approval of policy papers for the OCB tends to bear out his view. On some occasions, even months were consumed in this process; meanwhile, the situation under discussion had changed substantially.

Some experts, including Professor H. Field Haviland, Jr., and his associates at the Brookings Institution, hold that the task of unifying the policy and operations for which the President is responsible would be more effectively handled if there were a new "senior secretary" (see page 15); others with considerable experience conclude, however, that such a change is not necessary. Provision for this new "layer" of authority and policy-making would call for a considerable staff and introduce new problems of coordination. Moreover, jurisdictional disputes at such a high level would present the President, as final arbiter, with a whole new set of difficulties.

Although some phases of diplomacy are not dependent on large financial support, the importance of public funds cannot be ignored. The process of developing the balance sheet, which calls for careful analysis of programs and proposals, tends to keep theory and planning within acceptable limits.

Clearly, the President knows that important, comprehensive, detailed studies and analyses of foreign affairs are conducted in the State Department, but he must choose his own pace and timing in using this work and in arriving at conclusions. The system must be more flexible and responsive than the bureaucrat always finds comfortable. The volume of information, the multitude of studies, the number of experts and advisers who are available to the President, day and night, is enormous. His skill in using these resources spells success or failure in foreign policy for the President.*

THE IMPOSSIBLE JOB OF SECRETARY OF STATE

The Secretary of State, as he approaches the first days in his office, hopes to be able to avoid distracting details and concentrate on the main tasks of advising the President and shaping foreign policy. He recognizes that, as the government's leader in foreign affairs and as the coordinator of programs in this field, he also has adminstrative responsibilities; but he hopes that most of these can be delegated to a competent staff with clearly defined functions within the organization of the State Department. He is bound to be somewhat disappointed as he struggles with the difficulties of having brought to his attention what often seem to be minor problems, but problems which may bring major dangers. Thus the communist delay of a military vehicle in the Berlin Corridor, the injudicious statement of an American tourist in Paris, or the actions of high school students in Panama can increase international tensions and bring about critical reactions in a dozen capitals, all of which demand his immediate attention.

He has usually established close working relations with the President even before starting on his new job. In many instances he has not worked with the Washington bureaucracy or become familiar with the intricacies of the Department of State and the Foreign Service. Dean Acheson, Dean Rusk, and Robert Lansing were among the exceptions to this generalization, since they had held responsible positions in the Department. Cordell Hull, as a former Senator, had well-established relations with Congress. In general, however, the Secretary has had little familiarity with the apparatus which is the

---

*The U. S. Senate Committee on Government (John L. McClellan of Arkansas, chairman) has issued reports on the organization of the government, including detailed material on the Executive agencies that deal with foreign relations.

main tool at his disposal. The complexity of his task comes, therefore, as something of a shock. He wishes he could limit the scope of
his functions and devote his time to major policy.

It is natural that, as a man familiar with the main problems the
nation faces, he should seek first those ideas and programs that
would lead us to higher ground—where security, welfare, and the
fulfillment of national ideals could bring new hope and confidence
to the nation. These goals are difficult to attain when considerations
relating to scores of nations and the numerous demands of their
economic, psychological, and political conflicts claim his attention.

The Nature of the Job.   The Secretary's day begins with the summary of events of the past 12 hours. From Moscow to London, from
Delhi to Lisbon, politicians have been at work for several hours.
Unrest, which has brought trouble during the night, may threaten
many of his plans. As Dean Rusk said in testimony before a House
Foreign Affairs Committee, "The world is round. Only one-third
are asleep at any one moment, and the other two-thirds are awakened, somewhere or other, up to some mischief."[4]

All such matters of gravity are brought to the Secretary's attention
as he comes to his desk at 8:15—earlier, if need be—and may inter-
rupt his conferences throughout the day; hence, the schedule of the
Secretary varies from day to day with specific emergencies. First,
there is the intelligence summary, already mentioned, presented by
the Director of Intelligence and Research or his deputy. This is prepared between the hours of three and seven in the morning. It is
usually followed by the Secretary's staff meeting at 9:15; this is a
quick survey of the specific responsibility of each Assistant Secretary
(or his deputy), as well as comments from the Officers in Charge of
Congressional Relations, Cultural Affairs, Economic Affairs, Policy
Planning, and Administrative Affairs, and remarks from the Counselor and the Under Secretary. At times, this part of the meeting is
condensed to give way to a conference on immediate matters of
great urgency. The aides and secretaries then remake the schedule
for the rest of the day, adding consultations with the President, the
appropriate Cabinet officers and experts, as required, and taking
account also of meetings with Ambassadors, Congressional leaders
and the press, as these become necessary.

Thus, before 10 o'clock in the morning, the Secretary is made
aware, each day, of the difficulty of standing aloof from a particular

situation, the impossibility of sticking to his proposed plan of work, the many calls on his energy.

John Foster Dulles, who came to the job in 1953 after considerable exposure to the affairs of the Department, in 1949 and earlier, as special adviser to President Truman, looked apprehensively over the mountain of briefing books and "position" and "background" papers before he went to Paris for the Meeting of the Council of Foreign Ministers. He had for some time been aware of the growing complexity of the issues facing the Secretary. In fact, he seriously questioned—understandably—whether he might not have more time for thought and more influence on policy if he did not accept President Eisenhower's offer of the Secretaryship.

In a memorandum written in late November, 1952, before he took office, he listed most of the functions and activities of the office. These ranged, he said, "from the solemn and ceremonial to the bureaucratic." Of those on his list, he said that "making policies . . . is what I am primarily interested in."[5]

What Dulles called the "more important duties of Secretary of State" included, as he described them:

1. Protocol. Meeting on arrival and departure foreign Chiefs of State and Foreign Ministers visiting Washington.
2. Receiving Ambassadors of foreign countries and hearing their statements regarding matters affecting the two countries.
3. Attending international conferences in connection with UN, NATO, Pacific security, etc., and visiting foreign countries.
4. Selection of top-level personnel in the Department and abroad in foreign missions.
5. Relations with Congress, receiving Congressmen and testifying before the several Senate and House committees.
6. Preparation and delivery of public addresses for self, and for the President if dealing with foreign affairs.
7. Press conferences and meetings with press-radio commentators and like relations.
8. Consultation with top-level associates, as necessary to maintain Department morale, and seeing U.S. diplomats back on leave or for consultation.
9. Dinners, receptions, and social functions of diplomatic corps and as given by the U.S.
10. Settlement of policies and controversies with independent and

coordinate agencies such as Defense, Mutual Security Agency, Treasury, Commerce, Ex-Im Bank, Board of Psychological Strategy, Voice of America, Central Intelligence Agency, etc.

11. Approval (initialling) of important outgoing cables and reading important incoming cables and memos of conversations with important personages.
12. Handling the percentage of correspondence that requires personal attention.
13. Seeing important private persons who demand and are entitled to see a top official.
14. Attendance at Cabinet meetings and general White House talks, briefing and consulting with the President.
15. Dealing with current crises around the globe and calling for immediate reactions.
16. Making long-range policies.

The memorandum written before Dulles took office would probably have been substantially different if it had been drafted a year later. By the end of 1953 he had a different view, a change characteristic of most incoming high officials in Washington. He saw the extent to which the current emergency dominates the long-range plan. Inevitably, he, as others, became interested in the day-to-day decisions. A variety of military, economic, cultural, and political activities offers opportunities which in the short run limit progress toward longer range objectives. However, a detailed knowledge of specific issues is essential to the leadership and the coordination which the Secretary is called on to exercise. It becomes increasingly evident that conversations with Ambassadors, ours and those from other countries, and participation in conferences dealing with urgent matters of state are essential to his understanding. Moreover, addresses to audiences throughout the United States help to keep his thinking in tune with that of the nation and bring the moral force of leadership to bear on the general public.

Since minor matters might precipitate war, they cannot be delegated. The decision on priorities is crucial. The choice rests with the Secretary, who is aided by those who understand his point of view and manner of operating. This general situation prevails whether or not the organization chart is changed. In fact, there have been few rearrangements in the past 25 or 30 years that have substantially altered basic methods of operation. The Psychological Strategy Board is gone from the White House, as is the Operations Coordination Board. The White House staff has, however, taken on new functions —it is informed immediately of intelligence coming in from many sources.

There have been changes in the Department of State, many of them minor. Major ones have been expansions to take account of the relations with new nations and the growing importance of economic, military, and nuclear developments. The most important structural and procedural developments have been those initiated in 1947 when the National Security Council was established and the Central Intelligence Agency was asked to take over the work of the former Office of Strategic Services, with new and enlarged responsibilities. These made somewhat more definite the lines of authority among the White House, the Department of State, and the other agencies mainly concerned with cold war strategy.

No institutional modification or expansion could lessen the importance of close personal relations and sympathetic understanding between the Secretary and the President. The ultimate decision of the Chief of State, based as it is on the recommendations of his primary adviser, has to be molded by frequent consultations. These, whether they are formal or informal, are based on deep personal respect and confidence. If this is lacking, no substitute can be found. Members of the White House staff, competent, often brilliant, are not closely in touch with the many programs, problems, decisions, and agreements that make the web of international relations so comprehensive and so closely interwoven. To attempt by isolated decisions and proposals to initiate new lines of action can be extremely dangerous. Only those who are close to the existing commitments can say what will be constructive and judge whether innovation is a safe undertaking.

It is because of the organic nature of the nation's policy that the incoming Secretary, after a critical examination of what has gone before, makes fewer changes than may have been forecast. In many areas he is compelled to continue much as before. In some he can strive for improvement. In rare cases, he can reverse the direction in which we have been going and set new guidelines. It is not lack of imagination or absence of courage that dictates this situation. It is the delicate balance of forces, the impact of influences in one capital or another, and the weight of our authority that makes its use for change likely to cause miscalculation of our intent. This fact can lead to a sense of bafflement that would reduce an indecisive man to inaction. It is one of the several factors that make the Secretary's close collaboration with the President of prime significance.

If there were a job description for the Secretary of State, it would include some seven main headings, each of which would carry enough responsibility to occupy a man of extraordinary ability full time. Yet these different responsibilities must be combined and borne by one man, with the help of a competent staff, a well-ordered institution, and the support of other high-level government officers.

The separate headings would include:

1. Advising the President.
2. Formulating policy and modifying existing policy.
3. Coordinating the foreign affairs activities of the dozen and more departments and agencies with interests and responsibilities abroad.
4. Administering the Department of State.
5. As leader in the field, explaining and interpreting foreign policy to the American people.
6. As senior diplomat, representing the President in conferences and on ceremonial occasions.
7. Negotiating with other governments to improve understanding and to gain advantages for the United States.

All of these functions add up to the major responsibility of furthering the basic aims and safeguarding the vital interests of the nation. They sound more formal and take on a more classical symmetry if set forth in this fashion, but they correspond to the 16 points from Foster Dulles' memo that have been listed. No Secretary can completely delegate the major part of any one of them. Although he may anticipate selecting from among them, in fact, he is concerned with all.

Thus, it becomes apparent to each new incumbent that advising the President on both modifications and extensions of foreign policy, in general and in specific instances, requires work in the Department, with Ambassadors, with Congress, and with others, which he can only partially leave to his assistants.

A man who achieves the high position of Secretary of State— sometimes referred to as the most important job in the world— usually has an instinct for leadership and learns what elements in the institutions at his disposal help him in his conduct of foreign affairs. What he knows, and what the observer sometimes forgets, is that personal convictions and skill in diplomacy are the major tools of foreign policy. The ability to perceive when the antagonist may yield cannot be described in bureaucratic manuals, but it can come from experience and has been rooted in the character of the man.

It is because of a fear that the more subtle talents of the Secretary may be blunted by the multiplicity of his duties that some have urged that there be a "super Secretary." The Brookings Institution study, *The Formulation and Administration of United States Foreign Policy*, written for the Senate Committee on Foreign Relations in 1960, recommended a "new senior secretary."[6] This would be a "stronger Cabinet position for unified direction of the mainstream of foreign policy and operations." He would establish his own staff arrangements. He should be made Vice Chairman of the National Security Council to assure more effective direction of other departments, particularly the Department of Defense.

This suggestion, raised from time to time, has considerable appeal for those who know the "impossible job" of the Secretary; nevertheless, it was not supported by the experts conferring at the American Assembly at Arden House in 1960, nor by those who testified before the Jackson Subcommittee on National Security and Operations in 1964. The Secretary is now first in the Cabinet, does not need additional prestige, and would lose more than he could gain from being isolated from daily problems that might momentarily become crises. Dean Acheson has stated this objection to the suggestion, and in testimony stressed the importance of mutual confidence between the President and the Secretary as the key to the Secretary's effectiveness.

Thus the dilemma cannot be easily resolved. The burden of business is enormous, with approximately 24,000 persons on the Department rolls, 7000 or so of them in Washington—with the closely integrated Agency for International Development (AID) and the United States Information Agency (USIA)—with approximately 300 posts abroad and a cable traffic of 1500 messages in and the same number out on a typical day.[7] If contacts, direct and indirect, with all significant parts of this apparatus are important, then there is no foreseeable solution to such difficulties and no present prospect for lightening the Secretary's load.

Administrative Functions. Administration can, to a considerable extent, be delegated. The patterns of selection of personnel, assignment, budget, buildings, and the housekeeping functions of the Department have been well established and have changed only slowly over the years. The expansion of the staff, suggested in a special study under Henry M. Wriston, led to the inclusion of a large number of additional persons in the Foreign Service Officers Corps by special induction—lateral entry—and was so shattering to the "old school" tradition that the Secretary of State, in 1953, had to devote considerable time to the personnel proposals made then. Similarly, the attacks of Senator Joseph McCarthy on State Department officers necessitated a large expenditure of time by Secretary Acheson, and subsequently by Secretary Dulles, in seeking to defend the innocent from harassment. The increase in the volume of work after 1945, the expansion of space as personnel increased, the greater need for travel, the development of the material requirements for representation at the United Nations—all put strain on the system, but all were handled in due course.

There are some who think that a more aggressive financial effort to increase the Department's budget could perhaps have been pressed under the leadership of the various Secretaries in postwar years and that this would have led to a quicker modernization of communication and equipment in the Department. The Secretary is rarely an administrator, by temperament or experience, and is dominated by an intense desire to devote his capabilities to the other phases of his work. Fortunately, his door is open to the Under Secretary for Administrative Affairs, and a good working relation has usually prevailed, so that there is no dissonance in connection with such essential functions.

The appointment of Ambassadors and other high officials in the Department is, however, a matter in which the Secretary plays a part. The President and his staff are active in making the appointments of noncareer men, and some of these are, inevitably, political appointments. There are a number who, though recognized as having played a role in the election campaigns, are of a caliber and experience that fit them for the job, irrespective of political contributions. Though there is a tendency to assume that the competence of the noncareer men is lower than that of the lifelong diplomat, there are cases of remarkable ability which had refreshed the Service in a number of instances. The Secretary tries to see that there is no case in which the desire to pay off old debts leads to the assignment of a weak or uninformed person to a sensitive and difficult post. This is a part of administration which he cannot overlook.

The Secretary also has to lend his prestige and authority to the budget presentation, though he does not participate in many of these hearings. There are times when the lack of Departmental funds is a serious handicap to efficiency. Frequently, it has been a factor in delaying personnel transfers. It also discourages men of other professions from serving in the more poorly paid diplomatic jobs.

Representative Functions. The representation functions, which seem to consume an unwarranted amount of time, can in fact serve a dual purpose. Not only does the Secretary carry with him the full prestige of his office in casual conversation, but he also stands in a unique position to sound out opinions and convey the ideas of the President in a manner that is sometimes opportune for informal conversation. In the meeting that may take place at a state wedding or funeral, he can speak without a large company of aides. There is no need to include the many people who would have to be invited to a formal conference. Even a casual word at an airport, or before a dinner, may have meaning far beyond the occasion at which it is spoken. There are other instances when expenditure of time, energy, and physical resources are way out of proportion to the demands of protocol and the meaning of the event, but the sensitivity of the persons involved has to be carefully watched to avoid strained feelings—by the failure to take full account of rank and tradition. New efforts to have the Vice President take over some of these duties have already helped to relieve the pressure to some degree.

Official attendance at conferences has special requirements, and when the meeting needs to be at a high level, the Secretary cannot avoid the burden of participation. The conduct of international conferences can be crucial to security. Skill in this field comes only with experience, and the adroitness the Secretary shows in this function may be his most important contribution to the welfare of the nation. Here he can make offers and enter into commitments which, while they do not bind the President, are sufficiently authoritative to mold and modify policy on major issues. The help of those who work with him, the preparation of the Department and the embassies, the trust and instructions of the President all go into the diplomacy of the Secretary. The use of the total resources at his disposal requires an acute sense of what his antagonist is prepared to give and of where the lines of stiff resistance require diversion, surprise, or bold attack.

The negotiations, in spite of all the support that must be at hand, are essentially dependent on the leading personality, and this, in most cases, is the Secretary, speaking for the President. There can be no separation of this primary task from the myriad of minor plans, decisions, information briefings, conferences with knowledgeable individuals, and hours of analysis. It is because this part of the making of foreign policy is so intricate and so momentous that the extraordinary calls on the time and consideration of the Secretary, day by day and hour by hour, cannot be reduced. It is for this reason that the Secretary must seek out those who have ideas and information, whatever their rank, looking for proposals that add depth to his own assessment and to his developing decision.

Since the Secretary has these leading roles to perform, no one can take his place as spokesman in interpreting the intention and the meaning of foreign policy. He can send assistants to speak for him, and often their statements are impressive. If, however, it is necessary to make a pronouncement that will be heard in Moscow and Peking, that will echo from Europe to Asia and carry a challenge, a warning, or an assurance around the world, it must be made by the Secretary or by the President. Every man who holds this office comes to realize this fact and welcomes the opportunity to set the record straight. He knows that one of his major tasks is to lessen the danger of miscalculation.

The speeches which unfold new doctrines and which reemphasize fundamental principles are an important adjunct of policy. They make clear those parts of our strategy which we want known; they do not have to reveal facts that would give aid and comfort to those who oppose us. Television and radio make the official messages more effective now than they were formerly. In preparation for such speeches, the State Department frequently reviews the foreign policy aspects of Presidential statements, and the speeches of the Secretary are usually cleared by the White House at the highest level.

Coordinative Functions. Coordinating foreign operations as they concern the agencies of government outside the Department is a main responsibility of the Secretary. Only he, with the full

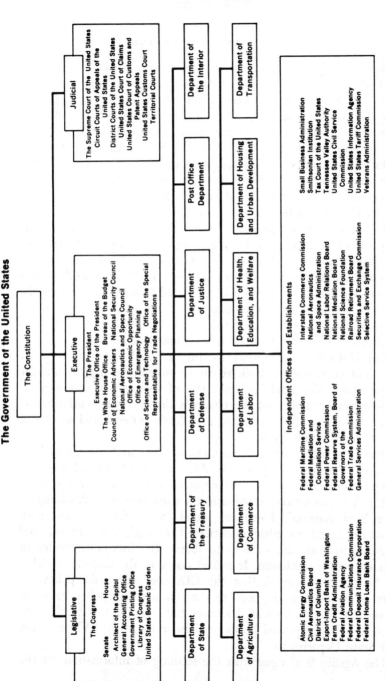

Organization of the Government of the United States (adapted from *United States Government Organization Manual, 1965–1966*). *Note:* All but a few of the departments and independent offices perform functions that involve, to a greater or lesser degree, foreign-policy considerations.

authority of the President, can assure government-wide cooperation. Conflicts are frequent, though some are of minor importance. The views held in Commerce, Defense, Agriculture, the Treasury, Justice, and the Atomic Energy Commission do not always coincide, but they differ mainly on short-range issues. Ambassador David K. E. Bruce, who served for a time as Under Secretary, said before the Jackson subcommittee, "The problem of interagency agreement is to my mind the most difficult of all to resolve."[8] In this area, as in other important matters, the stature of the men is likely to be the crucial element, rather than organizational arrangements.

The process of coordination goes on at all levels of activity. The desk officer is responsible for seeing that he is in touch with his opposite number in other agencies. The Assistant Secretary for the area and all personnel in between confer with those who deal with similar problems. No vacuum is permitted to develop between the agencies mentioned and the dozen others, such as the Tariff Commission, the Public Health Service, the Federal Aviation Agency, or even the departments of state governments.

The USIA and the Agency for International Development have in recent years been assimilated to a considerable degree into the Department. The tradition and habit of separateness is not likely to disappear entirely, but the channels through which information flows and plans are transmitted are clearly ordered and work efficiently for the most part.

Relations between the Department of State and the Central Intelligence Agency attract considerable interest. Occasional instances of operations in the field, not completely consistent with the views of the Ambassador concerned, and even differences in Washington, have been rumored. These are found to be, for the most part, criticisms based on little evidence. The legal, institutional, and operating realities are such as to reduce the inevitable shades of difference to a minimum. It is laid down in the division of labor in the executive branch that the CIA does not make policy. In spite of frequent assumptions to the contrary, the policy bases for action in Guatemala, Cuba, Vietnam, the Dominican Republic, and elsewhere were approved by the highest levels in the White House and State Department.

The Agency is charged with the securing of information for the

President and the Department. It is organizationally level with the National Security Council and is thus immediately under the President, who delegates a measure of his responsibility to the Secretary of State. "It is an established rule that the Agency should keep out of policy matters. . . ." "It is the gatherer and evaluator of world-wide facts for the National Security Council,"[9] wrote a former Director of the CIA. While every agency and every individual of outstanding capacity affect policy, there is no question as to where the responsibility for framing policy lies, and there has been no trouble among the leaders—only a mirage developing from the awareness of secret aspects of the activities of this Agency that confuses discussion. State-CIA relations may worry the public, but the Secretary of State has not been led to favor changes in methods of operation. He has relied on the coordination of the CIA and his own Department through the interagency Board of Estimates and other joint committees. The Board passes on all major intelligence documents and "estimates of the situation." At various stages of handling information and developing the story which is the background of decisions there is a fully articulated, working mechanism, so that the thinking and style of operation are similar.

From time to time, genuine differences of opinion within the executive branch do arise, and the manner of their resolution varies under different administrations. The methods of Franklin D. Roosevelt, of Harry S. Truman, of Dwight D. Eisenhower, of John F. Kennedy, and of Lyndon B. Johnson have been notably different. The extent to which the President takes over a problem of critical importance, or even lesser matters, affects the relations of the Secretary with the heads of other agencies. Truman and, to an even greater degree, Eisenhower leaned heavily on their Secretaries of State, and the result was a leadership that could not be challenged in Washington. Coordination of foreign policy in the last few years has depended to a considerable extent on the White House staff, lessening the importance of the Secretary of State to some degree. Nevertheless, in day-to-day work, as well as in times of special emergency, the system, the men, and the ideas generated in the Department continue to pull together the various elements of the executive branch and thus maintain the primacy of those who have the legal and traditional responsibility for policy.

PREREQUISITES OF POLICY FORMATION

This brief review of the secondary functions of the Secretary—the administration of the Department, representation, negotiation, explanation of policy, and coordination—indicates that they are all aspects of the two indivisible and major functions of the office: formulating policy and advising the President. Even when they can be delegated, one man still exerts an influence that is of enormous and continuing weight. He cannot shift the main burden to other shoulders. Though institutional inadequacy does at times increase the "foulup" factor, even organizational reforms cannot eliminate the requirement for the full use of the Secretary's power.

When Secretary Rusk appeared before the Jackson Subcommittee on December 11, 1963, he gave a comprehensive picture of the problems he faced. In speaking of organization, he stated that there should be constant striving for improvement, but added that "we would be deluding ourselves if we expected from such efforts miraculous differences in our relations with the rest of the world."[10] In explaining the difficulty of controlling affairs in a world of constant change, he said, "We do business now with more than 112 governments. During the present calendar year, there will have been elections or changes in government in more than 50 of them, including 10 of the 15 NATO countries." Five years earlier, when Foster Dulles was Secretary, the number of nations with which we had dealings of a significant nature was 60. The number has increased even in the four years since Rusk's testimony.

The elementary problem of organization, as Rusk outlined it, is to find men of the highest quality. He emphasized in particular the importance of the Assistant Secretaries and of the desk officers to the Secretary. The roles of the Under Secretary as to some extent his alter ego, of the Under Secretary for Political Affairs, and of the two Deputy Under Secretaries are obviously of great importance. He laid special stress on the man in charge of a particular country, usually called a desk officer: "He is the man who has the opportunity to brood 24 hours a day about the problems of a particular country. . . . It is he who is in the best position to alert the Assistant Secretary or the Secretary that a problem is festering. . . ."

Turning then to the Assistant Secretaries, who are close to the Secretary in all policy matters—and there are several in charge of the various Bureaus—he said, "The Assistant Secretary at any given time may have 50 or 75 or 100 matters which should be of concern to him which ought to be on his worry list." The art of policy is his decision as to by whom, when, and how these matters should be dealt with. Those higher up are dependent on these men.

All the work of the Secretary's subordinates and his associates in other agencies and the findings of the intelligence community have to be combined, assessed, and converted into recommendations for the President. Since only the important matters must be brought to that level, the detail needs to be transformed into the elements of the conclusions, so that a reasonable course of action can be outlined. These are the *requirements* for action in crisis which have been mentioned above. Those who support and advise the Secretary play different roles in meeting the requirements that lie behind decisions, which lead to modifications of policy and which turn the nation, if ever so slightly, in a new direction.

These prerequisites to action can be listed under six main headings. They could be further broken down, and must be in certain instances. The first is the *accepted position*, or general policy. With this the Secretary is in complete accord. It is his task, as has been stated already, to work constantly at making this position, and the principles which it represents, clear to the American people, to friends and to enemies abroad. In this effort he strives for the most impressive manner of making these ideas known. He himself inevitably gives constant thought to the need for modification in basic policy. In this he shares his burden with hundreds of his associates.

The second requirement, which is well provided for in the present institutions, is the *availability of background information*. This takes the specific form of intelligence estimates. These are full, analytical, up to date, and relevant to the problems that are likely to develop. These documents, for the most part highly classified— secret—are read by the Secretary and are also summarized and readapted for him as need arises. While there are many tangible elements that cannot be fully reflected in these formulations, the material can be depended on as a help in time of need. This the Secretary knows, even though he may ask for more data and various interpretive statements as, in an emergency, the danger increases. The facts brought before him in his staff meeting, during the day, and often during the night, come to him quickly and are usually concentrated on a few main issues. Essential to action is the third requirement, an *appraisal of the nature of the critical event*—the sudden change in international relations. In a time of constant turmoil, with many changes of government, with death and destruction in high places, with revolt and the threat to national security in many areas, it is often difficult to judge the importance of a particular occurrence. The top officials cannot be called on for action in cases of minor troubles when they have more serious concerns elsewhere, but delay in alerting the competent officer can be disastrous. In the feeling for these differences and the recognition of the time to cry havoc lies the possibility of effective action. Without the instinct and the courage that is called for, the risks which the Secretary faces would become intolerable.

Once the moment has been recognized and the flash information made available in a compelling manner, the *consideration of the values involved* becomes the fourth and immediate requirement. The issue has in all likelihood already been tagged as vital. All up and down the line, the significance of dealing with the new situation has been agreed upon. Only a brief review of its importance in the light of the global problems and total resources of the nation is needed before feasible options are outlined.

First, there is an agreed position for every case, which is the outline and formulation of general *policy* for that case. Second, after such issues and objectives are understood, attention is turned to the background of information, which gives to the recognition of a special moment or event a meaning in time and place relative to the basic position. Then, the value judgment, as to how this case fits into our vital interests, is made—the third step. There is, fourth, a review of the options which the government can reasonably consider.

In the course of making a choice, it is clear that a narrowing of the area of feasible action, by an event, a revolt, an assassination, a disaster, is necessary. Subsequently, in the crucial period, the fifth requirement consists of *recommendations* based on the four previous aspects of the developing situation; these are presented to the President, usually through the Secretary. There are, meanwhile, preparations for various operations on a contingency basis. The sixth phase is the *decision* itself—this modifies and influences, in greater or lesser degree, all future policy. It is followed by an explanation or adaptation of other phases of policy.

As seen from the viewpoint of one country and one critical situation, there is, for those working on the problem, the *narrowing triangle of choice*, already described. Thus, whereas before a special event the concern may be diffused among a host of considerations, the urgency of facing the new conditions leads to excluding some, and the specific incident may have eliminated others. This "narrowing triangle of choice" limits the decision to three or four of a myriad of possibilities which existed earlier, as planning was conducted over the past months. The contingency plans provide for more than one course, but the options tend to become fewer as the critical moment is at hand. Thus, in the time of need, only hours after the crucial event, the staff furnishes the Secretary with appropriate selected papers outlining several lines of action, with back-up material and with reports on the onward course of preparation that is being initiated according to tentative plans—if there are such plans. These recommendations as to choice, put before the Secretary or outlined by him as time permits, represent, as has been said, the fifth set of requirements that can be regarded as essential. It would be unrealistic to assume that he could not act in the absence of recommendations, but even when he takes the initiative in a crisis, staff officers prepare papers, make telephone calls, examine the extent of capabilities, and supply a varied "take" of materials and information. The recommendations are brought into line with his judgment, with previously accepted plans, and with known resources. They are made ready for the President.

The Secretary usually does not present the President with several recommendations; he is more likely to make a tentative decision and put this forward for approval, modification, or rejection, as the case may be. Since the President has been informed, from time to time during the preceding hours of work in progress, he may have arrived at his own conclusion before he hears the story from the Department of State. He has conferred not only with the Secretary but with his personal staff and he has been supplied with papers and information from various quarters.

This is the usual course of events, though the details vary. The officials who participate in the critical decision change from instance to instance; in recent years, the Secretary of Defense has been deeply involved. The Director of the CIA is usually present. Representatives of Congress are called in at more than one stage. The review and analysis is extremely comprehensive, and the ideas that emerge have been sifted and tested at many points. The air at the final meetings may be tense, but there is a superficial calm as the President hears the presentation, asks a few questions, and in perhaps an hour, calls the presentation adequate or inadequate. He is ready to issue instructions.

There have been, in the past 20 or so years, various styles for the relation of the President to the executive officers who are under his direction. There are also variations in the extent to which the Secretary confers hour by hour with his chief. Some of these differences will be seen in the account of what has happened in recent years. More would be evident if the narrative went back into earlier decades. Preliminary steps may be taken in task forces, in committees, in the National Security Council, or in the White House itself, with selection by the President's staff of where it will get its material and what persons it will consult. The requirements outlined here are always to some extent part of the picture, and the sequence of tasks is followed more or less as indicated over changing times.

The division of labor is something that a strong Secretary will control and dominate. The President relies on the Secretary's judgment, is governed by his advice, and then takes the risk with a knowledge of the nature of the preparation and the institutional foundations on which it is based. The Secretary in turn has to count on the support he gets from his subordinates, his associates, and the Ambassadors. As problem follows problem, the demands on him are relentless and overwhelming. He has to fight for time. He has only rare moments for contemplation. His swift comprehension depends on the resources which he has developed over the previous months.

Those who examine government pronouncements sometimes find what they consider to be inconsistencies, variations, and undesirable innovations. Sometimes their deductions are unwarranted, if they forget that the spokesmen for our policy address several audiences at once. They must speak to the informed official, to the less informed American public, to interested persons in friendly nations, to listeners in "nonaligned" countries, and to the leaders of the communist regimes. This calls for a shading of meaning, and sometimes an apparent lack of continuity, as conditions demand a stronger or a milder statement of our attitudes and plans.

Rarely do these variations indicate an abrupt change. The Press Club speech by Dean Acheson on January 12, 1950, on our Far Eastern defense and the withdrawal of aid for the Aswan Dam by Foster Dulles on July 19, 1956, have been so interpreted. In the one case, Acheson's speech on the defense perimeter in the Pacific, the communists misconstrued the United States' intentions toward Korea. In the other case, after Dulles' cancellation of American participation in the Aswan Dam project, President Nasser of Egypt thought he had a wide field of maneuver. Both statements had meaning as to policy, but the connotations were different in different capitals. There was miscalculation in both cases. The fundamental American policy, and its meaning for short-range action, was forgotten; the notion that our position had changed was exaggerated.

Those born in the early years of the century have lived under the policies of a dozen Secretaries of State. Many officers still in service have known eight—Cordell Hull, Edward Stettinius, James Byrnes, George Marshall, Dean Acheson, John Foster Dulles, Christian Herter, and Dean Rusk.* These men have differed widely in their methods of work, in their attitudes, in their relations with the Presidents whom they have served. All have been men of stature. They have devoted their entire energies to the enormous tasks that have confronted them. Several have left their mark on history. They have been, in some degree, the victims of inexorable circumstance; no one of them has been able to carry out his will to a full extent. In the past 20 or more years they have been largely concerned with the cold war and the threat of communism.

They have come to realize, sadly, that in a world of conflicting ideologies the aggressor has the advantage, and yet they abhor aggression. They have left a legacy of valor in times of stress. Those critics who focus on their lack of success may have done the cause of the free world harm, although criticism can sometimes be helpful; but it may also be costly in undermining the confidence of men who need support. A clearer understanding of their burdens, the

---

*The author has followed the work of these eight and others, including Robert Lansing, Charles Evans Hughes, and Henry L. Stimson.

limitations to their actions, and the ways in which they exemplify continuing American traditions may be a contribution that the outside observer can make to the clarification of foreign policy.

THE DEPARTMENT OF STATE

For the general public, the Department of State and the Secretary are one in their performance, their attitudes, their plans, and their successes and failures. Quite naturally, they do not see, behind the policy and aims, the elaborate machinery and the hundreds of persons responsible for its working; or, if they do see the detail, they associate it inevitably with the man who is in charge. This is proper and, to a degree, correct, since enormous effort is made to avoid a division of opinion. There must be cohesion and anonymous execution of the determination of the President as conveyed to the personnel by the Secretary. The first and overriding responsibility and function of the people in the Department is to give support to their chief.

Thus the main task is to support the Secretary in his formulation and execution of policy and in the development of policy recommendations. The second task is to carry out the programs and pursue the objectives which have been determined. For this purpose, a large and sprawling bureaucracy has been developed. The 24,000 persons, the 300 diplomatic posts, the many international alliances, the dozens of functions, and the multiplicity of positions and programs require the services of a network of people. Streamlining seems possible at times, but it usually is a prelude to new job proliferation: a job has innumerable aspects, and it is better, in these important matters, to have duplication than a vacuum. Thus the apparatus continues to grow as the work grows.

If the world were flat and the concerns local, the men and women in the Department could go home to dinner on time. As it is, there has to be a round-the-clock alertness to what is happening day and night all over the globe. The senior watch officer in the Operations Center serves to keep the lines open between the foreign posts and the men at their desks or in their homes. When the NIACT (Night Action Cable or Critic Cable) comes in, the first step is to call in the man on the desk. It is his responsibility to pass the word up the line without delay. He comes from home or wherever he is and usually has the cable in hand after the short time it takes to drive to the Department. He may have alerted two or three of those likely to be particularly concerned with the matter before leaving his house.

The simple and familiar steps are set in motion: reference to contingency plans, consultations at high and low levels, and perhaps, military preparations, or any other measures held to be necessary reactions in the emergency. If the matter is one that concerns only a few people or one that has been given urgency because of a meeting abroad of limited significance, the desk man may be able to handle it himself without calling on his associates. For this response also he has been prepared.

Geographic Administration. The administration of foreign policy is organized mainly on a geographic basis. Crises occur in particular countries and create problems that have a definite local import. This is why in State the geographic bureaus take primacy over the general functional bureaus. Of recent years, the functional offices have become increasingly important, but still, for the most part, they follow the lead of the country desks.

The manner in which the organization chart is drawn up reflects the growing increase of duties and the larger number of nations with which we have relations; but its general shape and the lines of responsibility have remained much the same in the past 20 years and longer. The main shifts in emphasis have been the occasional efforts to subdivide and subordinate the economic activities and some of the other functions to the country desks. This has proved useful in only a few cases. Where there is a large staff working on the affairs of the United Kingdom, France, Germany, or some other country, specialists in functional matters have been placed alongside the "political" officers. The divisions are comprehensive units.

The 80-page State telephone book is one of the best guides to the organization, which, as of 1967, is shown in the chart.[11] It shows the office of the Secretary divided into two sections. One section includes those who work in his central group of offices to aid him and the five special assistants, including the Ambassador at Large, the Special Assistant for NATO negotiations, two more for international labor and Vietnamese affairs, and the fifth special assistant, who is concerned to a considerable extent with public relations.

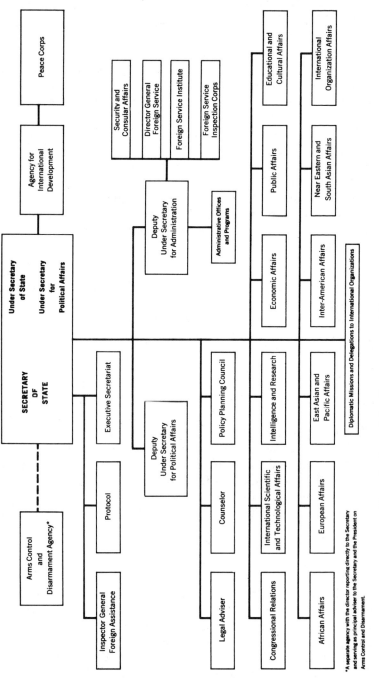

Organization of the Department of State (as of May 1, 1967).

The other part of the Secretary's office is called the Executive Secretariat (S/S). Through this center moves a large portion of the material prepared in the separate bureaus. Here it is screened for style and form and given priorities to smooth the flow to the Secretary's inner office. This process does not control the movement of the cables or the handling of the main intelligence information. It does regularize the more normal business of the Department and helps systematize material for special meetings and negotiations. In this office is the newly created Operations Center, which is staffed by senior officers day and night for immediate action and which is occupied with each special crisis. It is one of the significant organizational changes in the last six or so years. Those in charge, other than clerical and communications support, are assigned from the various bureaus for continuous duty over a number of months.

The next major subdivision is the office of the Under Secretary. He is a deputy and replacement for the Secretary on those occasions when the Secretary is not in charge. He shares a considerable part of the Secretary's burden and covers the entire field of foreign relations. There has been considerable discussion of the desirability of a "permanent Under Secretary." The British have used such a measure to advantage. While it is true that under our system the incoming chief has frequently retained several of the top officers to help him in the transitional stage, there would be considerable merit in the knowledge and assurance that such an officer would be in his post, irrespective of the other changes which the Secretary might wish to make. Legislation for this purpose, if passed, would constitute a radical departure from the traditional American system of government, since the new administration, elected by the people, wishes a unified and often a changed manner of performance. There is no doubt, however, that in foreign affairs, which relate to continuing programs beyond our borders, there are special circumstances that commend the idea. It is clear that the effectiveness of the Secretary, especially in his first months in office, is greatly facilitated and enhanced by the ability of his Under Secretary. The two men must have a cordial understanding, not only on operations in the Department but also on policy in its broadest sense.

The Deputy Under Secretaries for Political Affairs and for Administration have far-reaching responsibilities. The Secretary relies on the former for urgent and highly interpretive information on the most critical matters everywhere. He counts on the judgment of both on the recommendations to be put before the President. Nothing important happens anywhere without involving them and their various bureau chiefs and other officers. They are in constant touch with Ambassadors in trouble spots. Each is a leader and a policy-maker of the first order. He is usually a man of long experience who has been through the fires of negotiation and crisis.

As Secretary Rusk has said, "for all practical purposes" the "responsibility of the Under Secretary" and the Deputy Under Secretary for Political Affairs is coterminous with that of the Secretary for all tasks but administration. Purely administrative matters follow a somewhat different line. The top level men and their close associates constitute what is sometimes referred to as "the seventh floor." On this same floor are also the offices of the Policy Planning staff, the Counselor, and of Congressional Relations. Since these men and the various Assistant Secretaries are all close, organizationally and in physical location, to the Secretary, there is little ground for the statement that he "sits in the center of vastness . . . and has almost no staff which he can call his own."[12] There is no indication that the chief lacks assistants or is out of communication with the large organization which is at his service.

Another question, frequently raised, as to where and how policy is made can best be analyzed in connection with the requirements that have been noted above. This book will show, perhaps more clearly than abstract outlines, the various ways in which the term is used and the multiplicity of effort that is devoted to this work.

A change in coordination and supervision was outlined in Foreign Affairs Manual Circular No. 385 on March 4, 1966. This order set up the Senior Interdepartmental Group (SIG)* to assist the Secretary of State by:

1. insuring systematic consideration of policy problems requiring interdepartmental attention

---

*The SIG shall consist of the Under Secretary of State, Executive Chairman, the Deputy Secretary of Defense, the Administrator of the Agency for International Development, the Director of the Central Intelligence Agency, the Chairman of the Joint Chiefs of Staff, the Director of the United States Information Agency, and the Special Assistant to the President for National Security Affairs. Representatives of other departments and agencies with responsibility for specific matters to be considered will attend on invitation of the Chairman.

2. dealing promptly with matters raised by the member
3. assuring selectivity by areas and issues in the use of resources
4. and carrying out other duties and responsibilites of the Special Group (under NSC) which has been abolished

The Desk Officer. There is no doubt that in many cases the man in charge of a country—still usually called the desk officer— influences and shapes policy. His role in preparing position and policy papers designed to cover each set of problems area by area, and many functional matters as well, is generally recognized. As a result of efforts to assure the meeting of these needs, there is now a coherent structure of ideas and plans not formally in existence in the period of limited involvement 50 or even 30 years ago.

The desk officer is responsible for seeing that the formulation is available, that it is relevant to the current situation, and that appropriate action is initiated. He is, in a sense, a custodian of accepted policy. He also receives all incoming messages from the field, regardless of whether they were labeled "Eyes Only" for the Secretary, as in the past, or "ExDis" (Exclusive Distribution), or whether they come through in more routine fashion. Since he is constantly studying the problems of his country, he is one of the first to recommend modification of policy. This phase of the type of division of labor within the Department is unavoidable in a time when there are approximately 130 nations with which we are dealing.

The desk officer, although he is expected to take initiative, never acts alone, however. He must be in close and hourly contact with his division or office chief and, in important matters, with the Assistant Secretary who is responsible for his area. In most instances, he is likely to draft the answer to an incoming cable himself; but then he faces the problem of clearance, which, while it seems to delay action, is a way of keeping various bureaus and agencies in touch with what is going on in a particular country. There may be a score of telephone calls, an interagency meeting, consultations with officers at higher levels. Much of the work is, however, horizontal and is accomplished by men at about the same rank and degree of authority. Thus, much of the time-consuming movement of information and decision up and down through channels is avoided in the course of normal operations. Only the more critical issues go as high as an Assistant Secretary, and perhaps 95 percent of the Department's work is carried on without calling on the Secretary for his time. His information is complete but, in many cases, after the event. He and his staff acquire experience in swiftly skimming the hundreds of minor papers which have been prepared and acted on at lower levels.

The activities of the desk officer include meeting urgent requests, evaluating unexpected events, and, also, in the light of this constant flow, suggesting improvements in current programs and policy. He is trained to bring together quickly all the relevant considerations. When, either on instructions from above or on his own initiative, he undertakes a revision of the principal policy papers or specific position papers, he is influencing the formulation of policy. The extent to which his ideas prevail depends on the manner in which they are attuned to the national aims and the intentions of those of higher rank and greater authority. If he captures their thought, as expressed in more general terms, his recommendations may actually be carried forward with little change. Any suggestion he makes and any paper he writes is likely to be reviewed by dozens of others with experience and knowledge with whom he has been working for the months during which he has held this area of responsibility.

Frequently, the man who takes over this job is relatively junior and low in rank. He has been carefully selected and given orientation training for a brief period. His most significant education is probably on the job, where he has a high-pressure experience working with those who have already been in the country in question, who have been through a number of crises, and who know the workings of the Department. As he saturates himself in the information, the intelligence "estimates," and position papers, he gains the knowledge that helps him formulate his tentative appraisals and preliminary drafts of what may be a long series of revisions of texts to guide further operations. He attends meetings with the AID officers, with the security committees, with the CIA experts, and with lawyers, Congressional advisers, economists, and others working on the combined problems. He is expected to know well the political, economic, military, and cultural circumstances that affect our relations with the country in question. The more urgent the demands on our support or the more critical the dangers that arise, the more the levels of authority are telescoped. Every effort is made in times of emergency to see that the man who has the most direct, intimate, and full knowledge—and he may be a young man assigned to a desk—is brought into the deliberations and contributes his opinion on crucial matters.

In view of the unpredictable nature of events, it is fortunate that the Department is relatively flexible as to rank and assignment. The man who "knows" is usually made available to the Secretary, to the Operations Center, or wherever; here and abroad, the need is recognized. Although at times practical limitations on travel funds and personnel and vital functions may hamper prompt assignment, these obstacles rarely affect the more important reactions to sudden need. It is more in the general preparatory stages of the Department's work that budget considerations limit effectiveness. Much depends on the sureness of instinct of the Assistant Secretary who knows the staff who work under him and how they can best be used.

Desk Changes and Paper Continuity. Criticism is often directed at administrative policy on transfers within the Department and even more so overseas, as their frequency seems to upset the orderly workings of the system and to diminish familiarity with problems and break the continuity of personal contacts. Sudden changes of assignment are disrupting to associations and break the links established between the desk man and his colleagues in other agencies or between working partners in foreign posts. These transfers are required, usually, by the needs of embassies abroad and are a part of the natural hazards of the conduct of foreign policy. Some shifts could be postponed or perhaps avoided if there were a greater appreciation of the delicate relations involved. The fact that those who are called "substantive officers" are not usually consulted by the administrative staff leads to a sense of helplessness and may frustrate some of the current operations for a considerable time of transition. Continuity of a type is assured by the overlap of tenure, however, and men fill in where others leave.

The maintenance of a paper structure to cover past events and future contingencies becomes the more important because of the inevitability of transfer between the Department and the foreign posts. There is rarely a gap in the materials in the files, as the record of decisions, evaluations, positions, and operations is projected forward. Only as conditions change, new countries emerge, and new methods of acting in the outside world demand new formulations of policy is there a lag in the materials that guide future action. The mass of documents might seem excessive to the outsider, but it is the working material for the officer in charge. It brings him at once into contact with the varied aspects of his task and sets both the limits and guidelines.

The cable has already been mentioned as an instrument that calls for action and records decision. The single yellow copy of an incoming message which designates the location of responsibility in most cases goes to a desk officer, while simultaneously some hundred or more information copies are distributed throughout the collaborating bureaus in the Department and in other agencies. It is thus possible for any of several hundred individuals to inquire immediately as to what, if anything, is being done. Some of these men may volunteer suggestions and give useful help, setting in motion a score of inquiries or preparation so that the answer can be drafted with a minimum of delay. The reply, which coordinates action at many points, goes with the "yellow copy," and the pink "come-back" copies inform all those who participate and dozens of others as to what is taking place. If the Secretary is involved, his aides will follow through, so that in a meeting or by telephone he becomes a part of the act, or, in some cases, takes over from his subordinates and drafts the reply himself. In any case, the name of the Secretary—a practice different from that followed in some foreign offices—is at the bottom of every Department cable. It has been initialed in every case by an officer of sufficient rank and experience to have the privilege of signing the Secretary's name, and it shows the appropriate clearances, so that it carries full authority. It is a central element in the making of policy, the conveying of instructions, and the execution of programs.

The responsibility for assuring completeness in position papers, records of recent action, cables, estimates of the situation, and contingency plans rests to a large extent on the desk officer (and his Division chief). He produces not only the documents but his own ideas and the consensus, as far as he can report it, on short notice. He is the eyes and ears of the Department with respect to his domain, whether it be large or small—the United Kingdom or Togo, India or Panama. His work is supplemented daily by many associated with him and by the ideas and instructions of his superior officers, which help to bring his work to a focus. An examination of the channels of communication and the background and policy studies indicates that the Department can face its many preparatory tasks with a considerable degree of readiness. Nevertheless, the pressures are so great and come from such unexpected quarters that experience is under constant review in an effort to effect improvements.

One such improvement, which helps to meet the third requirement—appraisal—is the Operations Center set up after the Cuban crisis in 1962 and used for Berlin, Panama, Vietnam, the Dominican Revolt, and several other critical situations. It is to this center that special men are assigned as it becomes likely that emergencies will grow into major crises. Here, communications, "hot" information, round-the-clock watch are maintained. The men assigned to this work are freed instantly of other less pressing duties and insulated from the distractions that would lessen their availability for this special task. Both speed and concentration of effort have been gained by this innovation.

Instruments of Departmental Communications. The response of the State Department to the crises of the time, and the use of the new communications of the space age during the months after the Bay of Pigs, was spectacular. Those who used to stand at the window outside the code room on the fifth floor taking notes on the incoming messages to make the first quick decisions in the middle of the night would not recognize the facilities of the new Operations Center as a normal part of the conditions of present-day work.

Incoming cables decoded by machine are automatically transmitted by teleprinter from the nearby telegraph room and available "in the clear" almost instantaneously. The Senior Watch Officer (SWO), who is an experienced and knowledgeable man, well acquainted with current problems and advised frequently as to the major concerns of the Secretary and other senior officials, reads all the incoming messages. He can flash the desk officer or any other persons who, in his judgment, need to know of the latest information. On a nearby desk is a telephone console that has push-button connections with approximately a hundred desks and offices, so they can get the word without delay.

For the night and early hours there is an information blackboard where off-duty telephone numbers and addresses are posted. The Senior Watch Officer knows the business and social calendars of some dozen or more persons whose names are posted on the Board; they can be reached at any time—at a concert, at a dinner, or during a speaking engagement.

For the Pentagon, the Central Intelligence Agency, and the White House, there are direct wires that can be used by the Senior Watch Officer. This job is handled in shifts, with the telegraph position always manned. At a nearby office the editing is done of the cable summaries of the highest classification, which are to be circulated to officers close to the Secretary and to the Secretary himself. These are available twice daily, early in the morning and again in the afternoon.

There are a number of senior officers in the Operations Center to help with both incoming and outgoing messages. Direct "secure" telephones to some of the foreign posts are in a nearby room, and in another the teletype equipment which is used occasionally for interchange of conversation. Thus, the network of communications spreads over Washington in and outside the Department and overseas to many missions. There also are several "unsecure" telephones for less sensitive talks. The area can expand by minor adjustment to take in several groups of officers who need the facilities because of a sudden or anticipated crisis—a number of cubicles are ready for use; these connect directly with the core of the Center. There have at times been as many as three or four desk officers and their assistants in intense activity in this protected zone. The Secretary, whose office is not far away, walks in from time to time to look at the cables and talk with those who have studied them. At all times there is an officer from the Department of Defense at a desk in the Center. Those in the special briefing room with its large screen and comfortable chairs are protected from interruption by any person not immediately concerned, since the Operations Center is opened with a special key. (Provisions for those who stay overnight are infinitely better than they were a few years ago: there are a bedroom and modest facilities for making coffee, tea, and any simple meals that might be needed.)

The facilities provided mean that communications cannot readily be interrupted. Moreover, those working in the Center temporarily devote themselves exclusively to the priority problems. They do not encounter busy telephone lines, they have access to excellent maps and, with the help of the Senior Watch Officer, a comprehensive and clear grasp of incoming information. These improvements, long overdue, sharpen the cutting edge of our foreign policy by preventing delays and misunderstandings. Berlin is not cut off from Washington by distance. The Middle East or Africa can have a corner in the Department building. Any key mission can be alerted quickly of events elsewhere. The automatic decoding of Washington messages in many capitals makes communications more readily available to the Ambassadors scattered throughout the world.

The Subdivision of Responsibilities. The subdivision of the responsibilities of desk officers forms a type of mosaic, coterminous with all the countries and areas of the globe and functionally criss-crossed by the activities of those who work on finance, trade, aviation, labor, commodity agreements, public affairs, and other specialized problems that cross national boundaries. All the main Divisions are paralleled by offices in the Bureau of Intelligence and Research, which has close daily communications with the Central Intelligence Agency and thus helps to form a bridge between the information and the policy work.

Another manner of bringing about close cooperation is the recent decision to establish "back to back-ing," that is, direct and continuing contacts between the man on a political desk and the appropriate person in the Agency for International Development (AID), which is now integrated into the Department. It would lead too far into the detail of the institutions to attempt to describe the various ways in which coordination is accomplished. These illustrations serve to show the awareness of the importance of having a coherent, rather than a fragmented, approach. The essential element is the spirit of cooperation. The structure, like the lines on the chart, facilitates, but does not achieve the central purpose.

The interconnections are important, but so is the deliberate degree of separateness between the Policy Planning Council and the operating offices. This provision is designed to free the planners from routine tasks and to isolate them from the many diverse questions and decisions that have to be made on a day-to-day basis. The Council, established 20 years ago, was designed to fill a gap that was imperfectly recognized before 1947. Because of the swift succession of crises calling for immediate review, its attention has been devoted more to short- and intermediate-range issues than was originally intended. Even though it has not proved feasible to have the planners focus mainly on long-run objectives, it has been possible, however, to direct their energies to special problems and to stimulate the development of new ideas that might be unpalatable to those already committed to definite lines of action. It has been fortunate that those who are on this special staff have been able to think independently and to contribute their outstanding ability to the solution of what have turned out to be short-run problems, fitted as harmoniously as possible into the framework of the long-range national aims.

In one instance, Secretary Dulles asked the planners to outline more than a dozen ways to solve the Berlin problem and the reunification of Germany. On the first go-round, they were to propose novel and even extreme approaches in order to test whether conventional thinking was too sterile and unimaginative. Similarly, an officer is occasionally told to ignore existing papers and bring forward the most imaginative suggestions that are in any sense plausible, in an endeavor to see new angles to a persistent difficulty. Since plans are not permitted to circulate outside the staff until they have been screened and criticized, there is little danger that the proposal of impractical ideas will waste the time of the busy officers. Thus, much of the work is never aired, but it serves to set more clearly the limits of permissible action. Occasionally, a new idea, influencing our national security and chances for a reasonable peace, has been developed by the staff. Some will never be attributed to the Planning Council, but the results are nonetheless significant. One generally recognized product, in the early months of the Council, was the outline for the Marshall Plan, which brought to the war-devastated world billions of dollars of economic reconstruction in the years when deterioration might have destroyed the heart of Europe. This accomplishment alone would justify the setting apart of a group of men to carry on this special work.

In recent years, the work has been more informal than previously, less bound by paper work and "channels." There often are direct lines to top officials, to the National Security Council, to the White House, and to the office of the Secretary; they are used alternately or together—the methods depend to a considerable degree on the wishes of the President and Secretary. Under President Kennedy, the work with White House aides was extremely close.

The 17 or 18 men on the staff can establish contacts with the desks and offices as they wish, but they are not burdened with the responsibility for drafting cables or preparing programs. They seldom take part in public discussions. They are faced with no periodic reporting or routine assignments. They, almost alone in the Department, are given time for informal conferences and for discussing theory or far-ranging ideas.

In reviewing the resources of the Department, the varied ways in which requirements are met can be seen from these different elements in the organization. They do not add up to elegance in the system, but they have met the needs tolerably well over the past two decades. There have been improvements in the earlier rudimentary communication resources. There has been a moderate amount of adjustment to assure lateral and horizontal coordination almost without reference to rank and tradition. There have been an enormous increase in accessible information and improvements in the manner in which it is analyzed, classified, and stored. Further changes will undoubtedly occur, but they are likely to be along similar lines. It is inevitable that the geographic approach to problems, geared as it is to the embassies abroad and to the governments of other nations, must take precedence over the functional. In fact, changes in method in years to come may be more in appearance and terminology than in substance, as the requirements of foreign policy continue to set more rigid demands.

When a crisis comes, it has a country or area center. Each of the incidents examined in the later sections of this study called for decisions narrowly concentrated in the first critical hours, at the 38th Parallel in Korea; in and around Guatemala City; in Beirut, Lebanon; in Berlin, the strange walled area in the Soviet-occupied zone of Germany; in Leopoldville, in the Congo; or in the Dominican Republic. In each case, the Department had a broad policy and a considerable amount of information. The earlier experience made plain the need for more information, more contingency planning, and better evaluation of the material at hand. There may have been misjudgments of the threats to the peace that were developing in the Far East in 1950 and in Central America in 1952 and 1953. In

Lebanon, Berlin, and the Congo, the seriousness of the situation was recognized early and the extent of our interest realized.

The value judgment in the Department that precedes every important decision springs from a wealth of information that the Department accumulates over the years without interruption, but it depends in the final analysis on the understanding of two or three men. The essence of this requirement is that the men of ability operate from a solid base of supporting analysis and well-organized data. The stage of final decision is based on this preparation, conducted mainly at the higher levels; but in most cases the nature of this government's involvement and the existence of a vital interest have been thought out sufficiently in advance at various levels. The time required is short, therefore, and the procedures sharply focused with few visible preliminaries, even though the outcome is momentous.

Thus while the Foreign Service and Departmental officers of lesser rank are called on to keep policy and information available, and while they are the men who flash the knowledge of the critical moment, it may be the Secretary or someone else who spots the particular point of danger; and it is almost certainly the higher echelons that evaluate the meaning and call for the further fateful actions. The narrowing triangle of choice is recognized by a number of people. Some of the selection of options is automatic, since some possibilities are likely to have been rendered impossible by the new situation and by "the event." This process calls for skill, experience, and instinct as to diplomacy, operations, security, and political factors of various types. Here lies one of the greatest calls on the capacity of men at various ranks and in many different positions to coordinate their efforts. They must, in a matter of hours, bring to bear on the immediate issue the knowledge of the past, as well as of the meanings of the present.

In a moment of critical decision, when seconds are the measure of time, it sometimes seems as if the Department as an institution were playing an almost insignificant role, as a handful of men issue the instructions that may well change the course of history. Those who know the process are well aware that the work of the Department is aimed to meet such moments and that the thinking—the formal statements, the development of background and understanding of the issues—supports and aids the action.

After the series of steps that follows decision, it is necessary to move on to explanations to those persons not immediately involved

—Ambassadors from countries not directly affected, Congressmen and Senators not included in the smaller conferences, newsmen, the public in this country and abroad. Any change in programs or additional efforts will call, in the next few weeks, for major or minor adjustments that adapt the programs and positions in all countries to the changes in the locality initially affected. This work is usually inconspicuous but necessary. After the explanations and the adaptations, it is then urgently important to take a fresh look at policy and operations in the light of the experience of the crisis. These three aspects of the Department's work follow the decision and instructions that have been aimed to meet the situation in a particular country. At every stage in thinking and planning there must be a sophisticated appraisal of our capabilities based on experience. The men who have fewer years of service must of necessity be responsive to the views of those who have been through other emergencies and who can bring many intangible elements to bear on the problem. Without the continuing intense preoccupation of the expert and the "old hand," the intellectual judgments of new men could lead to serious dangers, additional and avoidable.

Even though in a more grave crisis, the State Department seems to have little control over the events initiated by a few men in the White House, this appearance is largely illusion. The work at desk, office, Division, and Bureau level lies behind the thinking and the information of the Secretary. The completeness of the routine work and the fullness of the detail form the bedrock on which action is based. In the case of Berlin, for example, there had to be a clear understanding of all facets of transportation in and out of the city. In the case of subversion in Guatemala and Lebanon, the methods, the political cliques, the resources, and our own activities had to be within the scope of our knowledge and subject to what influence could be exerted. Even in the less known area of the Congo, in 1960, there had been a substantial amount of work done on the problems already arising. There is never enough knowledge and, more significantly, there can never be a precise forecast of the timing or intensity of the pressure that will be exerted on our policy.

Throughout the Department, every officer—and this means several hundred—has to consider the likelihood of serious complications. While maintaining an attitude of calm and keeping his materials and ideas in an orderly fashion, he must be ready for war, revolution, or any other catastrophe. Because of the universal nature of most of the issues, the distribution of dispatches, intelligence summaries, and cables is much wider than is usually assumed. It has been considered wiser to have the large flow of paper than to take the time to trust the selections of those who might determine the nature of a more limited readership. The interests of cooperation are best served in this way. Even "Top Secret" messages go to scores of officers. A record of where they are and who has had access is part of the routine established.

The steps that have been described are facilitated and made more effective by the recently developed, and still growing, Operations Center. Thus, every recent crisis has been brought into this Center. The Secretary and the Under Secretary and officials at all levels meet in these seventh-floor rooms with the officers from the desks who carry on the continuing watch. There are lists prepared for action to be taken, some two score or more, in the case of a political kidnapping, a raid, an assassination, the fall of a government, or an ultimatum. If the event has not been anticipated, the system can still be put into action in a matter of minutes. There is little doubt that the state of preparedness in 1965 was immensely better than it was in 1941, 1950, or in 1956. It is likely that this emphasis on crises will continue for many years to come.

Selection and Training of Staff. Because of the inevitable dispersion of responsibility and a system that does not provide for rigid procedures and tight supervision, the selection and training of the officers is of paramount importance. There is a frequently recurring suggestion that there be a special academy for Foreign Service officers, perhaps along lines similar to those of the military schools, and there is a fairly widespread feeling that more should be done to assure the excellence of the individuals who face the difficult problems of foreign affairs. These views do not take adequate account of the special nature of the work and the kind of qualities demanded. When the question was raised in the hearings of the Subcommittee on National Security (88th Congress), the testimony was predominately against a "West Point" for diplomats. Ambassador George Kennan said:

> Like most of your witnesses, I am strongly opposed to the creation of a Foreign Affairs Academy at the undergraduate level . . . Drawing the junior recruits of the Service from the whole range of American

colleges and universities, and from many of the graduate schools as well, provides a far broader base and much better prospects of highly qualified entrants into the career.[13]

Ambassador Averell Harriman spoke of the great development in recent years of international studies in almost all of our important universities. Dean Acheson, in commenting on Senate Bill 865 calling for special training, stressed the fact that training for diplomacy cannot be equated to that for the military professions. He also said that there would be much hesitation on the part of government-paid professors to criticize freely, as can be done in our colleges, the acts and programs carried out by our President and Secretary of State. He indicated that "wisdom and proficiency" are best derived from responsible contacts with real problems. Ambassador Ellis Briggs, speaking in a lighter vein, suggested that such a special academy as was being discussed would become a colossal supermarket manned by Ph.Ds "into one end of which would be fed the ingredients of diplomacy" and from the other end of the hopper would come "solutions to the problems of foreign affairs." The fear was expressed by several in the course of the hearings that an academy for this special training would arouse public suspicion and decrease its confidence in action in a field of vital concern for every citizen.

It was clearly indicated by the experts that they held as most important a broad understanding of American conditions and a good general education which would provide perspective and a philosophical approach to the difficult work that would lie ahead. As for experience at the beginning of a Foreign Service career, it was convincingly stated in several instances that the consular service is the best discipline in the world and gives perhaps the most broadening experience. For specific phases of the work of the Department, specialized training is needed. Some need to have special preparation in economics, in law, in science, or in military affairs. There is opportunity to assure advanced education for limited numbers who are brought into the functional branches of the Department. This may occur early or later in the period of service, according to the needs of the Department and the interests of the individual. In recent years there have been hundreds of well-trained specialists, as well as many generalists, in the corps.

Selection of new officers coming in at the bottom of the Foreign

Service is made from the young men and women who survive a tough written examination and an oral examination designed to bring out many of their qualities of character, motivation, and personality. The number of applicants is narrowed down by the written examination to a few hundred who later take the oral. Of these, hardly more than one in three passes the test. The process of elimination of more than 95 percent of the applicants and final appointment of even a smaller number—less than 2 percent or approximately 200 a year—is discouraging to many young people, even though it serves to maintain the high mental and personal standard of ability of the Service. Moreover, the frequency of the final certification has to vary to some extent with the needs from year to year.

Lateral entry, from other government services or from civilian occupations, is possible, but has been used only sporadically. A large increase in lateral entry into the officer corps, however, resulted from the acceptance of the report of Henry M. Wriston and his associates in 1954.[14] Some who serve as temporary specialists and consultants are absorbed into the ranks at appropriate levels of salary and responsibility. The large additions to the staff have come mainly from special legislation taking in groups of workers from the Board of Economic Warfare in the mid-1940s, from the AID organizations, and from the information services. These changes in personnel have been considered by some to be dilutions of the spirit and special characteristics of the Foreign Service officer corps. As such, they have been resented and resisted by a few. But those who have opposed these moves have rarely proposed practical alternatives to meet the new needs of the complex specialties and the larger number of diplomatic posts to be manned.

The posting of young diplomats, as well as the more experienced ones, has long been the subject of jokes. Some even say that one should indicate on the form the choice of the assignment one does *not* want, since it would make more likely an assignment to a "desirable capital." Anyone who knows the complexities of manning a hundred capitals and of having a balanced staff in every mission recognizes that the knowledge of a language cannot guarantee the location of an officer. There are many men who know several languages, including the more exotic ones. The recent increase in the emphasis on learning to speak the language of the country of assignment, or one of the main dialects, has greatly added to the number of persons from whom one can choose. The theory is that the young officer can and should study for this part of his preparation as soon as the decision as to where he will go has been made.

The theory of assignments and transfers produces in most cases a type of circular motion. One is apt to return to the same countries several times in the course of a dozen different postings. Thus, the officers come back to familiar ground at a higher rank and with more experience, which gives them perspective to find old friends and study new and old problems. One criticism beginning to influence planning is the request for longer terms in one place and for less frequent changes. There has already been a shift in this direction. Some think that the Service can afford to have one or two persons who stay for many years in one place to become repositories of information and more sure guides to incoming Ambassadors. These men would not move on toward the highest ranks themselves, but might be willing to give up this opportunity for the satisfaction of expertness and the many amenities that would come with this type of career.

Cooperation with Economic and Information Services. It has been inevitable that, as the diplomatic use of informational and economic instruments has increased over the last two decades, the services that specialize in these fields should become more closely associated with the political offices. All the major relations between this country and Europe are affected by developments in the European Common Market, the OECD, NATO, and the financial interrelationships of the International Monetary Fund. Since one man cannot follow all the intricacies of the new organizations, it is important that institutional arrangements should bring the daily operations of different divisions close together.

For example, with the installation of the officers of the Agency for International Development in the same building as the geographic and political bureaus of the Department, with the higher officers in the quarters formerly used by the Secretary and his staff in the Virginia Avenue building, the close coordination of AID operations with the Department changed from theory to fact. Although the assistance programs are the continuing object of criticism and attack, they are now an established aspect of our diplomatic effort. We cannot win friends or control governments by grants of a few million dollars, or even by the larger sums which are frequently loaned or given; nonetheless, the Ambassador or the Secretary who has the financial means of helping a government in its efforts to achieve economic progress can speak with a more convincing voice and can persuade some who are reluctant to depend on the sincerity of our interest in their welfare.

In 1966, assistance was given in one form or another to more than 70 countries* and several organizations; it is therefore evident that Congress and the executive branch believe that this program is of importance in our foreign relations. In some cases, our willingness to extend substantial help may be crucial in supporting a government which is not only seeking to extend democratic practices but is also willing to lend moral and practical support in a time of communist pressure. As even the enemies of the aid programs realize, we are deeply involved in the affairs of other nations. Furthermore, even when there have been no apparent political results, our economic relations have, in many cases, been altered or improved by what we have done. Our major concern in these as in other matters is with our national security and after that with world-wide conditions.

Though many of the officers of AID perform functions that are highly specialized and have a minimum of political content, both their efforts and those of the country-oriented political experts are coordinated to further aims and programs that are, after all, essentially unitary. In recent years, the points of view of these two types have come closer together as there has been an increasing awareness of the usefulness of the varied tools that can be used. The earlier feeling that the economist is in a world apart has vanished.

The United States Information Agency, which is now linked more closely than in past decades with other aspects of foreign affairs, is still in a building some blocks away from the main State Department and has not been intermeshed with the political units, except in general orientation or in specific programs. In all important respects, the guidance that comes from the Secretary's office sets the tone

---

*The total of foreign countries assisted by AID and the four predecessor agencies, 1946–1966, is 120. This total includes Near East and Asia, 17; Latin America, 25; Far East, 14; Africa, 38; Europe, 17.

for information programs. After the separation of this work from the Department in 1954, it was felt by some that the gap had widened and that there would be difficulty in coordination. But coordination is being accomplished now by a number of arrangements.

In the field, the USIA and AID staff, as well as the representatives of CIA, are all part of the country team, under the leadership and guidance of the Ambassador. In the case of the AID mission, the head is, in some cases, also the economic counselor of the embassy. When he carries on these dual functions, he brings together the broader considerations affecting the commercial, financial, and other economic interests of our businessmen abroad and the representatives of industry, trade, and finance in the country where he is posted. Though some lines of communication with Washington remain open, in addition to those through the Department of State, there is no serious question of conflicting views or actions at cross-purposes. The functioning of the embassy will be described below, but it is important to note that from the missions in the field come much of the information, most of the requests, and many of the suggestions and warnings which are the raw material and the motive power to start action in Washington.

The coordination between the USIA program and the Department of State has been close. For a time, the RIAS—Radio in American Sector—Berlin was virtually a part of the State Department apparatus. There is good evidence from refugees and by correspondence to prove the effectiveness of the programs as they are heard in East Germany and in other border areas. (In the last four years, the Germans have been increasingly responsible for financing the cost and for developing the programs.) This type of activity has been made a part of foreign policy in the last two decades. The government has learned valuable lessons over the years about the proper nature and extent of these efforts to keep alive the hopes of the freedom-loving behind the Iron Curtain. It is equally important to communicate with the millions of interested persons in non-aligned countries and in friendly areas under continuing pressures from communist doctrines. The expenditures required are recognized as an alternative to military outlays, which are increased whenever we fail in the realm of psychological warfare.

Contacts with the American public are much more extensive than is generally assumed. There are the attempts, already mentioned, to explain aims and objectives—these would have astonished any old-time diplomat in the days of esoteric arbitration and negotiation at the turn of the century. The sizable delegations to the United Nations Trade and Development Conference (UNCTAD) and the General Agreements on Tariff and Trade (GATT) deliberations in Geneva, for instance, involve hundreds of Americans and many more delegates from other countries, with almost unlimited access of the press to meetings and information. The discussions in the United Nations in the General Assembly and in the specialized councils are open to the public to a considerable extent. Hearings on Capitol Hill help to make plain the points of agreement and disagreement with respect to military strategy, aid programs, and relations with allies and enemies. Most of the economic dealings, in fact, become known to the interested public as a debate on aid programs is fully aired. Although the early planning and proposals for new ventures by AID are sometimes kept secret and discussed in the context of the more highly classified work of the Department of State, it is not long before the broad outlines and even specific details of appropriation requests before Congress are widely publicized. On all these matters, the desk officers and their opposite numbers in AID work together closely. Divergence of views is not tolerable in a time when economic support is a major instrument of political objectives.

Another look at the Department's telephone book reveals the many different functions and shows that most of the work of many of the Bureaus is in the public domain. In addition to the special efforts of Political Affairs and the geographic bureaus to keep the public acquainted with the general nature of their activities, Congressional Relations, Economic Affairs, Educational and Cultural Affairs, Public Affairs, and Security and Consular Affairs are constantly dealing with the public. There are many specialized offices that are concerned with foreign private investment, financial arrangements, foreign building, and commodity agreements. These matters result in wide contacts and many meetings in which the businessman or expert participates in our foreign relations.

Cooperation with the Defense Department and CIA. The collaboration of the Department of State with the Department of Defense has been consistently close since the end of the Second World

War. The responsibilities in connection with occupation in Germany, Austria, and in the Far East, the increasing importance of the nine security treaties and the meetings they have entailed, and the work of NATO in its wide ramifications have all demanded coordination of policy and opinion in the foreign field. Some bureaus have daily contacts. Defense Department officers sit in on many State Department meetings, in some cases attending the small divisional staff meetings. The close interweaving of information, "estimates," and the preparation of data for the National Security Council all create a mechanism for bringing thinking and planning into close harmony.

Although the Central Intelligence Agency is a major source of information on both immediate crises and longer run threats to security, the Director is not legally a member of the NSC; he or his representative attends at the personal invitation of the President. In the nuclear age, the urgency of prompt evaluation of underlying tendencies, even before overt acts make the danger plain, has been greatly increased. Moreover, knowledge of the "denied areas" behind the Bamboo and Iron Curtains is critically important to those trying to make the official estimates. It is from the CIA that much of the subject matter for high-level discussions comes, and its information is drawn into the councils of those who carry on continuing diplomatic studies at the desk level and higher.

Since the Agency (CIA) is not responsible for the formulation and execution of policy, it is thought that its officers can view the situations which they are investigating without prejudice. They are as ready to reveal the weakness of the United States' position as its strength and so can help in providing a balanced account of what is going on. The myth that the CIA makes policy has been described by Allen Dulles as one of the most harmful and difficult to disprove.

> The facts are that the CIA has never carried out any action of a political nature, given any support of any nature to any persons, potentates or movements, political or otherwise, without appropriate approval at a high political level in our government outside the CIA.[15]

The necessity of avoiding widespread knowledge of the more delicate plans and contacts of this government excludes some who think they should know from access to the communications. Priorities are set by those in high levels of the Department of State who direct the intelligence aspects of our policy. Full explanations even of the *reasons* for secrecy are not possible, at least until long after the event. The communists are not unaware that this leaves them a fertile field for creating false impressions as to the activities of the more active and more covert agents—"spooks"—as well as the more scholarly "professors," and have stirred suspicion that feeds on the doubts of those who are not knowledgeable about the needs of intelligence in modern times. The many efforts of the Soviets, in particular, to penetrate our military installations, our intelligence operations, and our policy-making have led to tight security measures and attempts to reduce to a minimum the number of persons not directly involved who know of our estimates and plans. The Russians have used mechanical devices to "bug" embassies and have exerted pressure on individuals to defect or to become agents to an extent that cannot be ignored in the conduct of our foreign affairs. The instances in which they have succeeded in getting information of a highly sensitive nature may be few, but these few have been costly.

Problems of Security.   There is a tendency to make light of the strict measures taken to keep policy papers out of the hands of those who might misuse them or who might inadvertently pass on bits of information that would be helpful to the enemy. There are cases of overclassification of documents that seem to include little valuable data and contain only common-sense recommendations, but which are marked "Secret" or "Top Secret." It is hard to see how over-classification can weigh heavily in the scales against the possible harm of underclassification. There is no need for the public to have all the facts relating to Cuba, Vietnam, the Congo, Berlin, or Zanzibar. There are matters discussed in personal conversations which might seem of general interest, but, if such facts were likely to be spread abroad, conversations in the future might become restrained beyond the point of usefulness. The extra time and cost of handling highly classified papers is a small price to pay to avoid one damaging leak or the one case in which sources are revealed to the detriment of future intelligence.

Thus, the perennial complaint about secrecy has little solid basis. On all but the most critical issues, there are dozens of persons who know the appraisal of conditions and the proposals for action. It was said by Robert J. Manning, formerly the head of the Public

Affairs work of the State Department, that President Kennedy had only one week of secrecy in the case of the reaction to the missile crisis in Cuba, whereas Premier Khrushchev had about six weeks. This difference illustrates the degree of control which the Iron Curtain countries have in developing their programs. In some cases, the difference is even greater than in this special case in which President Kennedy placed a temporary embargo on the giving out of information. The Open Society operates under many handicaps in relation to the dictatorships. The State Department, which has a reputation for holding out on the public, suffers from the attacks of the more avid newsmen. It must keep its methods unaffected by any of these attacks as long as the security risks continue to be substantial.

The confidence which the Department and the other branches of the intelligence community places in its officers is far-reaching. Papers that deal with the conditions under which the government might engage in full-scale war are available to many with appropriate clearance. Intelligence operations of various sorts are known not only to those in selected parts of the apparatus, such as the Bureau of Intelligence and Research and some segments of the geographic divisions, but also in the offices of the Secretary, the Under Secretaries, the Assistant Secretaries, and elsewhere as needed. Because of the sensitive matters taken up at many meetings in Washington, the records must be meticulously complete as to attendance at meetings and distribution of documents.

There was an instance, in 1943, when a high-level decision on postwar boundaries was discussed in closed session with the Secretary, but the contents of the policy paper were published in the Washington evening newspaper that same day. It was never discovered how this news became available. Moreover, the publication, though accurate in many respects, was misleading in its emphasis and direction. Such revelations are rare. (A few have been traced to other embassies when there have been joint conferences.) The codes are guarded, and cables and position papers are locked in safes. The carbon paper used each day is burned. The officers and staff are enjoined to the unvarying caution necessary to protect our ideas, communications, and safety.

The problems of security are compounded because sensitive material has to be transmitted to far distant posts. It is never assumed that any telephone is "secure," although some conversations are "scrambled" to provide protection. The teletype is used now more than formerly, although it is still subject to breakdown—it has to be put through the "quick brown fox jumps over the lazy dog" routine test whenever the statements come through garbled. The variety of means of communication has increased, and the use of jet transport for airgrams is now feasible between many capitals. Every embassy, like the Washington offices, has a dependable routine for protecting secret documents. The preparations for burning the codes and the material that would be of use to hostile powers are well-known in all the missions.

Most of the work of the Department is open to public inspection, however. There are briefings for all comers several times a week. There are many pamphlets and reports that can be had for the asking. In general, the officers at several levels take time to talk to newsmen, to representatives of groups, to students, and to officers from other government departments. Though the expenditure of government funds for propaganda as such is closely restricted and limited in amount, the many speeches, television appearances, and contacts made by Department people continuously put before the public the basic facts. The United States Information Agency, closely connected with the Department of State, is restrained by law from using its resources for educating Americans about foreign policy, but the fact that it endeavors to set the record straight abroad helps understanding at home.

There are many who think that because the communists spend large sums on radio and other forms of propaganda, the United States should devote more resources to its foreign educational work. This country has not been able to compete with either the Eastern European countries or the Chinese in foreign exhibits and fairs— we have had to keep costs within a narrow budget and limit ourselves to a few exhibitions. Though a number of our efforts have been highly successful, it has been a surprise to some nations that we cannot participate in all the major expositions. There is evidence that in number of hours of broadcasting the communists have greatly exceeded what we have been able to do. American standards are high—the Voice of America gives out "hard" news and high-grade cultural programs in music and literature—but the volume, even when one adds Radio Free Europe and other private stations, has been smaller.

Cooperation with the Justice Department. The Passport Office, which seemed to have mainly routine functions in earlier days, now has become a subject of controversy because of problems connected with travel behind the Iron and Bamboo Curtains. The recent Supreme Court decision, giving more leeway in the granting of passports, has removed from the Secretary some of the responsibility that he formerly was required to exercise. Decisions on visas for immigrants, which raised difficult technical and political problems, have always been shared with the Department of Justice. The widespread agitation for revisions in the quota provisions of the law has produced pressure on the State Department because the provisions are administered by the consulates and embassies abroad. Actually, the officers in the foreign missions have had almost no discretion, and the granting of entry permission has been governed by the law and by the Department of Justice, with Foreign Service officers acting under specific instructions. The complexity of simultaneous action on applications in approximately 300 posts to arrive at approved combined national-origin totals has never been fully appreciated by the public. Even with more rapid communication and more elaborate mechanical devices, it is evident that a comprehensive system is needed to prevent pre-emption by one post of the chances of would-be immigrants elsewhere. It is agreed that there can be improvements in methods, but the new solutions undoubtedly will fall short of satisfying the hopes of millions who wish to come to the land of opportunity. No other nation has to meet the pressures we experience.

Summary. When one surveys the Department as a whole, one is impressed not only by its preparedness for action in crisis, but also by its attention to routine and continuing tasks. These routine tasks lay the groundwork for decisions that must be made in times of emergency. It is obvious that less public interest attaches to the continuing work, but it has to go on unimpeded in all areas—economic, financial, cultural, security, and administrative. Almost any officer, in the course of his lifetime in the service, may be challenged by sudden change; but most will be concerned with maintaining our strength, maintaining routine services, and watching relatively tranquil areas. Nothing can be taken for granted. Each officer must think of himself as prepared to take over the work of a colleague, to increase the area of his responsibility, to do the work of a minor clerk or even a janitor, if occasion demands. The future burdens on the Ambassador and his most junior assistants cannot be forecast in advance.

Twenty-four thousand men and women in the State Department dedicated to serving their country, thousands of others in the Departments of Defense and Commerce, in Central Intelligence, and elsewhere—all are charged with the delicate tasks of supporting our foreign policy and carrying out duties in conditions of hardship, weariness, and insecurity. The system endeavors to protect these people and their families. They are given moderate economic security and they are offered varied opportunities, but essentially they create their own destinies and pay in unflagging effort for their modest rewards.

The institution has met many a test and has supplied the sinews and brought forward the ideas that place us in the forefront of nations. Continuing improvement is always sought. Nevertheless, the Department of State is often the whipping boy of the journalist. It is held responsible for wars and revolutions, for waste of funds and sluggishness of action. There can be no rest for those who administer and plan, who select and train the personnel, who make policy and carry out programs. But only those who study their methods in detail and understand their responsibilities are likely to suggest constructive changes for the Department.

THE AMBASSADOR

An Ambassador is a man who has to do an indispensable job under impossible conditions. He must know what is going to happen before it happens. He must persuade heads of state to enter into agreements that may be unpalatable. He must be liked and respected even when his country is at loggerheads with the government to which he is accredited. He must be on good terms with warring political factions. He must entertain a stream of his fellow citizens with food and drink, which, perhaps, he cannot afford to furnish. He must attend social functions that drain his strength, and he must sit up all night to write cables or receive incoming telephone messages. He must run a large establishment—referred to as the "country team"—and must be the unquestioned leader of the staff. His successes may prevent a war; his failures can bring untold disaster.

This is the picture in many cases, but, of course, not in all. In some countries, instead of having a large group of officers under his administrative guidance and control, he is almost alone in an isolated mountainous area or in a tropical jungle—he may have to tend the "shop" with only one or two assistants. In emergencies, he controls supplies, decodes messages, and is perhaps the main channel of communication between the government to which he is assigned and the entire outside world.

In spite of danger, frustration, overwork, and underpay, an Ambassador is still the envy of every officer in the Foreign Service and the symbol of the almost unattainable peak of glamorous government service. The reason for his importance is that he is an extension of the power of the President. He is the voice of the United States speaking to the government abroad. He is the eyes and ears of his chief, gathering information and appraising the problems and attitudes, the strengths and the weaknesses of the country where he serves. Though he has a multitude of tasks, and, in the larger posts, scores of officers to carry out the diversified functions, the end product is his. He makes the judgment, he transmits the evaluation, he recommends the course of action to be taken.

In some cases, as in Guatemala in 1954, in the Congo in 1960, in Germany, in Vietnam, in Panama, in Lebanon, he stands in time of crisis as *the* American—the man who represents the Army, the Navy, the Air Force, the intelligence, and, above all, the President. It is he who says, "my country will not yield," "my country demands. . . ." This declaration is the policy of the United States. In some cases, he may be the only barrier between a hostile mob or an antagonistic delegation and his staff, his building, his lines of communication—his post, in both its physical and symbolic manifestations.

Of course, many Ambassadors have never been in a crisis. There is not one, however, who may not suddenly be involved in the unpredicted revolt, the sudden attack, the menacing coup, or the reversal of local policy that puts him in a perilous position and during which his services become of incalculable importance to his government. Those who are weighed down with administrative burdens may think back with nostalgia to the more adventurous posts they have held. Boredom may be the fate of some, danger the fate of others. But in essence every post is important.

The job of the Ambassador has three main aspects. First, he transmits the views and the wishes of his home office, the messages of the President and of the Secretary of State, interpreting our policy on occasions, making representations on other occasions. Second, he transmits to the White House, the State Department, and other agencies as required information varying from the extremely sensitive and secret to the more routine and technical. His communications bear the stamp of his ideas and give varying degrees of urgency to the suggestions he forwards. His cables and reports may be spontaneous and arise out of his experience and that of his staff or they may be in response to queries that call for his opinion or his appraisal. The reciprocating dialogue, the exchange of questions and conclusions, establish the background for the Washington "estimates of the situation" and lay the groundwork for decisions that have to be made at the center of power, the White House.

The important third area of activity, highly demanding in some cases—Bonn, London, Paris, and Tokyo—less so in others—Norway, Denmark, Spain, and Austria—is the general field of American operations. These may at times seem remote from the central core of responsibilities, but they can be vital, and they call for close supervision, under the guidance of the Ambassador. He can delegate, but he is ultimately accountable for all American aid and other operations conducted in the country of his service. These aspects of the Ambassador's job are new in this century, and they have grown markedly in the last 20 years.

In fulfilling these three groups of functions, the constant support and assistance of the Ambassador's deputy, his Foreign Service officers, his staff, and the Department at home bind the various elements in close association.

In representing the President, the Ambassador may be acting on direct word from his chief; more often he is carrying out instructions sent him by the State Department. Many of the messages are drafted by the desk officer or Division chief, who signs the name of the Secretary over his own initials. If the matter is of considerable importance, it is initialed by an Assistant Secretary, in rare cases by the Secretary himself. The authority to sign a cable is granted only to those with sufficient experience and rank. In all cases, there is clearance by from one to 20 or more persons concerned with the contents of a telegram. The Ambassador does not know who has written or initialed the incoming instruction (in a few cases, he can guess by the wording that the Secretary has done the drafting). He has to assume that the coordination at home is such that the incoming message does indeed represent the Department at all appropriate levels. If the President was directly involved, that is usually evident.

The flow of communications to an Embassy is varied, and, while most of it is from Washington, some is from other Embassies sending copies of special items that affect the Ambassador's country. The information about happenings outside his country varies from condensation of news items, Congressional actions, and top secret information on changes in "estimates" of contingencies to modifications of policy that affect his orders. The mass of materials in the field, as at home, is given an early screening and prepared for the Ambassador each morning and several times during the day. In connection with this work, as also in carrying out the second category of functions, he needs the help of officers in specialized sections of the embassy, and he depends heavily on his Deputy Chief of Mission.

Any time, day or night, the deputy or the head of the political section may seek out the Ambassador at home, in his office, or wherever he is to inform him of word from Washington. The heads of other sections, among which the work of the Embassy is distributed, and the military and other attachés have ready access. It is their responsibility to see that the Ambassador is immediately told of anything of urgency. In a large Embassy, such as that in London, with more than 500 American employees and approximately 40 units of government agencies other than the State Department, the question of coordination is paramount.[16] It is almost as complex in nature as that in Washington. While the channels of communication are largely centralized in the Embassy, the varied activities can pose problems of synchronization and harmony in executing government policy. The concept of the "country team"—a team that includes all the different American elements and missions in a country—has consequently been evolved, emphasizing the overall authority of the Ambassador. As Ambassador David Bruce has said,

> *An ambassador who does not control his own Embassy and all the elements in it ought to be fired, because you are dealing with people of goodwill and, except in extraordinary circumstances, I cannot imagine a dispute where even if there were a difference in principle it could not be resolved within the Embassy.*

In the field, the entire staff knows that the role of the Ambassador derives from his direct relations with the chief of state. They know that, as the Brookings Report says, he "can make a shambles of U. S. relations with another country or organization or can save it from irretrievable blunders." In a word, he can sometimes prevent a war or lose a nation.[17] It is for this momentous task that he is chosen by the President. He is not the one, usually, who complains that he has not enough scope or authority. His burdens are heavy, and he knows that without the directives from the President and the Secretary he cannot keep his post in line with global policy.

Criticism has been directed at the role of the Secretary of State in direct negotiations, the sending out of special ambassadors, and at visits by the President. The increase in travel by the men from Washington in the last decades has been inevitable, as has been the increase in return trips of the Ambassador for consultation. Moreover, communication by telephone and teletype has multiplied manyfold, as "secure" lines have become available, with the "scrambling" of words to provide for safe transmittal. The reason for some tightening of the reins between the capital and the field is not only the greater speed and facility of travel and communication, but also the fact that the United States is concerned with the affairs of more than 120 nations. There is a growing centralization of foreign affairs, accelerated by the knowledge that a failure of policy or inadequacy of information in Korea, the Congo, Panama, Lebanon, Germany, or Outer Mongolia may bring a clash that could set off a nuclear war. With the growth of the risk, the importance of prompt action from the center becomes imperative.

The President has chosen his man as an Ambassador with the knowledge of the grave responsibilities he must meet. There is little basis for the impression that the choices are frivolous. The so-called political appointments are, in most cases, of men who have had wide experience and who are known and trusted by the chief. If, occasionally, there has been a man without real merit who has been awarded a political "plum," he has not been likely to remain long in his assignment. The stakes are too high and the workload too onerous to permit toleration of evident incompetence.

There is no doubt, however, that the Department and the Foreign Service prefer to have career men in the posts. This is not only because they look on the openings as the goal of their own professional service, but also because the men who have grown up in the smaller posts, who have worked in the Department, and who have known each other and the system over many years deal more smoothly with the apparatus. They understand, almost instinctively, when a message from Washington is a high-level directive calling for precise and immediate action, and when it consists of the recommendations of a man with less authority, leaving an opening for further query and suggestions of modification. These are aspects of the relations between home office and outpost which the nonprofessional, however able, does not immediately grasp.

The basic requirement is, in any case, that there be at the head of the Embassy a congenial, responsive, and highly sensitive man, who can understand the thinking, the decisions, the aims, of the men in Washington who are guiding the worldwide conduct of foreign affairs. The fact that these are complex, many-sided, and often technical in nature imposes on the Ambassador the task of command ability. This he exercises over his immediate staff, the consulates, and the representatives of other agencies. As the Brookings Report states, "the talents of a brilliant innovator do not, of themselves, fill the bill on the quarter-deck."[18] Thus, those close to the Embassies and the Department, including the Ambassador himself, realize that while some of his functions may have been downgraded in recent years in that direct negotiation is shared with other men, both the variety of his tasks and the weight of his responsibilities have increased enormously.

It is fortunate that the caliber of the "political" appointees has usually been high, but, in any case, the proportion of men from outside has fallen from 65 percent in 1925 to about 29 percent in recent years; of these, only about 15 percent have had less than three years of government service, and most of them have had business or other experience abroad.[19]

In addition to responsiveness to the President, there is the work of keeping him advised about events in the foreign country and their meaning. At all times, the men making policy at home must know the views of the local government leaders, the extent of their willingness to cooperate, their power, and their intentions. As far as possible, the strengths and ideas of the minority parties, the influence on the head of state of pressures from abroad, and the prospects for the continuation of the existing policy must be made available to those who fit these pieces into a mosaic of overall planning. For this purpose, the Ambassador himself must have multiple contacts with critics, with dissident groups, with intellectuals who stand aloof from current policy, and with specialized centers of policy-making, such as the labor unions, the military, the scientists, the cultural leaders.

In carrying out these functions, he has the help of the Central Intelligence Agency, as well as of other members of the intelligence community, and the sources of information in other Embassies that bring in additional bits of information and help with its evaluation. Because of shifting changes in power and direction, the occasional report, or current information in a special telegram, is of more value in Washington than the routine studies that add to the burdens— and of which Ambassadors complain. The load is heavy, and sometimes his staff is prevented from pursuing the elusive clue or the intangible evidence that may help to forecast a coming emergency because they are required to hammer out a periodic report or a special agricultural, commercial, or financial round-up for which the post has been made responsible.

The enormous expansion of the Foreign Service is caused in part by the addition of emergency requirements to the routine tasks. Both have increased, and the administrators, seeing the opportunities for new authority, have not been slow to take advantage of the demands on the existing manpower by adding to the rosters. Neither the Secretary of State nor his Ambassadors have the time to perform the surgical task of cutting back the size of their establishments. The system works against them because the elimination of offices, while it may reduce the paperwork and enforce clarification of priorities, may leave them with insufficient staff in time of crisis. Only if the skill of the officer corps is increased can a responsible official cut down on numbers. The volume potential of work will always exceed the hours available, and there are few capitals where there is any time for idleness. In fact, the superimposition of the required reports on the need for ingenious efforts to learn what is going on under the surface, the social obligations, and the efforts to think constructively of the future problems and possible crises will always exceed the resources of most posts, large and small.

The Nature of the Job. Preparation for service in an Embassy is best achieved in most cases by experience in a variety of assignments in the Department. Work in various branches at different ranks fits the man for the tasks ahead. This training cannot be secured in schools, though a sound general education in a good university is of inestimable value. Much has been said about the extent of language capabilities of the officers, including the Ambassador, and more attention is paid to this qualification now than previously. Often the Ambassador, if he considers his facility inadequate, takes lessons in the language early in the morning before becoming involved in the day's work. Most of the junior officers know two foreign languages and endeavor to learn the local language or dialect, even though it may be exotic and difficult.

In many countries in Africa and Asia, as well as in Latin America, English is the second language and is spoken with fluency by the local officials. In many other countries, French serves as a useful means of communication. In matters of serious importance, American diplomats, like others, use their own language and employ interpreters to assure complete understanding on both sides. It is not considered wise to speak in an unfamiliar language when conveying vital information or when "making representation" for Washington, as every word has considerable weight in the communication. A knowledge of the local language is important, however, because it makes possible the reading of the local newspapers and facilitates the occasional ceremonial remark or short speech that is considered a courtesy. Certainly even a limited knowledge helps in understanding the mood and intentions of the people with whom one has to deal.

It has been urged by some that the establishment of a special "West Point"-type of institution for Foreign Service officers might raise the standard of performance of the officer corps. There are others, more experienced and more numerous, who think the result would be unfavorable. Several arguments against such an academy have been mentioned already (see pages 44–45).

There is a growing recognition of the intellectual demands on the officers in a foreign post. Those who watch the changing foreign scene know that without alert and discriminating men under him, even the ablest Ambassador may fail to keep the President fully advised. Independence of thinking on the part of the staff is of inestimable value to the Ambassador, even though for the most part his own personal view, after he has absorbed the pertinent information and varied opinions, is bound to prevail. There is special provision for exceptions to this rule. If an officer finds that his chief is unwilling to sign his report and loath to transmit it to Washington, he can invoke a service regulation and send it in without the concurrence of his chief. This minority report, as it might be considered, will be read in Washington and taken into account. Obviously, such reports are not frequently made, since only when there is a degree of harmony can a subordinate be useful to his Ambassador.*

The Ambassador, for his part, in fulfilling this, his most significant function, cannot be at war with Washington. He has various ways of pressing his disagreement with what seem to be the government's conclusions. He can send urgent cables, he can telephone, he can ask to come home on consultation to press his views in person. If, after having defended a position which, for any reason, is unacceptable to the President and which is not compatible with accepted programs, approved by Congress and in force in regard to his assigned country, he can make no headway, he finds he has little choice.

Ambassadors have on occasion resigned in protest. They have asked to be relieved of their duties because they did not think, under the circumstances, they could effectively represent the President. In one notable case, George Kennan left his post as Ambassador to Yugoslavia when he concluded that Congress was limiting his pos-

---

*In August, 1967, Secretary of State Dean Rusk invited junior Foreign Service officers to submit policy proposals and suggestions directly to the Department, bypassing normal channels (a junior officer's superior was not necessarily even to know that his subordinate had made a suggestion). A panel of 10 junior officers was set up to screen suggestions and send the best ones to the Secretary. Announcing the new program in the *Department of State News Letter*, Rusk wrote: "Innovation and creativity should be encouraged at all levels of the State Department and the Foreign Service. We must be sure that new policy ideas are not put to one side because of their unorthodox nature, or because they are not considered immediately applicable."

sibilities of action and failing to be persuaded by his knowledge and judgment. In his testimony before the Jackson Subcommittee he explained the issues as he saw them.[20] Joseph S. Farland found that his views on Panama were not heeded and left his post, which was not filled until after the subsequent riots of 1964. A number of Ambassadors, concluding that they were no longer effective, have resigned for "ill health" or for "urgent personal reasons."

The "mortality" of the men in the top diplomatic posts is increased on occasion by the hostility of the host government, which at times declares a man *persona non grata*. For instance, Kennan was asked to leave Moscow. This has not occurred often. We have been persuaded to withdraw our emissaries from countries which have shown a wanton disregard for international usage and human considerations, notably Hungary, Bulgaria, and Cuba. While this gesture may seem to lessen the prestige of the country that is left without our top representative, it has not noticeably altered the manner of behavior.

The long history of our diplomacy is one of good working relations between the President and his man in the field—a closeness of understanding that permits perceptive and persuasive reports. If we failed at times to get the correct "reading" on conditions and policies in Egypt, in Ghana, in Guinea, in Hungary, in Poland, in Cambodia, in Indonesia, in Cuba, in Iraq; if we have been in doubt about trends in India, in the Congo, in Brazil, in Turkey, and in Argentina, the results have been costly, though not always avoidable. It is not always easy to see what line of action would have been taken if our information had been more exact. Probably the Department of State could benefit by further study of the points at which information and interpretations have failed to warn the President of potential problems.

Exceedingly time-consuming, though in some ways less important, are the executive duties which the Ambassador must perform. While working conditions can make or break the morale of an Embassy and determine the readiness to respond to developments, they seem to require undue diversion of energy from the central tasks. They, rather than relations between Washington and the field, cause the uneasiness which is sometimes recorded and often misinterpreted.

Few Ambassadors want to be administrators, but unless they solve these problems of management, difficulties will plague them throughout their tenure. Inevitably, matters that seem of minor importance have multiplied with the new operating units, the aid programs, the host of military advisers, the many conferences and visitors, and the special scientific, cultural, and educational exchanges and exhibits. Thus, in addition to the traditional diplomatic functions and the Ambassador's contribution to policy-making, the Ambassador is expected to serve as a leader and coordinator of his country team while lacking influence over the budgets, personnel systems, reporting requirements, and operating policies of the field staff, theoretically subordinate to him. This the Jackson Subcommittee terms the Ambassador's dilemma.[21] If he leaves these important tasks to others, he risks losing essential control. If he performs them, he has little time for thought, negotiations, and policy suggestions that are of prime significance.

The Deputy Chief of Mission. The key to the success of an Ambassador in performing these new and onerous tasks may often be the performance of the Deputy Chief of Mission. He provides a degree of continuity and he brings to his duties a high degree of professional knowledge acquired from years of service in a variety of posts. He is usually on the threshold of being appointed an Ambassador himself, and he has the point of view and the experience that enable him to lift a share of the burden from the shoulders of his chief. In ideal circumstances, working in harmony with the man above him and with a loyal staff, he functions so as to leave the Ambassador somewhat free to read, think, and write. He takes over as chargé, in the absence of the Ambassador from his post; he often, therefore, accompanies the Ambassador on interviews with the prime minister, with the foreign minister, and with others of importance. Since the deputy's prestige and authority are recognized in the capital where he serves, he can on occasion substitute for the Ambassador at ceremonial functions. His relations with the staff are close because he is considered to be "one of them," and he knows intimately the intricacies of an Embassy and the problems that can make their lives difficult.

Staff Membership. In recent years, the usual Embassy staff has come to be made up not only of generalists, but also of specialists, supposed to know diplomatic procedure and foreign relations to some extent and to bring their particular skills in economic, scientific, or military concerns or in public relations to bear on diplomacy.

This change in balance is an outgrowth of the new undertakings of the American government. The wide range of activities can be suggested by listing some of the agencies in addition to the State Department and Foreign Service that are represented in the United Kingdom. For instance:

USIS—United States Information Service
AID—Agency for International Development
Agriculture, Department of
AEC—Atomic Energy Commission
CIA—Central Intelligence Agency
Commerce, Department of—including trade, travel, and maritime services
Defense, Department of—various attachés and security and administrative branches
FAA—Federal Aviation Agency
Justice, Department of—responsible for immigration and other services
NIH—National Institutes of Health
Treasury, Department of—including Customs, the Internal Revenue Service, the Coast Guard, and the financial attaché

There are also a number of specialized military units and a large number of American and local personnel employed on American undertakings. The total runs into more than 30,000 Americans, exclusive of their dependents, all of them under the general supervision of the Embassy.

London is a special case, considering also that there are five consulates in England and Northern Ireland.* Nevertheless, exceptional administrative problems of the same type occur in a dozen other missions. The number of persons under the Ambassador's leadership —requiring various forms of support, including communications, security, housing, and transport—necessitates a large staff of administrators and thus throws the diplomatic functions of the Embassy out of balance. The underestimation of the necessity for financial support of diverse requirements has been discussed by two critics, Ambassador Ellis O. Briggs and Professor James L. McCamy, men with vastly different experience. They paint a gloomy picture of the

*As of 1967, when two consulates had recently been closed.

situation. "Recent change has brought more action than thought to the conduct of foreign affairs," wrote McCamy.[22] Briggs stated that the main problem in this new and difficult situation lies with the Department, in that it has not established its primacy as the one voice in foreign countries conveying the United States' position. This failure to make the U. S. Ambassador "boss of all the operations being conducted in the name of the United States Government" is in spite of the efforts of both President Eisenhower and President Kennedy—in Executive orders and letters—to assure the clarification and centralization of authority.

Ambassador David Bruce, while recognizing the same problems, indicated that the chief could establish control.[23] He stated that the actions of the two Presidents had, in fact, been effective in creating the basis for unity. He mentioned the serious danger that demands from Washington would overwhelm a staff that was seeking to do a discriminating job. For instance, an official at home wishing a report on commercial dealings, raw materials, or railroad traffic cannot know the volume of other demands on the Embassy and is not in a position to judge the relative importance of his request. Thus a flood of paper and a host of operational problems can hamper the Ambassador in his role as adviser to the policy-makers in Washington.

The three main areas of responsibility are, therefore, both complementary and conflicting. While an Embassy staff inevitably feels the time pressures, and even at times resents the demands from different quarters, they inevitably also gain a sense of reality from the multiple contacts—the instructions and advice from Washington, the information and intelligence they gather in the field, and the exacting duties that arise in connection with the programs this government conducts abroad. In the struggle for the essential and the effort to contemplate the changing picture, some are swamped and bewildered; others maintain a position from which they gain a balanced view of the local national scene.

The Ambassador himself has to seek advice from his colleagues as well as from men in the government to which he is assigned. He learns to delegate responsibility as the activities increase. Some chiefs of mission struggle for more staff, some wish a cut in personnel. The comments of many who have studied the situation, however, indicate that it is difficult to conduct diplomacy "on a shoestring" and that the financing of foreign affairs has frequently been inadequate. Often an Embassy staff has been asked to work in buildings that are inadequate and even insecure. The problems involved in locking up papers and cables after each reading put a strain on the officers and secretaries that could be partially avoided by safe and substantial quarters. Some of the new buildings with their large glass windows, as in the Congo, are an invitation for rioters to attack. The fine, modern structure in Ghana, with its open exposed stairway as the only entranceway, would cause trouble in times of unrest. The building in Saigon has for years been unsuitable for government use and has proved impossible to protect. Some years ago, the Embassy in Laos carried on most of its activities in a tent. For some reason, a nation that prides itself on efficiency, and which has built some of the finest structures in the world, has not allocated the talent and money to construct proper facilities for the Foreign Service in a considerable number of capitals.

The United Nations Post. The United Nations in New York is in many ways a desirable post, but there is no doubt that the work load is varied and burdensome. There the Ambassador—from 1961 to 1965, the late Adlai E. Stevenson and, since 1965, Arthur Goldberg— with the help of a considerable staff, represents the President and carries out instructions from Washington.

He, for his part, reports to Washington on the progress of our policy, the attitude of other representatives, and the particular problems of the organization, its Secretary General, and the special subordinate agencies. These agencies include permanent bodies such as UNESCO, the Special Fund, the Children's Fund, and a number of *ad hoc* committees and organizations, such as those devoted to disarmament. His diplomatic duties are considerable, and, in spite of the fact that he is geographically close to the capital, parallel those in other parts of the world. His duties and responsibilities are important to all phases of our foreign policy.

The Consulates. The work of the consulates, under the Ambassador but somewhat removed both from the point of view of policy and geographically, in many cases, is interesting and important. Several of those testifying before the Senate Subcommittee (the Jackson Committee) stated that this work was the best possible apprenticeship for diplomacy. The consular officers acquire an intimate knowledge of foreign conditions and problems without the complexities of the larger establishments.

Much of the consular work is to protect American citizens and their interests abroad. Although millions of Americans go abroad and return in safety, some become stranded, destitute, injured, or detained by foreign authorities. A consul is supposed to know his way around and to deal with these situations. In case of accident or death, he notifies the family and acts for them. An instance of extraordinary work of this kind was reported when the consul in Ecuador, Harry Lofton, went into the Andes to explore the mountains in search of two lost Americans. His instructions from Washington were: "Go find them." In a 10-day search in constant danger, he and his companions first found one of the two men, and when all hope for the other was nearly given up, they found him, too, and brought both out alive.

Much of the work concerns American business. Technical negotiations, contacts, advice, and legal assistance with property, inheritances, and the execution of legal documents, and other matters call for a variety of competence and give valuable experience to a young man or woman at a consulate. They have a considerable degree of independence along with their responsibility. They, like the officers in the Embassy, have representational duties and can play a useful and constructive role in the country of their assignment. Some of their work is routine, having to do with passports and visas; some is unpredictable and demanding, such as the protection of sailors and travelers who get into difficulties. All has a human-interest factor and brings with it much excitement and variety.

There are between 250 and 300 consular posts scattered around the world. (Some have recently been closed as an economy measure.) They are all under the Bureau of Security and Consular Affairs, in which the Passport Office is one of the main elements. In a number of places, often because of the status of the area, we have no Embassy. In such places the consulate or Consulate General* assumes a special importance. This is true of Geneva in Switzerland, Mozambique in Africa, Hong Kong, and, for many years, was true of Singapore. Berlin, which has a consulate, also has a special mission

---

*There is little distinction in type of responsibilities but some in the scope and volume of business and the size of the office.

which performs some of the functions of an Embassy in the occupied city, though under the Bonn Embassy. In Hong Kong in particular, because of the importance of the information coming from Mainland China, there is a large and busy staff. They maintain close relations with the British High Commissioner and share with him the entire "take of information" that relates to developments behind the Bamboo Curtain.

The information gathered by the consulates is of extreme importance. In many cases, the collaboration with the CIA is active. While reporting is not a primary function, in a few cases it is given a major emphasis. Thus, in several cases, except for questions of legal status, rank, and protocol, the consulate is like an Embassy. The dozen or so larger consulates are charged with many duties and manned by scores of officers. Service in these posts is often of more interest and a greater challenge than in a quiet Embassy. Examples of these significant posts are the offices in Calcutta, Bombay, São Paulo, Strasbourg, Marseilles, and Bordeaux. The men and women who have served in such consulates have found their work rewarding.

In many of the countries, while the interest is great, there are real hardships to be faced by our representatives. In Angola, Consul General William Gibson was faced by an angry mob in 1961; the rioting people threw his automobile into the sea and invaded his office. In the Congo, in 1960, the Ambassador was confronted by an irate crowd ready to stone and burn and shoot down foreigners of whatever status. In Korea, the Embassy staff had to flee for their lives in 1950. In the Vietnam Embassy, the dead and wounded left a record of heroism as testimony to the courage of those who volunteered for transfer to this post. Frequently, in Moscow, the Embassy has been stormed by protest groups, throwing bricks and ink bottles. In China, in 1949, Consul General Angus Ward was seized and held a prisoner for months.

In the stately entrance to the State Department building on C and 23rd Streets in Washington there is a bronze tablet with the names of some 40 men in the Foreign Service who have given their lives in acts of heroism. Those who died of disease after their service or whose families suffered fatal accidents are not listed there. An officer who is sent to a faraway post knows that it may be exotic, pleasurable, glamorous—or, perhaps, bring mortal danger. He cannot ascertain in advance.

The Demands of Social Life. In normal times the social life of which so much has been said is a necessary part of the job. Not only the Ambassador but officers at all levels have to develop an informal and easy relationship both with the people of the country where they serve and with their opposite numbers in other Embassies. The time required is in most cases in addition to a long working day, not to mention weekends; the money for even simple entertaining is often beyond the normal capabilities of officers.

In the social aspects of the work, as in others, the wives play an important part. They are asked to improvise in creating a home, to share the unusual local conditions, to learn the language, to get to know their associates, and to contribute service and ideas to the life of the community. There are few professions where the whole family shares in the work to the extent of the families of officers in the Foreign Service. They participate in unusual experiences that make the life attractive and in difficulties that make the life hazardous. They are asked to learn the language if it is at all practicable. Occasionally, where the posts are thinly manned, they work in the Embassies, though this practice is limited to special cases of unusually heavy work loads or emergencies, when there is a need for manpower that cannot easily be supplied.

In every instance, the family has to make adjustments which are taxing and which frequently more than offset the pleasures of life abroad. Schools are frequently unsuitable, and sometimes the health conditions make it inadvisable to keep young children with the rest of the family in a tropical post where disease is prevalent or where medical care is inadequate.

The Inspection System. The Department's inspection system, which is set up both to maintain the level of efficiency and also to protect the interests of the officer and his family, takes some of these matters into account. Because the men in the field are not able to consult with the Washington personnel office and because needs, conditions, and types of problems are so varied, the work of the inspectors is considered essential to the maintenance of good working standards and also for the welfare of the officers and the proper evaluation of performance on the job. Thus, a corps of senior officers is constantly on the go, traveling to all of the several hundred Embassies and consulates—visiting each one about once in two or three years—and talking privately with every officer with a view to securing a comprehensive understanding of the work performed and of the men and of their families. George Kennan in his testimony before the Senate Subcommittee stated that "Foreign Service work breeds its own morale."[24] There are, however, situations in which an officer needs special assistance, perhaps a transfer to a different post.

Staff Transfers. In the attempt to keep the whole system in operation there are sudden transfers. The apparently arbitrary procedure is the subject of one of the main complaints that come to the fore. Although the shifting of officers is often required by a special need in some area where a vacancy has developed, the hardship suffered by the individual and his family may be great, and the loss in effectiveness may mar both his career and the operations of the post which he has left. Almost all of those who testified before the Senate Subcommittee on Government Operations indicated their view that a tour of duty of three or four years, rather than the shorter span of time frequently typical, would benefit the standards and provide a greater opportunity for learning about the country and the language, as well as the people. The determination on the part of the administrators in Washington to assure a variety of experience and to prevent the men at a post from becoming too deeply involved in the problems of one country has almost certainly sacrificed some of the values of deeper insight which could increase understanding of local issues and also build up a smoother working relation with Washington. The strain on living arrangements for the family is often severe when they are asked to pull up stakes and move to a different climate, a new political scene, and a strange language area.

Of course, it is necessary to transfer those in hardship posts more frequently than might be desirable under easier conditions, particularly where there is a "claustrophobia" that comes from living in a hostile country. A long stay behind the Iron Curtain affects the attitudes of the individual and makes it necessary to give relief to keep perception sharp. Similarly, the physical conditions in some areas are debilitating and may make a short tour of duty necessary. This hazard applies alike to the Ambassador and his family and to the men on his staff, though the Ambassador returns home for consultation more frequently, thus enjoying respites from a difficult situation. The Department takes account of some of the special conditions by paying a substantial differential in hardship posts. In many cases there are rent allowances which make it attractive to serve in countries where costs are lower than in the United States, even though the conditions present difficulties. In any case, the salary scale is low compared with jobs of similar responsibility and work loads in private business. There are few men who earn above $20,000. Even the salaries of the Ambassadors, with all the allowances and funds for representation, are far below what such men could earn outside the Service. It is notable that diplomats from many small countries earn, at the various levels, considerably more than our officers of comparable rank. They also are usually kept at one post for longer periods of service, sometimes running to 10 or even 20 years.

Women Staff Members. In our Service, as in those of other countries, there have been few women at the higher levels. Even taking into account the various reasons why this is considered wise, the proportion is so small that it is difficult to find justification. For many years there was only one woman career Ambassador, Frances Willis, who served her country with distinction in many posts. The few women political appointees, who performed notable service, have had brief periods of duty for the most part. The number of able women who are given positions of responsibility below the top levels suggests both the availability and the competence of those who have joined the Service. The fact that danger and special working conditions that demand strength of mind and body are not major factors can be judged by the large number of women secretaries and junior officials assigned all over the world. They have measured up to the standards set them with distinction and a high level of accomplishment.

Summary. Many difficulties confront the Ambassadors who represent the President far from home base. Efforts to increase the support of these men in their arduous work are not always successful. The obstacles they must surmount have not, however, prevented them from adding greatly to our strength and prestige abroad over the years. Many have served in several posts, and often their experience and their ability have been used in special assignments of major significance after their service as chief of mission. In reviewing the past, it is evident that as requirements have multiplied, the level of performance has risen.

The most serious Departmental complaint, however, is illustrated by George Kennan in his testimony after his resignation as Ambassador to Yugoslavia. He said his staff was a group of "exceptionally able and loyal assistants." He testified that he had no difficulty in exerting his authority over the establishment in Yugoslavia, adding that the authority of an American Ambassador is just about whatever he wants to make it. He found, however, that Washington's limitations on his policy were intolerable:

> If I had known, for example, when I was offered the job in Yugoslavia how little value the Congress would assign to my own judgment, in the light of experience of nearly 30 years in the affairs of the Eastern European area, I would not have accepted the appointment. . . .[25]

RESTRAINTS ON POLICY-MAKERS

The analysis of the development of foreign policy has focused largely on the interrelationships and working arrangements of the main American institutions responsible for plans and decisions. An understanding of the full story requires at least a brief look at some of the limits that set off action not acceptable to the public at home or to the makers of policy abroad, from action that is.

These limits are set by various institutions that exercise restraint. Three of them—to be discussed here—are the American Congress, the press and public opinion, and the United Nations. Even in times of most dynamic and flexible action, the limits lie somewhere within the area of agreement determined, in part, by these three institutions. The President, the Secretary of State, and others may seem, at times, to act without regard for public opinion as expressed in the legislative branch, by the press, and in the world forum in New York; nevertheless, unless they can persuade, they must in fact compromise or capitulate. At the very least, these institutions warn of potential danger and suggest a further examination of the direction of policy when it moves into new ground.

Congress. It is evident that Congressional concern with foreign policy has grown markedly in recent years—it has become more active as the extent of our involvement has increased. The legislators are aware of the many ways their constituents are affected by aid and trade, by defense expenditures and cooperative ventures, by negotiation or conflict, and consequently, they have increased the number of their investigations, hearings, and debates, both in committee and on the floors of the two houses. The President and the Secretary of State always follow these inquiries in great detail.

Congress, under the Constitution, has a watchdog function that gives it access to all foreign policy information except that bearing on the most delicate issues in negotiation or that which has to be withheld to protect sensitive sources. In sudden emergencies it is sometimes necessary to confine early consultation on such issues to the leaders of the two Congressional parties, who are called into a White House conference for conversations that are never fully revealed. Even in swiftly developing crises, such as Lebanon, Suez, and Cuba, however, the Congressional leaders were consulted early. Thus, though the President made the decision, he had the benefit of consultation with the lawmakers. (The Korean action is sometimes cited as one of the occasional exceptions to prompt consultation.)

In long-continuing investigations, such as those of the Armed Services Committee and the Subcommittee on National Security and Staffing Operations of the Committee on Government Operations, the time taken for hearings during one year has surpassed that taken by most other committees in the entire previous decade. In the course of such debate on the more controversial matters, those who wish to restrain foreign activities can establish positions contrary to executive policy, and the resultant publicity leads to public questioning. Frequently, the Secretary is called on to explain and defend the current policy in person—often many times. In 1962, for instance, it is reported that the Secretary appeared before Congressional committees in formal session 25 times. In addition, he conferred with members of Congress, in committee and out, no fewer than 90 times. He was supported in this work by other members of the Department, particularly by those in the Bureau of Congressional Relations. Meanwhile, at least 87 other officers met with members of Congress 224 times.[26] The main Congressional interest has been in security, defense, finance, and commercial relations. In past years there has been a considerable amount of discussion about the appointments to posts abroad. An enormous amount of time is diverted from other duties by these inquiries and debates.

The power of the Senate is felt particularly in connection with its Constitutional prerogatives of advice and consent on treaties and approval of diplomatic appointments. These responsibilities involve its members in many negotiations and lead the President to appoint Senators to numerous international delegations. The Senate and House exercise considerable control over the national purse and thus initiate scrutiny of both the aims and the execution of special programs carried out as part of our foreign policy. Congress has been particularly watchful of East-West trade in the last 20 years; it also has on occasion attached special conditions to appropriation bills for foreign assistance with a view to a recipient nation's attitude toward communism.

The discussion of the meaning of approving aid for Vietnam in 1966 is an example of warning as to limits and yet giving hesitant approval to the Administration's program. Action on the authorization by chance coincided with the period of hot debate on the American action in Southeast Asia. To some, the attacks on the President's policy seemed to threaten the success of his program. To others, the bitter discussion was held to be a healthy manifestation of a vigorous democracy. To the veteran diplomat who knows of the serious—almost inevitable—difficulties involved in studying problems in depth, such a disagreement causes alarm. Lack of information may be a handicap for those not directly concerned with foreign affairs, but it is hardly characteristic of those on committees dealing constantly with foreign policy. Furthermore, recent threats to American security have increased the problem of the Executive branch in dealing with Congress. Though closed sessions protect the secrecy of some of the hearings, the Secretary of State and his top aides are always seriously worried for fear delicate aspects of controversial issues may be reflected inadvertently in conversations reported to foreign embassies or to the press.

In spite of occasional conflict, however, dependable Congressional support of foreign policy requires frequent consultation. In recent years it has enabled four Presidents to reshape programs and redirect aims along new lines. NATO, the Truman Doctrine, the Marshall Plan and other aid programs, the Eisenhower Doctrine, the Korean police action, nuclear development, and space programs are cases in point. The reluctance of some to support our worldwide involvement —particularly in the Far East—has been outweighed by general approval and the availability of funds, which have permitted a wide latitude for action. The Vandenberg resolution of June, 1948, which gave Republican cooperation to the security measures of the Democratic administration, was one of the early moves to lessen partisan struggles and to speed up the agreements which made possible not only many new ties with Europe but also action elsewhere.

Since Presidential power in the foreign field has taken on new forms with large financial commitments and many alliances—some involving the loss of American lives on foreign battlefields—it has been the practice of recent administrations to seek the support of Congress in the form of special resolutions. The resolution of January 29, 1955, on the defense of Formosa and related areas is one instance. Such resolutions are not designed so much to extend the powers of the President as to indicate clearly, to the American people on the one hand and to the potential aggressor on the other, the will and the capacity to defend friendly nations seeking help. As Secretary Dulles said in his testimony on the Middle East, the Eisenhower doctrine of Congressional support was designed to add the extra thrust.[27] The responsibility and the capability of the President stems fundamentally, as President Johnson said in 1966, from his position as Commander-in-Chief of the armed forces and as head of state charged with national security. Such resolutions have bound Congress more explicitly than formerly to the Executive branch in critical issues. In the debates on special resolutions the advice and consent of Congress, as well as the expression of critical views of opponents to proposed action, have been sharply focused and brought before the people for their information.

Some of the controversial issues before Congress have been accentuated by fears that the growing power of the President, and thus of the Secretary of State, would lead to national bankruptcy or plunge the country into war. There had been a new trend under Franklin Roosevelt to engage the nation in foreign activities on the basis of executive agreements and decisions made in special international conferences, such as those at Cairo and Teheran in 1943 and Yalta in 1945—all of which have been seriously criticized. The decisions about China in 1948 and 1949 were made while President Truman moved toward closer dealings with Congress and sought through consultation with the Republicans, Senator Arthur Vandenberg and UN Delegate John Foster Dulles, an increased degree of bipartisan support. There were complaints on the Hill about the delay in bringing Congress into the decisions in 1950, when the President turned to the United Nations before fighting in Korea. The objections raised by Senator Robert Taft and others to the war without a declaration of war led President Eisenhower to commit himself to consultation in emergencies before any similar action.* (During the postwar years there has been markedly less use of the executive agreement than in the Roosevelt years.)

Another recent development increasing the interest by Congressmen in foreign problems has been travel to foreign countries, facilitated in considerable measure by the aid programs. Part of the funds generated in national currencies by the sale of foreign aid goods by recipient governments has been available for United States uses; therefore, substantial amounts over the years have been drawn from these funds to finance travel by legislators. Although the trips are frequently referred to as "junkets," they have brought useful contacts and information to American visitors that might not otherwise have been available.

In spite of occasional efforts to restrict the President's powers, there has been no significant reduction. For example, the measure proposed by Senator John W. Bricker in the 1950s to circumscribe the President's powers to enter into agreements or to make treaties was not adopted. The modified Bricker amendment, first submitted in 1951, was defeated by one vote short of the required two-thirds majority in 1954. The scope of Presidential action has thus not been curbed by law but has continued to be subject to a variety of pressures which have set outer limits. Only because of the strenuous efforts of four Presidents and eight Secretaries of State have the opportunities for action remained largely unhampered. Indeed, in one instance the authority of the President in the commercial field has been notably extended. Congress passed the Trade Expansion Act of 1962, which gave the President unprecedented authority to cut tariffs by 50 percent under specified conditions and greatly enhanced the bargaining power of the United States in the forthcoming Geneva negotiations on trade and tariffs, known as the "Kennedy round" (1963–1967).

---

*This commitment restricted the Administration's response to the request for help by the French in Indochina in 1954.

The role of the Central Intelligence Agency in foreign affairs has been debated frequently, with divergent views. Some have sought legislation which would give Congress a larger share in the oversight of its operations affecting policy; others have adhered to the idea that a more limited scrutiny was advisable in the field of intelligence. The safeguards provided by the Special Committee and the review of the budget have seemed to the majority to assure conformity with the intent of Congress and the guidance of the Department of State. In other words, although various proposals have been brought before Congress to increase supervision, they have not received wide support. A special advisory board, in existence for some years, which consists of representatives of the President (that is, the Secretary of Defense and Secretary of State), has been given the responsibility of advising the Director of Central Intelligence on operations that involve policy considerations and thus are subject to its approval.[28] In 1967, a new inquiry to assure adequate supervision was conducted by a group headed by Under Secretary of State Nicholas Katzenbach. Thus, in spite of occasional criticisms of what has been referred to as the "invisible government," the record shows that both the contacts with Congressional leaders and the machinery for coordination and control are adequate.[29]

In fact, with regard to most current problems, the difficulty facing Congress is not too little information, but too much. The process of screening and sorting the large volume of material—the published hearings, the special reports, the budget presentations, and all the technical and special data which comes before the legislators and their staffs—imposes a large burden and presents the men on the Hill, otherwise busy with their legislative duties and political problems, with an insurmountable task. It has been estimated that more than half the 36 standing committees are concerned with international issues.[30] Dealing with these matters calls for familiarity with the history of past conflicts and negotiations and for technical competence in defense, finance, commerce, and other specialized fields. For instance, the complexities involved in legislation on the Test Ban Treaty of 1963 and approval of the sale of surplus wheat to the Soviet Union later that year are reflected in the many pages of testimony given before the legislation was enacted.

Though the Senate and House share the responsibilities of the Executive in the shaping of national policies, their members cannot have the day-to-day familiarity with policy of those who are constantly dealing with Washington agencies, diplomats, intelligence agents, and others involved in current programs. Congressmen are not usually in direct contact with leaders abroad; thus they receive their impressions of foreign political developments from various other sources, unofficially from the press, officially as they inquire of the officers working in the field. Fortunately, they are aware of their dependence on the foreign policy apparatus for most of their access to background information. Though they try to keep a balanced view of conditions and though they criticize the policy line from time to time, their degree of support for existing policy outweighs their restrictive attacks on it. It can be said that the capacity of the President to act, although modified by Congressional views, has not been paralyzed. Rarely in the past decades, perhaps not since the disastrous conflict between President Wilson and the Senate over the Versailles Treaty and the League of Nations in 1919–1920, have the basic policy and fundamental decisions of the head of state been thwarted. The extent to which Congress may in the future prevent action similar to the police action in Korea or the fighting in Vietnam cannot be forecast. Their willingness year in and year out to support the Chief Executive has, since the late 1930s, permitted the growing leadership and the widening scope of activities that now characterize American foreign policy.

The Press. In the interaction of Congress and the Executive branch the voice of the press plays a major part. The newspapers and television and radio constantly report to the people; this broadcasting of controversy and opinion has resulted in an alert and increasingly responsive nation. In this country, more than elsewhere, there is a continual stream of information and a flood of opinion, both expert and naïve, to keep the public interest alive.

Because of the importance of the educational efforts of the press and the manner in which an individual's views on policy can, if not fully explained, reach the public in a version that distorts the facts, the Secretary of State devotes considerable time to discussing with newsmen the meaning and direction of foreign policy. He is aware of the importance of securing the support of an informed opinion and also of the moral right of citizens to know of the decisions that affect their well-being and their survival. Thus, the press and the diplomat are not in opposition, although both are under considerable pressure for information that is often difficult to provide.[31] Though only occasionally can the news media alter a short-run decision taken in Washington, there are many ways in which the longer-run trends are modified by the majority opinion of the people. In a democracy, these outer limits to action are established so firmly that a statesman cannot long ignore them.

The journalist, aware of his power, seeks to increase it by heightening the more dramatic aspects of events he reports. The diplomat, on the contrary, tries to keep discussion of difficulties and even of successes to a low key. He deplores the sensational and shuns headlines. He does not agree with the reporter who urges, on many occasions, that the public interest is best served by maximum disclosure; rather, he attaches a high importance to privacy.

In October, 1962, there was a serious complaint about the cutting off of news at the time of the Cuban missile crisis. For a few days there was a news blackout, at President Kennedy's request, which was explained only later by the White House. Thus Kennedy was given a brief period in which he had almost complete control over our international relations, during which the public waited in suspense for the outcome of the crucial negotiations between Kennedy and Khrushchev. This was a striking case in which the critical nature of the situation made it essential not to reveal any confusing bit of information and not to enhance the risk of miscalculation by leaders in the Kremlin. When these crises arrive, it is too late and the situation is too critical to allow prolonged debate. Our system places the responsibility squarely on the shoulders of the President, for this phase of security as well as others.

The sharp distinction between a period of crisis and a period of more normal operations makes all the more imperative efforts to explain policy aims and methods to the public. The State Department, more than any other agency of the government, continuously and in many ways tries to inform the public of the nature and significance of current and prospective foreign policy. The Bureau of Public Affairs issues descriptive pamphlets, free for the asking, on almost every phase of our foreign affairs. There are frequent briefings of groups representing various segments of educational, business, and cultural life, the weekly *State Department Bulletin*, and the published documents, speeches, and releases, which form a large mass of material widely accessible and comprehensive in scope. The Bureau deals directly with the working press in Washington and with other representatives of the public, here and abroad. There is liaison with churchmen, veterans, Chambers of Commerce, universities, 4-H clubs, Boy Scouts, visiting foreign students, and a variety of citizens' groups. In Public Affairs there is a Speakers' Bureau which supplies qualified officers to address gatherings on appropriate occasions through the country.

Public attention focuses primarily on the high-level contacts between prominent journalists and the President, the Secretary, and others. Actually, the daily news briefing is an important source of information and gives the writer many clues which he develops later in various ways. At noon every day the press chief or his deputy is available in the easily accessible news room in the Department. He often gives a "handout" to the reporters. Frequently, there is a question-and-answer session, during which reporters can ask for fuller explanation and amplification. The newsmen have desks, telephones, and files. Nearby is a counter where all the recent releases are laid out for his taking. Moreover, he can look for friends in other bureaus or wait outside the Secretary's office or the conference rooms to see what he can glean in the way of casual information. The "white papers" and the special leaflets are given to him at his request. These, issued from time to time, cover all the major issues, conflicts, conferences, and policy formulations, as well as containing dozens of speeches by the officers. Much information is also available in the *Congressional Record* and the reports of hearings on the Hill.

The most dramatic aspect of the public relations of the Department of State is the Secretary's press conference, held fairly regularly when the Secretary is in Washington. The Secretaries have differed in the frequency of their sessions with the press and also in their manner of conducting the discussions. Andrew Berding has described the press conference in his book *Foreign Affairs and You*, where he says of Secretary Dulles:

> . . . he regarded the press conference as an opportunity to put some of his thinking across to our own and other peoples. He felt that the press conference, because of its informality and because what he was

*saying was in response to questions, gave him an opportunity to speak
out and say certain things it would be difficult to say in formal
communications.*

Berding adds that when Dulles stood up before 150 to 175 correspondents and fielded their barrage of questions he gave no sign of
apprehension.[32]

He says that Secretary Herter felt that the "press conferences for
a Secretary of State 'were dangerous.' He eschewed them as much
as possible." He says of Secretary Rusk that he "has been sparing of
press conferences. The correspondents have been somewhat disappointed. . . ." He adds that, in his opinion, "Mr. Rusk has handled
the answers well and has gone as far as he reasonably could."[33]

With regard to the significance of these debates, Berding adds,

*Secretary Dulles said to me that the most important feature of the
press conferences was the transcript as published the following morning textually by The New York Times. This, he believed, was read
word for word by every Embassy in Washington and many foreign
offices overseas and by thousands of influential people in the United
States and abroad.*[34]

Before the meetings, which sometimes are held once a week on
Thursday, sometimes less frequently, and sometimes during special
crises, there is preparation for the Secretary throughout the Department and frequently consultation with the President. The day before
a scheduled conference, each Division in each Bureau decides
whether questions in its area of activity are likely to be posed and
whether it is desirable for the Secretary to volunteer a statement.
After the conclusions are reached, possible questions and reasonable
answers are drafted in brief form and included in the Secretary's
briefing book. This is given to him the day before the conference,
with special additions, if necessary, the following morning. He has
the opportunity to review this book and refresh his memory on a
wide variety of problems and factual situations. The Assistant Secretary for Public Affairs has the book under his arm as he follows the
Secretary to the platform to face the audience of eager newsmen.
Rarely, if ever, is the book consulted once the session is open. Occasionally, the Secretary may instruct his aide to supply additional
information which he thinks should be in writing or which is too
detailed for appropriate oral discussion. On the whole, however, the
questions are met with quick and ready answers—and in a few cases

with a "diversionary action" that stimulates, even if it fails to satisfy.

The preparation of the briefing material for the news conference sometimes brings to the attention of the Secretary material on emerging problems that would not ordinarily have been available to him in this easily accessible form on a few hours' notice. It is not a substitute for the intelligence briefing, but it may give a policy slant which is valuable to him in informing the journalists and in keeping the public up to date. The transcript of the conference is immediately gone over with great care, and, since it is handled in separate sections, it is available to the newsmen within an hour or so of the meeting as a basis for checking their stories. This mimeographed record, with minor changes in punctuation and perhaps the breaking up of a sentence that seems too long, makes it possible for the reporters to make direct quotes. (In the case of the President's press conferences, no changes in sentence structure or wording are usually made. Indeed, President Eisenhower arranged for a private court reporting company to make the notes and issued the transcripts without prior White House scrutiny.)

Another, and probably more difficult, way to inform the American public, and many abroad, comes through the informal press briefings held from time to time. (Secretary Dulles scheduled more of these than his successors.) These dinner meetings and other group discussions are off the record. They are designed to give a more philosophic and extended analysis of the major problems of current concern. They are a great strain on the Secretary, as the discussion tends to penetrate deep into purpose and motive. Question follows question, and the Secretary has to be both frank and wary. It is always dangerous to give views of the President's thinking or to look into the future as to the probable negotiating position of the government. Since these talks furnish background that colors later comments, they seep through into the public press, even though without direct quotes. Only rarely has there been a serious leak of a confidential discussion which may have harmed our foreign relations. The journalists are a sophisticated group who understand the problems of the official —few sacrifice their contacts with top-level officials for the sake of a scare headline.

Special requests for personal interviews, particularly by those who are developing a comprehensive story, are sometimes granted. The requests present problems, since it is not considered good policy to favor those men who represent the large metropolitan dailies, as contrasted with those from the smaller cities. Nevertheless, it is inevitable that a few papers should have special advantages by reason of their larger staff and foreign representation. The newsmen seek information also from the foreign embassies and from the other departments of government. The problem is not so much a dearth of news as one of balance and selection to give the public a sound perspective on what the national leaders are trying to accomplish. In this effort the newsmen also pay considerable attention to the views and information of leaders of Congress concerned with foreign affairs.

There is a tendency on the part of some of the writers to be more than observers of the quickly changing scene and to exercise an influence on decisions. Professor Bernard Cohen discusses their roles as critics, as representatives of the public, and also as "policy-makers." He calls them actors in the process "very close to the stream and structure of policy-making."[35] While this aspect of the journalist's influence is perhaps felt more in Washington than outside, it is a not negligible part of his influence both between and during election campaigns. Even the most objective reporting involves choices, and editors and columnists exert considerable pressure on the public, on Congress, and at times on the officials themselves.

In the interests of security, on occasions the newsmen have withheld information until its official release. They have had problems in connection with the U-2 affair, Cuba, and other crises during which some aspects of the conduct of foreign affairs had to be kept secret during the time of the greatest interest. The area of public understanding is one where a high degree of cooperation is needed to achieve the desired result. Without an informed public, men cannot be expected to appreciate the objectives for which they fight and die. Even the lesser demands, which call on a large share of the taxpayer's dollar, depend for adequate legislation and support on effective education of the public.

It is for this reason that the Department devotes many hours to assistance of the press and the publication of explanatory material. In no other country is there a comparable effort. The supplementary activities of the United States Information Agency, which are directed to foreign nations, help, but in an indirect manner. They do not issue material in this country and cannot act as a propaganda agency. Their role is clearly limited and defined.

The broadcaster, the journalist, and others who put foreign policy issues before the public all play a part in making the statesman a familiar figure as they bring their criticism or praise to bear on his actions. Their long-run contribution is sometimes forgotten in the hot controversy over short-term issues. In the immediate present, they suggest the limits which the public can set to a policy which they do not understand or will not tolerate. The State Department is acutely aware of the constructive and destructive possibilities.

The United Nations. Other limits arise out of world public opinion. This opinion is most widely represented by statements in the United Nations. No survey of foreign policy and how it is made can be complete without a recognition of the influences that come from the leaders in other nations. Opposition or support inevitably modifies the lines along which the President and Secretary of State proceed. All major programs and alliances receive attention either in the General Assembly, the Security Council, or in some regular or special committee. Here our positions are debated and our intentions challenged.

Those who conceived the UN at Dumbarton Oaks in 1944 and who brought it into being in San Francisco a year later expected that it could eliminate many misunderstandings and harmonize the aims of the leading nations. The experts, even the most optimistic of them, did not expect that it would end conflict or reconcile major differences. They considered that in providing a forum for discussion and the exchange of views, action would be moderated and time gained for adaptation to changes which could not be avoided. To a considerable extent, the United Nations has accelerated the pace of change. It has also cushioned many of the shocks which would have had a disruptive effect. In fact, among the many functions it performs, the dissemination of information and the increase in communication have been among the most significant.

The UN's negotiating activities have been sharply curtailed by the dichotomy between the aims and principles of communist nations and those of the Western democratic world. Moreover, the failure of the communist countries to share in the financial and security burdens on other nations has hampered many of the efforts which the United States and the European countries have wished to make in the interests of economic, scientific, and cultural cooperation. The struggle over many issues has set barriers to American policy.

Thus even though its capabilities were limited in the situation which developed after Yalta and Potsdam, it has been both an addition to the apparatus which the President and the Secretary could use and has in some respects limited their action. It has been a meeting place where persuasion and criticism could bring international leaders into line or make plain their differences. Here the heads of state from the new nations of Africa and Asia have gained a sense of world problems. UN committees have developed technical programs and made investigations of difficult issues. They have taken over a number of aid and trusteeship functions and served as a midstation between colonialism and independence.

In performing its many tasks, the United Nations relieved the United States, to some extent, of responsibilities which would have been burdensome at a time when we were already expanding our activities in the occupation of conquered areas, in European reconstruction, and in security alliances. The fact that many of the functions performed became multilateral and international lessened the likelihood that the United States would be blamed for imperialistic activity. Criticism, which was bound to come with our predominance in many economic and political affairs, was thus diluted.

The scope of the United Nations in widely diversified fields is suggested by the names of some of the specialized agencies which have been coordinated under its charter.* Fifteen of them are:

International Telecommunication Union (ITU)
Universal Postal Union (UPU)
World Meteorological Organization (WMO)
International Labor Office (ILO)
International Monetary Fund (IMF)
International Bank for Reconstruction and Development (IBRD)
International Finance Corporation (IFC)
International Development Association (IDA)

*These vary as to degree of importance and autonomy.

Food and Agriculture Organization (FAO)
United Nations Educational, Scientific, and Cultural
 Organization (UNESCO)
United Nations Industrial Development Organization (UNIDO)
International Civil Aviation Organization (ICAO)
World Health Organization (WHO)
Asia Development Bank (ADB)
Intergovernmental Maritime Consultative Organization (IMCO)

Much of the work and the many facilities which these organizations make possible are of importance to the smooth working of international relations in the less controversial fields. In all of these agencies the United States has played an important part, but in some of them the tasks have been shared to a degree with other nations, which have supplied staff, ideas, and even some financial resources. The communist bloc countries have participated in this work, as well as in some of the *ad hoc* commissions, but the part they have played has been limited.

In the Monetary Fund and International Bank, as well as in the other financial undertakings under multilateral control, the United States has been in the forefront in contributions, leadership, and in the quotas—the shares allotted which determine both financial participation and voting. In these organizations, as contrasted with the General Assembly and the Security Council, American predominance has therefore been reflected in the management and guidance of the organizations.

In public discussions, however, most emphasis is usually placed on the frustration of peace-keeping efforts by the use of the veto in the Security Council. This has been a bitter disappointment to many idealists who felt that a sure road to peace had been found with the acceptance of, and widespread membership in, the United Nations. From 1946 through 1967, the Soviet Union cast 104 vetoes and thus blocked actions of many different kinds. All other vetoes have totaled merely eight, and the United States has never vetoed a proposal. At the outbreak of the Korean War in 1950, the Soviets were still out of the Security Council, which they had boycotted since January.* Their absence facilitated the immediate condemnation of the

---

*They walked out in protest over the continued presence of Nationalist China.

North Koreans in the Council and the initiation of the police action to save South Korea. In other cases, where chance did not favor the free world's plans, action in the General Assembly has been a partial substitute for agreement in the Security Council. Nevertheless, many of the moves by the United States have been frustrated; this has led some skeptics to question the value of the organization. The crisis of 1964 and 1965 over the financial arrears of the U.S.S.R. and several other nations had an inconclusive end, as this breach of the rules was allowed to be overlooked. In spite of the Soviets' defiance of the majority will on occasion, there is no evidence that they wish to withdraw.†

Why, ask many observers, should the United States, with its large financial contribution and its efforts to assist the tentative and often fumbling actions of many of the members, tolerate a situation in which the vote of Togo, or of Mauretania, is equal to the vote of the most powerful economic and nuclear power on earth? The answer is clear, though not satisfying. There is no formula for voting which will satisfy the democratic notions and the aspirations for power of the other members, except the present simple and inequitable arrangement: one nation, one vote. The acceptance of this situation can be construed as an indication that criticism in the UN may represent opposition that would emerge in other forms if there were no UN.

In spite of the frustrations and disappointments in the performance of the UN, it is still an addition to the diplomatic machinery and the means for working toward a world of law and order. Here the increasing demands for harmony and compromise are debated. Here methods of cooperation are tried and applied to various situations. Those who have studied recent history understand that the finding of solutions to such questions as the Israeli-Arab disputes, Cyprus, Algeria, and the Congo will long elude the best endeavors of any international organization. The fact remains that many a quarrel has been kept within manageable bounds and that the safety valve of General Assembly debate has given a useful pause for reconsideration and, in some cases, for retreat. In this body, the United States, while acting quietly and without fanfare, has availed

---

†Indonesia's withdrawal in 1965 has been the only case; it returned in 1966. Syria lost a seat in 1958, when it was joined with Egypt in the United Arab Republic, but regained it in 1966, when it seceded from the UAR.

itself of opportunities for securing support and has tolerated debate, knowing that at times it has been a substitute for more violent conflicts.

Fortunately, in the framing of the charter, precautions were taken not to exclude already existing means of cooperation and alliance. Regional organizations were expressly recognized as proper developments between members and nonmembers. NATO, OAS, SEATO, ANZUS, and CENTO were all consistent with the letter and the spirit of the organization. So far, there has never been a two-thirds vote against the United States on any question to which we were committed.

Thus, in this critical period, there is at hand for our use a multilateral organization. Through its many subagencies and highly expert inquiries, it can supplement some of our American expenditure of time and effort. For instance, the Special Fund, now in the United Nations Development Program (UNDP), while small in its contribution to development, has performed valuable service in a number of countries.* Then again, we have often applauded the Secretary General's stand before the court of world opinion, one made all the more effective because he was in the forefront of the international debate.

The lines of action of our Ambassador to the UN are laid down in Washington. They are the guides to our debates, our votes, and our diplomatic persuasion in New York. This facet of diplomacy, which is an art, is very much like that performed in our missions abroad. Our Ambassador has a complex and many-sided responsibility. He is exposed to pressures from all over the world. He is in close touch with Washington. He reports continuously on the opinions, attitudes, efforts, and abilities of the representatives of each of the approximately 122 other nations. Like other Ambassadors, he receives telegraph instructions from the Department of State. He is joined, as are other Ambassadors, by the Secretary of State from time to time. On rare occasions, the President may address the General Assembly. The Ambassador is near, and yet he is separate from the organization in Washington. He faces the same requirements for initiative and for subordination to Presidential decisions. However, there are new facets to our foreign policy and new chances of growth in our ability to work with other nations in the UN.

---

*Expenditures as of 1966 totaled approximately $500 million.

The power of Congress in fulfilling its responsibilities to the will of the people, partly reflected in the press, and the challenge of world opinion, expressed in the United Nations and elsewhere, set concentric circles about our action in foreign affairs. They tend to define the scope of policy as reflected in daily work and decision in crisis. The President, the Secretary of State, his Department, and all the cooperating services are aware of the necessity of conforming to the conditions set by these outer limits.

CRITICISM OF THE STATE DEPARTMENT

Every few months there appears in some major daily or monthly an article discussing "what is wrong with the State Department." Each one is occasioned by the growing awareness of the importance of action in the foreign field and by a frequent sense of frustration among writers, like that which confronts the student and the expert. No one likes to acknowledge the persistent difficulties or the impossibility of finding dependable and enduring solutions to foreign policy problems. The Secretary of State and the Department are, therefore, the obvious subjects of criticism.

While refutation of general charges is impossible, one can say in rejoinder that there has not been a nuclear war and that there has been a rising standard of living in the years just past. Nevertheless, many inadequacies must be admitted—yet no one knows better than the official or the diplomat the shortcomings in the system. The number of persons employed by the Executive branch who are involved directly and indirectly in the formulation of foreign policy runs into the hundreds of thousands; the tasks are multitudinous, and the recent expansion of functions presents new and special problems.

One of the main areas of dispute relates to the selection, promotion, and degree of specialization of the personnel. Those who discuss this aspect of the Department frequently condemn its lack of imagination, of flexibility, of ingenuity, and of foresight. The charges may be well-founded, but the correction cannot be prescribed in terms of categorical changes in the system. The desired improvement can only come with gradual evolution and patient effort.

Another criticism recently heard among the professionals is that the speed of communication and the increasing power of the President have almost paralyzed the possibility of quick action in the Embassy abroad. This uneasiness does not apply so much to the Ambassador in his normal functions as to the Embassy, operating in an emergency under contingency plans and general guidelines.

Then again, some observers decry the extent to which the White House staff call on Departmental officers at various levels, in an attempt to bypass channels. Usually, these contacts have actually complicated the process of inquiry or action by necessitating extraordinary steps to coordinate action after the unusual contacts have started the wheels turning by what seemed to be the more direct approach. The familiar interconnections in the apparatus which have been established are not without meaning and cannot be ignored without cost.

Finally, when a situation develops which causes the officers in the Foreign Service abroad or in the Department in Washington to conclude that the Secretary of State is not in fact the chief adviser to the President and not in control of the major aspects of foreign affairs, the tone and morale of the personnel deteriorate rapidly. There have been such times in the last few years. With such a situation there comes a serious danger to the effective execution of our policy, which weakens it in the short run and even more in the long run.*

The main thesis behind the description of the process and the survey of recent action is that though there can be many negative criticisms, constructive suggestions have been few.

NOTES

1. Theodore C. Sorensen, *Decision-Making in the White House*, Columbia University Press, 1963, p. 24.
2. Edward Hallett Carr, *What Is History?*, Knopf, 1962, p. 55.
3. H. Field Haviland, Jr., ed., *The Formulation and Administration of United States Foreign Policy*, Brookings Institution, 1960, p. 45.
4. Temple Wanamaker, *American Foreign Policy Today*, Bantam Books, 1964, p. 25; U. S. Congress, House Committee on Foreign Affairs, H. R. 12169, January 26, 1966, p. 16.

---

*The uncertainties of recent years may be partially put to rest by State Department Circular No. 385 of March 4, 1966, reaffirming the authority of the Secretary and his staff.

94   FOREIGN POLICY IN THE MAKING

5. Eleanor Lansing Dulles, *John Foster Dulles: The Last Year*, Harcourt, Brace & World, 1963, p. 34.
6. Haviland, *op. cit.*, p. 3.
7. Jackson Committee, U. S. Senate Committee on Government Operations, Subcommittee on National Security Staffing and Operations, *Administration of National Security*, 88th Congress, 1965, pp. 34, 35.
8. *Ibid.*, pp. 235, 386–389.
9. Allen Dulles, *The Craft of Intelligence*, Harper & Row, 1963, pp. 256–263.
10. Jackson Committee, *op. cit.*, p. 386.
11. Haviland, *op. cit.*, p. 48.
12. Jackson Committee, *op. cit.*, p. 400.
13. *Ibid.*, pt. 5, p. 376; also parts 1, 2, 3, 4.
14. James L. McCamy, *Conduct of the New Diplomacy*, Harper & Row, 1964, p. 171.
15. Allen Dulles, *op. cit.*, pp. 188, 189.
16. Jackson Committee, *op. cit.*, pp. 236, 239, 242.
17. Haviland, *op. cit.*, p. 110.
18. *Ibid.*, p. 111.
19. McCamy, *op. cit.*, p. 236.
20. Jackson Committee, *op. cit.*, p. 360.
21. *Ibid.* ("The Ambassador"), p. 65.
22. McCamy, *op. cit.*, p. 249.
23. Jackson Committee, *op. cit.*, p. 239.
24. *Ibid.*, p. 362.
25. *Ibid.*, p. 360.
26. Wanamaker, *op. cit.*, p. 20.
27. *American Foreign Policy, 1950–1955, Current Documents*, Department of State, 1957, pp. 2363, 2486.
28. Allen Dulles, *op. cit.*, p. 258.
29. David Wise and Thomas B. Ross, *The Invisible Government*, Random House, 1964, pp. 258–263.
30. Haviland, *op. cit.*, p. 22.
31. Bernard C. Cohen, *The Press and Foreign Policy*, Princeton University Press, 1963, pp. 224–247. This analysis is a useful summary of the relations of the Administration and the Press.
32. Andrew Berding, *Foreign Affairs and You!*, Doubleday, 1962, p. 171.
33. *Ibid.*, p. 171.
34. *Ibid.*, pp. 171, 172.
35. Cohen, *op. cit.*, p. 39.

II

TWO DECADES
OF FOREIGN POLICY

PROSPECTS FOR RESPONSIBILITY, ACTION,
AND LEADERSHIP: EUROPE

For more than 20 years, the United States has been working, in
various ways, to equip itself and to shape its course to meet the new
responsibilities and the increasing challenges of the latter half of
the twentieth century. The changes, which have been many, have
been continuations, fitted to a new environment, of long-term policy
and fundamental principles. They have been demanded by the great
threat to our security and by the worldwide opportunities to increase international cooperation. The nature and extent of the new
elements in the making of foreign policy have been discussed in
Chapter I. The manner in which they have been revealed in the
swift flow of history, since the Second World War, can be reviewed
in the story of our diplomacy and our foreign programs.

This account inevitably highlights our impressive economic activities in the fields of aid and financial and commercial cooperation;
our extensive part in military government and defensive measures
abroad; the new efforts in the fields of education and information;
and the expansion of our leadership in agreements and alliances to
safeguard the peace. It includes the use of multilateral organizations,

especially the United Nations, and the attempts that have been made to limit and control armaments and to prevent the spread of nuclear danger. All of these aspects of our international involvement and our acceptance of the leadership position which was thrust upon us are evident in specific events, decisions, agreements and crises. The degree of success or failure can be variously assessed. Only history can give a clear verdict. Time will alter opinions, but the facts can bring lessons for today.

The temper of these years is compounded of various emotions, aims, and fears. They include pride and a sense of obligation in a world striving toward an equitable and peaceful unity. The increasing determination to moderate local, tribal, and even national differences is reflected in many programs of cooperation. The will to hold back the tyrannical ideologies of aggressive powers is evidenced in a readiness to defend Berlin and to fight in Korea and Vietnam. A sense of our limits, of our vulnerability, of our inability to control restless and rebellious areas—these disturbing thoughts partially explain clashes between the executive and the legislative branches of our government. (A case in point is the frequent conflicts over spending for defense or for aid.) The evidence of our present position is not always clear; nor can future trends of opinion be predicted with any confidence. Moments of hesitation have followed times of firm and decisive action. Thus, there have been miscalculations on the part of our enemies and doubts on the part of our friends.

The drama of these years is heightened by the fear of nuclear conflict, the mystery of the conquest of space, the sense of widening human perspective, and the rapid changes in the expectations held by large segments of people in emerging nations. So far, we have not fully absorbed the meaning of the recent past, but this understanding is necessary if we are to deal effectively with the problems of the present.

The division of the last 20 or so years into meaningful periods has a limited usefulness because some of the changes have been gradual, as attitudes and practices have been progressively modified. It is possible, however, to single out a number of events and decisions as of special importance in that they changed the course of our policy. These occurrences are outlined here as marking shifts of emphasis in four distinguishable phases.

The years from the end of the war and the Yalta Conference to the establishment of the North Atlantic Treaty Organization were marked by changing estimates of communist aims and the resulting danger to Western democracies. This was a period of disillusion and growing apprehension. The next few years, from the outbreak of the war in Korea, were characterized by determination to resist communist aggression and the development of a series of treaties and alliances. The third period, from the mid-1950s to 1960, was a time of repeated Soviet probes to find weak points in the Western position, met by increasing commitments and changes in security measures on the part of the United States. The fourth span of years, from 1960 to 1967, was a time of reappraisal of the intentions of the communist world and growing concern as to the direction of the newer nations. The crisis in the Congo sets a significant turning point for this chapter in the increasing involvement which has no acceptable cut-off date—as our involvement in Vietnam carries us further into the defense of nations under pressure in Southeast Asia.

To give an account of the 20-year period through which we have just passed is a demanding task because selection and classification has to be made to assure the emphasis on changing response to events. Much of the American strategic planning is addressed inevitably to the Cold War struggle. There are other challenges that require attention, notably the issues raised by some 60 newly independent nations in Asia and Africa. Similarly, changes of a less dramatic character in Latin America must be considered. In the fields of science and economics there are a host of recent developments that affect diplomacy. New resources are available. Some bring orderly institutional arrangements into world affairs; others arouse fear and occasion a restlessness that is difficult to restrain.

The successes and failures of the United Nations, which seemed in 1945 to promise new ways to peace and security, have brought added burdens for the statesman and placed the United States in a new position with respect to both friendly and hostile nations. Many new problems have emerged which call for greater diplomatic skills and larger financial resources.

The account to be sketched here in broad outlines is intended as a background to the understanding of six critical moments in our policy-making, which will be presented in some detail in Chapter III. This whole account of foreign policy in the making is developed from the point of view of American aims, institutions, and personalities. Its scope is limited as compared with worldwide positions and intentions. Moreover, because it is necessary to condense and summarize, many interesting events and background considerations have to be omitted.

YEARS OF HOPE AND DISILLUSION

In the months before the end of the Second World War, diplomats and experts were working feverishly to prepare for the conditions expected to confront the Allies after victory. There was a keen sense of the material needs and a consciousness of political problems of unprecedented scope. Along with apprehension, there was also a hope that the United States and its allies could seize the opportunity that would come with the first days of victory to build new institutions and reach dependable agreements for cooperation and a stable peace. It was assumed that two of the warring countries, Germany and Japan, would present the main difficulties and that the period of adjustment would pose many thorny questions between belligerents and their neighbor nations, fearful of resurgence.

The planning conducted in Washington from 1942 to 1945 was a new attempt to anticipate the future and reflected a realization that the United States would have to carry a considerable share of the task of achieving order and prosperity after victory. The State Department's Special Division, under the direction of the Division Chief, Leo Pasvolsky, was given the task of preparing planning documents. After they had been cleared by the State-War-Navy Committee and the White House, they were sent to London to be incorporated into international plans being made by the European Advisory Commission; there the British, the Russians, and, occasionally, the French conferred with American representatives. These papers were aimed at the requirements of the first two years after the war, while our troops would remain abroad. A few had a longer time perspective, and some were to have a lasting impact. Others had to be discarded as conditions after the surrender of the Axis powers developed along unexpected lines. The Cold War had not been a part of the projections into the years that lay ahead.

OVERLORD—the landings in Normandy on June 6, 1944—was

recognized everywhere as a decisive step on the march to victory. Rome had been taken on June 5, and an Italian government was approved two weeks later. These triumphs were accompanied by varied and complex political problems. They involved the establishment of provisional governments and brought to the forefront the questions of elections and political freedom—issues that were to increase the frictions in Central Europe even before recognition of the Cold War. The problems of Belgium and the Netherlands were less acute. Those of France, Greece, and particularly the Balkan countries became increasingly serious in the years 1945 and 1946. The issues in Yugoslavia and Poland were special causes of strain between the communist and noncommunist powers. While spheres of influence had been informally sketched in the conversations among Churchill, Roosevelt, and Stalin at Yalta, the unsatisfactory nature of the assumptions that led to the Soviet domination of Central Europe was evident immediately after Potsdam. The debate over the responsibility for the spread of communist domination over the countries which the Western powers had helped to liberate will long trouble historians.

The inadequacy of political planning, as contrasted with economic, will be blamed for many of the obstacles to unity of effort in the postwar years. Clearly, the United Nations had not the power to remedy the errors made while the fighting was still going on. The changes in national conditions were too great to be anticipated. Moreover, the diplomatic negotiations failed to reflect the views of the more impartial experts. In the heat of battle the decisions were made at the top and resulted from the views and estimates of the few statesmen dealing with each other in times of great peril. The priorities were chosen in the name of victory. The choices were not always wise.

Behind the economic forecasts and projections of the early 1940s lay years of bitter experience which had brought certain lessons to the forefront of thinking among statesmen. The failure of the international financial policies of the interwar period, culminating in the depression and the collapse of the gold standard in 1931, had brought home to many the economic interdependence of nations. The rise of Hitler and the aggressive intentions of Japan and Germany had demonstrated the weakness of even the stronger nations standing alone. The interrelation of all major economic, security, and political policies and the increasing threat to civilization drove home the impossibility of isolationism. These lessons were unmistakable, even before Hiroshima. Then, in 1945, the special nature of the nuclear age gradually became apparent.

The United States was aware of the nation's relative economic strength, which was to increase worldwide responsibilities. This knowledge was fundamental to the proposals for the United Nations Relief and Rehabilitation Administration (UNRRA) and to the "double standard" which the United States was to accept in its large contributions to all the postwar economic efforts. UNRRA, a stopgap relief measure, was devised in November, 1943, at the same time that the charter for the United Nations Organization was being outlined at Dumbarton Oaks; it was designed to meet some of the more urgent needs for food and shelter and also to care for the millions of refugees displaced during the war and occupation by the Japanese and the Germans.

A sense of the magnitude of the problem was reflected as UNRRA was considered in a complex of other economic measures. The conference at Bretton Woods, New Hampshire, in July, 1944, met to consider proposals, already widely discussed, for monetary, investment, and trade organizations to deal with the longer term needs of devastated and debt-ridden countries. It was then expected that the Soviets would share in this work. They took an active part at Bretton Woods, promising at the time a large gold subscription to the projected financial institutions—a promise greeted with cheers at the final banquet presided over by Secretary of the Treasury Henry Morgenthau, Jr. The measure which was to bring the agreements for the International Monetary Fund (IMF) and the International Bank for Reconstruction and Development (IBRD) into existence was approved by the Senate and the House on July 31, 1945. The U.S.S.R. never adhered to the agreement for the institutions.

The proposed International Trade Organization, which was also discussed at Bretton Woods, never came into being, but the General Agreement on Tariffs and Trade (GATT), which undertook work on liberalization of trade, has taken over some of the intended functions of the proposed organization and has been the basis for conferences reducing restrictions and lowering tariffs.

The importance of the United Kingdom in this effort to aid

reconstruction and the U.S. wish for partnership with it were recognized in the $3,750 million loan to Great Britain on December 6, 1945. Though the loan was substantially below the amount requested by John Maynard Keynes, the financial genius with whom the United States experts had worked closely, it was still large when measured on the scale of earlier economic support.

Thus, the economic foundations for a far-reaching cooperation were laid even before the war was over. One of the first organizations to be set up, ICAO, grew out of the International Civil Aviation Organization Convention and was established by the final act of the Chicago Conference ending in December, 1944. Other agencies started in the early postwar years—some of the results of the extensive planning—included the United Nations Educational, Scientific, and Cultural Organization (UNESCO), the World Health Organization (WHO), the International Refugee Organization (IRO), the World Meteorological Organization (WMO), and the Intergovernmental Maritime Consultative Organization (IMCO). The International Telecommunication Union (ITU), the Universal Postal Union (UPU), and the International Labor Organization (ILO)—three organizations dating from before World War II—were revised in 1946 and 1947.*

These organizations, and others that followed, represent the willingness of this government to carry a large share of the postwar burdens and also an awareness of the importance of economic instruments in the conduct of foreign affairs. They have provided schools in the arts of international cooperation and have given a solid basis for economic expansion which would not otherwise have been possible. In spite of the enormous strain on the economies of war-devastated lands and the pressures exerted by technical and scientific changes, there has been no world depression. The stability of currencies has been more dependable than could have been expected, and the progress toward economic integration has continued steadily since the war.

This, then, is the favorable side of world affairs. The other side

---

*The many resolutions, Acts, agreements, and treaties of this period are included in A *Decade of American Foreign Policy, Basic Documents, 1941–1949*, prepared at the request of the Senate Committee on Foreign Relations, Document No. 123, 81st Congress, pp. 1381, Government Printing Office, Washington, 1950.

became evident even before the war had ended. The Soviet demands for large reparation payments from Germany had given hints of their lack of appreciation of the economic emergencies that would follow victory. This was first officially brought into the open in the conversations of Secretary of State Cordell Hull in Moscow in October, 1943. There was only vague knowledge of the "Katyn Woods massacre" and of the failure of the Red Army to come to the help of the Polish underground in 1944. As the war in Europe moved toward its climax, however, reports of the behavior of the Soviet troops as they moved westward began to reach American Army centers.

Franklin Roosevelt on his last trip abroad sought to reach constructive agreements with Stalin at Yalta. He knew of the military estimates of the expected heavy losses to our troops in the Pacific, predicted to exceed a million men. He knew of the suffering which would be endured if the war in the East were to continue for many months to come. Mindful of these facts, he tried to settle the many problems relating to Europe and assure Soviet help in the Pacific war.

The Yalta meetings were cordial during the first days. Winston Churchill reports the speeches and conversations in some detail in *Triumph and Tragedy*.[1] There was agreement over the United Nations, and the difficult problems of the future of Germany caused no rift. Indeed, there seemed to be a measure of general agreement —though the manner in which crucial questions were disposed of and others left for later decision is hard to understand even now. The main tensions developed over the future of Poland. Yet even this seemed to Churchill to have been disposed of in a satisfactory manner. Roosevelt had indicated that he could get along with Stalin. Churchill expressed his view that the Soviet leaders wished to live "in honorable friendship and equality with the Western Democracies." (He was to change his impression in a few short weeks.) The United States was gratified that the Soviets had agreed to enter the war against Japan.

The hopes with regard to Polish independence and eastern boundaries deteriorated as the Soviet leaders failed to keep their Yalta agreements. Churchill's letter to Roosevelt on March 13 indicates his profound disillusionment: "Poland has lost her frontier. Is she now to lose her freedom?" The Soviets became suspicious about our negotiations for the surrender of the German army in Italy, in which they had been invited to participate. Stalin sent a message to Roosevelt that was considered insulting. Roosevelt in his reply referred to "vile misrepresentations of my actions" by informers. Thus, it is clear that the shadows of troubles to come were already evident. Meanwhile, General Eisenhower wrote to Churchill on April 1 that "if at any moment collapse should suddenly come . . . we would rush forward, and Lübeck and Berlin would be included in our important targets." These were the thoughts of the world's greatest statesmen.

On April 12, President Roosevelt died. The many questions in Europe and in the Far East which had not been completely thrashed out and which were to trouble the world for the next decades pressed for early decision. The problem of German dismemberment was put aside. The American intention of capturing Berlin from the West was dropped. President Truman took up the heavy burdens and waited to hear whether or not the atomic bomb was ready. When the German surrender came at Rheims on May 8, the tasks of military government began.

It was a month after Roosevelt's death, on May 12, that Churchill wrote to President Truman of his "deep anxiety because of their [the Soviets'] misinterpretation of the Yalta decisions . . . their overwhelming influence in the Balkans . . . the difficulties they make about Vienna," their techniques and their armies. He said: "An iron curtain is drawn down upon their front. We do not know what is going on behind."[2]

For some leaders, 1945 was a turning point. For most political observers, it came later, after the Fulton, Missouri, speech of Winston Churchill in the spring of 1946 and after Secretary of State James Byrnes' speech in Stuttgart in September of that year. In fact, programs and operations in the first years after the war were governed by a series of contradictory views, plans, and commitments. The assumption that the military occupation of Germany and Austria would be brief explains the nature of the temporary arrangements, considered serviceable for a short period.

Meanwhile, the rapid change in the situation in the Far East came as a surprise. President Truman had left for Potsdam on the cruiser *Augusta* before the successful explosion of the first atomic bomb at Alamogordo flats in New Mexico on July 16, 1945. The cable to the President told in code of the "arrival of General Groves' lusty infant with the flashing eyes." The conversation between President Truman and Joseph Stalin at Potsdam, in which the success of the experiment was reported, reflected slight realization on the part of the Soviet leader of this major turning point in history. He is said to have made no comment. President Truman, on his side, seemed to be little influenced in his plans for the future. There had not been a firm decision to drop the bomb on a Japanese city, and the military effectiveness of such an action was still to be demonstrated.[3]

Potsdam, which was an extension of the conversations of the Yalta Conference, has been blamed for agreements which in fact took place earlier. There is little doubt, however, that if Winston Churchill had not had to return home after the first few days, thrown out of office by the electorate, a new look at many of the postwar problems might have been initiated.* Truman had been newly thrust into a position of power and had been insufficiently prepared by Roosevelt. In fact, those who had been working on these problems in the departments in Washington had been acutely aware of the extent to which the decision-making process in Roosevelt's time had been dominated by one or two men—the Vice President and the Secretary of State had known little of the trend of thinking or the conditions on which agreements were based. (Furthermore, Cordell Hull had been succeeded by Edward Stettinius on November 27, 1944. The new Secretary's knowledge of current diplomatic issues was less even than that of his predecessor, who had been excluded from many of the conferences by President Roosevelt.) In spite of these handicaps, however, Truman at Potsdam showed a businesslike attitude that impressed his associates.

The order to drop the bomb on Hiroshima, which had to be the decision of one man—President Truman—led not only to the surrender of Japan, but also to a new world of international relations. The long-range consequences were for some time obscured by the immediate consequences: there was peace in the Pacific, but there was awe at the tragedy of the terrifying power of the bomb.

The State Department knew before the Potsdam Conference that

---

*He was replaced at the conference by Clement R. Attlee, the new Prime Minister.

many of the Japanese leaders wished to sue for peace. It was feared, however, that the warlords had the power to prevent capitulation. There was an announcement regarding surrender terms by the Allied leaders on July 26 in an effort to shorten the war.[4] The reaction to this move was not encouraging. It had been estimated by many military leaders that the war might continue for 18 months more if the invasion of Japan were executed without the use of the atomic bomb. The consideration that more than a million Americans and countless Japanese would die was conclusive for President Truman. After the successful July 16 test, he gave the command that the atomic attack should be launched as soon as the weather permitted. A bomb was dropped on Hiroshima on August 6, and another on Nagasaki, three days later.

The Japanese surrendered unconditionally on August 14; the formal surrender document was signed on September 2. The occupation of Japan under General Douglas MacArthur, which followed at once, was not complicated by the Soviets' participation, as it was in the case of Austria and Germany. There was no need to negotiate with Moscow on such matters as access or control agreements. Nevertheless, though we were successful in preventing Soviet interference with our policy in Japan, we lost other positions of strength as the Soviet invasion of Manchuria laid a basis for the communization of the Chinese mainland. The plans for disarmament, reconstruction, and democratization moved forward promptly in Japan, however. The Basic Initial Post-Surrender policy directives to the Supreme Commander were issued on November 1, 1945. They defined the scope of authority and control of the country and covered political and administrative organizations, demilitarization, prisoners of war, education, the operation of the economic system, and other related matters. The Emperor, an important symbol for the Japanese, was retained.

In these postwar arrangements the United Nations was established to keep the peace and to assist in the diplomatic settlement of disputes, but played no part in postwar occupation. The new organization of "peace-loving nations" had wide scope, but its strength was no greater than the will of its members. Since it had no military or financial base on which it could operate, it could not intervene in a significant manner in postwar occupation, negotiation of peace treaties, or adjustment of the disputes between the major powers over the spheres of influence in Central Europe and the Far East. This instrument of foreign policy, thus fashioned in a time of growing tensions, was not able to expand its activities and develop a tradition—it was surrounded by controversy and beset with difficulties from the start.

This was a period of disappointment as in international and national organizations channels of communication and allocation of responsibility did not keep pace with the rapid succession of events, which necessitated decisions that could not be delayed. The expertise of many working on the proposals for restoring order and reestablishing governments and economic relations was not adequately focused on the new power problems. The men in the leading foreign offices and in the United Nations operated in the midst of confusion. Their capabilities were not coordinated, and the basic aims were distorted as conditions changed more swiftly than the plans and documents which were to govern their actions.

In late 1945 and early 1946, a few diplomats disagreed with most of the others on the emerging pattern of Soviet intentions. Negotiations had begun in Paris on the peace treaties for the Balkan countries and Italy. The first of 104 Soviet vetoes in the Security Council of the United Nations suggested a serious limitation on its power, recognized initially only by these few. In February, a resolution proposed by the United States on the withdrawal of foreign troops from Syria and requesting a report to the Security Council on the results of negotiations was vetoed by Andrei Vishinsky. (As has been mentioned, the United States has never cast a negative vote in the Council. The veto has been used only eight times over the years by other countries than Russia—by France, by the United Kingdom, and by China.)

A further blow to the hope that the United Nations would be a major instrument in disarmament and especially in atomic control came when the Soviets refused the proposal of Bernard Baruch to bring atomic weapons under international control. This plan was put before the Commission and approved by the U.S.S.R. in December, but later, Soviet rejection brought the effort to a halt.

Meanwhile, the Council of Foreign Ministers, established as a result of Truman's suggestions at Potsdam, was having comparable difficulties in trying to settle the postwar problems of the Big Four. The group (CFM) held its first meeting in London in September,

1945. The ministers and their deputies were to hold a series of meetings on the occupation of Austria and Germany. It was considered more effective to have the postwar questions with which they were concerned handled in a smaller body than the unwieldly General Assembly of the United Nations. Moreover, many members obviously had no jurisdiction over these specific matters.

The Moscow CFM meeting in December, 1945, has been termed an "Eastern Munich," since Secretary of State Byrnes made a number of concessions to the Soviets which were reported to have annoyed President Truman.[5] The President became increasingly aware of the Iron Curtain, which was to be brought to world attention by the speech of Winston Churchill in Fulton, Missouri, in the spring of 1946. Here, Truman heard the former Prime Minister call for a tougher policy toward the Soviets. Meanwhile, he was being informed by his representatives in Austria and Germany of the many difficult negotiations which revealed the opposition of Moscow to the reconstruction of Europe and the settlement of the war problems.

A change in Washington's policy in Europe became evident in September, 1946, when Secretary Byrnes made a major speech in Stuttgart, indicating that America would help reconstruct Germany and that our troops would remain in Europe. General George C. Marshall was in China, studying its problems, at the same time. The occupation of Japan was proceeding according to schedule. In other words, demands on American resources, both in diplomacy and in economic assistance, were increasing in both the West and the East.

The directives concerned with the occupation of Germany and Austria had been prepared by the planning committees and approved by the European Advisory Committee in London; they were now in the hands of General Lucius D. Clay in Germany and General Mark Clark in Austria. The two generals had tried during the summer to work out operating arrangements with the Soviet generals to facilitate rapid denazification, disarmament, and establishment of democratic control in the assigned zones of occupation. They had both met with baffling obstructions at unexpected points. The question of *access* was handled in somewhat different ways in Germany and Austria, and the political and economic questions varied, mainly because of the theory of differences in the legal status of Germany, the aggressor, and Austria, "the first victim of Nazi aggression." The variations in arrangements were not regarded as serious at the time because of the assumption that the occupation would bring heavy burdens for only a few months, until a treaty draft would form the basis for further action in each instance. The contrast between the Pacific area and Europe is best illustrated by the fact that though the Japanese treaty was signed in 1951 and the Austrian State Treaty in 1955, the German treaty has continued to escape our grasp.

From the outset, the special status accorded Austria proved vital for its reconstruction. The Soviets, apparently misunderstanding the meaning of "socialism" in Austria, a nation which had constructed the *Karl Marx Hof* as a contribution to the living standard of the workers, chose Karl Renner, the venerable philosopher, as President. Their conversations in Vienna at this time indicated that they were not aware of his moderate and pro-Western views. The beginnings of a central government to be effective in all four zones were thus achieved early. It was soon apparent that the Soviets had made a number of other miscalculations in their dealings with Austria. Foremost among these was their acceptance of the "veto in reverse," which permitted the laws passed by their legislative body to go into effect 31 days after enactment unless unanimously disapproved by the four occupying powers. When adopted, these laws were valid throughout the land. The Soviets also permitted free elections. The Russian political representative told his American counterpart that he would be content with a 20 percent communist vote —he got 4 percent, a demonstration of strong anticommunism in the land. At about the same time as the elections, a monetary reform which helped make democracy operable in Austria was approved. After preliminary difficulties in agreement among the four powers as to the technical methods to be used, the modified American plan was adopted. Thus, in regard to leadership, the veto power, elections, and monetary reform, the Austrian government was allowed to start its long march toward independence and freedom, which culminated in 1955 when the State Treaty ended the occupation.

The Russians who had come in as liberators had allowed their soldiers license that often resulted in brutality; this alienated a population that might have been friendly. Even after the first period of disorder was over, there was a tragic story of kidnappings, economic exploitation, and political intimidation designed to bring the officials to submission to communist authority. Such stalwart men as Prime Minister Leopold Figl and Minister of the Interior Helmer stood up against threats and pressures of various sorts. The jeep that toured the city with officers of the four powers—French, British, Russian, and American—was a constant reminder of the pledge of unification and Allied support of the new government. So was the internationalized sector of Vienna, the inner city over which the Soviets never had control.

Vienna was thus both an evidence of the success of United States planning and a sign of the continuing gap in philosophy and intentions between the East and the West. It took a little time to demonstrate the extent of the progress that was being made and to develop confidence in the future of the country. The great difficulties in Germany had led to doubts in some centers about the viability of the smaller, long-suppressed country in the Danube River valley. A few loans and some industrial raw materials and coal from Army sources gave their stalled industry a chance to begin operations, even in the bitter cold of the early winters. Austria proved ready to respond to the opportunity offered by the Marshall Plan in June, 1947.

Policy had dictated a harder line for Germany. But conditions became intolerable because of large-scale removals of plant equipment and restrictions by the Soviets. During the first months, the discrepancy between the programs of the United States and the Soviets had not been as evident as in Austria. Then removals of plant and equipment, which virtually paralyzed early attempts to revive economic life in the eastern provinces, exceeded the EAC agreements and stirred the Western allies to protest. By 1947, the unwillingness of the communists to work toward a united economic system had become glaringly apparent. In the frustration of the requirements for a monetary reform came the first direct and serious clash between the two major postwar powers.

Work toward peace settlements continued in Paris and elsewhere. The signing of the five peace treaties for Italy, Hungary, Bulgaria, Rumania, and Finland,* as the result of early negotiations, had done almost nothing to settle the growing dispute as to the freedom to be accorded to Austria and Germany. In fact, they served to stabilize

---

*Since the United States had not been at war with Finland, this treaty was not signed by the United States Government.

the position of the Soviets in the center of Europe. As we look back, the failure to recognize the growing menace to the free world seems strange, though it can be explained by the preoccupation with the new tasks of occupation and the emphasis on the restoration of economic and political institutions in France, Belgium, and the Netherlands. The uncertainty over the communist influence in Italy and the clouded fate of Trieste were seen as immediate problems. Meanwhile, the large unmet requirements of England and her inability to assume the same share of the international burdens as that carried in the prewar period were emphasized by the speed with which the funds loaned in December, 1945, were disbursed. England, in spite of a rigorous austerity program, found the $3,750 million from the United States insufficient to provide for the imports and other urgent needs of 1946. The government began the year 1947 with a profound sense of weakness.

The communist penetration of Greece and the implied threat to Turkey could not be ignored. The insurgents supplied from the north were disrupting conditions and threatening the Western-oriented leadership in Greece. In February, 1947, England turned to the United States, saying that it was no longer possible for its government to supply the millions needed to keep Greece and Turkey from falling prey to the revolutionaries. The United States was faced with a dramatic new challenge.

The outcome was the Truman Doctrine of March, 1947. This decision to act marked a major shift in United States policy; it also was the outstanding case of theoretical planning in the Department of State. The story of the events in the 15 weeks between the presentation of the two British notes and the final development of the ideas behind the Marshall Plan is extraordinary for imagination and scope.[6]

George C. Marshall, recently returned from an arduous mission to China, had been sworn in as Secretary of State to succeed James Byrnes. He was taking a brief vacation when the British notes were presented to Under Secretary Acheson on February 21. When Marshall returned to Washington on Monday, February 24, work had already begun on the planning to meet the new requirements. Those who knew of the developments had recognized immediately that, if the Soviet advance was to be halted, the United States must move promptly into the void which was being created by the

British withdrawal of support. A documented statement of the situation had been prepared and recommendations formulated for the consideration of the Secretary. Meanwhile, a special working party, under Dean Acheson's guidance, drew up a detailed program of action that described the inadequacy of funds; emphasized the need for authority to assure military, technical, and economic assistance; and outlined a number of the extraordinary measures that would be necessary.

These requirements were discussed in a meeting on the evening of February 24. The main attention focused on Greece, though agreement on the importance of Turkey was assumed.[7] There had been a Cabinet lunch that day; the issues were then explained to a larger group of officials on the next day. There was an impressive unanimity of view and a sense that this moment in time was a turning point in American history. On February 26, the final version of the "Position and Recommendations of the Department of State Regarding Immediate Aid to Greece and Turkey" was prepared. The core of the recommendations had been developed by a small group of men who were to be the central figures in the Policy Planning Staff a few weeks later. On the basis of their paper, the further document, the President's message to Congress, was drafted. Inevitably, as in all matters of prime importance, this document went through several versions. There were almost continuous meetings, in the Department of State, the Departments of War and the Navy, in the Cabinet, and with Congressional leaders.

The delivery of the speech and the promulgation of the new doctrine came on March 12. Secretary Marshall had already left for Moscow, where the Council of Foreign Ministers had started meeting on March 10 to begin discussions of the postwar settlements for Austria and Germany. Although there was a degree of bewilderment and surprise in Congress, it was not long before the President secured the support of his own party and of most of the minority leaders. (The outstanding Republican, Senator Arthur Vandenberg, indicated his view that the active policy was necessary, while another outstanding Republican, Senator Robert Taft, did not approve of the new line.) During this year, the whole direction of our policy shifted—with the Truman Doctrine, the Marshall Plan, and the National Security Act, adopted in July, 1947. The Truman Doctrine was described in the President's declaration in the message to Congress: "I believe it must be a policy of the United States to support free peoples who are resisting attempted subjugation by armed minorities or by outside pressures."[8]

Changes in both emphasis and procedure came in Washington. New legislation set up the National Security Council "to assess and appraise the objectives, commitments and risks of the United States in relation to our actual and potential military power, in the interests of national security, for the purpose of making recommendations to the President . . ." The newly created Central Intelligence Agency was made directly responsible to the Council. Much of the intelligence work and a large part of the personnel were taken over from the Office of Strategic Services, which had functioned actively during the war.

The Truman Doctrine was clearly a part of a general reorientation of our foreign policy, perhaps the most significant change in the decades since the turn of the century. This redirection of our intentions was not to become completely evident until after the Korean War had forced on us not only economic and political challenges but also direct aggression which had to be countered by force.

The unsuccessful meeting of the Council of Foreign Ministers in Moscow had convinced Secretary Marshall that the U.S.S.R. was not ready to cooperate in the reconstruction of Europe. No progress was made toward treaties for Germany and Austria. In an attempt to push, somehow, toward positive results, it was agreed that the ministers' deputies should meet in Austria for the drafting of a treaty for that country, to be presented later to the ministers. The disappointment in Moscow undoubtedly confirmed the impressions of the American diplomats; it also set the tone for the article, whose author was identified only as "X," in the July issue of *Foreign Affairs* that introduced the term "containment" as a guide for our dealings with the communist world. The article, later revealed to have been written by George Kennan, echoed the ideas expressed by President Truman on March 12, that the aggression of totalitarian states, whether direct or indirect, undermines the security of the United States. This was to be a keynote of our action in the next two decades, as the hopes felt during the first elation of our wartime victory gradually dimmed.

In these decades, new tasks were undertaken in the pursuit of continuing aims. The involvement of our military personnel in reconstruction and training in Greece began promptly. Deliveries of supplies from warehouses in Europe were possible even before shipments from the United States further supported our words with deeds.

There was what might be considered a last attempt to heal the growing breach with the Soviets. Foreign Secretary Ernest Bevin is said to have begun his diplomatic efforts which led to transforming a suggestion into a practical plan by telephoning several leading personalities the night of Marshall's speech. The British and French accepted the Marshall Plan at a meeting in Paris on June 27; the Soviets showed a hesitant interest. Invitations for a general conference, including the Soviet satellites, but not including Spain, were then issued on July 31. Fourteen European countries accepted. The answers of Czechoslovakia and Poland were at first in doubt, even though *Pravda* had attacked the Marshall Plan on June 16. Then the order came that they could not participate, and the Soviet Union turned its back officially on the reconstruction of Europe. The Committee on European Economic Cooperation (later the OEEC and then the OECD) was to continue in existence for more than two decades. It was an important economic arm of the free world diplomacy in this critical time. As it studied the specific needs and developed plans for rebuilding the economies of the member nations, work in Washington proceeded for the European Cooperation Act of June, 1948. This in turn was to build a foundation for the coming North Atlantic Treaty Organization.

These first years after the end of hostilities were marked by various attempts to negotiate the differences between the communist and democratic worlds. In Moscow, London, Paris, Vienna, and elsewhere we met with rebuffs. We were to register gains in the Atlantic area, but our position on the mainland of Asia was less clear. There, crisis was worsening rapidly in 1947. We were unwilling—and, many think, unable—to stem the tide of events. Our position was in sharp contrast to that in Europe. Our atomic capabilities were already beginning to be considered unusable. Also, as early as January, the State Department had announced abandonment of efforts to mediate in the Chinese Civil War.

With a view to a treaty for the Pacific and a settlement of the future of Japan, the United States suggested, on July 11, an 11–nation Far Eastern Advisory Commission. The refusal of the Soviets to go along with this proposal led eventually to the independent course which was pursued by the United States in drafting the Japanese treaty in 1950. The American experience in attempting to move on treaties for Germany and Austria made the Soviet desire to throw the matter of the Japanese treaty into the Council of the Big Four completely unacceptable to Truman.

Other changes in this period signalized the closing of the colonial era and the emergence of new, independent nations. The announcement by the United Kingdom in February, 1947, that it would withdraw from India in June, the termination of the British mandate over Palestine and its independence, the creation of the Moslem state of Pakistan, and the cessation of fighting between the Dutch and Indonesians were followed by an increasing drive for self-government elsewhere.

In October, in a secret meeting in Poland, the Cominform (Communist Information Bureau) was established by the communist parties of the U.S.S.R., its East European satellites, and Italy. Its stated aim was to exchange party experiences, but it was dominated by Russia.

Interest in regional security pacts was also growing in the United States and the rest of the Western world. Truman had called a high-level conference in Washington, with bipartisan support from Senator Vandenberg and John Foster Dulles, consultant to the State Department and adviser to the Republican party, to consider the threat to our security and the fear inspired by Moscow. In August, 1947, the Treaty of Rio de Janeiro for hemispheric defense was adopted by the delegates from 19 nations.

The year 1948 was to be momentous: the Soviets pressed on bordering countries, and the United States prepared to respond not only with the active development of the Marshall Plan but also with the North Atlantic Treaty Organization for collective defense. This effort began even before the United States knew that the Russians knew the secret of the atomic bomb. On December 19 of that year the President asked Congress for $17 billion for a four-year period for the European Recovery Program.

Signs of communist infiltration of the Czechoslovak government had been obvious to close observers before the turn of the year. After their participation in the October, 1947, trade union confer-

ence in Prague, Austrian officials feared they might also be sub-
verted. The communist pattern of gaining control in the key departments of information and internal security in Czechoslovakia
was paralleled by pressures in other countries. The ability of Czechoslovakia to resist was undermined, and on February 22, 1948, when
the communization of the top offices was evident, President Beneš
was forced to resign. A peaceful coup had been maneuvered without any resistance from the Western powers or the people in the
nation. The communists gained another nation but lost, from that
moment, any chance of victory in Austria or in West Germany.
Nevertheless, the Soviets continued their opposition to the three
Western occupying powers in Frankfurt and Berlin, as they rejected
the monetary conversion which was to make possible the rebuilding
of the country and the establishment of a pro-Western Federal
Republic of Germany.

In spite of growing political difficulties in many places, those
working on the details of the economic unification of Germany
were not mentally prepared for the Russian rejection of the monetary reform. It was clear that the rebuilding of industry, the mining
of coal, and the lifting of Germany above the subsistence level
would not be possible until the Reichsmark currency was eliminated
and a new banking system established. The United States had
stopped dismantling industry in the west and had demanded a cessation of Soviet removals of plant equipment from the east. The
American and British zones were combined by the Bizonal agreement of January, 1948—later to become Trizonia as the French
joined the combination; it permitted a united economic policy and
provided for appropriate legislation and assistance in the establishment of local government. Political life was thus reviving at the
time of the financial reform. An immediate favorable result was
an increase in production of coal in the Ruhr.

Plans for the currency reform proceeded at a feverish pace, and
the required law was promulgated on June 18, 1948. It was drastic
in scope: it wiped out approximately 90 percent of the currency and
credit and introduced a new unit, which was to serve as a dependable
medium of exchange and put an end to "cigarette currency," thus
destroying the basis of the black market, which was undermining the
feeble beginnings of reconstruction. Overnight, the whole aspect of

the economic life changed and there were, at last, motives for working and saving. A new start was being made in the western zones for the postwar strength and the *Deutsche Wunder*. For some months the Soviets had been harassing the West and Berlin by sporadic interference with access to Berlin. On June 24, the land routes to the city were effectively blocked. This direct challenge to the United States by communism was the first in a series of confrontations during these years. But there were also political pressures on the citizens and the Allied diplomats from the Soviets occupying Berlin. These increased through the early months of 1948 and reached a high point in July of that year. The Soviet commander had walked out of the Kommandatura on June 16, but the withdrawal was not official until July 1. The attempts to incorporate Berlin into the East zone of occupation had been characterized by the political activities of the SED—the socialist, later communist, unity party, using methods similar to those employed in 1947 in Czechoslovakia. The protests of the Berliners in mass meetings on March 18 and May 1 indicated an awareness of the dangers.

Lucius Clay, Commanding General, felt certain of the anticommunist views of the leaders he was dealing with and also of the citizens in general. It was Clay who was urging, on an apparently hesitant Washington, the advisability of sending an armored column down the road to challenge a Soviet command which did not, in his opinion, want war. Meanwhile, he had been preparing as best he could for the air lifting of supplies to a Berlin that was low in essentials of all kinds.[9] His telephone call to General Curtis LeMay on June 24 is described as follows:

> "Curt," said General Clay, "can you transport coal by air?"
> General LeMay replied: "Excuse me, General, would you mind repeating that question?"[10]

All available aircraft, mobilized after this conversation, prepared to start lifting supplies into Berlin the following day. The flow of coal, food, and various sorely needed items began as a trickle and increased steadily until it reached a record high of 12,490 tons in one 24-hour period in April, 1949. By the time this operation was well underway, it was also performing the important function of flying the products of Berlin's active industry out of the city, as well as providing raw materials.[11]

The city was, of course, on an austerity program. No one was sure at first that the water and sewage systems, electric power, and minimum food and fuel requirements could be supplied. The Soviets undoubtedly were confident that they could destroy the will of the people and overtax the resources of the Allies in the city. They made an offer of food to the population in July, requiring only a general registration in East Berlin to acknowledge their authority. Only a few responded. Although the city leaders were not completely convinced that the Allies would remain in the city as the difficulties increased, they were so aware of the dangers of yielding to the Soviets that they showed no sign of weakness. Caution and delay have been reported as characterizing the attitude in Washington, but the decision there on July 28 to send additional bombers to Germany indicated a growing firmness. General Clay, in Germany, was backed by both the Berliners and the Allied forces and their dependents in the city. They did not wish to be evacuated and faced the deprivations of the period without flinching. The doubts about the ability of the Air Force to keep the necessities flowing through the dark and foggy winter months were partially dispelled as the number of flights increased daily.

The attitude of the Allied personnel and their dependents, as the shared restrictions and dangers became more evident, has been fundamental in the development of the friendship between West Germany and the United States. The blockade days and the heroic airlift demonstrated an understanding of the meaning of the Berlin position in relation to Germany and Europe. On the experience of these 11 months were built the later acts of cooperation with the West.

When the first signs of trouble had begun, weeks earlier, General Clay had said:

> *We have lost Czechoslovakia. Norway is threatened. We retreat from Berlin. When Berlin falls, western Germany will be next. If we mean to hold Europe against Communism, we must not budge. . . . I believe the future of democracy requires us to stay.*

Feelers put out in Moscow by our Ambassador, General Bedell Smith, led to the conclusion that the only terms that could be negotiated at that time included our giving up Berlin. As attempts to secure an acceptable agreement continued, Washington began to recognize the meaning of this challenge, the morale of the Berlin population, and the potentials of the air lift. The Western commitment increased.

The behavior of the Soviet leaders in Berlin indicates that they understood neither the point of view of the Berliners nor the determination of the Americans to resist further communist encroachment. Moreover, they were not convinced of the will of the leaders in the West to halt the forward march of communism. Pressure of a milder type was being exerted in Austria, but the installation of the central government and the operations of the Allied Control Commission were such as to limit the threat; in any case, the cutting off of access to Vienna was of doubtful value to the Soviets, at least unless the Western powers were forced out of Berlin.

The drama had several elements: the stream of planes flying into the city, cheered by the populace, welcomed by the children; the fate of the men who were killed in their mission; the cooperation of the people of the city and the soldiers and civilians of the occupying powers—all focused world attention on their courage and will to resist. This time of suffering and danger marks emergence of Berlin as a symbol of the linking of America's fate with Europe and a transformation of the attitude of Germany toward the conqueror from overseas.

The end of the blockade signifies also a shift in Soviet tactics and a recognition of the developing ties of the Atlantic Alliance. The excuse for the termination of the blockade was ostensibly the desire for a meeting of the Council of Foreign Ministers, which took place in Paris in April. The first intimation of a change in Stalin's intentions came in an interview with the journalist J. Kingsbury Smith on January 29, 1949. More than a month later, there was a partial agreement between Jacob Malik, Soviet representative on the Security Council, and Philip C. Jessup, the U. S. Ambassador to the UN. These informal talks had begun on February 15. They are among the several instances showing that, when the Soviets wish a change in approach, they find easy means of communicating their intentions. The Foreign Ministers convened in Paris in April, and an agreement to normalize access to Berlin was soon reached, subsequently to be broken in various ways by the communists. On May 12, "Operation Vittles" came to an end, and the reconstruction of the city and its democratic development gained a new intensity and vigor. The end of this important episode was followed by a new Soviet maneuver attempting to divide the Western powers by the promotion of neutralism.

There had been a profound change in American and British intentions with respect to Germany and a new impetus to the preparation for a security alliance during the blockade. The Brussels treaty of March, 1948, was influenced by the events in Europe, the communist take-over in Czechoslovakia, the failure of treaty negotiations for Austria, communist politics in Italy and France, and Soviet threats in Germany and Berlin. Britain, France, and the Benelux countries entered into a 50-year agreement to collaborate for collective self-defense. The Western European Union (WEU) created the Consultative Council, which was a forerunner of the North Atlantic Treaty Organization, in which the United States became committed—for the first time in peacetime—to continuing military cooperation on the Continent. Thus, in April, 1949, these five nations were joined by five other European countries, Canada, and the United States to form NATO. Greece and Turkey joined in 1952. It was agreed to bring the Federal Republic of Germany in on October 23, 1954. American leadership and participation would hardly have been possible if there had not been bipartisan support. Senator Vandenberg and Foster Dulles had been working with the Administration for some months. The Vandenberg Resolution, passed by the Senate on June 11, 1948, indicated the support that could be marshaled for cooperative security measures then being prepared in concert with the major European powers. It declared that the U.S. would "exercise the right of individual or collective self-defense . . . should armed attack occur affecting its national security." General Eisenhower was chosen by the NATO representatives as the first Supreme Commander.

Politically, this development meant a manifestation to the communists and to Europe that the United States would not withdraw but, rather, would assume large responsibilities in military matters paralleling the economic contributions under the Marshall Plan. These NATO developments led Moscow to accusations of Western provocation and to threats of reprisals, none of which was carried out. The evident concern of the Kremlin was followed by the Warsaw Treaty in 1955, after the Germans had been brought into the alliance.

Technically, the security treaty brought many changes to the military operations in Europe. There was a coordination of methods and an exchange of views, bringing close together the details of preparation for joint action in emergencies. Much of this work, which has gone on without interruption for almost 20 years, has been overlooked by those who focus their attention on occasional disagreements and who see the problems of holding together a military alliance when there is no immediate threat of hostilities. The progress in communications, in standardization, in common manuals and procedures is a major achievement which increases the solid foundation of a forward strategy and a strong foreign policy. In this period, more than ever before, the work of the diplomat is dependent on the accomplishments of the soldier in resisting direct and indirect aggression.

All this progress in NATO was shaken by the French withdrawal of troops and their demand that U.S. installations be removed from French soil in 1967. The final outcome is yet to be seen. The Western European nations' determination "to achieve a greater unity" was to move forward rapidly from 1948 and 1949 onward. Some of this drive was expressed in the Council of Europe, with its seat in Strasbourg. The membership of the group of 10 was later expanded to 15. Thus, a number of overlapping associations—which were to foster security, stability, economic growth, and freer interchange—wove the fabric of present-day European cooperation, in which the United States participates with members or observers. The first meeting of the Council in 1949 in Strasbourg elected as President Paul-Henri Spaak of Belgium.

The importance of Germany requires a further comment on its rebirth as a nation. The first postwar elections were held on August 15, 1949. On September 8, the first government of the German Federal Republic was formed. Immediately thereafter, with the support of the Allied High Commissioners, Konrad Adenauer was chosen as Chancellor. Military government by Britain, France, and the United States in West Germany ended, though the occupation of Berlin was to continue for many years. The Contractual Agreements were signed in Bonn, the capital of the new state, on May 26, 1952, when the Allied High Commission was abolished. The contrast over the next 15 years between freedom in the West and oppression in the East, where approximately 400,000 Russian soldiers were in tight control, became increasingly apparent. This was the cause of a constant stream of refugees fleeing to the West, more than 3 million between 1952 and 1962, the largest voluntary migration in recent history. The Soviet communists found themselves frustrated by German policy and the NATO alliance.

The View from the Far East. The situation in the Far East was vastly different. Here the United States and the other Western powers both underestimated the seriousness of the communist advance and discounted their own capacity to resist the onward sweep. The Communist Chinese captured Nanking in April and Shanghai in May, 1949. The People's Republic was proclaimed in October and immediately recognized by Moscow. The Nationalist defense in South China collapsed.

In December, 1949, Chiang Kai-shek, with an armed force of 650,000 men and a civilian population of 1.5 million, took refuge on the island of Taiwan. Here, threatened from time to time by invasion and beset by various political and economic difficulties, he and his people struggled with the help of American aid for years, until they became self-sustaining in the early 1960s, leaning always on the West for their security, hoping for eventual return to the mainland.

Another advance of the communist world was the explosion of an atomic device in the U.S.S.R., announced by President Truman in September, 1949. The prospect of this event had been foreshadowed, but it brought the free world to a new phase of diplomatic relations. The atomic monopoly which the United States had enjoyed, and which had seemed to give strength to the nation as our conventional forces were weakened and the apparatus dismantled, was over. A new threat had to be met by increased vigilance in Washington and by expanding alliances abroad.

The speed with which, after the end of the first postwar period of adjustment, the colonial empires of European states began to fall apart, brought new problems. India, Pakistan, Indonesia in 1947, Burma in 1948, were forerunners of a host of countries, approximately 70 in the next 20 years, that emerged as sovereign powers with new hopes and ambitions, not easy for the more highly industrialized and older countries to meet.

President Harry Truman had some of these countries in mind

when, in January, 1949, after being elected President in his own right, he announced the technical assistance program, to be known for many years as "Point Four" because of its position in his inaugural address. This marked a transition in the emphasis of our aid program which, though focused partly on mutual security, was to move further into the field of economic development.

The years from the end of the war were characterized mainly by the growing understanding of Soviet intentions of expansion and our assumption of new tasks. We had no desire to dominate the nations of the free world, but we were the only people who had the atomic bomb and the human and financial resources that were so urgently required. Thus, while we ignored the early moves of the communists to spread their influence in Europe and in the Far East, we woke to the dangers of the situation in 1947 and became strong in our resistance and our support of the European bastions in 1948. The oppression in East Germany and in Hungary became more onerous, but it was balanced in part by a growing sense of the need to resist in Austria, Italy, France, and elsewhere. The United Nations, which had a part in the withdrawal of the Soviets from Iran in 1946, had been plagued by their vetoes in the Security Council. The Soviet representative had cast 43 negative votes by December, 1949. The Soviets blocked attempts to carry out the agreements as to United Nations action in Korea. They boycotted the Korean Commission and closed their zone of occupation to outsiders; then they announced the withdrawal of their troops on December 30, 1948.

There seemed to be no front on which the free world found cooperation possible. The bright hopes of 1945 were dashed.

TESTING GROUND: THE FAR EAST

Thwarted in the Atlantic area, the communists exploited what they erroneously assumed was American indifference in the Pacific. They observed our unwillingness to halt their advance on the Chinese mainland in 1947 and 1948 and concluded that we would not take large-scale risks in that area. This miscalculation was confirmed in a measure by the statement of President Truman on January 5, 1950, barring military intervention to aid the Nationalists on Taiwan.

Communists in Peking and Moscow undoubtedly also noted the speech by Secretary of State Dean Acheson a week later, to the National Press Club; this speech gave the impression that the American defense perimeter excluded Korea. It has been reported since that time that a review of the intelligence material available in the early months of 1950 indicates an adequate forecast of the plans for an invasion in force over the 38th Parallel, with the intention of imposing communism on the whole of the nation.

Meanwhile, on January 10, Jacob Malik, the Soviet representative, had walked out of the UN Security Council in protest over the failure to expel the Chinese Nationalists from the Council. This boycott was to continue through a momentous period.

The May announcement in Paris by Secretary Acheson that we would give economic aid to the pro-French regimes in Indochina was not taken seriously by the communists as a demonstration of our interest in freedom in the Far East. Nor was the beginning of the work on the Japanese peace treaty by John Foster Dulles, acting as consultant to the State Department. The cooperation of Peking and Moscow was close at this time. The joint decision to carry the communist offensive into the Far East was in a sense an answer to NATO, and it was also a move to offset unilateral action in restoring economic and political rights to Japan in a treaty of reconciliation.

The North Koreans, urged on by communist leaders elsewhere, crossed the 38th Parallel and attacked South Korean forces on June 24 (EDT), 1950, precipitating our "police action" response, which was to continue until July, 1953. The risks taken by the Chinese and the Russians then were greater than they realized. So, some thought, was the danger of atomic war as our conventional forces were steadily pushed back; indeed, some clamored for the use of our atomic potential. This never-declared war had the support of Congress, but President Truman avoided legislative debate on Capitol Hill. In his early decisions he had not engaged in wide consultation and kept the deliberations in the hands of a few.

The tide turned in September, when the bold landing of American troops at Inchon made possible a successful cut through to the capital at Seoul. Despite this success, bitter fighting continued during the following months. As the troops moved northward, on September 15, the Joint Chiefs of Staff in Washington authorized operations north of the 38th Parallel. Soon thereafter, the UN General Assembly voted 47 to 5 to create a new committee on unification of Korea, thus further supporting General Douglas MacArthur in his drive. The General was optimistic and in early November declared that the war was almost won. He did not anticipate the intervention of the Communist Chinese. There was evidence of the presence of Chinese troops, but it was not until later in November that they attacked in force and thereby discouraged hopes of an early victory.

The more controversial aspects of the campaign began to open a breach between MacArthur and the Administration. The General asked for support in a more aggressive action. He was told there could be no blockade of mainland China, no bombing of their industrial complexes, and no use of the Nationalist forces on Taiwan. The concept of limited war was accepted by many in Washington, but not by General MacArthur. In reply to a question, he wrote Joseph Martin, the Republican leader of the House, a letter that was released in March. It stated his views with regard to the necessity of taking a more vigorous line and used the words so often associated with him, "There is no substitute for victory."

President Truman, who was seeking negotiations, feared that the Army would pursue a policy divergent from his line and, more important, he believed that the military were asserting independence of the supreme civilian command, which was in his hands. On April 11, 1951, he dismissed General MacArthur and requested his immediate return. From that time on, until the change of administrations after the 1952 election, the political issues and domestic politics relating to the Korean war divided American opinion. The stalemate in Korea intensified the feeling of frustration. The official position supported the world view that nuclear power was unusable —and the weary conflict dragged on.

Meanwhile, one of the fears in Europe was that the engagement of the United States in the Far East would diminish the American contributions to the newly created NATO. Even though arms and planes had been sent to the Atlantic alliance, preoccupation with the fighting abroad and the domestic conflicts at home over the dismissal of MacArthur were drawing attention from the cooperative developments just getting underway.

It was in 1950 that the Schuman Plan was advanced as a serious proposal to unite the coal and steel potential of the German Ruhr and of neighboring countries in a large combination of a productive community to be known as the Coal and Steel Community (CSC). This plan followed the ideas of various leaders as to ways of assuring peace. (In fact, economic cooperation had been discussed as early as 1947 by Foster Dulles, Jean Monnet, and Robert Schuman.) Such plans for basic economic cooperation followed naturally on the early and continuing success of the Marshall Plan in rebuilding devastated areas of Europe, bringing with it the practical working arrangements of the Organization of European Economic Cooperation (OEEC) and the European Payments Union (EPU). In the many committees, practical arrangements with respect to raw materials, transport, power, and the stabilization of financial relations had brought to the front talent and resources which were to develop new strength. The treaty setting up the European Coal and Steel Community was signed in Paris on April 18.

The United States continued to foster the ideas which were designed to make the European nations active partners in commerce and finance, as well as in security measures. The new word *infrastructure* described to some extent the economic base of security and the need for adequate communications and material foundations for a common military policy. We were increasingly intermeshed in the problems of the Atlantic partners. All of the new American agencies, such as the Information Agency, the Central Intelligence Agency, the Administration of Foreign Aid (by various successive organizations), and the Atomic Energy Commission, as well as the older departments, such as State, Defense, Treasury, Commerce, and Agriculture, were carrying on important functions abroad. The National Security Council, the President, and the Secretaries of State and Defense had multiple concerns throughout these years. The Cold War was extending the Soviet aggressive intent ever farther, so our efforts at cooperation had to be stepped up at many points. Our personnel abroad increased, and our budget reflected the growing demands on our resources.

The conduct of national policy had been shaken from 1950 to 1953 by domestic controversy. Senator Joseph R. McCarthy had determined to fight what he proclaimed as the danger of communism and subversion in government, particularly in the Department of State and the Department of the Army. Alger Hiss, who was blamed for part of our failure in the Far East, had been convicted of perjury in the trial to determine his dealings with the Soviets. Klaus Fuchs in Great Britain had confessed to treason in connection with giving the Soviets atomic information. At about the same time—January, 1950—President Truman announced that he had ordered the production of the hydrogen bomb.* The troubled reactions to these events and to the Korean war, along with a widespread feeling that there must be some explanation for our difficulties, laid the foundations in public doubt on which "McCarthyism" was built.

Many informed people believe foreign information and the development of foreign policy were seriously damaged in these years from 1950 to 1953 by the attacks on men in the Foreign Service and in the Defense Department. Little known and relatively unimportant events were dragged out by McCarthy as evidence of disloyalty. Some instances of incompetence were uncovered (perhaps some officials were unprepared for the heavy responsibilities placed upon them), and some government servants confessed to improper conduct. A *few* seemed actually to have been involved in treasonable activities. In any case, some were forced to resign. The campaign was waged mainly for partisan political reasons, but some of McCarthy's followers honestly believed they were fighting a menace to our security. The attacks continued at their height for several months, then were carried on less intensively. The insinuations that accompanied these attacks caused untold suffering to many who were honest and dedicated in their work for their country.

It was not until 1953 that the resistance of Secretary of State Dulles to interference with State Department personnel and of Secretary of the Army Robert Stevens in Defense and his counsel, Joseph Welch, became effective. The subsequent condemnation of McCarthy by the Senate halted the attacks, and conditions began to return to normal. Estimates vary as to how deep and lasting the scars have been. Certainly, to the individuals affected there is no compensation for unjust attack. For those who were guilty, the penalty was overdue. The consideration of the foreign policy of the early 1950s is not complete without considering the extent of

---

*The United States exploded its first hydrogen bomb on Bikini on March 1, 1953.

possible damage. The time of bitterness must be taken into account by the historian who is studying such difficult questions as the rise of Soviet atomic power, the threat of communist China, and the slowness of the United States to recognize the significance of the Cold War.

The fight against communism in other countries in 1951 was a natural concomitant of the action in two major areas. The completion of the draft of the Japanese treaty was one example of the sense of urgency and the suppression for a time of minor issues. The document, finished by Dulles and his associates on March 26, was laid promptly before the cobelligerents. There had been consultations at various stages of its preparations, but these had not been serious distractions from what was basically a one-man job. The coherence and the simplicity of the text were evidence of the feasibility of this new method of arriving at a workable draft in a relatively short time. The subsequent changes introduced, mainly in bilateral conversations, did not divert Americans from their aim to have a treaty of reconciliation which would quickly strengthen the position of the free world in the Far East. The questions of reparation and settlement of claims, always difficult, had to be negotiated with patience, but only minor changes were made in the early U.S. document. The peace conference was set for San Francisco in September.

The U.S.S.R. had blasted both the procedure and the proposed treaty itself. Japan had become an informal ally of the United States as the war in Korea increased Japan's importance for us as a staging area. The rigors of the first months of occupation had been relaxed and the compliance of the Japanese had rendered our task there much easier than had been anticipated. Soviet officials were alarmed by these evidences of growing American-Japanese cooperation.

The Seven-Point Memo, which had been made public on November 24, 1950, had outlined the provisions of the proposed settlement. It indicated that the United States would make a peace treaty for itself and for any or all of the nations that had been at war with Japan, that its sovereignty would be restored and its security safeguarded, that membership in the United Nations would be provided, and that there would be military aid, territorial readjustments, and a direct procedure for negotiation. After the first-draft document had been put forward in March, 1951, Dulles visited the Philippines, Australia, New Zealand, Korea, and Japan. A new text was issued as the result of conferences in those countries and elsewhere and after reviewing a draft the British had submitted in April. Invitations were then sent to 49 nations to submit their views and, subsequently, on August 14, the final document was published. The Soviet Union's opposition was evidenced by a demand for a five-power treaty as a substitute for the American draft. The Soviets expressed extreme displeasure, viciously attacking the document. The crisis occasioned by this move was nevertheless more fictitious than real. Dulles let it be known that the invitations to the conference were to *sign* the published treaty and not for further discussion. The Soviets were invited to sign. The Japanese had indicated that they were ready to accept the proposed peace terms and that Prime Minister Yoshida would attend the conference on September 4. Unexpectedly the U.S.S.R. accepted the invitation and sent delegates to the conference. It can be supposed that they hoped for some last-minute delay that would give them room to maneuver.

The sessions were chaired by Secretary of State Dean Acheson; President Truman addressed the representatives of the countries present. Yoshida has described the proceedings, saying, "though some expressed dissatisfaction . . . [with] the reparations, none said anything that could be construed as anti-Japanese."[12] The troublesome problem of "which China" should sign had been handled with adroitness—the Japanese were to decide, and there was little question as to what their decision would be. At the meeting, Dulles and Acheson worked as a team. A British writer summed up the success by saying "the plan of campaign was gloriously neat and wholly Dulles'. It worked like a charm and turned Gromyko, the Soviet delegate, apoplectic with fury."[13] (The contrast with the situation in Germany, where the treaty was blocked for decades, is striking.) A defense treaty between the United States and Japan was also signed at this meeting. Japan was on the way to becoming a loyal ally.

In the course of negotiating the Japanese Treaty, to allay fears of a possible resurgence of Japanese aggression, the United States had promised various defensive alliances. These promises led to the creation of ANZUS, the organization set up by a treaty with Australia and New Zealand, and to a pact with the Philippines.

These pacts recognized that an attack on any one of the parties endangered the security of the others, and there was agreement to consult whenever the territorial integrity of any was threatened. The completion of the network of treaties came later, with the conclusion of the negotiation of the treaty with South Korea after the armistice in 1953, the treaties with Nationalist China in 1954, and the development of the South East Asia Treaty Organization by a treaty signed on September 8 of that year. SEATO was not patterned after NATO; in fact, it was scarcely an organization in the usual sense. Its members included, besides the United States, Great Britain, France, Australia, New Zealand, Pakistan, the Philippines, and Thailand. Nehru, pursuing what was generally called a neutralist line, did not favor the inclusion of India. The Pacific Charter, which set out principles as to rights and self-determination, was a sign of the desire to remove all traces of colonialism from these protective arrangements.

Many diplomatic consultations were necessary to conclude these mutual security arrangements and preparations for meeting danger wherever it might strike. They were expressions of expanding American commitments and also signs of the far-reaching threat from communism. Even these loose associations and generalized statements of shared interests served to express the will to resist aggression in the Pacific.

The preoccupation with security, which became vital with the Korean war, was to intensify; Dulles had been prominent among those advocating increased efforts in this field even before he became Secretary of State in 1953. In this area, there was, in 1951 and 1952, a smooth working bipartisanship which, though not with complete unanimity, brought together the outstanding leaders of both parties. Only Senator Robert A. Taft stands out as continuing to doubt the wisdom of these security measures. His death in 1953 was a loss to the conservative wing of the Republican party, the wing whose members wished to restrict our foreign obligations to a minimum.

The Baghdad Pact of February 24, 1954, which became the Central Treaty Organization (CENTO) after the revolution in Iraq in 1958, developed as the weakness of France and the United Kingdom required their withdrawal from active support in the tumultuous Middle East. This was a new and unaccustomed region for our diplomatic efforts and meant a further extension of our already multitudinous obligations. In contrast, the Rio Pact of 1947 had been concluded with countries for which we had an evident interest and continuing association. A total of nine defensive and consultative arrangements, varying from NATO, which was highly operational, to looser and less definite associations, marked the years from 1947 to 1960 and underscored the new diplomacy. They were the occasion for large increases in personnel and missions abroad.

The Colombo Plan had been initiated within the British Commonwealth countries on January 14, 1950. It was later endorsed by the United States as non-Commonwealth countries were brought into its consultations. It created one of the first organizations to devote itself to the development of the economies of South and Southeast Asia. After 1951, its scope expanded, and though its work was not large as compared with other aid programs, it embarked on a number of worthwhile joint projects, notably the Mekong River development. The Economic Commission for Asia and the Far East (ECAFE), a research and planning association with its headquarters in Thailand, was to further this type of program. Meanwhile, the Point Four Technical Assistance Program announced by President Truman in 1949 was extending its work in cooperation with these other international groups.

The growing troubles in Indochina were so grave at this time that the nations affected seemed to require more than economic support. The war there was going badly for the French, and leaders in Washington proposed military help to halt the advance of communism. The sudden decisions of the United Kingdom and the French not to cooperate in this new effort made our proposal unacceptable to Congress, and we were forced to watch the division and weakness which would lay the area open to aggression in later years.[14]

NATIONAL AND MUTUAL SECURITY

During these years, the air was full of theories as to how to achieve national security. There were feverish efforts to assess the communist potential, and there were attempts to fit our nuclear capabilities into the new world in which the Soviets also had an atomic bomb.

Thus the statement of January, 1954, in which Dulles stressed the "capacity to retaliate instantly by means and at places of our choosing," already foreshadowed in a *Life* article in 1952, stirred a debate that continued into the 1960s.

The frustrations of the Korean war had brought a sense of weakness. The developing programs in NATO raised a number of controversial issues. The failure of the French to quiet the troubled areas in Southeast Asia and the unrest in the Middle East made us acutely aware of the need to review our strategy. No hope for escape from the new burdens came with the discussions and actions in the United Nations. The establishment of an international security system and attempts to regulate armaments as proposed in the UN Charter seemed remote. The increasing fears of uncontrolled nuclear development caused growing concern.

Our government had committed large funds to the Mutual Security Program, which picked up where the Marshall Plan left off. The first shipments under the Mutual Defense Assistance Program were made in January, 1950. The Mutual Security Act of 1952 authorized more than $4 billion for military purposes and almost $2 billion for economic programs. Furthermore, appropriations for national defense jumped in 1952 to $27 billion and in 1953 to $36.8 billion, from previous levels of $11 and $12 billion. This increase in defense expenditures represented a shift in priorities in our foreign relations. Although the expenditures did not mean that there was a rapidly increasing sacrifice in terms of percentage of gross national product, which increased throughout the period, they did indicate a changed attitude toward military strength, in our own country and abroad. They indicated an unprecedented concern for cooperative security in NATO and otherwise.

The Mutual Security Act of 1951 was the first of several in which economic aid and military aid were commingled deliberately and administered by the MSA organization in collaboration with the Department of Defense.* The changes in American public opinion that were necessary before this new policy could be initiated had gradually become apparent. It was obvious that economic instruments alone were not sufficient to bring security; they must be

---

*Foreign aid totaling more than $116 billion from 1945 to June 30, 1965, included Marshall Plan aid of over $13 billion before 1952.

accompanied by more specific short-range action that would give confidence to those fearful of communist aggression. The competition between those who advocated emphasizing economic requirements and those who advocated emphasizing military ones was sharpened by the election campaign of 1952, but the turning point had clearly been the outbreak of hostilities in Korea.

The seeming remoteness of the Western Hemisphere from the theater of struggle in Europe permitted a neglect that was to cause increasing trouble in years ahead. The gap in our policy was not complete—rather, it was a question of emphasis, which is not easy to assess at this time. Much effort was given to relations *within* the Western Hemisphere. For instance, there was a meeting of the foreign ministers of 21 American republics on March 26, 1951. The discussion of common problems was helpful, though not of primary urgency. There had, in fact, been a series of meetings to knit ties between the nations of North and South. Among these was the Ninth International Conference of American States, which had met in Bogotá from March to May of 1948.[15] The conferees endeavored to outline the duties of hemispheric institutions. As a result, the delegates developed the Pact of Bogotá and the charter of the Organization of American States (OAS) (this charter did not go into effect until December 13, 1951). The Inter-American Conference, the "Supreme Organ" of the OAS, was set up by an agreement ratified by the United States on August 28, 1950. The Pan-American Union in Washington provided the center for the secretariat.

Thus the "good neighbor" policy developed an institutional framework. The concern with economic action initiated in the discussions in 1948 was stimulated to some extent by the more active programs under the Marshall Plan in Europe and led to the Alliance for Progress. In spite of evident needs, however, many years were to elapse before the United States would exert effective leadership in the development of the countries to the south. Even the Alliance for Progress was slow in building up momentum. It was not until 1958 that President Kubitschek initiated its predecessor, Operation Pan-America. There was no inclination among the American states to form a counterpart of NATO. The conflict between the free world and communism seemed remote in South America. Few took note of the growing danger in Guatemala, where the communists were becoming active, building on the revolutionary movement of 1944.

The tone of international discussion in Latin America was conditioned by a feeling of neglect. Those who looked beyond their own border struggles and their social and economic problems had concluded that the United States was indifferent, as its preoccupation with NATO, European reconstruction, and the Korean conflict increased. Washington, for its part, did not have the capability—or so officials there concluded—to turn toward the nearby problems, which were of growing importance.

Setting up the Organization and adopting the Pact of Bogotá to settle disputes peacefully and to increase cooperative action were not enough to assure the effective functioning of the new machinery. No inter-American conference took place in 1951 and 1952, though Secretary Acheson did convene a meeting of the Consultation of Ministers of Foreign Affairs in April, 1951.[16] The Declaration of Washington drawn up at the meeting took note of the "common danger" and reaffirmed inter-American solidarity in the Korean war emergency.[17] This act followed the policy evidenced by token contributions to General MacArthur's command from 17 republics in June, 1950.

Our relations with the nations to the south have for years been complicated by the activities of private investors. Although it was clear that they were having an important influence on the economic development of various sectors of the economy—copper, steel, coffee, and others—the businessmen were thought to be high-handed and to ignore the true long-term interests of the nations of the Western Hemisphere. The foreign exchange that came from the key industries was largely squandered, and the local leaders seemed at times to care less than the foreign investors about the economic future. The politicians were ready to blame the Americans for expropriation as nationalist sentiment grew. The natural jealousy felt for the more prosperous republic to the north, and the evident heavy commitment of the United States in Europe, fanned the flames of a sentiment that was to continue for decades. The effort to overcome the sense of injustice and neglect was difficult, and the programs that came into existence later were only slowly successful in building a solid foundation for cooperation.

This was the unhappy mood that confronted us when the communist penetration of Guatemala brought us face to face with the danger of a hostile beachhead within a short distance of our shores. The new Eisenhower Administration that took over in January, 1953, quickly became aware of the danger. Even in the midst of efforts to terminate the Korean conflict they decided that a more active concern was needed. The first act was to shift Ambassador Peurifoy from Greece to Guatemala, with the express intention of watching for infiltration such as he had encountered in Greece. There, under the Truman Doctrine, he had dealt effectively with subversion. A similar task lay ahead of him in his new post. The course of events in Guatemala (to be described in Chapter III) brought a new sense of solidarity to the Western Hemisphere.

In March, 1954, the resolution of Caracas helped to lay a solid foundation under our policy of opposing the communist regime of Arbenz and gave warning of our support of Colonel Castillo Armas. Although the activities of the communists in Central America were well known, there was no focal point for resistance until the revolt of June, 1954. After the successful halting of this subversion and the establishment of a pro-American regime, there was no serious communist effort to take over the control of any area until the Cuban missile crisis of 1962. Nevertheless, the progress toward understanding and toward economic measures of significant size and continuity was to continue to be disappointing.

While military and scientific techniques were developing at a rapid rate in the Western Hemisphere, the problems of diplomacy were becoming more difficult. There had not been in the immediate postwar years the same bold and unrestrained provocation as that which characterized the 1950s. Most of the more conspicuous incidents occurred in Europe. Here the Soviets forced down planes close to, but not (in most cases) over, their territory. Men and women disappeared from German and Austrian soil, never to return—kidnapped by the Soviets. There was constant harassment and often the use of force in violation of international law and custom. All this time our growing capacity to retaliate lessened, rather than increased, the preventive capacity of the United States. The world was faced with a situation where the strongest nation had to suffer frustration up to the point where our prior commitments and vital interests brought the possibility of nuclear war within the realm of current possibilities.

Two cases in point were the arrests of William N. Oatis, Associated Press representative in Prague, and Robert A. Vogeler, in Hungary. These cases, examples of the arbitrary action of a police state, revealed that there was little or no fear of United States reprisals. The holding of airmen who crashed, either under attack or by accident, was comparable in a number of instances. These all strained the ingenuity and the negotiating techniques of the State Department and the embassies abroad. No adequate formula to protect people and interests was devised. The results of our actions depended on a complex of international relations and the mood of the men in the Kremlin, always hard to anticipate. It seemed that such incidents had been easier to handle before the nuclear potential had arisen and before the determination of the communists to dominate a large part of the world had become apparent.

Vogeler, after being held for more than 17 months, was released from prison on April 28, 1951. The resulting understanding between the United States and the communist government in Hungary caused the United States to allow the consulates in New York City (Hungarian Mission to the UN) and Cleveland to be reopened (the closing had been more symbolic than material as a deterrent). It also announced that American passports would be validated for travel in Hungary. Restitution for goods in the U.S. zone of Germany was resumed.[18]

It was not long after this that Washington protested the mass deportations of thousands from their homes in Hungary in "flagrant violation of the human rights provisions of the treaty of peace" which we had signed in 1946. One of several incidents involving the holding of downed airmen was resolved in December, 1951. Four such men had been arrested without having access to any American officials, but they were released after the payment of "fines." This was another episode in which the Budapest regime had "ignored the basic rules of long-established international conduct." The flaunting of these rules was evident in so many cases that, to all intents and purposes, in the conflicts in Eastern Europe, the normal rules could not be assumed to prevail. The validation of American passports for travel in Hungary was no longer permitted. Somewhat later, in 1953, the travel of Hungarian diplomats in the United States was restricted, though these rules were modified as the Hungarian rules affecting American diplomats were altered. These various episodes were symptomatic of the tensions and harassments that surrounded our relations with the communist governments in the early 1950s. This was the Stalin era, but in spite of some tendency to moderation after Stalin, similar episodes occurred under Khrushchev.

The general atmosphere of these times can be underscored by referring to the speech of Secretary Acheson in 1950 in which he discussed "tensions between the United States and the Soviet Union" and the note from the Secretary in March, 1952, on "travel restrictions on Soviet officials in the United States," imposed because of the new restrictions on American diplomatic and consular representatives in the Soviet Union.[19] In October, the Ministry of Foreign Affairs in Moscow sent a note to the United States government indicating that Ambassador George F. Kennan was *persona non grata* and requesting his immediate recall. This act was based on objections to statements by Kennan to the press in passing through the Berlin airport.

In his State of the Union Message in January, 1952, President Truman emphasized the "terrible threat of aggression." In 1953, just before leaving office, he described how the "communists seek to fish in troubled waters, to seize more countries, to enslave more millions of human souls." He referred to the 13 million square miles of the Stalinist world—where police were everywhere, with their authority unlimited, and terror and slavery were instruments of government. In speaking of his own job, Truman said that "the bundle of burdens is unique; there is nothing like it on the face of the earth." He recalled the new measures for collective security, the grand design of the Marshall Plan, a Europe moving rapidly toward political and economic unity, and the urgent economic and social problems of Asia and Africa where "hundreds of millions of people are in ferment." He reminded his listeners that Lenin was a preatomic man and emphasized that in the search for peace, the need for strength as well as for retaliation had been greatly increased since the Soviets had developed their atomic capabilities in 1949.

At the conclusion of Truman's term he had recognized the importance of continuity in foreign policy. The sharp debate during the campaign between Eisenhower and Stevenson, in which each party accused the other of inadequacy and mistakes, did not, in fact, lessen the importance to both parties of building on the constructive work of the past. The Constitutional issue raised by the fact that a President continues to be responsible for foreign affairs between the election and the inauguration of his successor made essential special efforts to establish liaison with the incoming Administration. Woodrow Wilson had tried to plan a solution to this problem in 1916, when he feared he might be defeated by Charles E. Hughes. The problem in 1952, however, because of the serious conflict in Korea, was a real and especially demanding one. After talks between President Truman and President-elect Eisenhower, a statement was issued on November 18 on "Continuity and Responsibility in the Conduct of Foreign Affairs." It announced that arrangements for liaison and cooperation had been made in the spirit of the Constitution, though without any sharing of responsibility, which could not be shifted until the new President had taken the oath of office.

A reassuring start on arrangements was made. These were the easier because Secretary-designate Dulles had been working with the President and the Department of State in connection with the meetings of the Council of Foreign Ministers, the Japanese Peace Treaty, and other matters. His association with policy-making officers in the Department had been close and of considerable duration. The points of agreement were more substantial than the differences. Thus, a smooth transition could be expected, even though changes were inevitable.

THE POST-STALIN ERA

The year 1953 was one of change for the Soviet Union, as well as for the United States. On March 5, Joseph Stalin died. This brought many questions to the leaders in all countries and a new unrest to the peoples behind the Iron Curtain. It was impossible to be sure whether basic policy in the Soviet Union would change significantly or not. The new premier, Georgi Malenkov, was a man of less striking personality than his predecessor, and the relative power of the potential rulers grouped around him was uncertain. Others who had for a time shared responsibility included Molotov, Beria, Nikolai Bulganin, Kaganovich, Zhukov, and Nikita Khrushchev. Zhukov was to become Defense Minister, Bulganin succeeded Malenkov in 1955, and Beria was executed in a few months. These were changes which it was difficult for the outsider to interpret. The intensely centralized government of Stalin, which had developed during his 25 years of unquestioned control, gave way to a less sharply centralized regime, in which changes were to take place every few years after 1953. During these years, Khrushchev gradually emerged as a leading power—in 1958, he assumed the two key positions of Party Secretary and Premier of the Government.

In discussing the "preconditions for accommodation with the Soviet Union" in the post-Stalin era, Secretary of State Dulles stated that "nothing that has happened, or which seems to me likely to happen, has changed the basic situation of danger in which we stand." He noted three facts: the Soviet Union was heavily armed, it was deeply hostile, and it had no moral inhibitions against the use of violence. He urged active efforts to bring the European Defense Community into being.[20]

The issues before the new Administration were in most respects the same as those of the previous eight years. The attempt to deal with them brought few changes in basic approach; the differences, with a few exceptions, were in pace and tone. One of the exceptions was the determination, by use of a military or political offensive if need be, to end the fighting in Korea. This decision, which had been announced by President Eisenhower during the campaign, was thrown into sharp relief by his brief visit to Korea—in fulfillment of a campaign pledge—in November, 1952. He and Dulles had determined on a course of action that was set forth in part in Eisenhower's report to Congress on February 2, 1953. He said that the Seventh Fleet "would no longer be employed to shield Communist China." He added that this implied no aggressive intent but that we were under no obligation to protect a nation fighting us in Korea. At about the same time, jet fighters were added to the Far Eastern Command, and nuclear missiles were moved to Okinawa.[21]

Although those on the inside knew that the President had not accepted General MacArthur's proposals and was more than reluctant to act to reunify the peninsula by force, the possibility of going further and facing additional risks was implicit in 1953 policy. It was shortly after his report to Congress that word was sent to

Peking by way of Nehru in India that if other means of halting the fight in an honorable truce should fail, the United States could not refrain from using the force at its disposal. Some interpreted this statement to refer to nuclear weapons.* It was believed that this message—and the fear of Chiang's intervention from Taiwan—was effective in breaking the deadlock over truce conversations.† An agreement for the repatriation of the sick and injured captured personnel was reached on April 11.

Troubles still attended the negotiations, however, at home and abroad. Both Senator Knowland and Senator Taft denounced the prospective truce as dishonorable. In Korea, President Rhee, restive over the caution of the United Nations Command, permitted some 25,000 of the North Korean and Chinese Communist prisoners to escape. It was admitted by United Nation headquarters that the South Korean security forces had made little effort to prevent the men from breaking through the barricades and disappearing into the civilian population. American Ambassador Ellis O. Briggs called this a serious incident and one that might interfere with an early armistice.[22] As so often, the bad news came through in the middle of the night. Dulles telephoned President Eisenhower immediately upon receiving the news.[23] This was one of the instances when the United States stood at the verge of war. The moment called for unquestioned determination, and the result was the willingness of Peking to agree to an armistice.

The resolution of the conflict was embodied in a cease-fire agreement, signed by the field commanders on July 27. The new demarcation line was set at the stabilized front, cutting diagonally across the 38th Parallel. The end of the fighting left many unsatisfactory issues, both for the communists and the free world. It failed to constitute a real victory in the eyes of many. The basic lesson which came with Truman's decision of 1950 had been learned, however. Similarly, the willingness of the new Administration to carry the war to the north, and even to threaten the mainland, made an impression that was not ignored by the communists.

During this time, Winston Churchill, who was again Prime Minister and who had met with General Eisenhower shortly before his

---

*This report cannot be proven.
†The conversations had begun in 1951.

inauguration, was urging a meeting "at the summit." Though this type of diplomacy was not new, having been resorted to by Woodrow Wilson in 1919 and by others, it had a new feasibility in view of the increasing speed of travel. Churchill urged the President that solutions for Europe in particular might be found in a meeting of heads of state. Eisenhower, supported by Dulles, insisted that there would be few prospects of success unless there were signs of good intentions on the part of the Soviets. The e hopeful indications would appear if hostilities in Asia were ended, if captive peoples of East Europe were freed, or if there were steps toward the conclusion of the treaties with Austria and Germany.

Berlin and Germany. With a view to testing the Soviet attitudes and to making progress on these essential aims in Europe, the United States in July invited Russia to participate in a conference of the Four Power Foreign Ministers (CFM). After many exchanges on this proposal, the Soviets agreed in November to attend a meeting that was scheduled to take place in Berlin in January, 1954. There was hope in some quarters that the new leaders in the Kremlin would in fact take a different line and that the Berlin meeting could be followed by a summit meeting. The conversations in Berlin, however, revealed an adamant position at that time on both Austria and Germany. (It was not until more than a year later, in order to achieve their desire for a summit conference, that the Soviets acceded to our proposal for the Austrian State Treaty. This was at least a contributing factor in the willingness of the President to go to Geneva in that same year—1955.)

Rumors and oppressive acts in East Europe were disturbing the Germans behind the Iron Curtain. The situation in the Soviet-occupied zone in the winter of 1953 was far from reassuring. The result was that thousands of refugees were streaming into Berlin, fearing that their chance for escape might be cut off. It was easy to get to Berlin, and there were no obstacles to walking across the political line of demarcation which separated the two parts of the city.

The refugee receiving center was always crowded. Factories were taken over for temporary shelter. Hundreds of men, women, and children, who had left home with a few possessions, were bedded down on straw and held for interviews, pending their travel into the Federal Republic of Germany. While some of these persons wanted to stay in Berlin, the German authorities feared that too large a concentration of persons who had been under communist domination for several years and who, for the most part, hoped for eventual return to their homes in a free East Germany, might lead to disturbances. The policy was that most of them should be flown out to the west.[24] There they were given civic rights and assistance, and, as the economy expanded, they became an important part of the labor force. The Western allies did not interfere in the conduct of this policy. They did not officially grant aid to the fleeing thousands, though general aid financing did contribute to new housing, made extremely tight by the additions to the population in the badly destroyed city.

Aid to industry had been furnished Berlin in considerable volume.* By dint of harmonious and well-planned support, the city's factories were beginning to produce, and the reduction of unemployment from more than 30 percent toward the goal of full employment, achieved some nine years later, was proceeding rapidly. Berlin was gaining its former status as a highly productive center.

Though the workers in West Berlin were earning good wages and beginning to see the results of the economic cooperation between the city, the Bonn authorities, and the American aid programs, the workers in the East were under pressure to produce more for less money. A system called "norms" was imposed on them to speed up their production. Meanwhile, with less cash income and higher food prices, they were feeling the oppression of the Soviet rulers whose soldiers kept in line the servile authorities in Pankow, Berlin, the seat of the East German regime. There had been no chance for labor bargaining in these years. The contrast between the industrial conditions in the two parts of the city was disturbing. Many of the workers lived in their former homes in East or West and worked in the other section. The labor unions in the West were active and vocal. The Iron Curtain did not seal off the Soviet zone.

Early in June, 1953, the masons who worked on the buildings of *Stalinallee* (now *Karl-Marx-Allee*) decided to protest their worsen-

---

*The total was more than $1030 million between 1945 and 1960; this figure includes aid of all types.

ing conditions. They asked for a meeting with the authorities and were refused. On June 16, they went to work in an angry mood. They said they must fight for their rights. Conditions were becoming intolerable. They decided to march to the headquarters of the Soviet authorities in *Leipziger Strasse*. Some dozens of men, still in their white smocks, came down off the scaffolding and went along in a body, to be joined by several hundred as they walked through the streets. When they got to the office buildings to make their demands, they were refused admittance. Furious with the arbitrary decision, they began tearing down propaganda posters and setting them on fire. The crowd was shouting "freedom," "we won't be slaves," "down with the norms." Their clash with the Soviet-controlled Peoples' Police became violent. The Vopos, not armed with guns, tried to beat the people back. Excitement spread through the sector and into the Soviet zone from the Baltic to the southern borders.

The news of the Berlin revolt spread quickly by word of mouth. Many of the telephone workers and railroad workers were pro-Western, and almost all were anti-Russian. The hope of throwing off the communist yoke spread like wildfire. In more than 200 towns and cities, the citizens broke down the doors of the jails and let the political prisoners go free. The headquarters of the communist parties were sacked and burned. Revolutionary groups took over the town halls, and the suppressed expectation of independence and victory over the occupying forces inspired thousands to acts of bravery.

The uprising had been generated without leadership and without plan. The hatred for the foreign rule led to a desperate desire to strike out, and for several weeks the zone of Soviet occupation was in a state bordering on war. But the people had no weapons and no outside support.

In Berlin, the decisions of the night of June 16–17 were inevitable. The commandants of the three Western powers, meeting in closed session to decide on their course of action, were joined, early on the 17th, by Mayor Ernst Reuter, who had been in Vienna, but had returned with all possible speed to his city. The commandants and their political advisers issued orders to keep their troops, some 20,000 soldiers, back from the stormy areas at the sector border. They instructed the Berlin police to restrain violence. They forbade the use of the RIAS (Radio in the American sector) to incite a widespread revolt. The station was to issue only factual accounts of what had happened. The brilliant labor leader, Ernst Scharnowski, was told he could not broadcast an appeal for the workers to rise.

The generals and their political advisers knew that the Soviets were moving in tanks and heavily armed soldiers. They knew that 22 or more divisions, probably more than 400,000, well-equipped troops, were closing in on the centers of revolt. In Berlin, they were not leaving the suppression of the uprising to the Vopos; the more ruthless, trained soldiers would serve better to reestablish control. If the Allied troops, with NATO backing, were to attempt to support or even permit Germans from East and West to overthrow the Soviet army, there would be not only a blood bath in Germany, but a serious clash between the Soviet Union and the Western allies. The fate of the whole satellite world would be in jeopardy. Only a nuclear war would have settled the issues set aflame by such an uprising.

There was little time for consultation—either national or international. The decisions as to the posture of the occupying forces, the behavior of the Berlin police—then unarmed—and the use of the radio had to be made at once. The information went out to Washington, but the orders were given locally, before there was a genuine chance to know what the home governments thought of the revolt. The Soviets had strung their barbed wire across the main streets joining the two zones. Tanks bristling with guns were at the intersections. Heavy vehicles were driving through the crowds, mowing down the brave young men throwing rocks. Some of them did not survive to know that they were heroes. The dead of the 17th of June demonstrated the spiritual strength—and the physical weakness—of the victims of the police state.

Berlin was to make clear many of the elements of the conflict of the postwar decades. It was to show the ability of men to live in the shadow of danger. It was to bring together diverse views and different philosophies in a cooperative effort. It was to produce doubt as to whether the capitals of the world could clearly navigate the troubled waters in which they found themselves in their confrontation with the communist intentions and strong, unyielding doctrines. It was to show the continuing desire for freedom and the force of guns to crush the physical manifestations of rebellion. The policy of "rollback," the conviction that the United States could go beyond containment to liberation, had to be viewed in the cold light of facts.

The Soviets had the military capabilities to face an emerging NATO. They had the beginnings of a nuclear potential, which no one wished to have used. They had the will to destroy Berlin in the interest of establishing their system. Thus the brutal dilemma of the atomic age was put before an anxious public by the Berlin revolt of 1953. The West could not encourage the slaughter that threatened to come. A war between the armed and the unarmed was impossible. There was no plan for such a contingency. The years of waiting for liberation must stretch out even beyond rearmament and beyond the cementing of alliances, to fundamental changes in the estimates and aims of the communist leaders. From 1953 to 1967, the will to freedom would have to be perpetuated by a far distant hope, a belief in the ultimate return to a different set of values and to a time when compromise would not destroy those conditions essential to human decency.

As a gesture, which had no military meaning but which gave a distraction to the embittered Germans, who had hoped to find Allied support and called for guns with which to fight, the United States inaugurated the food package program. Borrowing from the stockpile which had been built up to feed the city if there should be a new blockade of the access routes, the Americans gave parcels of food to visitors from the Soviet Zone. Many, wishing by their contact with the Allies to show their unbroken spirits, traveled for many miles to pick up the packages in West Berlin. This presented the communists with a dilemma. Finally, to stop the demonstration, they decided to risk adverse propaganda. They began to arrest travelers from the East and the surrounding zone, and travel to Berlin became hazardous. The United States stopped the program and, replacing the stockpile food, sent additional supplies into the zone by other means. Meanwhile, several hundred of the so-called ringleaders were jailed for many months. The refugee stream into Berlin continued.

Here again, as in other cases, the greater strength of the West was thwarted, not by lesser capabilities overall, but by the unrestrained aggressive will of the adversary. The determination to bind together the democracies and to increase their potential, not only military but also economic and psychological, was given an added impetus. The struggle to reestablish freedom in the areas behind the Iron Curtain was seen in terms of the "long haul." The short-run advantages of the police state were evident.

In dealings with Germany and Austria and in the attempts to establish the European Defense Community, the Eisenhower-Dulles policy was almost identical with that of Truman and Acheson. If there were differences, they were changes in style, including the increase in pressure on the French. Paris was suffering from wars overseas and from frequent changes in leadership which introduced an element of uncertainty into French actions.

Germany, having had elections and set up the Federal Republic, with Konrad Adenauer as Chancellor, in 1949, signed the contractual agreement abolishing the High Commission in May, 1952. This agreement ended the occupation, except for the city of Berlin. At this time the three Western occupying powers issued the tripartite declaration, often reissued since,

> The security and welfare of Berlin and the maintenance of the position of the three powers there are regarded as essential elements of the peace of the free world in the present international situation. . . .[25]

An agreement on debts was signed in London on February 27, 1953. In October of the following year the North Atlantic Council approved Germany's entrance into NATO. The membership became an accomplished fact in May, 1955, after Germany had been declared a sovereign state on May 5. It is interesting to note that in September of that year (1955) the Soviet Union accorded the Federal Republic of Germany full diplomatic recognition. Meanwhile, the efforts of the U.S.S.R. to demonstrate the sovereign independence of the regime in their zone continued.

The action to make possible the incorporation of German troops into the NATO defense force was to be fraught with difficulties before success was achieved. The original plan had been put forward by René Pléven as early as October, 1950. There was to be no separate German army and no general staff. The European Defense Community (EDC) was to be supernational. The United States accepted the proposal. The draft plan was signed in Paris on May 27, 1952, by France, Belgium, the Netherlands, Luxemburg, Italy, and West Germany. The progress toward German rearmament was so impressive that the subsequent setback came as a shock. Washington had realized that the ultimate success of the program was not a foregone conclusion, but the changes in the French attitude were more disturbing than anticipated.

The meeting of the three Western Foreign Ministers in Paris in July addressed itself both to the German-Austrian problems and to the situation in Korea, where the end of the fighting was expected in a matter of days. There also was discussion of the distressing situation in Indochina. It was after this meeting that the United States offered increased aid to help France in the struggle to halt communism in the Southeast Asian countries. France had promised independence to Laos, Cambodia, and Vietnam. Churchill had expressed a wish for a conference "at the summit" to deal with these urgent problems with the U.S.S.R., but at this time he suffered a mild illness, known by some to have been a stroke, which made such a plan inadvisable. It was decided to postpone the more formal meeting and to meet in a three-power conference in Bermuda in the fall. There were new men in Washington, confronting many old problems, seeking more effective solutions than those which had already been advanced. There was always a chance that new approaches might yield impressive results.

A European Defense Community. The urgency of moving forward with EDC* was evidenced by the unsettled conditions in the Middle East, in Southeast Asia, and in the Far East, as well as in the center of Europe. Negotiations could hold promise only if the strength of the alliance were assured by the incorporation on some basis of German divisions, which would enhance the power of NATO. Eisenhower and Dulles emphasized this need to Churchill and Eden in Bermuda when they met there in the first week in December. They also stressed the restlessness of Congress over the inconclusive state of the defense measures. The Bermuda Communiqué, along with various optimistic affirmations, said: "The French Minister of Foreign Affairs [Bidault]

---

*The EDC was an outgrowth of the Pléven Plan (René Pléven) of October 19, 1950.

explained the problems facing his government in regard to the European Defence Community."[26] The ministerial sessions of the North Atlantic Council, meeting in Paris the following week, asserted that "including a German contribution [in EDC] remains an essential objective for the reenforcement of the defensive strength of the Alliance."[27] In a statement in Paris on December 16, 1953, Secretary Dulles said that if the EDC were not ratified soon, the United States would have to make an "agonizing reappraisal" of the situation.

These words made such a stir that the Secretary was led to expand on them in an address to the National Press Club in Washington on December 22. He said that the statement had, in his opinion, "reflected a self-evident truth." He went on to mention the three factors which he believed made EDC essential.[28] One was the possibility of a strategy with American forces in Germany, a second was the importance of having German contingents under international control to avoid the spectre of a new German militarism, and the third was the importance of healing the breach between France and Germany.

Alternatives had been discussed, but diplomats held that there was no justification for bringing out in the open those less desirable possibilities while the prospect of gaining the primary objectives still existed. Dulles remarked: "Of course, if EDC fails, there will be things to be done. We are not blind to that." In spite of his further amplification of the intent of his pronouncement, many termed it a "brutal threat not only to the French but to everyone in Western Europe."[29] Some called it an indication that the United States would pull out of Europe. Those who were working closely with Washington, though they may have decried the statement as it was interpreted abroad, hardly credited the more extreme ideas, which were repeated even after later events proved them false. The vigor with which the commitment to Berlin was asserted was evidence enough to counter these fears.

The nature and vitality of the United States defense program over these years were under constant scrutiny. There were moments when some wondered if the new Administration was as determined as the former leaders in Washington. The nervousness and excitement over an occasional phrase was illustrated again, after the "agonizing reappraisal" incident, by the stir caused by the speech in which Dulles spoke of security being largely dependent on "the capacity for massive retaliation at times and places of our own choosing." Those who were searching for signs underlying the direct meaning extrapolated these words to mean that the United States would place its major reliance on nuclear retaliation and would underemphasize the necessity for conventional forces. Dulles' discussion of our defense posture in "Policy for Security and Peace" in the April, 1954, issue of *Foreign Affairs*, however, indicated that no aspects of our defense potential could be neglected.

Dulles' efforts in addressing himself to these questions were to lay a foundation for the delicate conversations between the foreign ministers in Berlin in early 1954. He feared, apparently, that the many notes being exchanged between the Soviets and the Western allies about this meeting and a possible later summit meeting might lead to uncertainty as to the firmness of our intention to halt aggression by cooperative means such as EDC or even by means of atomic weapons, with which the United States was well armed. Little was accomplished during the days of arduous conversations. A quadripartite communiqué, issued on February 18, proposed a meeting in Geneva to settle certain Korean questions,[30] and a tripartite communiqué, signed by the French, British, and Americans, was released the next day. This concluding statement concerned Germany, the main question before the meeting, and—as has been mentioned—the Soviets were adamant on that topic and thus did not concur in it.[31] In fact, in contrast to the typical cheerful communiqué that smooths over differences, the one issued by the four Foreign Ministers on February 18 contained the following brief summary:

> The Four Ministers have had a full exchange of views on the German question, on the problems of European security, and on the Austrian question. They were unable to reach agreement upon these matters.[32]

During the four weeks of dueling, the United States placed on the record the full picture of the Western efforts since 1945 to aid Europe, to restore democracy, and to find security. Similarly, the Soviet Foreign Minister, Vyacheslav Molotov, outlined in emphatic terms the conditions they required in their dealings with postwar Europe. They intended to hold on to East Germany, to permit unification only if they could control the election machinery in all of

Germany, to maintain troops in Austria indefinitely, and, in return for a Soviet-controlled Europe, to permit the United States an "observer" role.[33] As far as Korea and Indochina were concerned, the resolution to meet in Geneva to seek a solution to the division of Korea and the establishment of peace in the area was phrased in American terms and conformed with our policy of nonrecognition of the communist regimes.

The long-drawn-out discussion, while leading to no material progress, did serve to clarify the elements of the two sets of problems in Europe and the Far East which were to limit action for many years. The Eden Plan for the reunification of Germany in five stages, beginning with free elections and ending with a peace treaty, was rejected completely by Molotov. The interplay of initiative and proposal between the three Western allies was effectively handled and further cemented the unity of the three powers on major questions.

The first year of the new Administration can be considered to have ended with this Berlin Conference of 1954. These months were of great significance in the shaping of free world policy. For 20 years the Republicans had been the minority party. Because of the new emphasis on bipartisanship, however, they had been in close touch with the Democratic leadership since 1942. As usual after an election, there was no abrupt change in direction, and all the major programs in the fields of aid, security, and economic cooperation were carried on with no interruption. In connection with Korea and the possible use of nuclear power and the Seventh Fleet, as well as the tone in dealing with the communists, differences were noted and, on the whole, well received. It had been assumed that the new men could act more aggressively, for they had made many promises. Experience with Soviet policy and the firm hold which the communists had established on East Europe led to disappointment in the new foreign policy which, after all, could not change the basic obstacles to peace. The new men had to learn the lesson, still puzzling to the student of foreign affairs, that there are stubborn underlying conditions on which the communists can capitalize —for the very reason that they do not observe the same limits to the use of force central to the doctrine of the free world.

The year 1953 had been one of both success and failure. It was a time for reviewing past efforts and attempting new courses of

action. In sum, the changes were outnumbered by the reaffirmation
and reinforcement of former decisions and efforts.

Already the issues stood out in sharp detail. Indochina was becoming one of the points of serious difficulty. The weakness of the
French in their time of trial was emerging as a serious problem for
the United States. Paris, distracted by the struggle in Algeria, could
not maintain a position of strength in the Far East. Dulles endeavored, with what he thought was success, to secure the participation of the British in action to hold the line in Indochina and began
preparations for a show of strength in the area.

The story of the Dulles-Eden understanding of the early spring of
1954 will never be completely known. In later years, Dulles did not
wish to air the facts because, in his view, knowledge of them would
not further the understanding between England and the United
States which he deemed so important. No public statements are
available to explain what seemed to Eisenhower and Dulles a shift
in position. The growing awareness of the vulnerability of the
French defense in the area was discouraging others, and the defeat
seemed almost inevitable by early April. Sir Anthony Eden concluded, apparently, that an agreement at Geneva would better
further security than a more vigorous action by the Allies.[34] He
supported this conclusion by his indication that the Commonwealth
countries were fearful of any efforts by the United States and England which might risk a global conflict. Because of the Korean war,
in which our losses were heavy, he is said to have thought that we
might withdraw from Indochina if the going became hard and
leave the British in the lurch.[35] The mutual misinterpretations by
Eden and Dulles weakened their confidence in each other and thus
placed obstacles in the way of genuine cooperation in the months
ahead.

The conference proposed in Berlin convened in Geneva on April
26, 1954, to continue until July 21. The French had appealed to
the United States for help in the distressing emergency developing
in the tragic defense of Dienbienphu. Here the heroic garrison was
facing complete defeat. The will of Dulles to come to the defense
of the defenders was far from being a bluff. Some have called it
an empty threat without the determination to act. The reason for
what seemed a reversal of Washington policy lay, however, in the
reluctance of the British to intervene and of the French to press the

military effort with more vigor. It has been reported that Dulles discussed with them the use of atomic weapons. There is no doubt that if the Secretary had received support from the Allies, he would have gone a long way, and the future of the area would have been markedly different. Some still think that the risks he would have taken were too grave, but the unsolved questions are likely to remain in the realm of the unknown.

The Geneva meeting in which the United States reversed its position has been called "one of the strangest episodes in postwar history."[36] Secretary Dulles returned from the conference the first week of May. On May 7, Dienbienphu fell. In an address in Washington "midway in the Geneva conference" the Secretary paid tribute to the "gallant defenders."[37] He explained that his return was not connected with developments in the conference, where he had left General Bedell Smith as the "highly qualified head of the American delegation." He stated that he had been out of the United States for a large part of the past six months. He had attended conferences in Bermuda, Berlin, and Caracas, and two NATO meetings in Paris, in addition to the meeting in Geneva. He had also traveled to a dozen countries on other missions. He said that his further presence was impracticable in the long-drawn-out sessions.

Congressional Resistance to Alliances. The work of developing other much-needed alliances, which now appeared more urgent than before, required convincing Congress and, in particular, the Foreign Relations Committee of the Senate that we were taking the right course in halting communist aggression. This was not easy. Members of Congress knew that there were weaknesses in the Allied position and noted our inability to use force. They were suspicious of many of the earlier pacts, knowing that some had taken the form of executive agreements that had bypassed the Senate in recent years. The isolationists, led in some instances by Senator John W. Bricker of Ohio and including from time to time Senators Connally, Knowland, and Taft, wished to restrain the Executive branch. (Senator Vandenberg had changed his policy, adopting a constantly more progressive attitude since his resolution of June, 1948.)

Bricker therefore proposed an amendment to the Constitution, a key clause of which stated: "A treaty shall become effective as internal law in the United States only through the enactment of appropriate legislation by the Congress." The amendment was first introduced in September, 1951. Ultimately, it was reintroduced by Bricker and other Senators in various versions and with numerous modifications designed to meet strong opposition from the Administration and others. It failed to pass the Senate in any of its forms. In 1954, President Eisenhower indicated that the intended curb on the power of the President would make it impossible for the nation to deal effectively with friendly governments for mutual defense. In February of that year, the measure was again defeated (by only one vote). Senator Bricker continued his fight, but there was no serious danger after that of passage of such an amendment. In any case, Bricker was removed from the Senate in 1958 by the Ohio voters. The Administration could proceed without serious obstacles to the conclusion of a number of treaties.

The eight treaties which served to set up a system of cooperative defense had been signed between 1947 and 1954. They included:

The Rio Treaty	21 nations	September 2, 1947
NATO	15 nations	April 4, 1949
The Philippine Treaty	2 nations	August 30, 1951
ANZUS	3 nations	September 1, 1951
The Japanese Treaty	2 nations	September 8, 1951
South East Asia Treaty	9 nations	September 8, 1951
Korea	2 nations	October 1, 1953
The Republic of China	2 nations	December 2, 1954

These treaties spanned the globe. They were within the spirit and the letter of the United Nations Charter. Forty-three nations were involved, all bent on the prevention of aggression. The United States was closely associated with the Central Asian Treaty Organization, first established as the Baghdad Pact in 1955 and changed to CENTO in 1959, but did not become a member, attending the meetings as adviser and as a member of some of the committees. Many of the smaller member nations could not have withstood attack without the support of the larger powers, but it was hoped the vacuum of power had been filled and danger averted by formally accepting the obligation of mutual defense.

While we limited our association to some of the undertakings, we recognized the necessity for giving economic and military support over a wide perimeter. We were not willing to sign the armistice agreement of July 20, 1954, which halted the fighting in Indochina, and did not join in the declaration of the Geneva Conference, as we were pressing for collective defense in the area. We had regretfully concluded that some areas were impossible to save from communism, at least under prevailing conditions. On August 8, we announced that we would aid in the evacuation of the areas north of the 17th Parallel, the newly established dividing line. We also said we would grant material aid. Thus we became involved in Vietnam. The losses in the Indochinese region were humiliating to the French and distressing to the entire free world.[38]

The establishment of SEATO thus appeared to be an urgent task, and the pact was signed on September 9, 1954. Ramon Magsaysay, President of the Philippines, declared that in establishing SEATO the nations were "seeking the welfare of Asian peoples and . . . not promoting 'colonialism.' " SEATO cannot be compared in military significance with NATO, but its consultations and meetings, cultural programs, medical research, and countersubversion seminars have coordinated thinking and cemented relations in these far-flung areas. Military exercises (maritime, sea and air, air-ground) were conducted several times between 1955 and 1962. There is a military planning office at the headquarters in Bangkok, Thailand.

The sensitivity to colonialism, which was growing each year, increased rather than diminished as more countries gained independence. The Department of State established the Bureau of African Affairs, splitting it off from the Near East-Africa bureau in 1958. For the officers in this area, work was increased steadily, and the attention of the highest officials turned in this direction. New Embassies were established as, successively, colonies gained independence.

Some of the significant dates were: the independence of the Philippines in July, 1946; of Burma on January 4, 1948; of Indonesia in December, 1949. Korea and Israel declared themselves republics in August and May of 1948; Libya became an independent federal kingdom in December, 1951; India and Pakistan became separate dominions in the British Commonwealth on August 15, 1947; India proclaimed itself a sovereign republic in January, 1950, and Ceylon was granted dominion status in the British Commonwealth in

February, 1948; Vietnam, Laos, and Cambodia became independent states in the French Union in March, July, and November, 1949. The full independence of these Indochinese nations came after July 3, 1954.

A Retrospect of Diplomacy. The difficult conditions that faced many of these countries and others gaining independence in the years to come made more important the assistance of the United States and the former colonial powers. They also opened the way for communist penetration, which was to develop in the form of offers of supplies, money, and technicians in the years between 1954 and 1967.

The year 1954 had also been one of significant action in Central America. When the tenth Inter-American Conference met in Caracas, Venezuela, on March 1, Eisenhower and Dulles were very much disturbed by the growing communist pressure on Guatemala. The efforts of Moscow to indoctrinate and to subjugate the leaders and key organizations in the country had begun in 1944. Because of preoccupation elsewhere, the United States had not observed these developments closely. Not until 1953 did Washington become deeply concerned. The efforts to meet the challenge, which began with the sending of Ambassador Peurifoy from Greece to Guatemala, intensified throughout these weeks. It was an essential purpose of the meeting in March to secure adherence to a declaration of solidarity; it was adopted in Caracas by 17 out of a possible 21 votes. While some critics have written of the reluctance with which this agreement was reached, closer inspection of the problems and the aftermath of United States intervention in June shows that this was an important element in the prompt and effective support the United States gave the rebels under Colonel Castillo Armas. The menacing possibility of a communist beachhead in Guatemala was ended in June, 1954. The impression made on Moscow by our support of the anticommunist leader Castillo Armas is reflected in the fact that the Soviets ceased for about eight years to attempt to set up a communist-controlled government in this hemisphere. (See Chapter III.) Meanwhile, the troubles in Latin America continued to smoulder— many of them would resist efforts at solutions for several decades.

Acute problems elsewhere continued to command the primary attention of Washington. The French defeat in Indochina and pressure in Algeria were to shake the plans for the European Defense Community in August of that year. Though not unexpected, that was a serious setback. Since the Berlin conference had not made progress, the search for a treaty had to be put off again. The new arrangements for German participation in European affairs included a contribution of a significant share of the forces needed to build up NATO; to this Dulles and Adenauer agreed.

Alternatives to this approach had been envisaged with the Eden Plan, brought forward in Berlin in January. If the plan had been accepted by the Soviets, it would have provided a means of reunification, with a five-stage provision for reestablishment of a democratic government for all Germany. The question of European armament would have taken on a different form. As it was, the German forces were to form the backbone of the North Atlantic Treaty Organization. While appraisals of the French attitude toward Germany and the United States vary widely, the more understanding took account of the cost of successive wars. The more enlightened recognized the potential importance of an integrated Europe with a revived French Republic and a strong Federal Republic of Germany. It was with the dangers and the possibilities in mind that Robert Schuman had proposed the European Coal and Steel Community in 1950, and it was with the success of this first venture that the six nations on the continent of Europe went ahead with plans for the European Economic Community or the Common Market. The Treaty of Rome in 1957 followed the establishment of the Coal and Steel Community and the vigorous development of economic cooperation, which were to give economic foundations for defense as production and prosperity increased beyond the hopes of war-devastated nations in the immediate postwar years. Germany called her young men into the armed services, and the economy of the Federal Republic became the strongest in Europe.

Nuclear developments in the years between 1945 and 1955 changed the scope and importance of diplomacy. On January 21, 1954, the United States launched the submarine *Nautilus*, the world's first atomic-powered ship. There was a new urgency to consideration of controls and limitations of armament. From Hiroshima and Nagasaki, which demonstrated superior United States potential, to the proposed MLF (Multilateral Nuclear Force), which in 1963 shook the Western Alliance, the significance of the new approach to warfare was a major preoccupation. Because of the enormous threat of destruction, the concept of limited war as a way of checking wars was increasingly discussed, as the strongest nation in the world found itself restrained in the protection of its vital interests. From Korea to Berlin the situation brought frustration—the idea of "no win" conflict baffled the courageous and confused the weak.

The approach of the mid-1950s was twofold. On the one hand, there were attempts to curb and reduce the nuclear danger. On the other hand, there was the continuing effort to redirect offensive and defensive weapons so as to lessen encroachment and deter aggression. Proposals to place the atom under international control, while we still had the monopoly, had been put forward by President Truman and Bernard Baruch in October, 1945. These were rebuffed by the Soviets. There was a resolution in the General Assembly of the United Nations in January, 1946, to explore the possibility of the exchange of information and the development of peaceful uses. The Soviets brought forward a suggestion for the destruction of all nuclear stockpiles. This would have wiped out our position of power. The Soviets were then, and continued to be, against international inspection of their capabilities and military activities.

Our own proposal, elaborated by the Acheson-Lilienthal Committee (1946), suggested the creation of an international authority which would own all "dangerous raw materials," carry on its own activities, and inspect "nondangerous" operations. This plan put forward in 1946 was overwhelmingly approved by the United Nations in 1948, but continued to be rejected by the Soviets.

In 1949, the Soviets exploded their first atomic device. In 1952, the United Kingdom and, in 1960, the French also exploded their nuclear devices. In 1964, Communist China announced that it had successfully set off its bomb. The age of *proliferation* had followed the time of discovery, as the danger to civilization increased. The concept of "peaceful coexistence" put forward by the Soviet leaders seemed to some to offer an escape from imminent danger.

Meanwhile, the problem of fallout was given more importance. In 1954, the growing number of tests had brought an awareness of the threat from the pollution of the atmosphere. During these years the scientific work had gone on steadily. In 1950, President Truman had authorized the production of the hydrogen bomb, and in December, 1952, the first such bomb had been exploded in the Pacific. Then in August, 1953, the Soviets announced that they, also, had exploded an H-bomb.

In an effort to shift the emphasis and to bring international authority into the picture, President Eisenhower presented his "atoms for peace" proposal in December, 1953, and the plan was accepted by the General Assembly unanimously just a year later. A further effort to bring about inspection and control, which would lessen the danger of atomic development, was made by President Eisenhower in his "Open Skies" proposal of July, 1955. This suggestion involved the exchange of blueprints of military establishments.

President Eisenhower had also decided, in September, 1954, that even though the Soviets refused to participate, the International Atomic Energy Agency should be established. This was discussed in a technical conference in Geneva in 1955 and in further negotiations which led to agreement by 27 nations in late 1955.[39] The problem of testing and the many-sided effects of increasing numbers of explosions were highly disturbing. Various approaches to the questions were attempted. The long arduous road to the Test Ban Agreement of 1963, in which the Soviets concurred in the limited action, was begun early. A new phase was to emerge with the space age. This changed the possibilities of detection and shifted the balance in regard to observation in a new direction. After Sputnik (1957) and Explorer (1958), the problem had begun to take on different aspects.

During these momentous postwar years, beginning after Potsdam in 1945 and continuing until the spring of 1955, there had been other grave disappointments. One was the failure of the Soviets to agree to a State Treaty for Austria. After the serious effort in Moscow in 1947, it had been decided by the four powers to ask the foreign ministers to name deputies to prepare the way for an acceptable document, clearing up many of the technical aspects of the settlement.

The first series of meetings was held in Vienna in the summer of 1947. The debate was prolonged and almost fruitless. The greatest amount of time was devoted to defining "former German assets." These were properties in Austria which were deemed to be German and thus subject to reparations. The Soviets wished to stretch the definition to include industries created in considerable measure by Austrian labor and partly financed by Austrian funds. A problem of categories would have existed even if there had been a will to achieve a settlement. It soon became evident, however, that the Soviets did not desire a treaty.

Some progress was made when it was proposed that Austria make a lump-sum payment which would be taken as the counterpart of the "former German assets"; the sum of $150 million was to be paid to Russia. The restitution of various properties taken from France or elsewhere, including *objets d'art* and identifiable items, was to be carried out in addition to this payment. Even though the simplification of the problem in the "short draft" removed some of the negotiating pitfalls, hundreds of meetings were held in Vienna and New York as the Soviets raised objections which made the discussions of little use.

It became evident that they were not ready for a treaty on any basis which would free Austria from their influence and control. Further conversations were meaningless and had to be postponed until their interest in other unrelated issues changed. In 1952, the United States addressed an appeal to Moscow on the basis of the short treaty draft with the simplified financial formula. The United Nations also addressed itself to the four governments in December. These, and other, efforts were of no avail. There had been 379 meetings at various levels. The situation was regarded by many as hopeless; they did not see any likelihood that the Soviets would withdraw from occupation. It was possible that they still hoped for political gain, although the Austrians had shown a steadfast anti-communist attitude since the "liberation" in 1945.

Then, as often in dealing with dictatorships, the situation changed suddenly in the spring of 1955. The declaration of the United States, the United Kingdom and France on April 5, 1955, is revealing:

> The three governments have followed closely the recent exchanges between the Austrian government and the Soviet government on matters relating to the state treaty. From these exchanges it appears that the Soviet Government may now have certain clarifications to offer regarding their policy toward Austria. . . . It remains the earnest desire of the Governments . . . to conclude the state treaty as soon as possible. . . .[40]

The three powers said that the Ambassadors in Moscow could handle the matter if Austria accepted the invitation to negotiate in that city.

The United States had indicated earlier in a note to the Kremlin that the matters in dispute which might be the subject of a future summit conference included not only broad security issues, but also the resolution of the German and Austrian treaty issues. There is reason to conclude that the granting of the Austrian treaty at this time was considered by the Soviets to be a low price which they could afford to pay to achieve such a meeting. Their reasons for wanting to have the conference lay partly in the changing leadership in the U.S.S.R. At this time, Nikita Khrushchev was taking over increasing power.

One of the aspects of the final settlement of great importance to the Soviets was the neutrality of Austria. The provision adopted did not raise serious difficulties for the Western allies. There was no reason for a large army or air force. Austria was not needed in NATO and did not wish to be a possible battlefield of later conflict. If it were to be in the path of advancing armies, violation of its territory by any party to the treaty would free the others from restraint. Moreover, there had never been, in the minds of the Americans, any doubt as to where the people's loyalties lay.

The agreements between the Austrian Premier and the U.S.S.R. in Moscow did not preclude last-minute demands by the Soviet representatives in Paris just before the signing of the treaty. There were two days of anxiety for fear the U.S.S.R. was reversing its position.[41] When Secretary Dulles, in Europe for the NATO meeting, refused to relinquish the accepted position with regard to the status of Austria, the Soviets, who had failed to block the entrance of Germany into NATO, dropped their demands. The memorandum of Moscow, April 15, 1955, stood, and the foreign ministers went to Vienna for the signing on May 15. Ninety days after ratification, the foreign troops left Austrian soil, and almost immediately, Austria joined the United Nations. (There is no statement of neutrality in the state treaty. It took the form of a declaration by the Austrian Parliament on November 5, 1955.)

THE KHRUSHCHEV ERA

During these years, in spite of the monolithic aspect of the communist bloc and the apparent unwavering allegiance to the doctrines of Marx and Lenin, there were changes and conflicts within the leadership. In 1955, there was a shift, with the decline of Nikolai A. Bulganin and the rise of Nikita Khrushchev.

On February 14, 1956, at the Twentieth Communist Party Congress, Khrushchev delivered a speech. Our intelligence service was convinced that a text of the speech must be available, so a document hunt was instituted.[42] As a result, the text, never published in the U.S.S.R., was found far away from Moscow and promptly made available to the free world. The speech emphasized the crimes of Stalin and was a step in the take-over of control and the strengthening of Khrushchev's position as a dictator. This shift within the hierarchy, beginning to be evident in 1955, did not take on definite form until 1958. After Stalin's death, the inner conflicts and changes remained obscure until the emergence of Khrushchev. The seeming flexibility in diplomacy and the relaxation of intellectual barriers, with more numerous relations with the West, brought one of those periods of partial "détente," which led to hope and willingness to negotiate on the part of the leaders in Washington and other Allied capitals. After Malenkov fell from power in February, 1955, his successors, Bulganin and Khrushchev, pressed forward with their request for a high-level international conference. In addition to the conciliatory move in agreeing to an Austrian treaty, they put forward new disarmament proposals on May 10, 1955.[43] These seemed to be some improvement over earlier suggestions, even though as presented they were unacceptable.

On May 26, 1955, the proposal of the British, French, and American governments for a conference of heads of state was accepted by the U.S.S.R.[44] On July 15, President Eisenhower announced his trip to Europe in the interests of peace and conciliation. The hope that the Soviet intentions had changed for the better was based in considerable measure on the success at Vienna. The phrase "summitry," used in connection with this meeting, is derived from Winston Churchill, who, in May, 1953, said that there should be a meeting "at the highest level." The term usually refers to negotiations between heads of state and the Soviet leaders. It has also been used in a less specific way to refer to conferences where the communists were not present.

There has been serious doubt about the advisability of having direct discussions between the heads of state, the men who make the *ultimate* decisions. Since there is, in such cases, no fall-back position, the whole gamut of major choices and agreements is exposed to the manipulations of the adversary. For the communists, the position is vastly different. They do not have to explain their actions either to their own people or to the outside world. They can put themselves on display without danger of weakening their position at home. In fact, the clash with the heads of other governments gives them an advantage, as it seems to show a strong position, and they can always claim a victory. The facts that the stage is conspicuous, the meeting dramatic, and that the non-communist world appears almost as a suppliant with proposals and compromises can be a help in shoring up their strength in the Soviet bloc.

It is almost impossible, in contrast to this situation, for the Western powers to seem flexible. They must face the crossfire of criticism both in the communist and in the free world. A change of attitude may be construed as weakness, and the failure to win a substantial gain is termed ineptitude. The President is in any case peculiarly handicapped in the United States by the fact that he cannot be long away from the country.

There is no instance in which a congenial atmosphere has permitted the leaders of opposing systems to reach a new and constructive understanding in the years since the war. In fact, it is difficult to find an instance when discussions between the heads of the Soviet and American states have yielded fruit.

Secretary Dulles, who was less optimistic about the Geneva Conference than President Eisenhower, had seen the difficulties in which President Woodrow Wilson had found himself in Paris in 1919. The struggles in which he became engaged enhanced neither his reputation abroad nor his power at home. The bargains put before him led to confusion, and he returned to America weakened and depressed to face a hostile Congress. This was a tragic case; Wilson found his extraordinary abilities and noble purposes of little aid in seeking to master the negotiations.

Though the later conference was simpler in composition and narrower in scope, it did little to improve our standing or to further the development of a foreign policy acceptable to the American people. The British had been eager for the meeting, both for domestic political reasons and because they hoped for some accomplishment.

However, the two main problems—the nuclear threat and the division of Germany—did not yield to negotiation.[45]

On the German question, a sentence was included in the Directive of July 23. It said

> The Heads of Government, recognizing their common responsibility for the settlement of the German question and the re-unification of Germany, have agreed that the settlement of the German question by means of free elections shall be carried out. . . .[46]

The foreign ministers were to make further arrangements. Their meeting in the fall which resulted from this directive ended in complete frustration of the alleged agreement in Geneva. The optimistic communiqué did not really conceal the failure of the meeting. The pictures of a smiling Eisenhower seated next to a stolid Bulganin were propaganda displays in Leipzig and elsewhere, blown up bigger than life—the British and French leaders had been cropped from the photograph. The "spirit of Geneva" was exploited by the Kremlin in many ways.

In September, a few weeks after the conference, President Eisenhower suffered a heart attack. His rapid recovery ended a period of dismay; the conduct of foreign affairs was only briefly ruffled by the event. His "open skies" proposal, attacked formally by Molotov in October, was approved by the UN General Assembly in December, as a minor dividend from the otherwise unproductive meeting in July. It was a forerunner of other proposals which showed the suspicion and rigidity of the Soviets in regard to the threat of nuclear war.

The French were struggling with the difficulties of the Algerian conflict, and Africa was beginning to stir with new claims for freedom. The stage was set for the aggressive demands of Nasser, who was to dominate the problems of the Middle East and North Africa for months to come. The rumbles of his increasing activities in the Arab world led to fear in the Mediterranean and to hatred on the part of the Israelis. The Baghdad Pact (later CENTO) was formed as a stabilizing influence.

In spite of the Soviet dissolution of the Cominform—established in September, 1947—as part of the new post-Geneva strategy, there was no substantial progress on any of the open questions. The Cold War was to become colder as the year wore on.

Suez and the Middle East. There are few crises in which so many different lines of policy and practical strategy are involved as the Suez tragedy of 1956. In the week between the attack by Israel on October 26 and the acceptance of a cease-fire by the British, French, Israelis, and Egyptians on November 6, many issues involving the balance of power in the Middle East, the rise of Nasser, the survival of the Israeli state, the use of the Suez Canal, oil, the spread of communism, and the prestige of the United Nations stirred the passions and aroused the fears of millions. Negotiation, threats, persuasion, and force had combined with other ingredients of diplomacy in a struggle that left deep scars. The shock to the Western Alliance was serious. The impression on nations emerging from colonialism was far-reaching. Although the story has stimulated many volumes of debate and analysis, several aspects of the incident have not been revealed. The controversy goes on.

The United States had been little involved in the problems of the Middle East in the years before the Second World War. It had watched the changes and recognized the many problems there, but, until the Truman Doctrine of 1947 brought us directly into the affairs of Greece and Turkey, we considered that the burdens rested on the shoulders of the British and French. After the war, our interest in the founding of the Israeli state in 1948, increased by strong Jewish support from financial and cultural circles in the United States, led to a keener observation of what was occurring. The growth of economic dependence on oil also turned attention to the importance of the nature of the control of Arab lands.

On May 25, 1950, the United States had joined England and France in a declaration designed to increase stability and to moderate tensions between the Arabs and the Israelis. They proposed a Middle East Command to protect the security of the region, but Egypt refused to take part, and the plan collapsed. The Egyptians were striving intensely for independence and, in particular, for ending the influence of England. A group of young officers in 1952 ousted King Farouk. Shortly thereafter, Colonel Gamal Abdel Nasser forced out General Naguib to become the unchallenged head of the government. His vigorous program to build up the strength of the Arab world and to unite its people threatened not only Israel, but also many less dynamic interests in the Mediterranean, the Middle East, and Africa. In the face of this obvious danger of growing power, the United States could not be indifferent; neither could the Soviet Union.

The agreement by the United Kingdom to leave Egypt and to close its military base at Suez was concluded in October, 1954. For Nasser, it meant the culmination of a long effort to free the land of foreign troops. For England, it was a further step in the break-up of her overseas influence. For the rest of the world, it meant a disturbing uncertainty as to the future of a troubled area. Washington had urged the signing of a pact and proceeded to work on the alliance that was known for several years as the Baghdad Pact. The Baghdad Pact or Middle East Treaty Organization,* as it was called officially, was signed by Turkey and Iraq in February, 1955. It was adhered to by Britain, Pakistan, and Iran later that same year. In 1956, the United States agreed to support the treaty organization, but not to be a member.

During the years since the proclamation of the state of Israel in May, 1948, there had been continued hostility between the Jews and the Arabs, leading to a short and terrible war, mediated by the United Nations. The armistice came in July, 1949. Approximately a million Arab refugees, even now, live in camps in Jordan and the Gaza strip; most of them had fled during the fighting in 1948. There were many raids along the Arab-Israeli border and in the Gaza strip. These are said to have convinced Nasser that he would do well to capitalize on the Soviets' annoyance over the signing of the Baghdad Pact. Thus he signed the barter arms agreement with the U.S.S.R. in September, 1955, and mortgaged a large share of the cotton crop in return for arms. With these arms he hoped to counter the demonstrated military superiority of the Israelis. Unfortunately, the United Nations truce observation machinery failed to inspire confidence in the region, which seethed with hatred. Disputes over water, in the Jordan River basin, seemed insoluble.

The tensions increased steadily, with indications that Nasser would act aggressively, with the presumed support of the U.S.S.R., if there were serious interference with his intentions. The United States had meanwhile indicated that consideration would be given to financing a portion, roughly half, of the High Dam at Aswan.

---

*Later this became the Central Treaty Organization (CENTO).

Britain offered $14 million. Nasser delayed his acceptance of the offer, bargaining with the Soviets for help of various types. Congress, noting the growing influence of the Soviets in Egypt, stipulated in July, 1956, that no funds from aid appropriations could be used for financing the dam. The efforts by American officials to woo the Egyptians from their growing involvement in Soviet aid were thus thwarted—the attitude in the United States was well known at this time.

The episode of July 19, when the offer to assist in building the dam was withdrawn, has frequently been misinterpreted. The record of uncertainty in the negotiations for a period of months suggests that the American decision could not have been regarded as "abrupt" by Nasser. The denial was foreshadowed long in advance; the United States Congress and the British Parliament had both raised serious objections.

Dulles had discussed the prospective loan with the British and the French during the NATO meeting of the previous December. It was announced then that the Americans and the British would associate themselves with the International Bank for Reconstruction and Development in assisting Egypt. There followed prolonged negotiations with the IBRD. It was tentatively agreed that there would be a grant of $70 million, of which Great Britain would furnish $14 million. The further stages of aid would be in annual installments from the World Bank, England, and the United States as a loan. The remainder, estimated at $760 million, would be Egypt's contribution in labor, materials, and in other forms. Repayment was to be over a 40-year period, with the interest rate set at 5 percent. Dulles, in his press conference of December 20, 1955, said he had discussed the matter in Cairo in 1953. He added that it "was a cheap price to pay for peace and progress." He admitted a relation between the offer and possible Soviet aid to Egypt—this it was desirable to counteract.

As arrangements for the loan proceeded, Nasser raised various objections to the Bank's conditions, which he said offended the dignity and sovereignty of Egypt. The British were having trouble in the Middle East at this time; on instigation from Cairo, Glubb Pasha was ousted from his post in Jordan as British military expert. Some in London urged withdrawing the loan offer.

In the United States, Congressional pressure increased. Nasser's provocative dealings with the Soviets were well known. There were also questions as to whether the commitment of cotton, the main export of Egypt, to repay the U.S.S.R. would not imperil both the local financing of the project and the servicing and repayment of the loan. Perhaps because of these rumors, Ambassador Hussein asked for a meeting with Dulles on July 19. He was to report to Nasser on the status of the loan. Hussein was a friendly, allegedly pro-American diplomat, a physician and social worker before he became a government servant. The conversation was between men who could talk easily with each other. The Secretary is reported to have shown Hussein a draft press release which was to be issued that day. It read in part:

The United States joined . . . in an offer to assist Egypt in the construction of a high dam on the Nile at Aswan. . . . Developments within the succeeding seven months have not been favorable to the success of the project, and the U. S. Government has concluded that it is not feasible in the present circumstances to participate in the project. Agreement by the riparian states has not been achieved, and the ability of Egypt to devote adequate resources to assure the project's success has become more uncertain than at the time the offer was made. . . . The United States remains deeply interested in the welfare of the people. . . . It is prepared to consider at an appropriate time . . . what steps might be taken for a more effective utilization of the water resources of the Nile for the benefit of the peoples of the region. . . .[47]

The press release was issued after the visit of the Ambassador. The Secretary left a few days later for a ceremonial visit to honor the President of Peru at his installation. On July 26, Nasser announced the seizure of the Suez Canal. It was known that he had already begun training navigation pilots to operate the Canal. His act did not come as a surprise to everyone, but it was nonetheless a shock. Secretary Dulles never explained or defended his action in July.

Those who followed events and who understood Nasser's drive for power realized there was no possibility of satisfying his aims. There was no assurance that the dam project could be carried through smoothly and without serious conflicts. The denial of support could scarcely have been avoided and seemed in line with our overall strategy. The trap which had been laid by the Egyptian leader tended to shift the blame on the United States for his aggressive push. The press, which played up the final act, ignored the long and tortuous road from the first plan to final impasse and overlooked the pitfalls that would have followed if we had been engaged in a 10-year program of extreme complexity. Some of the difficulties we would have found have been encountered by the Soviets—who then offered to help build the dam—but neither the communist nor the Arab press has given them emphasis.

The rising crisis of 1956 led to a feverish response in Europe, fearful that oil would be cut off and that the flow of goods through the Mediterranean would be stopped. The power and the prestige of the West were seriously threatened and its economic life damaged. A series of meetings was begun to attempt to reach a practical solution. The problem of how to react to the seizure of the Canal tortured the diplomats and was the subject of hot debate in the press. During the next three months there were innumerable meetings. The first plan was to have a gathering in Geneva, to which Nasser would be invited. The site was changed to London at the request of the British and French. The British had taken the line that *immediate decisive action* was essential to safeguard economic conditions, political prestige, and the sanctity of agreements. The United States, while recognizing the urgency of these questions—as indicated in the travels back and forth across the Atlantic by high officials, including the Secretary—warned that the use of force would be destructive, rather than remedial.

A tripartite statement had been issued by the British, French, and Americans on August 2. They spoke of a threat to the freedom and security of the Canal as guaranteed by the convention of 1888 and proposed a conference of 24 nations, including Egypt, to be held on August 16 in London. Russia and India were among the nations attending. Egypt refused; it was recognized that Nasser could not come to the capital of the country most hated by the Egyptians.

At this time, Dulles proposed a Canal Users Association in a cable to Prime Minister Eden. Eden put the plan before Parliament, and he was reported to have agreed. There were, however, differences in the conceptions of the two men on this course of action. The threat of war was hanging over Europe and the Middle East. Some in Britain urged immediate military action, but the British parties were divided. The French advised fighting. The Americans continued to urge negotiation. Nasser was reported as meticulous in his efforts not to interfere with transit in the Canal during those weeks.

Dulles is said to have urged the handling of the Canal issue in such a way that "Nasser should be the one to take the hostile or obstructive act" and then the British and French would have a case to bring before the United Nations. The two governments, however, wished to press the matter more urgently, so they lodged a complaint with the Security Council. The issue was considered from October 5 to 13. As a result of these deliberations, on October 10, four men began discussing the problem: Dag Hammarskjöld (UN), Selwyn Lloyd (England), Christian Pineau (France), and Mahmoud Fawzi (Egypt). They came up with six principles:

1. no discrimination against transit through the Canal;
2. respect for Egypt's sovereignty;
3. insulation of the Canal operations from the politics of any country;
4. fixing the Canal tolls by agreement between Egypt and the users;
5. allocation of a "fair proportion" of the revenues for Canal improvements;
6. arbitration of the compensation to be paid to the old Canal Company, which Nasser had expropriated.[48]

These principles were approved unanimously by the Security Council in a night session, October 13–14. A meeting was scheduled to be held in Geneva on Monday, October 29.

Events elsewhere, some little known and some widely proclaimed, heightened the drama of the moment. The British had, it appeared, deployed their fleet in such a way as to indicate the support of military action. Our intelligence, however, noted that the forces had subsequently been shifted to suggest a lack of intention of aggressive action. Mobilization in Israel was observed, but this was said to be purely defensive. At this critical moment, revolt in Hungary led to dramatic headlines and stirred the sympathy and hopes of many on both sides of the Iron Curtain. Suez was almost forgotten in the hours of intense excitement. There was a request for an emergency session of the Security Council on October 27. News from Warsaw indicated further uprising against the Stalinists there. The whole satellite world seemed about to burst into flames.

The Suez crisis was not to be delayed, however. On October 29, the news came in to Washington that Israel had launched an invasion of Egypt's Sinai Peninsula. On October 30, the British and French issued an ultimatum, and the British-French air attack on Egypt began on the next day. There had been an emergency meeting at the White House on the 29th, after which the President had summoned the British Chargé * to warn the British government of the gravity with which we regarded the threat to the peace —a peace shattered two days later. The British fleet was steaming toward Cyprus. The "plot" to seize the Canal has been hotly debated and variously reported. The cease-fire ended the plot on November 6, after the full danger and tragedy of one of the most momentous events of the postwar years was revealed to an anxious world.

On Thursday, November 1, the Israeli forces had cut off the Gaza strip and were penetrating the Sinai Peninsula. The General Assembly was scheduled to meet in New York. The secrecy which had surrounded the plans, only slightly penetrated by United States intelligence, led to conflicting estimates of the probabilities of war and suggests the skeptical view taken in London, Paris, and Tel Aviv of the United States attitude toward the use of force.

On Wednesday, October 31, President Eisenhower had delivered an address to the nation. He referred to the debate of the political campaign and said that the situation in the Middle East caused serious concern,—passion "threatened to prevail over peaceful purposes." He reported "the essential facts":

> . . . relations of Egypt . . . kept worsening to a point at which first Israel—then France—and Great Britain also—determined that, in their judgment, there could be no protection of vital interests without resort to force.
>
> Upon these decisions events followed swiftly. On Sunday the Israeli ordered total mobilization. On Monday, their armed forces penetrated deeply into Egypt and to the vicinity of the Suez Canal, nearly 100 miles away. And on Tuesday, the British and French Governments delivered a 12-hour ultimatum to Israel and Egypt—now followed up by armed attack against Egypt.
>
> The United States was not consulted in any way about any phase of these actions. Nor were we informed of them in advance.[49]

---

*The new Ambassador, Sir Harold Caccia, had not yet arrived.

The Security Council of the United Nations met that same evening. In view of the failure to secure unanimity, they called an emergency session of the General Assembly, which convened on November 1 and 2.

There had been a virtual blackout of communications between the British, French, Israelis, and Americans in the weeks preceding the attack. None of the three Ambassadors was in Washington on the fateful days. Intelligence sources had given mixed and confused reports. Information, usually flowing freely between allies, had virtually dried up. The maneuvers of the British had been misleading and did not evidence a clear purpose. President Eisenhower had endeavored to make plain that no considerations related to the Jewish vote in the election would alter his opposition to the use of force. Then, the sudden strike left us little alternative to action through the UN.

The special session of the General Assembly met on November 1 and in the early morning of November 2. Bad weather made Dulles late, and Sir Pierson Dixon of Great Britain was already speaking when he arrived. This meeting was the culmination of a long fight to prevent war and to moderate the tense conditions in the Middle East. Dulles' speech was one of the most momentous of his life:

> I doubt that any delegate ever spoke from this forum with as heavy a heart as I have brought here tonight. We speak on a matter of vital importance, where the United States finds itself unable to agree with three nations with whom it has ties, deep friendship, admiration, and respect, and two of whom constitute our oldest, most trusted, and reliable allies.
> The fact that we differ with such friends has led us to reconsider and reevaluate our position with the utmost care, and that has been done at the highest level of our Government. Even after the reevaluation we still find ourselves in disagreement.[50]

He continued to describe the situation and to analyze its gravity and then introduced a resolution which called for a cease-fire.

> I believe that at this critical juncture we owe the highest duty to ourselves, to our peoples, to posterity, to take action that will assure that this fire which has started shall not spread but shall promptly be extinguished. Then we shall return with renewed vigor to curing the injustices out of which this trouble has arisen.

The resolution calling for a cease-fire and withdrawal of troops to the armistice line was adopted by a vote of 64 to 5, with Australia,

France, Israel, New Zealand, and the United Kingdom opposed. There were six abstentions—Belgium, Canada, Laos, the Netherlands, Portugal, and the Union of South Africa.[51] (That same night, the resolution on the Hungarian situation was discussed.) After Resolution 997, a cease-fire followed on November 6, with the Alliance shaken, but not shattered.

Secretary Dulles arrived home in the evening of November 2. That night he was stricken with the first of two serious attacks caused by cancer, and he was operated on during the afternoon of the next day. Under Secretary Herbert Hoover, Jr., took over in the Department of State.

The Soviet threat to join in the fight to support Egypt had spread apprehension. As the bombing continued, the United States exerted its full influence to bring a halt to the fighting. All the troops were not withdrawn until a short time after November 6. A resolution had been adopted in the United Nations on November 5 to establish an Emergency International Force to "secure and supervise the cessation of hostilities."[52]

There were many difficult conferences and communications over the phased withdrawal. The tension in the Alliance was distressing to all. The NATO meeting of December 10, attended by Dulles, who had largely recovered from his operation, was held in a difficult atmosphere but marked the end of the crucial phase of the episode. The troops were out of Egyptian territory by December 23. The United States was helping Europe with supplies of oil, and the clearing of the Canal was underway. The Secretary said, two years later, that "I do not . . . try to explain the reasons or defend myself for that because I cannot do that without reopening old wounds . . . which we are trying to heal and which, in my opinion, have been healed, for which I thank God."[53]

The Suez crisis highlighted the three main tests of *accepted* action. First, there is the application of abstract principles which leading nations endeavor to establish as systems and codes of conduct which will bring nearer a world of law and order. Second, there are standards of behavior within alliances, without which there can be no basis for confidence. Third, it is expected that there be a reasonable assessment of the stakes involved which give a justification for the use of strong measures and which make recourse to arbitration or negotiation unsatisfactory.

The major variations of opinion, in the case of Suez, center around the appraisal of the threat to vital interests. Britain, and also France, came to the conclusion that the threat was serious enough to justify action outside the Alliance. Their efforts were, however, insufficient to achieve their objectives. Thus, they were left vulnerable to the criticism of cynics and idealists alike. Moreover, later events demonstrated that the economic loss was less than had been feared. The problems of Algeria, Cyprus, Israel, and Africa were not altered in character, though increased in intensity. The Middle East was increasingly disturbed, as the United Nations Force was only partially effective. The Canal was restored to use, more rapidly than had been anticipated.

What some have called a détente in the cold war was brought to an abrupt end in 1956. The restless in East Germany had been held in check, but signs of revolt erupted as desperate riots in Poznan on June 28 and 29. These were suppressed by shootings which shocked the United States and public opinion in the free world.[54] In September, news reached Washington that some of the people arrested were to be given trials; the demands to right the grievances continued, and, to the surprise of many, Wladyslaw Gromulka gained a measure of independence which, though far short of freedom, permitted a degree of autonomy within the Soviet orbit.

There were even more intense expressions of revolt by the Hungarian people in 1956.[55] On October 23, when Washington, London, and Paris were preoccupied by the Suez crisis, young men rioting in Budapest destroyed Stalin's statue. At first it seemed as if the angry young people, influenced to some degree by events in Poland and also by the return to Budapest of Erno Gero, the Stalinist First Secretary of the Hungarian Workers, had risen in rebellion. Gero's return from Yugoslavia occasioned public meetings on October 22. A relaxation of labor conditions was demanded. Demonstrators were under fire on the 23rd from Hungarian security forces, who were reinforced soon by Soviet armed units. Although information coming through was incomplete, there were some signs of hope that the revolt would succeed, at least to the extent of the Polish gains.

The Freedom Fighters of Budapest aroused the admiration of the world as, with crude weapons and often with bare hands, they fought in the streets of the city. The new Prime Minister, Imre

Nagy, demanded the immediate withdrawal of all Soviet forces from Hungary; this demand did not seem so unlikely to be met as it would have before the departure of Soviet troops from Austria in October of the previous year.[56] At the same time, Nagy announced the withdrawal of Hungary from the Warsaw Pact and appealed to the United Nations for assistance in restoring Hungarian independence. On November 1, however, the soldiers who had withdrawn from the city under heavy pressure of the street fighting on October 30 began to reappear. Reinforcements from Soviet occupying forces in Rumania helped them as they surrounded the city. On November 4, the most massive artillery barrage since the Soviet army had hammered Berlin in the last days of World War II was thrown against Budapest.[57]

In New York, the United Nations Security Council, meeting at this time, discussed a resolution requesting the withdrawal of Soviet forces from Hungary. The move was defeated, but it was followed by a similar resolution in the General Assembly, adopted by a vote of 50 to 8.

By November 3, the Soviet forces had completely surrounded the city. The next day they began a frontal attack on the barricades manned by students, workers, and certain military units. Nagy was forced to resign as Prime Minister; he was replaced by Janos Kadar, the new First Secretary of the Hungarian Workers Party. The two weeks' fighting was over, the streets were cleared, and thousands of refugees fled to Austria and beyond. "The tragic effort of Hungarian men and women to regain freedom for themselves and their children . . . [and] the brutal purge which followed their heroic struggle will be long and sorrowfully remembered. . . ."[58] This was the echo of sad events as the United States opened its doors to 5000 refugees and made an initial allocation of $20 million for relief.

There was little that could be done in the free capitals of the world to alter the situation. There are some who conclude that if there had been no crisis over Suez, the NATO powers, presenting a united front and acting quickly, could have forced the communists back. Diplomacy would have had a keener edge, and counter measures might have been devised. This may be true, but it is unlikely that sufficient force would have been brought to bear in Hungary to have halted the Soviets' military drive against the city. The fact that young boys and girls had, for a brief time, routed the soldiers of the occupying divisions was an intolerable affront that the leaders in Moscow could not let stand unavenged. They had reason to expect that if Hungary gained a measure of freedom by these actions, the whole satellite structure from Belgrade to the Baltic might soon be aflame. Here there is little doubt that vital interests of the Soviets were to be defended with the full use of conventional forces, perhaps even with nuclear weapons. Moreover, the United States had no access to the area.

The perilous position of countries in the Middle East—under pressure from the Soviets and feeling the aggressive ambitions of Nasser—forced the United States to turn its attention to that situation. Thus, President Eisenhower in January, 1957, defended an increased budget and put forward his request for the power to use economic and military aid in the Middle East, a special resolution to be known as the Eisenhower Doctrine. It was accepted by Congress only after prolonged, and often heated, debate. The tragic circumstances of the defeat of the Freedom Fighters in Hungary and the differences over Suez had caused dismay among many nations in the Middle Eastern area. The United Nations Emergency Force had moved into the Suez area on November 12, 1956. In response to an appeal from the UN Secretary General for support of this force, the United States, anxious for the early opening of the Suez Canal, contributed $5 million to an international fund—almost half of the amount contributed by 11 nations. The U.S.S.R. made no contribution.[59]

On April 24, 1957, the government of Egypt announced the reopening of the canal to "normal traffic," but Israeli ships were still barred, and unrest prevailed along the Gaza strip. The decline of British and French prestige opened up a power vacuum which the Soviets were exploiting by various means. Nasser, in spite of the poor showing of his armies, emerged from the crisis with enhanced influence. Special responsibilities to maintain Western influence devolved upon the United States and were reflected in the Congressional passage of the Eisenhower Doctrine resolution of March and in the dispatch, announced the same day, of the Richards Mission to study the situation.*

---

*Former Congressman James P. Richards was named Ambassador for the mission in the Middle East.[60]

The Beginnings of Space Age Diplomacy. This was the year of the Sputnik and of growing concern over the adequacy of U.S. defense. In spite of the strong statements of President Eisenhower —reelected for his second term—calling for increased defense expenditures, there were doubts, later expressed in the theory of the "missile gap."

Confusion in Western thinking came not only because of differences over Suez, but also because of the controversy over the alleged reliance of the Washington leaders on "massive retaliation" and deterrence and because of views on "the spirit of Geneva" since 1955 and Khrushchev's Twentieth Party Congress denunciation of Stalin in Moscow in February, 1956. The Secretary of State endeavored to set the record clear by various speeches and articles. For instance, in 1957 he reviewed the situation, saying that the "de-Stalinization" proclaimed in 1956 had led to a fierce reaction in Poland and Hungary but that there had been no more brutal episode than the suppression of the Hungarian people.[61] He said that the basic communist doctrine precluded changes of its own accord and that the pronouncements were mere stratagems.[62] The answer open to the free nations was collective security. He stated that the level of armaments could go down only when the danger of surprise attack was eliminated.

More trouble in the Middle East developed in May, 1967. On the 23rd, Nasser took action which threatened the peace when he denied the use of the Gulf of Aqaba to Israeli shipping. While the world's leaders contemplated what action should be taken, the Israeli army, harassed on its borders, acted to forestall an Egyptian attack; it drove swiftly into the Sinai peninsula, bombed Egyptian planes, and scored a decisive victory. In the north, confronting the Jordanian troops, the Israelis gained physical possession of all Jerusalem. Although the question as to who shot first has not been determined, most observers were impressed with the tactical and moral victory which gave the Israelis a position they are not likely to relinquish without dependable guarantees of future security. In this disturbing clash, the United States took a reserved position and did not extend its commitments. The end of the controversy in the area is not yet in sight.

Returning to the events of 1957, it is important to recall that we entered the Space Age when Sputnik I was launched by the

Soviets on October 4, followed by Sputnik II on November 3. Explorer I was sent up by the United States on January 31, 1958. During this year there was an increasing interest in Africa, as the new countries pressed for attention and for membership in the United Nations. The fighting in Algiers turned the spotlight on North Africa, where the difficulties of the French had been steadily increasing. The United States maintained bases in Morocco and agreed to supply small arms and ammunition to Tunisia. These facts brought a delicately balanced policy with respect to France.[63] While the United States supported efforts in the United Nations to further a peaceful solution, care was needed to avoid making the French position more difficult.

"The Emergence of Africa" was the title of the report made to Congress by Vice President Richard M. Nixon on his return from a nine-nation visit in February and March of 1957. One purpose of his trip was to represent the President at the celebration of the independence of Ghana on March 6. He stated that this area was a priority target for international communism.

The challenges to American policy were pressed with special vigor in 1958, the year when Nikita Khrushchev emerged as the head of both the government and the party and directed these attempts to shake the Western position. There was feverish activity in international relations throughout the year. The Soviet proposal of December 10, 1957, for a meeting at the summit was answered by President Eisenhower in January. He recognized the wish in many quarters for such a meeting and, responding to this interest, he stated that advance preparation would be essential to assure any progress in a top-level meeting. After an active exchange of notes, the Western powers presented an agenda including disarmament, European security and Germany, international cultural exchanges, and methods of improving international cooperation by strengthening the United Nations.

Conversations, notes, and technical talks on the detection of nuclear explosions were energetically pursued in this period. The United States, at the end of the first Geneva Conference of experts that began meeting in October, 1958, announced that it was ready to suspend testing provisionally on a year-to-year basis.[64] The Soviets had stated on March 31 that they were suspending testing. Later, it was revealed that they had set off at least 14 test explosions, in spite of their often-expressed concern about the harmful effects. The effort to suspend testing collapsed; the line of hostile probing evidenced by the actions in the Middle East, the offshore islands in the Formosa Straits, and elsewhere was evidence of the attitude of the time. Khrushchev was flexing his muscles in the foreign field.

The maneuvers in the field of summitry and disarmament were confusing to some observers anxious for peaceful relations, but the actions in the Middle East were clearly menacing. General Charles de Gaulle had made his spectacular return to power in May, just at the time when trouble was brewing in Lebanon and elsewhere. As President, he was to retrieve the French policy on Algiers, but not to retake lost ground in the Middle East. A vacillating President Chamoun of Lebanon, frightened by the revolt in Iraq and the assassination of the royal family in July, asked for American help in the civil war then raging in his own country. This gave the basis under the Eisenhower Doctrine for our landing several thousand Marines in Lebanon, thus demonstrating, to Premier Khrushchev, and to the world in general, that we intended to pick up the burden laid down by Britain and France. Moreover, we were willing to risk a serious clash with the communists in Lebanon rather than relinquish the area to communism. The crisis of July was spectacular, but the conditions were stabilized in a matter of hours.

The second major probe by the Soviets came in the Formosa Straits. In this case, Moscow, in close collaboration with Peking, tried to push back the Western allies, to expose the further island nations to attack and open the way for the Chinese communists. This was in fact the last phase of coordinated foreign policy which could be observed before the widening split which developed in the two main communist camps in the next six years.

The shelling of the tiny islands of Quemoy and Matsu was a typical maneuver, in that the initial stake seemed small in comparison with the risks the United States would have to take to prevent their seizure. Many, on both sides of the Iron Curtain, were of the opinion that these were worthless "pieces of real estate" for which endangering even a single American life would not be justified and that they could be abandoned without a serious setback. This was not the view in Washington. It was noted there that this was an explicit threat to Taiwan (Formosa). The unwillingness to protect these positions, however insignificant they might seem, would indicate an unwillingness to fight. Fear would spread on one side and confident expectation for further gains would, in all likelihood, lead to early hostile action of a more daring character. Therefore, the United States decided that the challenge must be met.

There had been a joint resolution in Congress in 1955, which, like the Eisenhower Doctrine resolution of March, 1957, laid the basis for our support of the position in these waters. These actions were fundamental to our deployment of the Seventh Fleet. It was instructed to convoy supply ships to the island and to fire if fired upon; we were willing to use force, if necessary. There were several troubled weeks from the middle of August until October, 1958. It became clear that the Red Chinese and the leaders in Moscow were aware of the strong position of the United States. The situation was disturbing to the Soviets, who did not wish a serious clash but at first acted as if our bluff in the area could be called; later, they were cautioning the men in Peking. The strange denouement of October 25, took the form of the announcement that, in order to assure the residents of the islands of adequate supplies and in the interests of humanity, there would be a cessation of bombardment on alternate days. This bizarre decision was followed soon by a halt in the attacks, and the incident was over. No American lives were lost. The gambit was won.

The third effort of serious intent and significance came in November, when Premier Khrushchev had made a speech in Poland indicating a new move on Berlin. The issue was joined two weeks later: on November 27, a note proposed the internationalization of the city. This suggestion was accompanied by the threat that the signing of a peace treaty with the Soviet-occupied zone would eliminate our rights to pass through the so-called "German Democratic Republic" and thus put our access to the city in the hands of the East German communists. The note referred, somewhat casually, to the possibility of United Nations control. To those who did not understand the legal and political history behind our position, this did not pose a menace. Actually, the whole structure of relations in West Germany was under attack. The immediate rejection of the suggestion and the reaffirmation of our intention that the three Western powers would remain in the city led first to a blurring of the issue by the U.S.S.R. and then to the statement that they had not intended the ultimatum. By the time of the December NATO group meeting in Paris, which indicated the unwavering stand of the West, the world was convinced that the U.S. would be firm.

It was in these three major probes of Western commitment that the Soviets tested our determination. While the issues of nuclear testing and meeting at the summit were less clear-cut, in Lebanon, in the Formosa Straits, and in Berlin the U.S. held its ground.

The year 1959 was a time of quieter relations. There was a pause and an exploration of possibilities for further negotiations between East and West. John Foster Dulles resigned on April 14; his death came on May 24, at the time of the meetings in Geneva.

The Foreign Ministers had discussed the German problem during the period when the Russian ultimatum ran out and rejected it on December 31, 1958. The three allies did suggest that they were ready to "discuss the question of Berlin in the wider framework of negotiations for a solution of the German problem, as well as that of European security." It may have been that the Soviets thought they had gained in world opinion. In any case, the invitation to Khrushchev to attend the September Camp David meeting in Maryland and to tour the United States was accepted. The Soviets agreed to participate in a new study of the detection of underground tests. President Eisenhower was invited to the Soviet Union, and plans were laid for a summit meeting in 1960.

Much has been said of "the spirit of Camp David," where, from September 25 to September 27, 1959, Khrushchev and Eisenhower conferred. It was here that Khrushchev and Eisenhower agreed to an early summit meeting and a postponement of Eisenhower's visit to Russia until the following spring. Actually, though the talks progressed in a friendly atmosphere, no concessions of consequence were made on either side. What impression was made on Khrushchev by his visit, it is impossible to say. This was the year when in the United Nations he was to pound his shoe on the desk in angry protest; a year later, in 1960, he embraced the bearded Castro with a bear hug as the Cuban leader came into the General Assembly hall. Khrushchev was advocating "general and complete disarmament" in four years, a proposal which seemed appealing to some, completely impractical—a propaganda gesture—to others. Cuba was moving swiftly to the left, and the Chinese were fighting in Indian territory on the northern border. Resistance in Tibet was crushed as the Chinese took over and the Dali Lama fled. De Gaulle was endeavoring to make some kind of settlement of the Algerian rebellion. There was anti-European rioting in the Congo on the eve of independence.

This has been called a time of détente by some. They compare it with 1955 and the harsh repression of the Hungarian revolt in 1956. These different "atmospheres" reflect the zigs and the zags of Soviet tactics. Actually, in the later period, tension was mounting in Africa, where the Soviets continually fished in troubled waters. Their interest in the Caribbean was more noticeable than at any time since the Guatemalan ejection of international communism. Their relations with India, where they were giving substantial aid, notably to the Bilhai Steel Mill, were somewhat equivocal. The troubles in Laos and in the rest of the Indochina area were again causing apprehension. Thus, the year was not one of unbroken calm; it was a period of growing Soviet strength, accompanied by a few signs of disharmony with the communist Chinese.

President Eisenhower, in an effort to cement relations with our allies, had undertaken a visit to Italy, Turkey, Pakistan, Afghanistan, India, Iran, Greece, France, Morocco, Tunisia, and Spain in 1959. His triumphal appearance in India greatly impressed Nikita Khrushchev, who had visited New Delhi earlier with a much less spectacular reception. It has been speculated that he concluded at that time that an Eisenhower visit to Moscow would be a danger to him. By the end of 1959, the position of the U.S.S.R. among advanced nations had become more evident to many, as the complexities of the Soviet strategy were analyzed by the experts. On both sides, the show of strength had been impressive since 1955.

Troubles in Latin America and in Africa were already evident in the last months of Eisenhower's Administration. These posed new problems for the United States, already committed heavily in the Far East, Southeast Asia, and the Middle East. Moreover, the situation in Europe, with problems involving the further evolution of NATO and the German issue, allowed no relaxation.

In February, 1960, President Eisenhower began a tour of four Latin American countries, Brazil, Argentina, Chile, and Uruguay. Washington realized that, in spite of visits by Secretary of State Dulles and the President's brother, Milton Eisenhower, and the attempt by Vice President Nixon to demonstrate our interest—which had ended in riots—we had not succeeded in developing the friendly and constructive relations so sorely needed. Seizures of American property in Cuba were signs of increasing difficulties there. We announced the termination of our aid to Cuba in May. Activities aimed at supporting a revolt against Fidel Castro were being carried on secretly.

A 10-nation disarmament conference that opened in March was holding long and fruitless sessions, but plans had been made for a summit meeting in Paris, and the heads of state began assembling there in late April. It was on May 1 that the U-2 crashed in Soviet territory. The United States reconnaissance plane was brought down by mysterious means. Flights of these planes had been known to Khrushchev since 1956, and he had chosen to ignore them, apparently because he was powerless to halt their crossing of the U.S.S.R. Finally, through flame-out or some other accident, one came within range of his fire. The circumstances were never fully explained. The United States reaction in Washington was confused—a denial was followed by an admission of the nature of the intelligence operation. The President assumed full responsibility. Anger and indignation, expressed by Khrushchev in an almost convincing fashion, accompanied his explosive departure from the Paris meeting. The heads of state, assembled for the summit, dispersed. The projected visit of President Eisenhower to the Soviet Union was canceled.

Continuing efforts in the field of security included a new treaty of mutual cooperation and security with Japan in January, 1960. The "missile gap" controversy of two years earlier took a new turn as Defense Secretary Gates declared that there was no evidence that Russia had the advantage but that on the contrary there was a clear balance in favor of the United States. In February, there was a successful firing of an American Titan Intercontinental Ballistic Missile (ICBM) down a 5000-mile range. Shortly thereafter, another Pioneer satellite was put in orbit from Florida. Thus, although we were behind the Soviets in the space field, progress continued to be made. General Lauris Norstad, Supreme Allied Commander in Paris, was working on agreement among the British, French, and Americans to form an integrated NATO conventional and nuclear armed task force. The economic strengthening of Europe was progressing, as demonstrated by the growing success of the economic union between Belgium, the Netherlands, and Luxemburg (Benelux), which had been established in 1948.

Toward the end of the year, the Organization for European Cooperation and Development (OECD) took the place of the former OEEC, formed under the Marshall Plan, continuing the joint efforts in Europe for 18 nations, plus the United States, Canada, and a number of African countries. The rising growth rate under the European Economic Community, which had begun to function in 1958, was impressive as the nations on the Continent became more cohesive and productive.

The communists, aware of the increase in unity and the progress in defense and space, were, in this period, making strong efforts in the east and south. They had conditionally accepted President Eisenhower's above-ground test ban proposal in March, but, after resuming negotiations in May, they walked out of the Geneva disarmament conference in June. Meanwhile, Khrushchev had signed an aid agreement of $250 million with Indonesian Premier Sukarno earlier in the year and had agreed to purchase a large amount of sugar from Castro, thus extending the Soviet influence in two vulnerable areas. The construction of the Aswan Dam by the Soviets began in January. Relations between communist China and Burma, Nepal, and Laos became closer.

This was the year of African political upheavals and new nationalism. Many countries gained independence. These included, in the time sequence of their new status:

Malagasy Republic	Niger
Togo	Dahomey
Senegal	Upper Volta
Mali	The Congo (Leopoldville*)
Somali	Nigeria
Ivory Coast	Mauritania

*The city is now called Kinshasa.

The major danger came with violent uprisings in the Congo in June, 1960. These brought new dangers of communist action and Western losses. The problems could not be solved definitively, but a temporary victory for the West resulted from the United Nations action in response to American efforts. The story, which told of bitter fighting and tribal conflict, is an example of the troubles ahead as the new forces in a rapidly changing world confronted the former colonial powers and the antagonists in the Cold War with conditions that were largely uncontrollable. (The account of action in a crucial week is given as a case history of crucial decision in Chapter III.)

During this year, the Republican party lost the Presidency, in a closely contested election, to John F. Kennedy. Foreign affairs issues were hotly argued during the campaign. In fact, Cuba was the subject of one of the spectacular television debates between Vice President Nixon and Senator Kennedy. The delicate issues, which were to become even more controversial later, were connected with secret operations under the Central Intelligence Agency. The changes in the handling of foreign affairs made by the Kennedy Administration after it took over were more in style, detail, and emphasis than in basic policies. Nonetheless, the Soviets felt there was a basis for testing the new men and their policies. Several crises resulted from this expectation of some new advantage.

THE KENNEDY ERA

The buoyant spirit with which John Fitzgerald Kennedy assumed the Presidency in January, 1961, carried through the first weeks in office. Kennedy gathered around him a notable group of young and intellectual advisers, most of whom had been battle-tested during the election campaign. He added others experienced in domestic and foreign affairs. He gave out the word that ideas were welcome and let it be known that he would receive them directly in some instances. He created the impression that the customary regard for established channels could hamper initiative and that the shackles imposed by those who attached importance to tradition could now be cast aside. New hope and creative imagination could get the country moving with a new acceleration. This was the time of euphoria.

Even before his inauguration, he had turned his attention to the problems of Laos, Berlin, and Cuba. These matters, and questions regarding NATO, nuclear weapons, and the balance of payments, had been discussed with President Eisenhower, Douglas Dillon, Adlai Stevenson, Allen Dulles, and various outgoing officials, as well as with the continuing staff. In his appointments and outlines of plans Kennedy had shown his concern for Africa, for Latin America, for the Far East, and for new administrative approaches, notably for the newly conceived Peace Corps. There was a clear intention to increase flexibility in relation to the communists, to put increasing emphasis on newly emerging nations, to revitalize programs for Latin America, to press for freer trade, and to give prompt attention both to defense measures and to disarmament efforts. In the early briefings, the new President showed a striking ability to grasp a multitude of facts.

It was not many days before the magnitude of the job became overwhelmingly apparent. In February there was violence in Angola, directed in part against the American consulate. From the Congo, the murder of Lumumba, earlier in January, was reported to the outside world. Conditions in Southeast Asia, Laos, and Vietnam were highly disturbing. Kennedy's aides pointed out to him the need for decisions about Cuba. Meanwhile, he was thinking actively about his plan to visit Europe and a possible meeting with Nikita Khrushchev. Reorganization of procedures in the State Department and in Defense was not proving easy, in spite of the President's determination and the concern of those about him to achieve quick results. The obstacles to effective action which his predecessors had faced at home and abroad came to him as a rude shock.

The need for action in Laos was brutally apparent in March. The Soviet pressure had continued to mount, regardless of warnings from Washington. In a press conference on March 15, Kennedy said that we were determined to protect the people of Laos from communist interference in the local efforts to establish a neutral and peaceful nation. Later, on March 23, he said that "the security of all Southeast Asia will be endangered if Laos loses its neutral independence." He was convinced that the key to the situation lay in persuading the Russians that we regarded the danger to the security of the free world to be of great magnitude. The Seventh Fleet was moved into the South China Sea, Marines were alerted, and several hundred were flown into neighboring Thailand. There had been discussion in the National Security Council of large-scale troop intervention. Representatives attending the SEATO conference in Bangkok on March 27 pledged military support.

As the tension mounted, the President made a new approach to Foreign Minister Gromyko. This conference impressed the Russian, who seemed at last to be aware of American determination and of the danger of miscalculation. Finally, Russian leaders clearly understood our concern, and the crisis ended in a temporary reliance on the British proposal to revive the International Control Commission. Kennedy had survived the first ordeal of diplomacy under pressure.

The most troublesome and controversial issue, as became increasingly apparent in these early weeks, was the decision with regard to plans for the invasion of Cuba by refugees trained in Guatemala for a return to the island. In a briefing of the President-elect on November 18, 1960, Allen Dulles and Richard Bissel of CIA had described the plans and the developing eagerness for action in the refugee camp. The Cuban situation in general had been discussed with President Eisenhower and others. The overall planning was considered almost daily for months in the high-level Special Group, established under the National Security Council, but operational problems were handled by CIA officers and instructors selected by them. The first plan was for guerrilla action; this was abandoned in late 1960 in favor of an invasion and direct action. After the November briefing in which details had been put before the newly elected President, the Director of CIA was assured of Kennedy's interest. He was told to go forward.

The need for a further decision became imperative shortly after the inauguration. In theory, several options were still open, but the difficulty of restraining the liberation army was becoming evident to the President and his advisers. In a cabinet meeting on March 11, Kennedy agreed that the arguments for letting the Cubans return to the island were cogent, but he directed attention to the importance of minimizing the risks for the United States. He ordered avoidance of direct troop involvements and gave instructions to prepare the way for a liberal political regime.

Official consideration in early April was largely directed to the chances of success of an operation that seemed to have high-level approval. Even now there are wide differences of opinion with regard to the estimates of support from resistance groups and allegations that there would be a significant uprising of rebels in the hills. The Director of CIA, Allen Dulles, said later that he knew of "no estimate that a spontaneous uprising of the unarmed population of Cuba would be touched off by the landing."[65] Some of the Special Group, however, apparently concluded that the expectation of success was justified by the part that would be played by resistance organizations.

The decisive Washington meeting is said to have been the gathering on April 4. There had been many changes in plans between November and April. The President knew that the Cubans in the training camp were impatient. The details of plans and alternatives—and supplements to refugee action—had been gone over in many meetings and by a variety of high-level officers. It is not clear that anyone at the April 4 meeting spoke out against the proposals, although some have said since that they were opposed to them then. The target date, several times postponed, was finally set for April 17.

The critical hours in the Bay of Pigs decisions were from Saturday, April 15, to Tuesday, April 18. The time, the place, and the manner of the invasion had been determined in the days just past. All the close advisers of the President knew of the proposed action; some who disapproved apparently thought they must, at this stage of affairs, acquiesce. The crucial new element in the plan is thought by many to have been the determination of the President to act in such a manner as to reduce to minimum proportions the involvement of the United States and to keep our role as invisible as possible. This decision limited the types of support we could give.

It is now known that even before the refugee brigade forces were committed to a point where withdrawal was impossible, Fidel Castro was aware that some form of resistance and a possible invasion were imminent. He had stationed troops at what he considered probable landing points. He knew the details of troop and plane activities. Officials in Washington were being quoted as repeating a presidential pledge that U.S. armed forces would not intervene in Cuba under any circumstances. Kennedy, in spite of the fact that elements of the plan were beginning to "surface," drove to his weekend home at Glen Ora, Virginia. He went to the Middleburg races with his wife, but after a brief interlude he found he could not stay and went back to Glen Ora to attend to his pressing work.

The following day, conditions became more tense, and he was often on the telephone to Washington. A first air strike of American planes against Cuban targets had been made, though apparently it was not fully anticipated by some of the President's advisers in the White House. The result was heated controversy over a projected second strike to follow. Meanwhile, the "cover" story had been "broken," and Kennedy, in Glen Ora, had issued orders designed to prevent another such "leak." The argument in the White House, through most of the night and early morning, concerned both air and sea support. There were sharp differences of opinion. To the men on the ships and those landing on the beaches, the desperate nature of the situation was soon apparent. On landing, they met opposition that they could not overcome. They were decimated or taken prisoner by the hundreds. It was all over in a scant two days.

To the men in Washington who had known of the plans, and changes in plans, these were grim days of frustration and anger. The threat of communist reaction seemed menacing. The defeat on the beaches of Cuba was to cast a long shadow over the coming weeks. The mood of recrimination in this instance was mixed with a growing realization of the complexity of operations both at home and abroad.

Kennedy's approach to foreign policy stressed new methods and new directions. He was little concerned with jurisdictional lines and suspicious of the traditional policies. He was urged to institute changes by those around him, but, except for shifting personnel and altering terminology, few were made. The Bay of Pigs disaster probably slowed, rather than accelerated, action along new lines. A spirit of urgency for tackling dangerous problems promptly, however, made the President the more anxious to face Khrushchev directly.

Since 1959 there had been increasing talk of coexistence and hopes for a better understanding with the Soviet leaders. Kennedy had written Khrushchev in February; on May 12, Kennedy received a reply to his letter indicating that, in spite of events since February, Khrushchev was willing, perhaps eager, to see the new President. The meeting was scheduled for June 3 in Vienna. At this time, Khrushchev was being pressed by Ulbricht to take action on East Germany; the Premier was prepared to make proposals to bolster the East German regime. But first he must test the determination of the new American leader.

Kennedy on his European trip stopped in Paris for a brief visit with de Gaulle. The two men apparently agreed on a number of points, including the support of Berlin, and talked frankly about other matters, such as the European Common Market, on which their opinions varied. The conversations were useful in revealing de Gaulle's position more clearly.

The talks in Vienna that followed are reported to have sobered and even shocked the President. He was not fully prepared for the hard words and the lack of agreement on issues where he hoped for possibilities of cooperation. The right to pursue the revolutionary process was asserted with brutal candor behind a wall of dogma which Kennedy could not breach. On specific problems, such as Laos, Berlin, and the test ban proposal, little progress was made. Khrushchev attacked the United States for its part in the Congo, in NATO, in Germany, and in Japan, not to mention Cuba. As they parted, Kennedy is reported to have said, "It will be a cold winter."

This meeting, which left the President temporarily shaken and discouraged, revealed difficulties in the handling of foreign affairs which could not be blamed on any small group of individuals and which were inherent in major world problems. He had said on June 2, "I go to Vienna with a good deal of confidence." Afterward he reported on "the somber mood [which] simply demonstrated how much work we in the free world have to do and how long and hard a struggle must be our fate. . . ." In this meeting it is probable that Khrushchev thought he had taken the measure of the new President—in October, 1962, he was to find his estimate wrong.

On June 4 in Vienna, Khrushchev had handed Kennedy an aide memoire on Berlin indicating the necessity of making the city a "demilitarized free city." Thus another crisis faced the new President in his fifth month in office. His conduct of foreign affairs at this time was complicated by the various statements made by Congressional leaders about the Berlin situation and by the difficulties which delayed the coordination of the French, British, and American response to the Russian demands. The increasing flow of refugees from East Germany through Berlin in early June was caused in part by uncertainty as to the exact nature of the U.S. reaction to the Soviet demands and in part by rumors that some action would be taken to cut off their escape route.

As the weeks went by and the fear of communist action grew,

the numbers registering at the Berlin refugee center exceeded even the totals in 1953 when, after Stalin's death, signs of change terrified the noncommunists in the zone of occupation. Those whose future depended so largely on their contacts with West Germany were apprehensive and expected some hostile move. The newspapers in Germany and elsewhere, between August 10 and 14, gave no hint of the kind of steps that might be taken to prevent flight from the zone. Intelligence items were gathered, but they were inconclusive. Saturday night, August 12, was quiet. Kennedy was in Hyannisport. In Berlin, the generals, soldiers, and diplomats enjoyed their usual time of relaxation and jollification. Toward midnight there was ominous news from various points along the sector border dividing Berlin. At 3 o'clock Sunday morning, there came an announcement that the border was closed.

The first barriers were largely of wire and wood with some stone and concrete. The several crossing points still open were patrolled by communist police and soldiers. Mayor Willy Brandt and other leaders rushed to the Wall. They were shocked by the event, though they could not at first be sure that the division was permanent and they could not envisage the high, 28-mile structure which was to rise in place of the first barbed wire and wooden barriers.

The British, French, and Americans, who had jointly respected the Khrushchev demands of early June, protested promptly, but took no counter action. The West Berliners who stood angrily at the Wall and threatened to storm the barriers waited for some sign of retaliation against the communists. After a week, however, it was generally conceded that the Wall was to remain, as it rose higher and became more impenetrable. The Western allies, concerned about problems elsewhere and knowing that the incentive to Ulbricht to cut off the exodus of workers was strong, accepted the situation.

Kennedy was preoccupied with problems in the Far East and also with the preparations for the conference on Latin America in Punta del Este that was to open on August 17. He was anxious to press forward with the Alliance for Progress which he had proclaimed in his earlier speech in March. He had recognized the need for further efforts to accelerate economic development and to bind the hemisphere nations in friendly cooperation. At the August conference the Alliance was formally organized to initiate many-sided action and to guide the use of aid. The $20-billion program was intended to be an instance of multilateral aid to result in a large degree of self-help. Secretary of the Treasury C. Douglas Dillon attended as head of the delegation. The message from the President was clear, and it was to be repeated several times in the next two years. The goals were to strengthen democracy and to spread "the fruits of the American revolution" and economic prosperity among the many. In order to coordinate aid programs and to take advantage of the experience of the past dozen years, the Alliance was set up within the Agency for International Development. During the following years it ran into obstacles of entrenched economic power to the south, ineffectiveness of operations, and political conflict. The aims set forth in 1961, which greatly expanded those emerging under the previous Administration, continued to define the Alliance's purposes and guide its actions into the Johnson years.

The progress in Southeast Asia, in economic development, in disarmament negotiations, and in relaxation of tensions was slow and often discouraging, but Kennedy's intentions became clearer as time went on. Thus, after the negative experiences of the Bay of Pigs, the Vienna meeting, and the Berlin Wall, the more positive aspects of the Kennedy program began to emerge. The Alliance and the Peace Corps represented action which he considered of great urgency and which would change the tone and direction of American foreign policy.

The Peace Corps had been set up by executive order on March 1. Sargent Shriver, chosen to head the new enterprise, had recruitment and training well underway by summer. Agreements with host governments were negotiated, and the enterprise, with more than 5000 young workers, was operating in many lands by the next year. In spite of doubts and criticism, it survived in growing strength through the following years. Its origins may have been in the Civilian Conservation Corps established by President Roosevelt in 1933, but it had the appeal of a new type of action, and it surged ahead with the interest and conviction of the young behind it.

Another constructive effort much in the mind of the President was the broadening and intensifying of the use of food as an aid to starving people. The effort was based on the well-known Public Law 480. Passed originally in 1954 and amended on various occasions, it took advantage of the existence of agricultural surpluses to give aid to needy countries, through both government and private programs. Under this law and the broadened Food for Peace program, billions of dollars' worth of food have been made available to Egypt, India, and other countries. Most of the counterpart local currency received by the governments for the sale of food imports was directed to development programs.

The Congo had continued to give concern throughout these years. In September, 1961, the world was shocked by the death of Dag Hammarskjöld in a plane crash during a trip to the Congo. He had sought to find remedies to the problem of the separation of Katanga from the rest of the Congo. His death intensified the critical situation in the United Nations, where the Soviets had been pressing their plan for a three-man direction of the UN, instead of the single Secretary General. They had first proposed this "Troika" in September, 1960. (It was named for the Russian sleigh with three horses.) They wished to use the "third world" of uncommitted nations to enhance their power or to paralyze action initiated by the noncommunist West. A solution was found, however, when U Thant of Burma was selected as Acting Secretary General on November 3. The Troika three-man directorate plan was not revived.

In December, Prime Minister Nehru, acting swiftly and without prior consultation, seized with force the small province of Goa. He ignored the legal and diplomatic aspects of the situation and overrode the obstacles to incorporating the area under Indian rule. There was only a short moment of surprise and objection. Portugal could do nothing to assert its authority in this distant place.

De Gaulle at this time had worked out the general lines of policy solution of the Algerian problem, and he announced the beginning of the withdrawal of troops. There had been notable progress on the Algerian question in 1961, as President de Gaulle, recognizing the intensity of feeling for independence, followed his earlier promises with a negotiated settlement. Eventually, after many weary months of conflict, the Evian agreement of March 18, 1962, became effective on July 3 of that year. Kennedy greeted the independence, which had been urgently sought by the rebels and which was essential for the restoration of peace in North Africa. It also brought an improvement of economic conditions in France and seemed to augur well for the future of Europe.

Nowhere in this first year was there assured tranquillity or promise of relaxation of tensions. The struggle for security had to continue in all areas. In a speech on September 25, 1961, Kennedy, looking back over the many events and the difficult crises of his first months in office, said, "This is a time of national maturity and understanding and of willingness to face issues as they are and not as we could like them to be." On November 11, speaking in Arlington National Cemetery, he said that "there is no way to maintain the frontiers of freedom without cost and commitment and risk." The buoyancy of the first period had been dissipated. A sober appraisal of the difficult realities had taken its place. In the next months, particular attention was devoted to the problem of checking the nuclear menace. The struggle for the Nuclear Test Ban Treaty was underway.

In his State of the Union message on January 11, 1962, Kennedy said that the "successes and setbacks of the past year remain on our agenda of unfinished business"—arms, peace, space, the United Nations, the Alliance for Progress, the Congo, Laos, Berlin, foreign trade policy, and other international issues.

The Philadelphia Fourth of July speech of the President on *interdependence* continued the drive for the Trade Expansion Act, which was passed in October, 1962. This measure gave a foundation for the United States conversations in Geneva on tariff reductions— known later as the "Kennedy round." The President was given the power to reduce rates by as much as 50 percent under conditions which would guarantee comparable advantages to American exporters. The provisional terms, which were scheduled to lapse in June, 1967, were the basis for months of discussion by the United Nations Conference on Trade and Development (UNCTAD). They were designed as a basis for the American position in the program of the General Agreement on Tariff and Trade (GATT). The crucial sessions were held in April and May of 1967, when, after more than four years of difficult and time-consuming negotiations in Geneva, the representatives of 50 participating nations, meeting under the auspices of GATT, came to an agreement on tariff reductions. These long debates of the "Kennedy Round" were completed on May 16, 1967, and the provisions accepted made it possible to benefit, just before the June deadline, from the legal provisions that had been adopted in October, 1962, by the U. S. Congress. This legislation permitted reductions up to a limit of 50 percent of the existing rates if reciprocal advantages were gained by the United States. Although some of the less developed countries were disappointed with their failure to gain preferential treatment, the leading commercial nations anticipated favorable economic consequences and an expansion of world trade.

During 1962 there were diverse efforts to deal with the Soviet communists, in spite of "extraordinary rumbles of discord." The problems of Cuba did not yield to our policy as the Russian involvement grew. The new crisis had a slow build-up and a dramatic climax. Fidel Castro had isolated himself from the rest of the Latin American community and was outside the area of our increasing efforts at economic assistance. In December, 1961, he had declared himself a Marxist-Leninist. In the next months his links with Moscow became stronger. Consultations in July led to the decision by the Soviets to install missiles secretly in Cuba, thus establishing a base less than 100 miles from our shore.

In late July the shipments of construction materials and equipment began to arrive. The CIA soon reported to the President that there were new developments in Cuba. Several thousand Soviet specialists were there, and military construction of some sort had begun. It was at first thought that the Russians would not go beyond the risk of minor defensive steps designed to protect Cuba from attack. The more desperate gamble planned by Khrushchev became apparent in September.

Not since the arms shipments to Guatemala in 1954, when the Soviets tried in vain to establish an international communist base in the Western Hemisphere, had they entertained serious hopes of a military position near our coast. But in August, 1962, it became obvious that they had embarked on a new and daring adventure. On September 13, a warning was addressed to Moscow stating that we would not tolerate the import of offensive weapons into Cuba. Gromyko replied on September 21 that their activities were strictly defensive and were occasioned by United States preparation for aggression against Cuba. In a press conference on September 13, the President said that the shipments to Cuba did not constitute a serious action, but that if they became a genuine offensive threat, we would do whatever was necessary to protect our security. Meanwhile, he increased the surveillance, including the U-2 over-flights, to watch the nature of the build-up. Officials who had discerned a softening of the Soviet line in some quarters could scarcely believe that Khrushchev would take the drastic step involved in the Cuban venture. Moreover, it was not known in Washington at the time that their technical progress had made it possible to shorten the time required to prepare missile sites. Reports from refugees, which had been frequent before, became more frequent and more disturbing each week. Photographic confirmation had been considered to be incomplete, but the negatives from the over-flight of October 14 gave a new meaning to the installations. They showed a series of buildings, a launching pad, and a missile on the ground.

The President called a high-level meeting to discuss the Cuban situation, the frightful risk of atomic war, and our possible reaction to the swiftly moving crisis. The group known as the EXCOM— under the National Security Council—assembled in the Cabinet room on the morning of Tuesday, October 16. It was to meet several times a day until the fateful decisions had been made. Everyone was aware of the danger of making a precipitate response and also of the impossibility of ignoring the shocking developments. Consideration was given to an immediate air strike, though the more cautious also brought forward other alternatives. Great secrecy was observed— so much so that many not concerned about Cuba thought that the President's television appearance scheduled for October 22 was likely to deal with the problem of Berlin.

On Thursday, the 18th, with more information at hand, Kennedy called Gromyko, the Soviet Foreign Minister, who was then in Washington, to the White House. The conversation was on both Berlin and Cuba. Gromyko said bluntly that he could assure the President that there would be no new steps until after the November Congressional elections. He complained of anti-Cuban activities in the United States. The President is said to have expressed doubts later as to whether or not he should have spoken plainly about our knowledge of the offensive missiles in Cuba.

Alerts were issued on Friday, the 19th, to the military commands. In the Department of State, studies were made of the legal basis for blockade. Kennedy, out of town for some speeches, returned on Saturday, giving the pretext of a slight cold. A television statement was set for Sunday and then postponed to Monday. Meanwhile, a meeting of the UN Security Council was called. It was also planned to put the blockade proposal before the OAS. Consideration was given by some to removing, our Jupiter missiles from Turkey, very near Russia; many thought they were obsolete, in any case. U.S. troops were moved to strengthen the Guantanamo base, and warships were ordered to new positions in the Caribbean. Steps were taken to inform the heads of state in foreign countries. In spite of all these actions, there was no disturbing "leak" to the press. A few bits of information had been learned, but the newspaper stories skirted the subject of serious developments.

Millions of persons in the United States remember the shock of the President's television announcement on October 22 of the Soviet missiles in Cuba and the fearful consequences that might come with United States demands for removal, with the order for support of U.S. military preparations, and the defensive quarantine of the island. The fear of nuclear war spread through the nation, and during the next three days the tension mounted to fever peak. The U.S. Navy had orders to board Soviet ships bound for Cuba. No one knew what Khrushchev's response would be. On Wednesday, October 24, Khrushchev sent a message indirectly to Kennedy, through an American businessman visiting Moscow, saying a clash of ships could mean world war. Then there came another and different indication of the Russian reaction to the United States demands—later that day some of the ships approaching Cuba stopped and altered course. The next day, October 25, the first American interception of a Soviet ship took place. Since after a search it was determined that the ship carried no missiles, it was allowed to proceed.

On October 24, U Thant, speaking for the United Nations, had asked for a voluntary suspension of both arms shipments to Cuba and the quarantine measures. Khrushchev answered that he agreed with the proposal. Kennedy replied that the missiles must be removed.

On Friday, October 26, Khrushchev sent a message direct to Kennedy. It differed markedly from earlier communications: it showed signs of recognition of the United States' determination, as well as grave fears of nuclear war. Thus the crisis had begun to abate.

Busy hours of negotiation and watchful planning followed. These were concerned with the shipment of missiles back to Russia, Kennedy's correspondence with Khrushchev, the return of Soviet bombers from Cuba, and the United States' pledge of no invasion. Khrushchev, speaking in December, said that "both sides made concessions—

reason was the victor—conditions in the Caribbean have returned to normal." The world realized that the young President of the United States had faced a challenge of the most ominous proportions and that his courage had brought a Soviet reversal of policy. These events came two years after his election—at the beginning of the last year of his life.

During 1962 and 1963, the effort to halt the nuclear race had intensified. The Soviets, after a brief pause, had resumed testing in 1961. Kennedy had thrashed out many aspects of the problem with Prime Minister Macmillan in Nassau. Their talks were followed by a letter from the British leader pleading again for the United States to continue to bar testing, urging that it was the only hope of saving mankind from the growing danger. The debate in Washington was heated as preparation continued for the explosion at Christmas Island in the Pacific. At the end of February, Kennedy informed Macmillan of the decision to go ahead, but he made one last attempt to persuade the Russians to accept a treaty which would mean the ending of all tests. Khrushchev declined the offer, and on April 25, 1962, the United States began a new series of test explosions.

Nevertheless, the struggle for disarmament went on. There were wearying sessions in Geneva and many discussions in Washington. Defense Secretary McNamara had denied the myth of the missile gap, but the notion still stirred debate in military quarters. Estimates of Soviet strength varied, but the possibility of annihilation by either side was the general assumption, and there was much talk of the philosophy of "overkill." It was not until after the missile crisis of October, 1962, that progress toward the test ban treaty was made. The treaty signed by Secretary of State Rusk in Moscow in August, 1963, was ratified in the Senate in late September. Although it was the subject of controversy among those who felt it hampered weapons development and put undue restraints on scientific exploration, it was the first and, for a long time, the only significant development in the field of limitation of armament. It had far-reaching psychological effects in this country and abroad. De Gaulle rejected the treaty. After some hesitation, the Germans in Bonn adhered. Thus in 1963 the first step on the "thousand-mile journey" had been taken.

In Washington during these months there was active exploration of areas of possible cooperation with the Russians. Without giving up our position of strength, it seemed possible in science, culture, and trade to expand relations between East and West. One proposal which seemed attractive in Washington, but which was rejected in Moscow, was a joint effort to land a man on the moon. The exchange of information on space was unfortunately not acceptable to the Soviet leaders, so prospects of a significant advance in that direction were excluded.

New troubles developed in January, 1963. The meeting of Kennedy and Macmillan in Nassau in December had been another of the cordial talks that resulted from a good understanding between the two men. They were concerned mainly with attempts to accommodate the desires of the foreign governments that wished to share in nuclear responsibility and thus were pressing for a dilution of the United States' monopoly of control. These governments were influenced by keen disappointment in Great Britain over the cancellation of the Skybolt plane program. The solution proposed was the Multilateral Nuclear Force (MLF). By providing for international crews on the Polaris nuclear submarines, it was hoped also to take account of the German pressure for a larger voice in defense arrangements. The tentative agreements reached, however, far from satisfied the wishes of European nations.

President de Gaulle, incensed by what he considered a betrayal by the two leaders, who had given him to understand that nuclear problems would not be discussed, moved now in the direction of French isolation from the European community. Although the sentiments of the French President were widely known, his press conference of January 14 came as a shock to those who anticipated steady progress and expansion of the European Economic Community. He stated that Great Britain was not suited for membership in the EEC, that it was not ready to adjust itself to the requirements of membership, and that care must be taken to prevent the dependence of the Atlantic Community on America, because of the danger that America would soon swallow up the European Community. Later in the month, in spite of appeals for a change in attitude, he indicated his firm opposition to the entrance of the United Kingdom into the EEC. From this time on he moved steadily away from participation in The North Atlantic Treaty Organization. His aim to restore glory and independence to France dominated his ideas of economic and military partnership.

Franco-German relations became closer as de Gaulle and Adenauer on January 22 signed a treaty of conciliation, thus contributing a constructive element to the European situation—which had been disturbed by de Gaulle's recent statements. Chancellor Adenauer was beginning to be critical of American methods and styles of diplomacy, and Germany turned in the direction of France, though not abandoning its fundamental reliance on cooperation with the United States. In this year Konrad Adenauer finally decided to step down as Chancellor and in October, 14 years after he assumed leadership, he gave up the post, which was assumed by Ludwig Erhard. The new Chancellor had a record of close cooperation with the United States.

In June, 1963, Kennedy went to Berlin; there he made a triumphal entry and won the hearts of Berliners by his spontaneous and whole-hearted support of their cause. This appearance, which stirred the emotions of the citizens of the divided city, partially eliminated the resentment over American failure to tear down the Wall and failure to act in the death of Peter Fechter—a boy who had hung bleeding on the barbed wire within sight of American MPs in 1962.

It was at about this time that the Soviets and the Chinese, meeting to reconcile differences in ideology, ran into obstacles in Moscow. There had been similar problems, observed by a few, in the previous years. In 1960, the Soviets had demanded repayment of loans, and there had been divergences of opinion which became more obvious in the following months. The time when, as in 1950 over the Korean war and in 1958 over the shelling of Quemoy-Matsu, the Kremlin could make its wishes known and the Chinese communists would obey, was over. The Chinese had not hesitated to express their disapproval of the action of Khrushchev in withdrawing the long-range missiles from Cuba in 1962. They made plain their support of wars of liberation, while the Soviets were pursuing a more cautious line in their dealings with the Western powers.

In his negotiations with the Soviet Union, President Kennedy sought ways to relieve tension and avoid a serious clash. One of these was the establishment of the special communications link with Moscow called the "hot line." This was agreed to on June 20 and operational in August.*

---

*The "hot line" was first used in May, 1967, when the Soviets and the Americans needed to clarify each other's intentions toward the Israeli-Arab war.

By late summer, the agricultural crisis in Russia had become acute. The Soviets wished to purchase American grain, as well as wheat and flour from other NATO countries. Kennedy announced on October 9 the decision to allow the sale of wheat from private stock to the amount of approximately 4 million tons or $250 million. These shipments were to be paid for in gold and sent forward in American ships. The matter was considered in the National Security Council and with Congressional leaders. The actual shipments began a few months later.

Meanwhile, the Middle East continued to reflect basic instability. Premier Kassim of Iraq was assassinated early in February in an army coup that brought memories of his own bloody take-over of the government about five years earlier. Pro-Nasser army officers overthrew the Syrian government in an extension of Egyptian influence there—a relationship which has fluctuated from 1957 to the present day.

The struggle between Indonesia and the Malaysian leaders continued throughout these months. The short-lived Federation which brought together Malaya, North Borneo, Sarawak, and Singapore came into being on September 16. Almost immediately, the relations between Malaysia and Indonesia were broken off. There also were demonstrations in Jakarta against the British, who had supported the move.

While there was comparative quiet in the Caribbean, as the United States showed restraint toward Cuba, there was uneasiness over conditions in Haiti. That impoverished and unsettled nation was ruled by President Duvalier in a term extended beyond his legal term of office. The United States severed diplomatic relations in a gesture intended to dramatize its disapproval, but resumed relations in June.

Signs of growing trouble in Vietnam were marked by a number of Buddhist demonstrations. The army seized control of Saigon on November 1, and the following day President Ngo Dinh Diem and his brother were killed. There were persistent rumors of the United States' involvement in the death of Diem; thus many concluded that the United States could have prevented the assassination. Elections long promised had been postponed, and the lack of central authority after the death of Diem became increasingly evident, with threats of Vietcong infiltration growing over the next three years.

In Africa, where American involvement was less direct, trouble still continued in the Congo, with the eventual reuniting of the ore-rich Katanga with the Republic of the Congo under Kasavubu and Adoula. In Togo, President Olympio was assassinated on January 13. The meeting that month in Ethiopia of the leaders of 28 states to work out cooperative arrangements raised the hopes of many but had little practical results. Only the economic institutions working on statistics and studies continued relatively undisturbed by the divergence of policies among the African countries and tribal warfare within them. In the north, Ahmed Ben Bella became the first President of independent Algiers on September 15 (he was ousted in 1965). Pro-Nasser contingents forced a change in the Syrian government in March, and a federation was established in Cairo on April 17.*

President Kennedy dealt with these and other varied issues with increasing knowledge of the capabilities and the limits which circumscribed his actions. He was gratified with the progress of the Peace Corps in its early months. The test ban treaty was considered a success. Relations with the Soviet leaders seemed to improve, as Kennedy's approval of the sale of wheat showed. He had devoted enormous time and attention to the political and developmental problems in Latin America. He had urged more contributions to the Alliance for Progress and had proposed a new treaty for Panama in response to some of their demands. His leadership had grown in scope and force—it was felt in all areas where conflict, poverty, and the will for more constructive action spurred him to new endeavors. His personality was making a deep impression in Berlin, in the Far East, in Africa, and in the Western Hemisphere, as well as behind the Iron Curtain. The days of hesitation seemed to be over.

Yet in no part of the world was there assured tranquillity. The President had been faced with scores of critical situations. His successes and failures were on a grand scale. The torch had indeed passed to a new generation, but they were finding it difficult to keep the flame alight as storms raged in international relations.

On November 22, 1963, the stunning blow fell with the assassination. Kennedy's promise and devotion were crushed in those

---

*This federation dissolved later.

disastrous moments in Dallas. The hopes that had lit expectations in many lands dimmed, and the sense of defeat brought a temporary halt to many bold ventures. Heads of government and chiefs of state from all over the world mourned as they walked in the funeral procession.

THE JOHNSON ERA

Lyndon Baines Johnson assumed his heavy burden immediately, as he took the oath of office at the Texas airfield. He had a clear knowledge of the nature of the problems, both from his association with President Kennedy and from his service in the Senate and Senate Foreign Relations committee. He had no respite to contemplate past events, however, as the continuing challenge of instability and threat in the Caribbean, Southeast Asia, Africa, and elsewhere called for the full exertion of power to protect the freedoms which, through long perseverance, had been achieved.

Entering his first full year as President in 1964, Johnson was much preoccupied with domestic concerns—the war on poverty, civil rights, and other urgent subjects of legislation. He would gladly have left most of the foreign policy problems to others, but he did not have this choice. The Panama crisis that broke early in January directed his immediate attention to the south. The prospects of growing unrest in Latin America and of the export of communism to many nations by way of Cuba were eminently disturbing.

The acute disturbance in Panama was relatively short-lived; it was brought under control in a few days, even though the destructive outbreak left continuing problems. The riots had been set off by high school students who injudiciously raised the American flag without the Panamanian flag, thus arousing the anger of the Panamanians. The hostility against the Americans had been growing for some time. The way in which the military ran the Zone and the extent of influence exerted by the U.S. presence and extraterritorial privileges under the treaty governing the use of the Canal were objectionable to the Panamanians. The situation was more difficult to handle because no Ambassador had been appointed to succeed Joseph S. Farland, who had resigned in August, reportedly because of differences with the State Department over American policy. During the five days of anti-American riots, diplomatic relations with the United States were broken and were not resumed until three months later.

Consideration was given in Washington to major concessions on the part of the United States, and the conflict turned to lesser complaints as President Johnson agreed that he would negotiate a new treaty. Inquiries into the best location for a new water-level canal or the extent of improvements in the existing facilities were accelerated, with a view to construction before the prevailing U.S. rights established in 1903 on the existing channel would terminate, according to schedule, in 1993. In spite of several commissions, some of the basic questions raised then were still undecided in 1967.

The growing troubles between communist China and the Kremlin stimulated speculation. These increased as Peking openly supported Pakistan in its dispute with India over Kashmir. Early in 1964, Chou En-lai visited several African states and then went to Pakistan, Burma, and Ceylon. He did not go to India. Although he visited Moscow later in the year, there was no basic reconciliation. Some thought that this development in the communist world would swing the Soviet leaders more in the direction of Western policy. They added this to a few other signs and talked of an increasing relaxation of tensions between Russia and the United States. The riddle became more provocative in October, with the change of leadership in the Kremlin.

The conflict in another area, Cyprus, became more acute in 1964. Throughout the year, in spite of talks between the Greeks, the Turks, and the Turkish Cypriots, which opened in London January 15, the conflict increased in intensity. Archbishop Makarios, President of Cyprus, rejected the compromise plan designed to stop bloodshed that was put forward in Geneva in July. Although the United Nations officials negotiated an agreement that went into effect on October 26, the antagonisms in the dispute were such that no complete reconciliation was possible. This critical situation was one that demonstrated the United States' intention to remain aloof when there is no specific commitment or when there is a possibility that other nations or international organizations would take the necessary constructive steps. It differed from those other situations, when the engagement cannot be shifted to others. The many cases of the latter type already strain our diplomatic, financial, and military resources to a degree that suggests the wisdom of limiting new responsibilities when possible.

The three major problems of the Johnson Administration in the field of foreign affairs in 1964 and 1965 became menacing in the early months. Perhaps the one least recognized by the general public at this time was the unrest and frequent changes in control in the Dominican Republic, a nation looked on by some as a "potential Cuba." The most serious of Johnson's difficulties was the growing burden and commitment in Vietnam. There, economic aid of hundreds of million dollars a year increased substantially, and military advice resulted in the commitment of approximately half a million men in the military contingents in 1967. The United States was engaged in fighting from the sea, from the air, and on the ground. The third major issue was that opened by de Gaulle in 1963; it was to compound the inherent difficulties in Europe over nuclear defense, the strengthening of NATO, and the relations of the United Kingdom with the EEC.

The plans for increasing support to South Vietnam were announced in February, 1964. In May, more support was given. In August, a joint resolution was passed by the House and Senate approving the Administration's Southeast Asia policy. The pressures from Saigon and the extent of involvement were increasing at a time when the objections from a vocal minority in the United States were still in a low key. In these first months, President Johnson had shown strength in his handling of the nation's business at home and abroad.

Vietnam received a large portion of our total foreign aid in the next three years. In addition to large sums for the military, loans, grants, and technical assistance continued. The appropriation for fiscal 1965 of just over $2 billion was approximately equal to the previous year. The communists gained considerable influence in Laos, which came under a coalition government in April. Relations between the United States and Cambodia deteriorated, in spite of U.S.-Cambodian talks in December that were intended to ease the situation.

Financial aid to Africa continued to be small in 1964 and 1965, partly in recognition of traditional support from the former colonial powers in Europe and partly because "feasibility studies" and reviews of conditions indicated the difficulties of constructive programming and the limited capacity to absorb aid of some of the less-developed countries. To the south, the Alliance for Progress was admittedly in need of improvement, and attention was directed to ways and means of increasing cooperation and achieving a degree of acceptable economic reform.

There were in 1964, however, a number of favorable developments in Latin America. In several countries, moderate or middle-of-the-road candidates succeeded those who were reported to have communist leanings. There was an improvement in the leadership of British Guiana when Forbes Burnham defeated the self-proclaimed Marxist, Cheddi Jagan. In Brazil, President João Goulart was deposed in April. He was followed in May by a more dependable military leader, Humberto Castello Branco. In Chile, Eduardo Frei, the moderate Christian Democrat, defeated the Communist Allende at the polls in September. In Presidential elections in December, 1963, Venezuela had elected the pro-United States Rómulo Betancourt.

Thus the changes in leadership in Latin America—in Brazil, Venezuela, Mexico, British Guiana, and Chile, were favorable to cooperation with the United States, while those in Vietnam and the Congo were less clear in their significance.

The threat of trouble in the Dominican Republic increased in early 1965. Generalissimo Rafael Trujillo, dictator for more than 30 years, had been assassinated on May 30, 1961. Since then, President Kennedy had considered it necessary to send naval ships to Dominican waters three times. There had been coups and countercoups. There were threats of civil war and evident communist subversion and machinations. There was reason to anticipate the overthrow of the dominant member of the ruling triumvirate, Donald Reid Cabral, in June. In fact, the revolt came in April. With the lives of Americans and other foreign nationals threatened, President Johnson sent in small contingents on April 28, reinforced and later joined by Latin American contingents under an OAS peace committee. Calm was restored, and after a year of provisional rule, a new President, Joaquín Balaguer, was elected in June, 1966. A degree of stability followed. (See Chapter III.)

The major change in control—a change that startled the world— took place in the Kremlin in October, 1964. The nine years of Khrushchev's domination came to an end. The meaning of his removal has been variously interpreted in its relation to communist policy. (The questions raised could not yet be fully answered in 1967.) There is little doubt that the Sino-Soviet dispute, the Cuban missile episode, the failure to expand agricultural production, and Khrushchev's own impulsive style of operation all played a part. What is less clear is whether the desire for rapprochement with the West, the determination to improve the standard of living of the average Russian, and the will to lessen the risks of war were major factors in the sudden change. The fact was that none of the experts had predicted this change, and even rumors of Khrushchev's health affecting his strength in the conduct of affairs had not led to widespread speculation of a take-over; thus it seems that no single reason can be assumed to have been the prime cause.

For a long time the students of Soviet policy will continue to assess the changes in Russia, as well as those in China, in order to seek guidance as to future American policy. The divergence of views did not affect the majority opinion in the United States, although the phrase "a pause in the Cold War" and talk of Russia's need for cooperation with the West were frequently heard and tended to stimulate criticism of the entire gamut of U.S. policy.

Shocking, even in this time of adjustment to new ideas, was the October explosion of a nuclear device by Communist China, with its threat of further dangers from this new member of the nuclear "club." This development, combined with a weariness on the part of those who had witnessed the fight over the barring of communist China from the United Nations and the anxiety over American involvement in Vietnam, led to mounting protest against foreign policy among students and in liberal and pacifist groups.

The year 1965 marked the expression of a sharp cleavage of opinion between leaders in the Senate Foreign Relations Committee and the Administration. From this time on, feeding on the events of October, 1964, the controversy over China and the Far East was to increase and to challenge Washington leaders. The reports of mounting strength and increasing boldness in Peking aroused fear in many quarters.

As a part of these changes in attitude, the fabric of restraints on trade between East and West was weakened in 1964 and 1965. The short-run economic interests of many countries and the political ambitions of some, particularly France, made it difficult for the United States to hold the line—even though the aggression of China in Southeast Asia and in the north of India was concrete evidence of a hostility frequently broadcast over the channels of propaganda. The economic strains that concerned Europe were accentuated by the deficit in the American balance of payments. The problem had been recognized in previous years, but the failure of mild measures to halt the outflow of gold led to growing worry, not only in America, but also in other countries depending on the dollar as a key currency and anxious that the whole network of exchange and investment be kept in good working order. Several study groups analyzed the problem, trying to determine the extent to which international liquidity was threatened and to seek solutions compatible with freedom of trade and exchange.

Preparatory meetings in Geneva from 1962 to 1964 preceded the United Nations Conference on Trade and Development (UNCTAD), which convened there on March 23, 1964, with 118 nations represented. It faced the commercial side of the problem with a growing awareness of the difficulties that had to be dealt with. And, in fact, little progress was made in the following two years. The attitude of the French, withdrawing gold from the United States and limiting the negotiating capacities of the European Common Market, was among the serious obstacles to agreement. The underdeveloped nations found their high hopes dashed by the problems preventing easy achievement of their desire for higher and more stable commodity prices. Nevertheless, when the Group of Ten met at Rio de Janeiro in September, 1967, they reached conclusions. This was a meeting of representatives of 10 leading financial powers and representatives of almost 100 other nations, all members of the International Monetary Fund. Here they came to substantial agreement as to new measures designed to increase liquidity and ease financial tension. The new drawing rights, which can serve as a means of payment, can lessen the calls on gold and reserves— at least in the short run—for all the member nations. The measures are no solution to basic economic problems but can improve the atmosphere and the mechanism of international payments.

President Johnson, like President Kennedy and Presidents before them, faced a constantly increasing number of responsibilities all over the world; as well as the burgeoning problems of outer space. There were a host of domestic political and economic challenges. Each President was limited in his ability to break through obstacles resulting from political conflicts, emotional hostilities, technical needs in less-developed countries, changes in institutions, and a multitude of shifts in power and policy.

The year 1964 ended, as it began, with trouble in Indonesia, Laos, Cambodia, Vietnam, the Congo, and many other areas. Uncertainty hovered over our policy-makers—uncertainty about commercial negotiations and international finance, as well as about the arms-control efforts. The strength of the United States was unquestioned, our economic resources were expanding, our will for peace was widely understood—but the manner in which our military resources and economic assets could be used to further world security was far from clear. Only in a few places—Brazil, Chile, North Africa, and some parts of Europe—was there discernible progress toward agreed aims.

The years 1965 and 1966 are so close to the contemporary scene that it is not possible to view them in perspective. The crisis over NATO posed increasing difficulties, as de Gaulle chose to assert an independence which undermined economic and military cooperation. Moreover, in the United States, protests over Vietnam increased, with the larger demands on men, supplies, and funds. The fighting in Vietnam intensified—and so did the protests—when General William C. Westmoreland was authorized on June 8, 1965, to commit American troops in direct combat. In July, North Vietnam rejected the proposal of a British peace mission to Hanoi. Toward the end of the year, President Johnson launched what was termed a "massive peace offensive" by sending envoys to many countries. Unfortunately, there was no favorable response.

In May, Communist China had exploded a second atomic bomb. Two weeks later, Chou En-lai began an extensive tour in Africa. Indonesians manifested their hostility to the United States in demonstrations and maintained their objections to the Malaysian Federation. In August, Singapore withdrew from the Federation.

The conflict between India and Pakistan reached the boiling point in the summer. By September 1, there was open fighting near the border. The cease-fire came later in September as the result of a United Nations resolution. In January, 1966, India's Prime Minister

Shastri and President Ayub Khan of Pakistan met with Premier Ko-sygin of the U.S.S.R. in Tashkent to consolidate the truce. Shastri suffered a fatal attack on this trip. He was succeeded by Nehru's daughter, Indira Ghandi. The ouster of Ben Bella in Algeria took place in a bloodless coup in June, 1965. His successor was Houari Boumedienne.

In France, President Charles de Gaulle issued his first ominous call for changes in NATO and EEC in September. He stood for election on December 5. In spite of his achievement in connection with Algeria and the revival of the French economy, the vote for him fell short of the necessary majority. Two weeks later, the run-off election gave him the necessary vote for another seven years. The course he was to pursue had become alarmingly clear, as he prepared to withdraw from NATO.

The death of Adlai Stevenson in July, 1965, had come as a shock to those who had been close to him over many years of service in the United Nations and other important positions. His keen mind and eloquent voice had brought him a host of friends in many lands. Arthur Goldberg resigned from the Supreme Court to assume the post of Ambassador to the United Nations.

The year 1966 was a time when Johnson had to face many dark problems. De Gaulle's threat to the security of Europe and the future of NATO soon became an actuality with his announcement of the withdrawal of French forces in February. The growing fight by Senator J. William Fulbright and others against the Vietnamese war complicated defense, aid, and domestic political measures.

The difficulties in international relations were not new, but took on new forms. Sukarno in Indonesia and Nkrumah in Ghana were stripped of their power. The foundations under the Ky government in Vietnam seemed shaky. India suffered increasingly from famine and drought, and conditions became acute in 1967. The Congo continued to be upset by rioting conflict. The struggle between Great Britain and Rhodesia over white rule was bitter, with neither side yielding as the fact of independence overwhelmed the legalities which could not be enforced by a partial boycott. South Africa and Mozambique gave economic support to Rhodesia's Ian Smith. The outbreak of hostilities between the Arabs and Israelis in June, 1967, was yet another reminder of the unsolved problems in that area and the precarious nature of world peace.

The concern for Latin America increased as the Alliance for Progress appeared to lag. The significance of the Punta del Este meeting in April, 1967, will not be clear for a decade or more. Already, however, the decisions made by President Johnson at this meeting with the heads of state have been enthusiastically welcomed. There is some basis for hope that in its emphasis on trade and coordinated production and administration, the meeting may have placed dollar aid in its proper perspective. The recognition of what Latin American nations can do, acting cooperatively, is a move in the right direction.

• • •

The lessons of the 20-year experience were clear. Not only do the communists zig-zag in their efforts to dominate the world, but the conditions and uses of power in the noncommunist world change and fluctuate—often in a disturbing manner.

Some critics of foreign policy say that we have done too little; others say we have done too much. A few judge our actions to have been approximately justified and adequate. For example, even in 1967, the intervention in the Dominican Republic was still hotly debated. It was viewed in the light of the Bay of Pigs disaster, the Cuban missile crisis, and the Vietnam involvement. But it was also viewed—as are most crises—in the light of the vastly differing descriptions and interpretations of it that appeared in the press.

Few of the problems of 1945 could be considered solved in 1967. Substantial gains had come from the reconstruction and rehabilitation of Germany. The Japanese treaty had brought the cooperation of Japan to our alliances. More important, perhaps, was the increased realization, made clear by bold actions, of the United States' determination to resist aggression in Greece and Turkey, in Berlin, in Cuba, in Korea, in the Formosa Straits, in Lebanon, in Vietnam, and in a dozen other areas. This consistency had left its mark on Soviet policy and was presumed to have been noted in Communist China. In the area of economics, the European Economic Community had contributed to the general strength of Europe.

There were many who deplored the wide-flung commitments of the United States. They felt there must be some better way to share the burdens. However, no President during the four decades since the late 1920s had found a way to shift the responsibility. The men in the White House and their Secretaries of State saw the only hope for security and cooperation in a firm position, in close working alliances, and in a willingness to risk war to save the peace.

NOTES

1. Winston Churchill, *Triumph and Tragedy*, Houghton Mifflin, 1953, pp. 346–402, 426, 449, 467.
2. *Ibid.*, p. 573.
3. The National Broadcasting Company's television documentary of January 5, 1965, "The Decision to Drop the Bomb" (NBC "White Paper" series), gave an impressive account of these events. The associate producer and the producer-director-writer have published a book based on material they developed for the program: Len Giovannitti and Fred Freed, *The Decision to Drop the Bomb*, Coward-McCann, 1965.
4. Senate Committee on Foreign Relations, *A Decade of American Foreign Policy, Basic Documents, 1941–1949*, Document No. 123, 81st Congress, 1950, pp. 49, 50, 633–659.
5. Alexander DeConde, *A History of American Foreign Policy*, Scribner, 1963, p. 660.
6. Joseph M. Jones, *Fifteen Weeks (February 21–June 5, 1947)*, Viking Press, 1955.
7. Walter Millis, ed., *The Forrestal Diaries*, Viking Press, 1951, p. 245.
8. *Basic Documents, 1941–1949, op. cit.*, pp. 1253–1257.
9. Lucius D. Clay, *Decision in Germany*, Doubleday, 1950, p. 358 ff. See also W. Phillip Davison, *Berlin Blockade: A Study in Cold War Politics*. Princeton University Press, 1958, p. 105.
10. Frank Howley, *Berlin Command*, Putnam, 1950, pp. 121, 198–236.
11. Davison, *op. cit.*, pp. 98–116.
12. Shigeru Yoshida, *The Yoshida Memoirs*, Riverside Press, 1962, p. 255.
13. Richard Goold-Adams, *John Foster Dulles: A Reappraisal*, Appleton-Century-Crofts, 1962, p. 51.
14. Dwight D. Eisenhower, *Mandate for Change, 1953–1956*, Doubleday, 1963, pp. 344–375.
15. Richard Leopold, *The Growth of American Foreign Policy*, Knopf, 1962, pp. 703, 776.
16. *Ibid.*, p. 704.
17. *American Foreign Policy, 1950–1955, Current Documents*, Department of State, 1957, p. 1293.

18. *Ibid.*, p. 2122.
19. *Ibid.*, p. 1928.
20. *Ibid.*, pp. 1962, 1963.
21. *Ibid.*, p. 64.
22. *Ibid.*, p. 709.
23. John R. Beal, *John Foster Dulles*, Harper & Row, 1957, p. 183.
24. Eleanor Lansing Dulles, *Berlin: The Wall Is Not Forever*, North Carolina University Press, 1967, pp. 56, 57.
25. *Documents on Germany, 1944–1959*, Senate Committee on Foreign Relations, May 8, 1959, U. S. Government Printing Office, 1959, p. 476.
26. *Current Documents, 1950–1955*, *op. cit.*, p. 1469.
27. *Ibid.*, pp. 1453, 1634.
28. *Ibid.*, pp. 1453–1457.
29. Goold-Adams, *op. cit.*, p. 107.
30. *Current Documents, 1950–1955*, *op. cit.*, p. 2372.
31. *Ibid.*, p. 1870.
32. *Ibid.*, p. 1870.
33. *Ibid.*, p. 88.
34. Anthony Eden, *Full Circle*, Houghton Mifflin, 1960, pp. 99–106.
35. Goold-Adams, *op. cit.*, p. 126.
36. *Ibid.*, p. 131.
37. *Current Documents, 1950–1955*, *op. cit.*, p. 2383.
38. *Ibid.*, pp. 2393, 2398.
39. *Ibid.*, pp. 2836, 2837.
40. *Ibid.*, p. 1884.
41. *Ibid.*, pp. 676–697.
42. Allen Dulles, *The Craft of Intelligence*, Harper & Row, 1963, p. 81.
43. Malcolm Mackintosh, "Three Détentes: 1955–1964," in Eleanor Lansing Dulles and Robert Dickson Crane, eds., *Détente: Cold Cold War Strategies in Transition*, Praeger, 1965, p. 103.
44. *Current Documents, 1950–1955*, *op. cit.*, p. 2005.
45. Jules Davids, *America and the World of Our Time*, Random House, 1962, p. 501.
46. *Current Documents, 1950–1955*, *op. cit.*, p. 2015.
47. *American Foreign Policy, 1956, Current Documents*, Department of State, pp. 603, 604.
48. Beal, *op. cit.*, pp. 270, 271.
49. *Current Documents, 1956, op. cit.*, pp. 651–657.
50. Goold-Adams, *op. cit.*, p. 649.
51. Beal, *op. cit.*, p. 284.
52. *Current Documents, 1956, op. cit.*, p. 666.

53. Eleanor Lansing Dulles, *John Foster Dulles: The Last Year*, Harcourt, Brace & World, 1963, p. 45.
54. *Current Documents*, 1956, *op. cit.*, p. 503.
55. *Ibid.*, p. 462.
56. *Ibid.*, p. 466.
57. Melvin J. Lasky, *The Hungarian Revolution*, Praeger, 1957, pp. 228–246.
58. *Current Documents*, 1956, *op. cit.*, p. 470.
59. *American Foreign Policy*, 1957, *Current Documents*, Department of State, pp. 992, 1008.
60. *Ibid.*, p. 831.
61. *Ibid.*, p. 35.
62. *Ibid.*, pp. 34, 35, 38; see also *Foreign Affairs*, October, 1957.
63. *American Foreign Policy*, 1958, *Current Documents*, Department of State, p. 1075.
64. *Ibid.*, p. 1332.
65. Allen Dulles, *op. cit.*, p. 169.

III

SIX CRITICAL
DECISIONS

A crisis is a turning point for better or for worse. It is decisive even if there is no clearly determined action on the part of those affected. Though a crisis may be the culmination of a long series of developments, it is sudden in its acuteness. In the case of a fever in the human body, it may be a change leading to probable recovery— or it may mean that death is to come. In foreign policy, it is a situation so intensified that, if it is not met with swift and adequate measures, there is likely to be a rapid deterioration.

In the following narrative, six crises will be described as they confronted policy-makers in the United States with the need for action. In these cases, although not unversally in recent American history, action was taken, with a degree of success that varied from case to case. In no instance was there a complete solution of the problems. The achievement of complete solutions is not possible in the present world situation. Only a temporary gain, an increase in strength, and a deterrence of hostile action, for a time, is to be expected.

In the selection of cases, both regional and chronological factors have been considered. Korea, representing some of the issues to be faced in the Far East, is the first of the six, occurring in 1950. It brought a series of critical phases, only one of which is analyzed—

the first. Guatemala, in 1954, which is important because of the efforts of international communism to penetrate this hemisphere, is the second case. It shows the newer applications of the Monroe Doctrine and the need for cooperation in the Americas. Lebanon, with the dangers to the free world of indirect aggression, was, in 1958, a key point in the Middle East. Berlin, a perennial problem, came under new attack with Khrushchev's diplomatic drive in 1958. This case shows that the defense of Europe must be a unified action, and in 1958 this unity was present. The Congo in 1960 revealed the numerous deep-rooted problems of Africa, where many nations achieved independence before they were ready for it. The Dominican Republic in 1965 is a case of intervention in a critical hour of chaos.

All these areas of danger continue to occupy our efforts in the fields of security and diplomacy. All call for continued watchfulness. Yet in these instances of quick decision and energetic response to mounting difficulties, the workings of our foreign policy-making are revealed in a generally favorable light. In all six instances, courage and an assessment of dangers and opportunities were fitted into the continuing realities of our national policy.

There were (in these cases) differences in the amount of information available and, above all, in the correctness of the evaluation of information. We were, at times and in some areas, slow to recognize the seriousness of the situation and also the extent to which our vital interests were affected. This delay came not so much from a lack of detailed study as from a failure to develop the worldwide perspective that would make our strategy equal to that of more aggressive nations. The American people were new to the world of international politics, and this fact influenced to some extent the views of both those who make decisions and those who criticize or support actions taken.

There are several phases that precede a moment of choice (see pages 23–25). These are: (1) an accepted policy or position, (2) background information, (3) knowledge of a particular event, (4) evaluation of its significance and relation to vital interests, and (5) recommendations. Then come (6) the decision, (7) its execution, (8) its explanation, and, later, (9) its review and appraisal. These aspects of the critical events of the past 20 or so years merit examination in an effort to understand how policy is formed and executed —where our strengths and weaknesses lie.

Each story is the more dramatic in that there is an hour in which the President and his Secretary of State give the word. The meeting in the President's study, with only a few men who share his confidence present—all looking beyond the papers on the desk, to the future of war or peace—this is the moment of history for which the world waits. This is the "eye of the hurricane," when a stillness comes before the rush of action is resumed. This is the consultation that will never be recorded, that will never be known. This is when the lines of power are charged. This is when the past is left behind, as the whole complex of relations is changed forever.

About such an instant of mental courage and leadership, little can be known at the time. We know the nature of the men, we can learn something of the considerations in their minds, we can weigh the capabilities and the dangers, but we cannot enter this room. It is only after the group disperses, after the orders have been given by telephone and in writing, that those not in the President's study can follow the course of action and associate themselves with the success and failure, whichever it is. The advisers give partial explanations of what has occurred. They do not defend or excuse their decisions or those of their chief. It is for those who are on the outside to wonder, to question, to criticize or praise. It is thus that the leaders of the government learn how much maneuvering room they have—what the people will tolerate. This is how a democracy responds.

The desire to know is strong, but even in a democracy, elements of secrecy are essential during a crisis. Our studies reveal much that had to be kept from the public at the time. We circle the central point, now looking inward to the mind of the President, now outward to the world of action.

In any crisis, the recognition of the moment of decision is crucial. If delay prevents early action, a later response is usually more costly. In these six cases, the choice was quickly made. Indeed, timing is perhaps the most important element affected by relations up and down the line. If there is close harmony among all those concerned with foreign policy, decisions are usually swift and firm. This means understanding among the desk officer, steeped in knowledge of people and conditions in one country; the Office Director, with an awareness of local conditions; the Assistant Secretary, with information on broad security issues; the Secretary of State; and the

President, with his sensitivity to Congressional, national, and overall values. It is the Secretary who spells out the ABC of the steps and who says to the President, "Now is the time." He calls for the meeting at which the die is cast. He carries back the instructions which then fan out over a wide field of action.

A study of these relations in special instances has more meaning if one is familiar with the apparatus—the Department, its lines of communication with the Embassies in the field, interagency relations, the men, their training, their functions, and their zones of responsibilities at various levels. Though only a few selected lights flash and telephones ring, it is this immediate activation of the relevant parts of the machine, the strong surge of power that thrusts some men and some materiel into the struggle, that commands our attention. It is to be ready for these occasions, as well as for continuing service to the people of the nation, that young men and women accept the drudgery, hardship, and long hours of work necessary in the conduct of foreign affairs. Without this sense of urgency, we could not operate at a high level. It is because of these special situations that some of the best young people in the nation look to the Foreign Service as a career. It is because there are these hours of peril that the public is interested in foreign policy.

In some cases, for example, Korea, a large part of our manpower, our security forces, and our economic potential is involved. In others, as in Guatemala, only a small effort at the right time and place achieves the intended result. In all cases, it is of crucial importance not to overlook the risks beyond the immediate hazard. This aspect of judgment, which may have been overlooked by the British at Suez (see pages 169, 170), requires that top officials have broad vision. Risk is always present, whether it comes from action or inaction. Some officials have to appraise the risks and make preparations for the likely contingencies.

It has been suggested here that the period after "the event" is different from that before. It is a time when there is a marked change in priorities and in the functions carried on by the officers involved in the response to the new situation. This has been illustrated by the concept of the "narrowing triangle of choice" (see pages 4–5). Many activities that were justified previously become of less importance or even completely inappropriate. Once the state of affairs has been faced, there follow recommendations which still further narrow the options and from which a selection is made. These proposals, though some or all may be discarded, usually form the basis for the decisions. Through all the stages, with more or less intensity, preparations in the military, economic, political, and public relations fields are being carried on. These have been adequate in some instances, inadequate in others. After the crisis is over, they can be appraised and criticized. Explanations, though important, do not always satisfy. The Administration in power may defend; a minority may condemn; the public may have a strong feeling, but it is not in most cases in a position to make a valid appraisal or estimate. Even if the public has a fair understanding of the risks taken and of the degree of success or failure, it can usually never know what might, otherwise, have been the outcome.

There is a tendency in retrospect to view many events as inevitable. This is a type of psychological protection from the intolerable burden of assuming responsibility for disastrous mistakes. This attitude clouds judgment and softens criticism in many cases—it seems to lessen the burden of responsibility. The student is not immune to this feeling. According to his temperament, allegiance, training, and aspirations, he throws much of the past into predetermined molds. He may struggle for intellectual freedom, but it is difficult to attain.

The cases described here are aimed to show decision, action, and free will. They are treated from the American point of view and they are colored by various assumptions as to national aims, programs, and capabilities. The treatments are not in any sense complete. They cannot contain the detailed evidence that might make it possible to say, "this was a success," "that was a failure." And yet these studies do endeavor to show the fruitfulness of prompt, well-targeted decisions and of willingness to "seize the nettle danger"—the power of men over events. Other cases might have been chosen, some more striking, some more controversial. These, however, may serve to show the conduct of foreign policy during critical days. Tools are in the hands of the heads of state; these tools the men of strength are compelled to use. Their achievements and their mistakes weave the web of history.

THE CHALLENGE OF KOREA: 1950

A Summer Night. June evenings in Washington can be laden with honeysuckle and fireflies. The mint juleps at the Chevy Chase Country Club are frosty. It was here that one of the State Department's high officers took his wife for a relaxing evening on the first day of his vacation, Saturday, June 24. He did not know that 1950 would be a year marked by memorable changes in United States foreign policy.

Tired after an exceptionally heavy week's work, Livingston Merchant decided that he would not leave town until Sunday afternoon. It would be better to have a good night's sleep and then a leisurely departure for Cape Cod. He and his wife reached home sometime after midnight. Their part-time maid had departed, but she had left several messages from the State Department to call without delay. One of the callers had been Philip Jessup. Normally, he was stationed at the United Nations in Lake Success, New York, but on this Saturday he had been called to Washington; he had arrived late in the evening.

"The North Koreans have attacked in force," Jessup said. "We are working out our moves because our action must be immediate. The President will be back from Missouri tomorrow."

Merchant offered to come at once, but Jessup told him to get some sleep and come in early in the morning, adding that he and his group would continue their work.

At about six o'clock in the morning, after only three or four hours' sleep, Merchant, who was Deputy Assistant Secretary of State for Far Eastern Affairs, went to his office. Several of the top men, including Secretary Acheson, were there. One or two of them left briefly, and Jessup returned to New York. The most recent recruit plunged into the critical work. He did not leave the building for more than 48 hours. His vacation and his outside life disappeared for the time. The urgent decisions were already being made.

The Response to Aggression. The meaning of the Korean attack and the American response has been clear since the first days. It was a major effort by the communists to drive the United States from the Pacific, beginning with an area which, perhaps, did not seem to be regarded as important and pushing on to other islands and continents after victory there. The attack was launched after indications earlier in the year that the northwest Pacific would not be held worthy of significant risks on our part and before the plans for the Japanese treaty had advanced to a firm position in the eyes of the world.

In meeting the aggression with force, the United States showed that it would not be possible to launch an attack there with impunity and that we were firmly committed to defend the area—that, even at the risk of the outbreak of World War III, we would not acquiesce in the conquest of Korea.

Morally, we were already engaged, although the Soviets had misconstrued some of our declarations. After 1947, we had recognized the interdependence of the areas which we had agreed to help and the dangers of further extension of the communist tyranny there. There was, in fact, no choice after the intentions of the North Koreans, sponsored by the Soviets and the Chinese, became evident. The only questions that had to be decided were the means, the timing, the various practical consequences of action. The large question was: having dismantled a large part of our military forces, would we be able to take a strong and effective stand against a swiftly moving enemy? There were to be many dark days between June, 1950, and July, 1953, when an effective armistice was finally achieved, though still leaving many questions unanswered and many problems unsolved.

Korea had been a center of conflict for generations before it became the battlefield in the war between the free world and communism in 1950. For centuries the peninsula had been a center or funnel through which people and traditions moved from the Chinese mainland to the island kingdom of Japan. It was a vassal state, paying tribute to various Chinese dynasties though it was ruled by its own kings and potentates. As Japan increased in strength, its interest in the "land of the morning calm" grew, and efforts to increase Japanese influence led to the clash which was the Sino-Japanese War. This conflict ended in 1895 with the treaty of Shinmonseki—a treaty negotiated by a former Secretary of State, the American John

Watson Foster.* It forced China to recognize Korea as an independent country.

Again, in the early twentieth century, Japanese dominance in the area led to the war in which the Japanese halted the eastward expansion of the Czarist Russians. America had a growing concern over the "system of balanced antagonism"[1] in the Pacific, and President Theodore Roosevelt succeeded in having the peace treaty signed at Portsmouth, New Hampshire, in 1905, under American "good offices."

The extension of Russian influence into Siberia and northern Manchuria had led to border conflicts with the Chinese. It was to lessen these dangers that there was agreement on a border in the Chinese-Russian Treaty of Nerchinsk in 1689. A later treaty permitted the Russians to build a rail line through northern Manchuria. As both Russia and Japan extended their spheres of influence, a protocol (Nishi-Rosen) was adopted in 1898 in which the independence of Korea was recognized, but in which Japan's predominant rights—a virtual monopoly—over the economic life of the nation were also recognized.

Even these early treaties had the effect of dividing Korea north and south at a line that cut across the peninsula in the valley near the now famous 38th Parallel, a region where Japanese and Russian influence came into close proximity. This was the natural demarcation that was later chosen to separate the zones of occupation. The Japanese worried about the problems of the growing influence of the neighboring powers and the strategic importance of the area, little imagining the changed situation that would develop 50 years later, with the United States combatting an incursion from the north and using Japan as a staging area. The challenge at the time was met in the Russo-Japanese War, which settled for about 45 years Japanese control in southern Korea. This state of affairs was recognized by the United States with the agreement that the Japanese would not harbor any aggressive designs on the Philippines; this understanding was embodied in the 1905 Taft-Katsura memorandum. The Korean peninsula was openly annexed by the Japanese shortly after a secret convention between Russia and Japan in 1910.

Thus the strategic value of the narrow Asian peninsula (about

---

*John Foster Dulles was his grandson.

the size of Minnesota) early engaged the major actors who were to clash in the later conflict, which was to impoverish this nation on the flanks of China and Russia. The southern half, the granary, was to a considerable extent cut off from the northern industrial and mineral-producing area. Gold, iron ore, and coal were to lay the basis for the industries and the proletariat of the north. Korea could not escape the strife in which the larger powers were involved.

The record of the negotiations over Korea from 1943 on reveals that efforts to make a dependable peace in the area were no more successful then than those of the preceding three centuries. The first decisions were made at Cairo in November, 1943. Of the discussions there, Winston Churchill later wrote: "Moreover, as will be seen, the President, who took an exaggerated view of the Indian-Chinese sphere, was soon closeted in long conferences with the Generalissimo [Chiang Kai-shek]." Churchill was urging Roosevelt not to permit other distractions to "cramp" OVERLORD, already planned for the following spring. He regretted the presence of Chiang and the importance given by the Americans to the "Chinese story, which was lengthy, complicated, and minor."[2]

The Allies early arrived at the decision to establish an independent Korea. Stalin was not at the meeting, but he met Churchill and Roosevelt a few days later at Teheran. Chiang was not at this second meeting, so these decisions were not fully coordinated. Moreover, at the Yalta Conference in 1945, a year and three months after these meetings, Churchill did not take part in the discussion of the Far East questions. He did associate himself later, at the end of the conference, with the famous secret protocol. The proposal for a trusteeship for Korea was apparently agreed on by Roosevelt and Stalin at this time, although this plan was never carried through.

The Protocol of Yalta, for many years "top secret," has become highly controversial. Critics have called it a "sell-out" and blame it for the later disasters in China and Korea. It provided for territorial changes in the Far East that would limit Japan and benefit Russia. It was made at a time when the expectation of a long and costly continuing war in the Pacific influenced thinking—it was thought that Russia's participation in that conflict should be assured. The atomic bomb had not yet been tested, and our approaching success with it was only the hope of a few men. In May, 1945, President Truman sent Harry Hopkins to Moscow. Stalin confirmed to him that he would keep his promise to the late President Roosevelt and join the Pacific war. Russian forces were not actually committed to that war, however, until August 6, two weeks after Stalin knew of the Alamogordo atomic test and eight days before the Japanese surrender. In this surrender the Japanese agreed to end their control of Korea.

The Potsdam Conference, meanwhile, had taken up some aspects of the Korean postwar situation. There is no published record of discussions of the international trusteeship idea, and the main considerations of the military occupation were left to the projected meeting of the Council of Foreign Ministers, which took place in Moscow in December. The Soviets appear to have taken for granted that their traditional role in Manchuria, their sphere of influence in northern Korea, and their participation, however tardy, in the war in the Far East would give them rights which they could eventually exercise. President Truman and Prime Minister Attlee announced at the end of the tripartite conference that the terms of the Cairo declaration had been reaffirmed. Stalin did not participate in this act. Chiang concurred by dispatch.

After the collapse of the Japanese Empire, the War Department submitted a draft to the Joint Chiefs of Staff providing for the surrender of the Japanese forces north of the 38th Parallel to the Soviets and those south of the Parallel to United States troops. The draft was issued at the headquarters of General MacArthur on September 2 and approved by Premier Stalin. American troops arrived in Korea on September 8.

Almost immediately after the establishment of governments in Korea—military government in the American zone and "peoples' committees" in the Soviet zone—relations between the two commands became strained. The situation reflected some of the same problems as those developing elsewhere between the two major powers. Here, as in Germany and Austria, the line of demarcation was intended as an aid to garrisoning and was not to divide the country politically or economically. Elections were envisaged for an early date in order to permit a centralized administration and to lay the groundwork for a new and independent democracy. As tension grew, it was clear that the Soviets and the Americans were each intent on preventing the other from gaining an influence over the entire peninsula. The subsequent negotiations from 1945 to 1947 were dominated by this purpose.

After the Moscow meeting of the Council of Foreign Ministers in December, it was agreed to set up a Far Eastern Commission. It was also agreed that there should be a Joint Commission to "elaborate the appropriate measures" for the formation of a provisional Korean government and to work out the agreement for a four-power trusteeship "for a period of up to five years." This Commission was also to be responsible for measures to coordinate administrative economic matters between the two commands. The representatives were to convene in two weeks. The Commission was directed by the Foreign Ministers to consult with Korean "democratic parties and social organizations" in preparing its proposals. The Joint Commission convened on March 20, 1946, and adjourned in early May without making any significant progress. President Truman had announced on September 18, 1945, that the building of a great nation was an accepted goal, but its realization was frustrated by the failure of joint efforts. The 42 later meetings of the Joint Commission (May to October, 1947) resulted in almost total disagreement. They paralleled a similar situation in the meetings attempting to frame a treaty in Austria during this same summer.

In August, 1947, Acting Secretary of State Robert A. Lovett proposed a plan of representation in a provisional Korean legislature. There were to be secret elections in each zone to choose representatives on the basis of population, and these representatives would then meet in Seoul to establish a united legislature. The whole process was to be supervised by the United Nations. Once established, the provisional government was to meet with the occupying powers to determine what needs should be met to assure a stable and prosperous nation. The whole problem was to be considered by an international conference of the signatories to the Moscow agreement. Since the South was more populous than the North, there would have been a larger number of representatives from the United States zone of occupation.

The proposition was rejected by Molotov, and the Joint Commission had to adjourn without an agreement even on a report of its activities. On September 17, 1947, Secretary of State Marshall, addressing the United Nations, reviewed the complete failure of direct negotiations on the Korean question. He said that after two years of effort and a series of agreements over the years, from Cairo to Moscow, there had been no progress toward the establishment of a democratic united Korea. He said that the inability of two powers to agree should no longer delay the rightful claims of the Korean people and proposed a resolution that was adopted by the General Assembly in November. A United Nations Temporary Commission on Korea was set up. It recommended that elections be held not later than March 31, 1948, and that after the elections a National Assembly be set up. The Commission was to expedite the withdrawal of the occupying forces. The Soviets failed to comply with the resolution. All efforts of the Commission to create machinery to observe the elections failed to make contact with the Soviet occupation authorities. The United States, taking note of the Soviet failure to cooperate and reporting that the Temporary Commission had observed the elections in South Korea, said that they were a valid expression of the free will of the electorate in accord with the General Assembly Resolution and announced its decision, on January 1, 1949, to grant full recognition to the Seoul government.

President Truman in June reported to Congress the entire history of the struggle to give a united Korea its independence and asked for aid to restore the debilitated economy. His request for $150 million was to mark the beginning of a continuing program of aid along the lines of the European Recovery Program. It superseded the Government Administration and Relief in Occupied Areas (GARIOA) program, which had kept the people from starvation. The President said:

> Korea has become a testing ground in which the validity and practical value of the ideals and principles of democracy which the Republic is putting into practice are being matched against the practices of communism which have been imposed on the people of North Korea. The survival and progress of the Republic toward a self-supporting stable economy will have an immense and far-reaching influence on the people of Asia.[3]

Thus, not only in Europe, through the ERP and the Truman Doctrine in Greece and Turkey, but also in Korea the United States had assumed comprehensive responsibilities. The United Nations, under influence from Washington and elsewhere, continued to concern itself with Korean independence; it adopted another resolution in October, 1949. The time of crisis was fast approaching.

Before the Clash. Support of the Rhee regime and the duly elected government in South Korea, in spite of its recognized weaknesses, was the only alternative to the loss of the area to communism.

The Joint Commission had failed. The United Nations had made no progress, though its moral support and the material aid provided by the United States gave the small nation a hope of developing into a stable democracy. Economic aid totaled about $181 million in the fiscal years 1946 to 1948 and $486 million in the years 1949 to 1952. The total of economic and military aid during the fiscal years 1946 to 1962 was more than $5 billion, of which $1,844,000,000 was military. These sums represented a substantial contribution compared with those made available to other countries—several times the amounts for all countries in Africa and Latin America combined. The normal time factors that delay shipments of aid procured from government appropriations, however, meant that less than half the sums allocated by then had actually become available to the Koreans in goods and programs when the 1950 attack came.

Controversy over Rhee's belief that the unification of the country could only be accomplished by armed intervention and Chiang's desire to return to the mainland in force lay behind the statements of the President and of Secretary Acheson in January, 1950. A White House release on January 5 ruled out military aid or advice to the Chinese on Formosa and added that the United States had no intention of involving itself in the civil conflict in China. This statement was followed on January 12 by Secretary Acheson's address to the Washington Press Club, in which he indicated a defense perimeter beyond which our interests were not immediate. He also gave the impression that we would not use force in the Pacific.

Some of those who have read the intelligence reports received during the months before the attack now wonder why they were not taken seriously at the time. The evaluation of menacing data always presents serious difficulty; danger lies at many points. In any case, the main preoccupation was with the newly created NATO, which was moving forward. A second and vital interest was the reestablishment of Japan as a new ally in the Pacific. Concern over China and Taiwan was reflected in the recall of Foreign Service personnel from Communist China, announced on January 14, 1950. This action was taken after the violation of American consular property and the "harsh and unjustifiable treatment of United States Consul General Ward and his staff at Mukden."[4] The various posts were closed within the next two weeks. Thus our diplomatic representation on the Chinese mainland came to an end.

At this time a "Treaty of Friendship and Alliance and Mutual Assistance" was signed by the Soviet Union and Communist China in Moscow on February 14. Secretary of State Acheson discussed the treaty on March 15, in San Francisco, referring to his "perimeter" speech of January 12. He described communist aid as equivalent to approximately $40 million a year and contrasted it with the grant of $400 million for a single year voted by the American Congress in 1948. He said: "We now face the prospect that the Communists may attempt to apply another familiar tactic and use China as a base for probing for weak spots which they can move into and exploit."[5]

Meanwhile, the Secretary, in reply to questions in Congress on February 9, had explained that "the seat of the Chinese Government is on Formosa . . . and that island, with Hainan, is the only remaining substantial territory now under its control"; he added that "it seems clear that any defense of the island would finally rest upon the United States." In response to further questioning as to what steps had been taken and what sums spent, he said State Department aid under the ECA program had amounted to approximately $18.5 million by December 31, 1949. He was then asked: "What areas in Asia come within the scope of the Truman Doctrine?" He replied that the concept of supporting peoples resisting subjugation is basic; he mentioned aid to the "recognized government of China" and to Korea and then referred to the January 12 speech: "There is a great difference between our responsibility and our opportunity in the northern part of the Pacific area and the southern part of the Pacific area." The communist authorities, Acheson said, had "publicly announced that the capture of Formosa is now a major military objective. . . ." It was natural that concern for the menace of aggression should have been focused more on Taiwan than on Korea. In this time, as on other occasions, the focusing of official attention on the demands that seemed most urgent led to an underestimation of the needs of other regions. The harassment of the border areas adjacent to the 38th Parallel was not taken as a sign of a large-scale attack, nor was it assumed that ground forces of the United States might play a considerable part in the halting of aggression in Asia. Our state of preparedness was at a low ebb.

Attention at this time with respect to Taiwan and Korea centered to a considerable extent on the economic rehabilitation that would consolidate our friendly political relations with those countries. In February, President Truman signed a bill allotting $110 million for economic rehabilitation of South Korea. The American troop withdrawal in June, 1949, made it possible to give the South Koreans large amounts of rifles and ammunition. Other military aid was granted, but limits were set on certain types of equipment, since President Rhee had threatened to invade North Korea; the United States withheld tanks, planes, and heavy guns suitable for offensive operations. There were objections in Congress that our policy in the area was not sufficiently strong, and the tide of criticism, which was to swell as political controversy increased and only to quiet for a time during actual hostilities, decried our "China policy."

The famous defense perimeter, supported by the Administration in 1950, which some think gave the communists "the green light," had actually been discussed by General Douglas MacArthur in March, 1949. Thus there are many diverse pieces of the puzzle of our position in that time that have not yet been put together. Reliance on the United Nations still seemed plausible to many, but they were about to experience a rude shock. The UN had been in large measure responsible for the idea that it could act in case of a breach of the peace; it was also responsible for the situation in Korea. The test was to come soon.

President Truman later summarized the situation in the two years before the attack. He described the establishment of the Republic of Korea, recalling that there had been free elections conducted under the auspices of the United Nations, but that "the Soviet Government had refused to allow elections to be held in the area under its control." The new government in South Korea had been recognized by the United States and by "a majority of the other members of the United Nations." He went on to say that "the Soviet Government stated that it had withdrawn its occupation troops from northern Korea, and that a local regime had been established there." United Nations observers were prohibited from going beyond the 38th Parallel to verify this fact or to supervise elections.[6]

A United Nations Commission composed of the representatives of seven nations was in the Republic of Korea in June, 1950. This Commission, having completed a two-week tour of the military positions of the ROK, stated that the army was purely for defense.

Their report on June 23 indicated that there were small bodies of troops and roving patrols to the south of the Parallel, but no indication of any capability or intention of attacking the North. There was no armor, no heavy artillery, no sign of air support. Thus, as they reported later, there was no provocation from the South and no warning of the attack. Calm was said to prevail along the artificial border. It was at this time that the American Embassy in Seoul took John Foster Dulles, representative of the President for the drafting of a Japanese peace treaty, to the 38th Parallel on an observation tour. There seemed to be no evidence of special danger at the moment.

Lines of Action Take Shape. Peace was abruptly shattered in the evening of June 24. A newsman called Secretary Acheson shortly after nine o'clock to ask what the United States would do about the attack in Korea. A few minutes later, word from the code room watch officer and calls from the Department's desk officer for Korea reported the receipt of a telegram from Ambassador Muccio in Seoul. These confirmed the news flashes and placed before the United States one of the momentous decisions of history. From this time on, our fateful involvement in the complex problems of the entire Far East became inescapable.

The attack had been launched at nine o'clock in the evening, our time (4:00 A.M., June 25, by Korean time). The crossing of the Parallel was made at several points. Ongjin was blasted by North Korea artillery fire. Amphibious landings were reported on the east coast. Tanks were taking part in the operation, and Kaesong was reported to have been captured in the first hours. There was no doubt in Washington of the seriousness of the situation after officials had read the telegram from Muccio. Secretary Acheson and several of his aides went immediately to the State Department. After a brief review of the information available, they telephoned President Truman, who was in Missouri. They advised him that their review and recommendations would proceed and that they did not urge his return until the morning. The American representatives to the United Nations were to be informed at once. Philip Jessup was asked to come to Washington, and contact was made with Ernest Gross, deputy to former Senator Austin, who was Ambassador to the UN; the Senator was in Vermont, and Gross was in

New York. The lines of action began to take shape by midnight.

It is not clear to what extent the deep involvement of the future was envisaged in the night hours of June 24–25. To some extent, the decisions of the next six days came step by step. Each phase moved in the direction which soon seemed inevitable. The first decision, to call the Security Council into session, was made almost immediately; this was logical and followed somewhat naturally from the responsibility which the UN had assumed in maintaining its Commission in Korea. The request for the meeting was forwarded to Secretary General Trygve Lie by Ernest Gross, first by telephone at 3:00 A.M., and then more formally. Gross asked Lie to transmit to the President of the Security Council this message from Secretary of State Acheson:

> The American Ambassador to the Republic of Korea has informed the Department of State that North Korea forces invaded the territory of the Republic of Korea at several points in the early morning hours of June 25 (Korean time).
>
> Pyongyang Radio, under the control of the North Korean regime, it is reported, has broadcast a declaration of war against the Republic of Korea effective 9 P.M. E.D.T. June 24.
>
> An attack of the forces of the North Korean regime under the circumstances referred to above constitutes a breach of the peace and an act of aggression.
>
> Upon the urgent request of my Government, I ask you to call an immediate meeting of the Security Council of the United Nations.

At approximately the same time, a telegram was received from the United Nations Commission in Seoul confirming the attack "in strength" at more than six points. It stated: "The latest attacks have occurred along the Parallel directly north of Seoul and along the shortest avenue of approach." The allegation that the South Koreans had attacked across the parallel was "entirely false." A few hours after the first aggression, "four yak-type aircraft strafed civilian and military airfields outside Seoul, destroying planes, firing gas tanks and attacking jeeps. The Yongdungpo railroad station on [the] outskirts was also strafed." The message referred to the signs of a full-scale war and suggested bringing the matter to the attention of the Security Council.

The swift course of events, which at the time seemed to come without warning—though one can now assume that they had cast a shadow before them—brought great pressure for action. Both in Washington and New York, thoughts turned immediately to the United Nations as the instrument for regaining the peace. There was no sign at this stage that military involvement was anticipated, but it was hoped, at least in Seoul, that the "Republican Army would give a good account of itself." Yet the tidal wave sweeping down from the north was too powerful to be held back by the unexpecting and unprepared forces in the south.

The Security Council met at Lake Success at two o'clock on Sunday afternoon in an atmosphere of apprehension. Its members did not yet know the extent of the intrusion of the hostile forces, nor that the fall of the capital of the ROK was imminent. The meeting assembled only a few hours after the first information, even before President Truman, back in Washington, consulted his advisers that evening at Blair House (his temporary residence during repairs to the White House). The Security Council expressed grave concern and termed the actions a breach of the peace. They voted 9 to 0 to call for a cease-fire and withdrawal north of the Parallel. The remarkable coincidence that Jacob Malik had boycotted the Security Council over the issue of seating Communist China made this action possible. The abstention of Yugoslavia was without material effect. There was no veto.

The evening meeting, where President Truman was briefed on the various items of information and the preliminary meeting of the Security Council, began to take account of American involvement. An order was drafted for MacArthur, requesting him to evacuate United States citizens. There was to be an increase in the arms and supplies to be furnished to South Korea; secret instructions were written to the Seventh Fleet to place it north of the Philippines, where it could protect the Taiwan Straits. The service chiefs were ordered to prepare the papers that would be needed if the military units of the U.S. forces were to be called into action.

There were reports that the invaders were only 15 miles from Seoul, though there was a news item on Monday in the New York *Times* saying that the South Korean forces had counterattacked. But there also was evidence that the South Korean forces were being outflanked. The news continued to be increasingly discouraging, and the signs of danger mounted. MacArthur headquarters reported that the South Koreans were unable to resist.

On Monday evening (Washington time), General MacArthur was ordered to commit U.S. naval and air units in direct support of the ROK army south of the 38th Parallel. The instructions were not to use ground forces in actual combat at that time. It was not evident that we would engage in battle, but we were supporting the part of the Security Council resolution that read: "The Security Council . . . calls upon all Members to render every assistance to the United Nations in the execution of this resolution and to refrain from giving assistance to the North Korean authorities." Thus the police action was initiated.

A further call for assistance came from the Security Council on June 27. It reiterated the "breach of peace" declaration, noted the continued hostilities in spite of the call for cessation and the request for withdrawal, and referred to the ROK appeal for help. The recommendation was that "member nations furnish such assistance as may be necessary to repel the armed attack and to restore peace and security to the area."

While the diplomats in New York were thus preparing for further action that now seemed necessary, those in Washington were equally busy. There had been relatively little consultation with Congress during these feverish efforts to meet the crisis. On the morning of Tuesday, the 27th, the White House issued a statement:

> At a meeting of Congressional leaders at the White House this morning, the President, together with the Secretary of Defense, the Secretary of State, and the Joint Chiefs of Staff, reviewed the latest developments of the situation in Korea.
> The Congressional leaders were given a full review of the intensified military activities.
> In keeping with the United Nations Security Council's request for support to the Republic of Korea in repelling the North Korean invaders and restoring peace in Korea, the President announced that he had authorized the United States Air Force to conduct missions on specific military targets in Northern Korea wherever militarily necessary, and had ordered a military blockade of the entire Korean coast.

This statement and the sequence of events from late Saturday night to Tuesday morning give the basis for the conclusion that Congress was informed but not consulted. There are many who think that however legal this procedure may be, it is inadvisable to move too far without close and full consultation.

No serious doubt exists, although the question was raised, as to the Constitutional authority of the President to deploy the Navy and call on the armed forces to carry out missions, either for specific objectives to protect the lives and property of American citizens or in the general pursuit of his foreign policy. In this instance, there was, though it was not needed from a legal point of view, the added justification of the call by the United Nations for assistance for the South Koreans.[7]

It may be regarded as unfortunate that the air strikes were not more immediate and in greater strength. By the time the orders had reached General MacArthur on the 28th (Wednesday), Seoul had fallen, and the soldiers of the ROK, some 50,000 men with light arms, were being driven toward the sea by the more than 100,000 North Koreans with tanks and heavy equipment. The rout was becoming a disaster. The tide could not be halted. It was only at this stage that American aircraft in Korea and Japan began operations. It was a week later that a small American force made contact with the invaders in the southern areas, where resistance still seemed possible.

On July 7, two weeks after the first attack, General Douglas MacArthur was made commander of the forces of the United Nations. At the same time, he was authorized to use the United Nations flag along with the national flags of the countries participating in the operations. The three-year struggle in the first acknowledged *limited* war to defend the principles and the very life of the United Nations, as well as continued freedom in the area, had begun in earnest. From July 8, 1950, until July 27, 1953, the lives of American soldiers were pledged in this distant battlefield for objectives only newly recognized but nonetheless stanchly defended.

The designation of General MacArthur as commander, to provide unified direction for all the assistance made available, was a further manifestation of the close working relations of the men in Washington and those in New York in this crisis. Fifty-two of the 59 nations who were, at that time, members of the United Nations (in 1967 there are 122) had supported the action to restore peace in Korea. Besides the United States, 15 nations sent military forces to aid the South Koreans. The first UN army, the widest collective security operation in history,[8] led to firmer UN action in following crises. This was prepared for by the "uniting for peace" resolution of

November, 1950, which gave the General Assembly the authority to take its own actions when a veto might paralyze the Security Council. It was recognized that the absence of the Soviets from the Security Council from early 1950 on had been fortuitous from the point of view of June events, but that it could not be counted on to recur in other circumstances. There has been some question as to the scope and binding nature of such General Assembly actions. Nonetheless, the crisis of Suez led to the dispatching of a 10-nation UN Emergency Force to patrol the troubled areas in 1956. In the Lebanon crisis in 1958, the UN sent an observer group (see pages 272–273). In 1959, Dag Hammarskjöld, the Secretary General, visited Laos in connection with "peace-keeping." More importantly, in 1960, the strong action in the Congo demonstrated the extent to which the office of the Secretary General had been expanded.

For the United States, the fact that the action was international and came to be considered a "police action" was of great importance in the legal, political, and psychological aspects of the situation. War was never declared, though on December 20, in Executive Order 10195, Korea was designated a combat zone as of June 27, 1950.

The United Nations appeal brought help, but the contingents from other nations were not large. The participation was small as compared with the large expenditure of money and lives by the United States. In the first days, only British troops were available. The size and nature of the British and U.S. forces were "sufficient only to perform the occupation duties in Japan."[9] They had to be regrouped and reequipped to be able to take on combat in Korea. MacArthur's first report to the United Nations spoke of the "end of the chance for victory of the North Korean forces" in spite of "the speed with which he could overrun South Korea once he had breached the Han River line and with overwhelming numbers and superior weapons temporarily shattered South Korean resistance." MacArthur went on to say:

> When he crashed the Han Line the way seemed entirely open and victory was within his grasp. The desperate decision to throw in piecemeal American elements as they arrived by every available means of transport from Japan was the only hope to save the situation. The skill and valor thereafter displayed in successive holding actions by the ground forces in accordance with this concept, brilliantly supported

in complete coordination by air and naval elements, forced the enemy into continued deployments, costly frontal attacks and confused logistics which so slowed his advance and blunted his drive that we have bought the precious time necessary to build a secure base.[10]

The speed and effectiveness, under adverse conditions, of the Eighth Army, the Seventh Fleet, and the Far East Air Force saved the United Nations from being driven into the sea at Pusan and opened the opportunity for the spectacular landing at Inchon not many weeks later, when a few hours of high tide gave us a moment which was firmly seized and boldly developed by amphibious forces.

A major decision had been the refusal to accept troops of the Chinese Nationalists on Taiwan. Some 33,000 had been offered for Korean combat on June 29. The Secretary of State in his note to the Ambassador of the Republic of China on July 1 indicated a fear of the threat of invasion by the Chinese Communist regime in Peiping as a reason for not accepting. The note indicated that MacArthur's headquarters would discuss with the Chinese military plans for the defense of the island before any decision was made as to the wisdom of reducing the forces on Taiwan by transferring men to Korea. There are some observers who have held that this decision prevented what might have been quick action to drive back the invaders. The opinion in many circles at the time, however, was that there was a serious danger of an attack by the mainland Chinese on Korea if Chiang were to be directly involved. In fact, it was assumed, as indicated in various speeches and reports to Congress, that if the action were handled in a limited way, the Soviet Union and China would not intervene directly.[11]

General MacArthur had cabled Washington on Friday, June 30, that there was urgent need for more strength. The South Koreans had been pushed back in confusion. He urged the acceptance of the troops from Taiwan. According to Eric Goldman, President Truman supported the recommendation, but Secretary Acheson persuaded Truman that the offer should be declined. Thus the note of refusal was dispatched and the order given to General MacArthur to use the troops he already had. On Friday, "full intervention had been decided on," and "Douglas MacArthur was in command in Korea."[12] By this time, Australia, Canada, New Zealand, and the Netherlands had offered aid. The critics of the Administration in Washington joined in support of Truman's bold response to the attack in Korea.

A *Sequence of Decisions.* The decisions that led to the three years of fighting fall into a number of successive choices. The Saturday night-Sunday morning determination to request the meeting of the Security Council, with the realization that this would lead to further fateful steps, was a necessary prerequisite. A telephone call from Jack Hickerson, Assistant Secretary of State, to Secretary General Trygve Lie transmitted the Washington conclusions and initiated the preparation for the second phase of decision. The inevitable next step on Sunday was the demand for a cease-fire and the call for the North Koreans to retire behind the 38th Parallel.

The third major decision came on Tuesday, June 27, when information from the Far East indicated that the invaders had neither held their fire nor begun to withdraw. On the contrary, they were continuing their march southward. The Security Council, in close collaboration with the leaders in Washington, recommended that UN members furnish the assistance needed to repel the attack.

The fourth decision, on June 30, was to decline the offer of the Nationalist Chinese to furnish troops for Korea. The fifth, and in some ways the most momentous, of the whole series of major and minor decisions was the order by President Truman committing ground troops for battle on the same day.

It is, of course, possible to outline various numbers of decisions (Snyder gives nine as of principal significance[13]). These five, however, seem to have been crucial in initiating the train of events which was to reach far into the future. Each of these five, in sequence, extended the scope and increased the weight of responsibility. As they are examined, one is compelled to wonder at which point there came a realization of the extent of the danger. There was not, probably, an early acceptance of the heavy expenditure, the loss of lives, which was to come later. There was no obvious preparation, in the first day or so, for the kind of warfare that was to come. There was no strong statement of the serious threat to the Western position. While opinions may vary as the history is further scrutinized, it seems apparent that the process of clarifying decisions and intentions continued throughout the week and did not reach a definitive stage until late on Friday, the 30th. There was, until that time, little appreciation of the extent to which we were committed.

This progress in meeting the strong and growing challenge to our national security required that the consultation and action be confined to a very few individuals. As is the case in dealing with most emergencies, the alternatives are few, and the persons considering them must be limited to those capable of wielding high-level authority. The narrowing of the field of choice makes inevitable the effective use of authority at this crucial stage. Plans must be unhesitating and increasingly conclusive in their meaning and in their guidance to all those who must follow the pattern.

The earliest "value decision"[14] was to the effect that the threat was serious and that extraordinary action would be required. Thus, as announced on Tuesday, June 27, "Initial measures taken by the United States in the Korean crisis" included the orders to United States sea and air forces to "give the Korean Government troops cover and support." The President had also ordered the Seventh Fleet to deploy to the north to "prevent any attack on Formosa." U.S. forces were to be strengthened in the Philippines. Moreover, Truman had directed "acceleration in the furnishing of military assistance to the forces of France and the Associated States in Indochina" and the dispatch of a military mission there. The extension of our concern over an enormous geographic area was thus made clear. The proposed involvement of U.S. troops in Korea was not clear until Friday. Only then was it quite obvious that our men would be involved in battle of a serious and continuing nature.

A New Role for the U.S. in Foreign Affairs. The world was shocked by the North Korean invasion of the South. Many nations seemed to be surprised at the prompt reaction in the United States and impressed by the Security Council and the General Assembly consensus. There had not been much publicity about the boycott of the Security Council by the Soviets; thus there was some puzzlement over the communist position in the UN and why they had failed to be present in the Council meeting. Perhaps instructions from Moscow were delayed. Those who were remote from foreign policy problems assumed the trouble in the Far East was local. Those close to the government looked, appalled, on the prospect of World War III.

Later, the controversial issues and the tragic course of the war brought sharp differences of opinion as to the policy of the government and the conduct of the campaign in Korea. These views on our strategy, pro and con, varied as conditions changed and overshadowed the appraisals and attitudes of the first few weeks. In general, it was evident to many responsible people that the United States should use the forces at its disposal. They had little idea of how insufficient they were or how great was the threat of their nearly complete destruction as the North Koreans swept down over the mountains and plains, capturing villages and cities in their drive to crush resistance. The first news at the end of June was inevitably confused. The interpretation of earlier observations and of intelligence reports had given little warning or guidance to understanding events after they had occurred.

As new action took shape, there were no signs of objection on the part of the public. Congress, at first inclined to criticize the way the Administration had crystallized its position, reduced its debate to a "growl" as the seriousness of conditions was revealed. The public responded affirmatively to the government's decisive action. The necessity to build up the Army and to accumulate stockpiles in the United States was quickly recognized. But only gradually did people generally become aware of the added burdens of U.S. engagement in the Far East. The fact that we had taken on burdens in the Far East in addition to those under the Truman Doctrine, the Marshall Plan, NATO, and the OAS and would be faced in South Asia with growing threats that could not be ignored—these were matters which the nation was not eager to face. The war, undeclared but costly and frustrating, in any case became real in a matter of days.

The press recognized the pattern of aggression. The New York *Herald Tribune* said that "if force were met only by words," as in the Hitler time, there would be bolder and bigger attacks. The Atlanta *Constitution* said: "If we don't resist here, we might as well write off the rest of Asia as well." The Denver *Post* wrote: "If the United States does not respond, the United Nations is doomed." The Portland *Oregonian* commented: "The U.S. has guaranteed the sovereignty of the republic; we have no choice but to fulfill our guarantee." The New York *Times* reported on June 27 that President Rhee had termed U.S. aid "too little and too late" and it said in a headline that "WAR SPURS SENATE ACTION," as the upper house accelerated the pace on passage of the arms aid bill ($1,222,500). There also were reports that the intelligence authorities had said the war was no surprise. The *Times* made reference to an *Izvestia* article under the headline, "NORTH KOREAN PLAN BARED 17 DAYS AGO." The Chicago *Tribune* asserted that Truman needed the war for political purposes and that he should not be given authority without consultation. On the whole, however, the American public showed a will to back the quick and decisive action of their President.

A few journalists were optimistic, thinking the United States could handle the affair without too much difficulty if Russia did not come in. But awareness of the sad state of preparedness came as a shock to many. Though changes were rapidly initiated, lost time could not be recaptured. It was at this time that the then Senator Lyndon B. Johnson, a "freshman" in the Senate after having been the head of the Naval Affairs Subcommittee during the House investigation of World War II, became active on the Preparedness Committee. He said: "Our big job is to get the defense effort away from the hardening of the arteries of imagination and ingenuity." There was much to be done, and it took many months to overcome the lag which had developed and to rebuild our armed forces. A closer relation between the executive and the legislative branches was required (see page 231).

Leland M. Goodrich gives several reasons for the uncertainty and weakness at the time, pointing out that our weakness was particularly unfortunate because "there was little in the record of the United Nations up to this time to indicate that its support would be effective."[15] The dependence on the United States became clear in view of the uncertainty as to the effectiveness of UN action. Another miscalculation by the U.S. is laid to the fact that there was no solid warning of the kind that had been impressive in the case of the Berlin blockade; there had been no statement that the nation "would not stand idly by in case of attack." This Goodrich terms a serious lack.[16] He also criticizes the Defense Department and the State Department for their failure to reconcile objectives; one, he says, was concerned mainly with the disposition of limited forces, and the other, State, with the fending off of communist control in Korea. The implication is that the necessity to use the armed forces was not recognized at the outset of the crisis.

Win or "No-Win." The weary years of fighting and the cost of the conflict must not be forgotten in considering the significance of the early decisions. The brilliant landing in September at Inchon, where the tide was high enough to beach the boats for only three hours, was the first major step in winning back the territory of the southern area originally under the control of the ROK. Then the entrance into the war of the Communist Chinese in November, after a preliminary skirmish on October 26, increased the risks and accentuated the fear that the world was faced with a global war that would lead to unimaginable horrors.

When General MacArthur then demanded an extension of the war, with Chinese troops already crossing the 38th Parallel, the most controversial element of the hostilities came to the forefront. MacArthur had concluded that if he were permitted to bomb the northern installations in Manchuria and elsewhere, he could win, and that otherwise there could be no victory. His troops had been pushed back in brutal fighting at the end of the year. Armies had been threatened with annihilation. The men were cut down on the high ridges, and in the barren valleys they were swept by snow and wind. The retreat started in November was not halted until January.

It was at this time that MacArthur wrote his famous letter to Representative Joseph Martin. The General's campaign for a loosening of restraints on his action had begun. On March 24, 1951, he issued a long statement indicating that he stood ready to "find any military means whereby the political objectives of the United Nations might be accomplished." MacArthur said the Chinese must be aware that if the United Nations abandoned its tolerant efforts to contain the war and we expanded our military efforts, Red China would be doomed to the risk of imminent military collapse. The State Department interpreted this pronouncement as presenting Red China with an ultimatum she must reject. On April 5, a communication from MacArthur in answer to a sharp order of March 20 from Truman indicated that disagreement had shifted to open challenge. There was a serious issue both as to the conduct of the war and the supreme authority of the President over the military. The question of supreme civilian authority was resolved on April 11, when Truman relieved MacArthur of his position and substituted Lieutenant General Matthew Ridgway.

The first question was not so easily resolved. There is still continued argument over limited war. A new concept, it frustrates the instincts and seems to deny the ultimate value, the goal of victory for which sacrifices usually are made. From the Caribbean to the jungles of Southeast Asia, the new type of warfare—new in that it is a conscious policy—is disheartening and unsatisfactory. The phrase "It's the war we can't win, we can't lose, we can't quit" was said to be the bitter refrain of the soldiers during the second retreat from Seoul. There was to be a victory of sorts, but no glorious triumph of right over wrong, of democracy over communism, of the United Nations over the forces of aggression. The nuclear potential and the masses of Chinese under the command of the dictators seemed to leaders on both sides to present too great a threat to risk full-scale war. As Robert Leckie has said, "Of Korea, then, it is enough to say: It was here that Communism suffered its first defeat. That was the only victory possible."[17]

The truce, when it became a lasting armistice, was won in 1953 by a word from Dulles to Nehru in New Delhi, by the release of Chiang Kai-shek from the restraining influence of the Seventh Fleet, and by the impression disseminated that nuclear weapons would be used against installations deep in communist territory. Which part of the three-pronged maneuver was most influential, it is not possible to say. Because of the attitude of the new Administration, which was able to shake off the myths and the assumptions that had gathered, rightly or wrongly, around the former leaders, the war was effectively stopped and the fighting men came home. Three years of struggle, bloodshed, and controversy won for an anxious world new concepts and showed the enemy that the strength of moral resistance could be fortified by military preparations and valor on the battlefield.

The Results of the Korean Challenge and Its Answer. All the later shifts and changes, difficulties and sacrifice, cannot dim the importance of the last days of June 1950. Here men of courage, recognizing terrible risks, knew that they would have to assume the burden of war. While the confusion of the first days, as the decision to fight was taken, now seems to be outlined in stark realism, closer examination shows the strengths as well as the weaknesses of the first hours.

The meaning of acting through the United Nations is paramount. It showed our determination, if in any way possible, to act correctly and to establish a system of international behavior in repelling aggression. The fact that successive instances have shown that the UN lacks some of the power and the capacity to accomplish this central objective, had to be discovered by experience. Nevertheless, the world is the richer for having tested the capabilities and the limitations of the new organization.

Moreover, the existence of the United Nations had been threatened, and its survival was now, for more than a decade or two, assured. This was the main result of the decisions that summer night in Washington. The United Nations was charged with the political rehabilitation of Korea. The Commission was reporting to the UN in New York. It is clear that the intervention of the United States did not necessarily have to be done through the UN but could have been carried out independently; judging by the votes, however, it is certain that the UN would have taken some stand in the matter and presumably would have associated itself with the United States. In fact, the Security Council would have met shortly after the attack, in any case, on receiving in New York the direct report of the aggression. This came at almost the same time as the request from Washington. The action of the Security Council was both more rapid and more clearly defined because of the leadership from the United States. The course chosen appears now to have been a life-or-death choice for the organization. It was still the hope of many nations that the institution created in 1945 could be the instrument for international solution of major disputes with the avoidance of armed conflict. Though this hope was not specifically realized, the UN was nevertheless saved in 1950.

The decision within the first few days—by some of the advisers within the first few hours—that Korea was important was a crucial choice among possible policies for the United States. Even though the peninsula had been declared "not within the recently defined defense perimeter in the Far East"[18] and thus a "soft spot" where the communists were given the impression the United States would not intervene, the challenge was recognized. Soviet probing at this point would, with near certainty, be followed by strikes elsewhere if it were not quickly frustrated. Moreover, the next act of aggression might find the Western powers in a less defensible position. At least in this area the Seventh Fleet was nearby, and there were occupation troops in Japan. This "value" decision was therefore of the utmost importance.

The extent to which this nation was unprepared for military action and the failure to interpret the intelligence reports which hinted, if they did not prove, the likelihood of serious attack, are best judged by the lines on the map showing the depth of penetration of the North Koreans. By September, 1950, the South Koreans and the United Nations forces held only a small circle of territory surrounding the port of Pusan; the land area was perhaps one-eighth of the peninsula south of the Parallel. The retreat had been swift and disastrous. There was serious question as to whether the troops could hold at this last position.

There had been no "integrated master plan." Our military strength was at a pitifully low level. Our commitments elsewhere were considerable. The strategic importance of Korea was slight, *if viewed apart from the political considerations* in the Far East.[19] There was no firm theory as to the extent of the Soviet commitment in this area, although their interest and their directing hand were recognized. Reitzel refers to the considerable segments of Congressional opinion that had advocated, months earlier, a stronger policy against Red China and in defense of our friends in the Far East.[20] The executive decision for a restrained "long-pull" effort and the avoidance of too wide an area of engagement influenced the planners. This was the conclusive reason for the failure to prepare for what later developed as a major threat. The newly created Policy Planning Staff, National Security Council, and Central Intelligence Agency did not seem to have been concerned with the possibility of aggression in Korea. They judged the harassments on the line of demarcation to be incidents of minor importance. Europe and NATO were the major preoccupation. The economic aid which the United States was extending to the ROK army was not taken seriously as a sign that we would become heavily engaged. The real danger, when we had to face it, however, had come from a grave miscalculation on the part of the communists. They apparently were convinced that we would not respond by means of force.

The basic decision of June 25 with regard to the importance of the issue was followed by the series of subsequent determinations already described. They came informally as the situation developed, as the range of possibilities narrowed, alternatives became fewer, and the need to accept large risks loomed as inescapable. The stakes included not only the United Nations' prestige and influence, but also the confidence in us and cooperation with us of small nations everywhere. The weakness of the United States in its military capabilities, while not to be disguised, could not be allowed to control our leadership and the free world's reaction to aggression; the time needed to build our strength was costly, but it was the price we were willing to pay. The policy of the United States was bent toward discouraging aggression, to forcing negotiation on reasonable terms.

In the long conflict that ended with the armistice on July 27, 1953, the United Nations had stood up to the attack, the United States, along with its partners, had paid the heavy cost of battle, the civilians had taken control over the military, and the principles of collective security had won a temporary victory. The whole network of alliances came after the end of the fighting in Korea, after the Japanese Peace Treaty of 1951, and the recognition in the United States that our security is inevitably tied with that of remote areas—in the Far East, in the Middle East, and in Africa, as well as in Europe.

In the history of United States foreign policy, Korea represented a strengthening of purpose and a proof of fortitude. The test was met. The line was held.

THE CHALLENGE OF GUATEMALA: 1954

On June 18, 1954, Danny, coming home as usual on the 12:30 school bus, burst into the Embassy residence gasping, "There's no school this afternoon because there is going to be a revolution at 5:00." As I mulled over this announcement, he dashed to the telephone to broadcast the news to his classmates. Danny's inside information had come from the older pupils on the school bus, a source I respect, because often the teen-agers are more accurately informed than their parents.

A few minutes later, Jack came home and confirmed the children's report. This was H-hour and the armies of Castillo Armas had launched the attack against the Arbenz Government. Even then the rebel forces were advancing within the borders of Guatemala.[21]

This is an excerpt from the description written by Mrs. John E. Peurifoy of the events in which the United States took a stand against communist infiltration of this hemisphere and in which her husband, the United States Ambassador to Guatemala, played a courageous and highly intelligent role.

In this picturesque, mountainous country in Central America, the United States was confronted with one of the outstanding policy dilemmas of recent decades. Not until 1961, when Cuba became a target of Soviet aims, was there a comparable crisis in this area.

Little that is definite is known about the early measures taken to aid Armas. "Revelations" have described "CIA's Banana Revolt."[22] The hand of the United States has been seen in various phases of the overthrow of the communist regime.[23] It is doubtful whether the outsider will ever know the full story, but the broad outlines have been fairly well filled in.

Our awareness of the threat to our national interests had led us to give a high priority to the expulsion of communism from this hemisphere. Important aspects of this new policy are on the record; they merit analysis. Our actions were varied and taken through several channels. Our underlying principles, reflected in the Monroe Doctrine, were amplified by a number of acts in the Organization of American States. They had been challenged by international communism. In response to the events of May, 1954, and earlier, we recognized a moment of opportunity and, facing genuine risks, supported the revolt of Colonel Carlos Castillo Armas and the overthrow of the communist-controlled President Arbenz. The days in June were not only dramatic, but important in our world position and in the resistance to Soviet aims.

Ten Years of Increasing Communist Intervention. The information at the disposal of the authorities in Washington during the months and years before the crisis was meaningful and conclusive. It went back for more than 10 years. Ever since it achieved independence as a nation in 1839, Guatemala has been susceptible to dictatorship and has suffered from serious political and economic problems. In the decade beginning in 1944, there were revolutionary efforts to achieve a different style of government. With this change came a new menace originating in communist ambitions, as Moscow saw opportunities in the new situation. The perennial hope of a foothold in the Western hemisphere led the Kremlin to efforts to infiltrate and to subvert.

The change that occurred in 1944 was the overthrow on July 2 of the last of the military dictators.[24] General Jorge Ubico, who had seized power in 1931 and ruled as a feudal chief, was thrown out when his front man, Federico Ponce Vaides, was ejected in an uprising of workers, students, and young officers. This was the critical turning point known as the "October Revolution." The lack of experience and vague idealism of the young revolutionists opened the way to communist influence, which was skillfully exploited by Moscow, as Ubico's policy was rejected.

The man who briefly was President in 1951, Dr. Juan José Arevalo, professed a philosophy which he called "spiritual socialism"; this was, in fact, close to communism in its tendencies.[25] Although he did not come to power with any significant help from the international communists, they began to secure positions of influence, with notable gains in the labor movement and in the press, in spite of his anticommunist statements—and the slow subversion of the country began.

Meanwhile, a communist-oriented party, the *Vanguardia Democratia*, led by Manuel Fortuny, at its first party congress in 1949 had adopted the name *Partido Communista de Guatemala*, but decided to remain underground. It is not clear, now, whether or not our "intelligence" noted the formation of the *Vanguardia Democratia* in 1947 or followed closely the rise in influence of Manuel Fortuny in what was to be the *Partido Communista de Guatemala* after September, 1949. In June, 1950, the periodical *Octobre* was founded by Fortuny, with the hammer and sickle as its emblems. Its aim was to support the peasants and workers through communist action. At about the same time, the *Partido Communista de Guatemala* came out of cover and adopted an openly communist line. It held its first public meeting in July, 1951. Meanwhile the Cominform, meeting in Bucharest, had recognized the Guatemala communists.

Explosive events had led to the rejection of President Arevalo and the election of Jacobo Arbenz Guzmán as President and his inauguration on March 15, 1951. The revolt, which is seen by a number of observers as a turning point, was set off by the murder of Francisco Javier Arana, popular chief of the armed forces; but it ended when Arbenz, definitely implicated in the attack, in which his wife's chauffeur was identified as the assailant, took over the government.[26] His lack of general popular support has been noted as the reason for his turn to the communists, and his debts to the leftist band of supporters who surrounded him were evidence of his vulnerability. The movement of the government toward the left, which from this time on became conspicuous, was increasingly characterized by terroristic methods.

Fortuny and a number of others who were interested in the *Partido Revolucionario Obero de Guatemala* (PROG), now openly communist, had backed Arbenz and were instrumental in putting him into power. The links with the Soviet leaders became clear in the trips of the Guatemalans to Europe and in published statements in Europe supporting the communist effort in the early 1950s. In 1953, a training school for communist cadres was established. While the positions of the leading parties shifted, it became known that four of the leaders who were communists and four fellow travelers were meeting regularly with President Arbenz. On April 4, 1954, Guatemala withdrew from the Organization of American States, when it became clear that the agenda of the coming June meeting would include consideration of "resisting the subversive action of international communism." The leftist organizations openly opposed the United Nations police action in Korea.

Thus, the movement of key persons and organizations to the left appeared to menace the freedom and opinions of the majority. Violence increased, and arrests and illegal seizures were followed by other acts of intimidation. The Agrarian Reform Law of 1952 led to considerable violence. Although the constitutionality of the law was questioned in the courts, Congress, acting virtually as a rubber stamp of the President, eliminated those on the Supreme Court who opposed the President and his supporters, so the measure and its application went unchallenged. Expropriation under this law directly affected the United Fruit Company, with its large land holdings. Ignoring the protests of the State Department, the Guatemalan government had by 1954 taken over more than 400,000 acres, with only nominal compensation.

Apparent indifference to these developments in the United States and elsewhere, which has been noted by many commentators, now appears surprising, in view of the fact that the communist methods of subversion bore considerable resemblance to their early efforts in Berlin, Czechoslovakia, and other areas. They could scarcely go completely unnoticed, in view of the direct interests of American business. Nevertheless, the articles by Will Lissner in the New York *Times* during June, 1950, attracted little attention. The first notable public statement was made on October 14, 1953, when Assistant Secretary of State John M. Cabot charged that "Guatemala is openly playing the Communist game."[27] This marked the beginning of active concern on the part of the United States government. Thus it was "in backward Guatemala that the Eisenhower administration first grappled with communism in the New World."[28]

Now, with the perspective of time, the steady progress of Soviet infiltration and subversion in Guatemala is clearly evident. Indeed, most of the key events could have been appreciated much earlier than they were. The fact that there was so little evidence of anxiety in Washington was attributable, in part, to the intense preoccupation with problems elsewhere—the needs of Europe, the disillusionment over Soviet behavior in Germany and Austria, the difficulties of the United Kingdom, the Truman Doctrine, the Marshall Plan, and the revolution in China. The attention to the Japanese peace treaty and the outbreak of war in Korea and a number of other problems of great urgency laid heavy burdens on a nation that had recently been isolationist and only in the years after World War II was assuming world-wide responsibilities. The developments in the years which were most important for Guatemala were of the utmost significance elsewhere. Nevertheless, there was a growing concern for Latin America—shown by the fact that President Eisenhower sent his brother Milton on a tour of several South American countries in June, 1953. He felt that the Good Neighbor Policy and the Monroe Doctrine needed to be re-examined in the light of current conditions.

In a retrospective account of the situation on June 30, 1954, Secretary Dulles told a national radio and television audience:

> For several years, international communism has been probing for a nesting place in the Americas. It finally chose Guatemala as a spot which it could turn into an official base from which to breed subversion, which would extend to other American republics. This intrusion of Soviet despotism was, of course, a direct challenge to our Monroe Doctrine, the first and most fundamental of our foreign policies.

He went on to comment on the Soviet techniques:

> In Guatemala, international communism had an initial success. It began ten years ago, when a revolution occurred in Guatemala. The revolution was not without justification. But the Communists seized on it, not as an opportunity for real reforms, but as a chance to gain political power.[29]

He outlined some of the steps taken:

1. Communist agitators infiltrated public and private organizations.
2. Recruits were sent to Russia and other communist countries for revolutionary training.
3. The trained recruits organized the peasants and workers under communist leadership.
4. Having gained control of mass organizations, they then moved to take over the official press and radio.
5. They dominated the social security system and the agrarian reform organization.
6. Through the technique of the "popular front," they dictated to Congress and the President.
7. They caused the Supreme Court to dissolve, by using the legislature, when it refused to sanction communist-contrived laws.
8. These steps were followed by the suppression of constitutional rights, mass arrests, brutal tactics. and the killing of opposition leaders.

When affairs had reached this pass, there was little hope of a peaceful solution. This pattern of Soviet tactics had succeeded in other countries. Could they be thwarted in this case?

It was not until the press coverage of early June, 1954, began to show the excesses of the Arbenz regime that attention was attracted to the growing crisis. People in the United States, preoccupied with urgent problems in Europe and the losses of men in the Korean war, had, except in a few circles, taken little notice of the deteriorating condition in Central America. There was no wide knowledge of the oppression under the Arbenz regime. Small notice was taken of the Soviet program of infiltration, through labor, agriculture, and political subversion. The public was little concerned either in the planning in 1953 or in the swift movement of events in 1954. One can guess that policy-makers in the Kremlin and also in Peking were watching events with intense interest. The effort to win a base for operations in the Western Hemisphere would not go unnoticed in the Cominform.

In this case (as in others, such as the Dominican action in 1965), the capabilities of the United States were limited. Action that would offend the other members of the Organization of American States, sensitive to the prosperity and power of the "Giant to the North," had to be avoided. Any intervention that might be construed as aggression was not consistent with principles strongly held and sanctioned by the United Nations. Any plan that was likely to fail would open the door to more extensive communist attempts to establish beachheads in the Western Hemisphere. Political considerations had to override economic and military ones. Overt and covert programs had to be skillfully coordinated.

The question that had to be faced in Washington, as the flow of information made it glaringly apparent that the Soviets were developing a base for later action in other Latin American countries, was when, how, and with what methods to act. There were, in this case, as in other instances, various possible courses of action. In 1954, the policy of postponement, sometimes justified, would have meant missing the promising opportunity offered by the rebellion of the dissatisfied citizens who wished to see communism ousted. The courageous but almost desperate efforts of Colonel Castillo Armas and two or three hundred fugitives, in exile in Honduras, were crucial to the execution of the United States' plan to maintain the principles of the Monroe Doctrine. The march of events in 1953 and 1954 quickly narrowed the choices and left the United States with the option of either granting support to Castillo or watching his bold attempt fail in the clash with an entrenched minority under the harsh dictatorship of the communist leader Arbenz.

Growing Apprehension. By the middle of 1953, the United States was alert to the situation and had arrived at the conclusion that the vital interests of the nation and the fundamental principles of our foreign policy were menaced and that action must be taken to prevent a base for international communism. These decisions were basic to all subsequent preparation.

At the year's end the options were: (a) to watch and wait; (b) to put psychological pressure on the communist-oriented government; (c) to act internationally through the Organization of American States and possibly through the United Nations; (d) to give limited support to those who were acting to weaken the communists in Guatemala; (e) to act directly and with force to overthrow the dictatorship. Since almost any action would come under the scrutiny of world opinion, quick to examine motives and criticize methods, the question of intensity and timing was doubly important.

In the six months immediately preceding the June crisis, the United States endeavored to gain its objectives through persuasion and international pressure. The first act pointing in this direction was to transfer John E. Peurifoy from Athens to Guatemala. This assignment was significant not only because of the personality and ability of the new Ambassador, but also because in Greece he had been dealing with problems akin to those he would face in Guatemala —communist infiltration, subversion, and civil strife.

He took a decisive stand from the outset. Arriving in November, 1953, almost at once he made a statement calling on nationalists and patriots to stop playing the communist game. On December 18, Peurifoy spent six hours with President Arbenz, trying to persuade him of the dangers of his course. The results were discouraging. *Time* magazine paraphrased his report on the result of his first week's experience with Arbenz: "Maybe this man doesn't actually think of himself as a communist, but he'll sure do until one comes along!"[30] Peurifoy was called home for consultation in January, and there was general agreement during the consultations that the threat was increasing.

Meanwhile, preparations were being made for the tenth meeting of the Organization of American States, to be held in Caracas from March 1 to 28, 1954. The groundwork for the meeting in Venezuela had been carefully prepared in the days preceding it. Earlier foundations had been laid at the fourth meeting of the Consultation of Ministers of Foreign Affairs of the American States in March and April, 1951. The ministers had declared their intention to adopt measures necessary to eradicate international communism as a force within their territories. They had referred to the resolution of the first meeting of the OAS at Bogotá in 1948, and they resolved to take action to end subversion.

The Caracas Resolution that emerged from the OAS meeting of 1954 was considered to be a notable step forward in the achievement of unity and in the multilateralization of the Monroe Doctrine. It declared that:

> . . . the domination or control of the political institutions of any American State by the international communist movement, extending to this Hemisphere the political system of an extracontinental power, constitute a threat to the sovereignty and political independence of the American States, endangering the peace of America, and would call for a meeting of consultation to consider the adoption of appropriate action in accordance with existing treaties.[31]

It also recommended some immediate steps to counteract subversive activities. Communist-oriented Guatemala voted against the resolution. Argentina and Mexico abstained, but the other states stood solidly behind the statement of the dangers and the affirmation of their foreign policy in opposition to alien influences. The United States' leadership had succeeded in developing the legal basis for the struggle which it knew was coming and in which it was determined to play a decisive role.

By March, 1954, the choices of action which have been noted had been narrowed to two. It was no longer necessary to search for clues as to what was happening; the story was plain for all who were concerned. Efforts to try and influence the Arbenz government had been futile. The feasibility of acting directly to overthrow the government by force was seriously questioned and had no substantial support in Washington.

Preparations for multilateral action were being carried forward in an active way, in Washington, in the OAS, in New York at the United Nations, and elsewhere. Measures were already being taken by the CIA to give limited and discreet support to those Guatemalan nationals anxious to overthrow the communist regime in their capital city. Thus the scene was prepared for the United States to stand behind the popular movement that was to come.

If we look at the sequence of events and actions, we can test them against the outline of requirements for decision-makers and find that there was an increasing improvement in preparation leading to the second, and perhaps crucial, decision in June. In this case, as in most other instances, there had been earlier decisions that were important. In a sense, the evaluation itself is actually a choice of major significance.

First, the reports, official and unofficial, as to the political, social, military, economic, and psychological conditions in Guatemala were adequate. They had not, at first, been interpreted with a view to their wider significance; indeed, they had not, at first, been appreciated, but by 1953 they were receiving considerable attention. There was by the end of 1953 a new alertness that meant that any specific item of information or event was likely to be put in its proper perspective.

Second, in 1953 there was an evaluation of the situation that brought a firm conviction that communism in Guatemala must not be tolerated and that strenuous efforts to prevent outside intervention must be made by all feasible means.

Third, various policy explorations, position papers, and contingency plans were in the works—some were related to the Caracas Conference, some to the continuing work of the OAS, some to the stopping of suspicious vessels on the high seas, some to the CIA activities, and some to consultations with Congressional leaders and others.

Fourth, there was a careful and, for the most part, secret appraisal of practical possibilities in the situation existing and expected to exist in the coming weeks. Thus the preparations began to come into focus with a view to timing and prompt action in a probable emergency.

There has been a natural desire to know the full details of the planning and assistance granted to the Guatemalans in Honduras and elsewhere. Full details have not been made known and will not be—at least in the foreseeable future. Officials say that in the conduct of foreign policy, there is no useful purpose served by exposing all the methods and the instruments used. The principle of "need to know" governs in this as in many other cases.

The Chips Are Down: May, 1954. In the spring of 1954, the Supreme Court ruled segregation unconstitutional. American diplomats were exerting their efforts in Europe to further the plans for the European Defense Community. They were engaged in the deliberations of the Geneva Conference to end hostilities in Indochina and they were concerned with the aftermath of the Korean armistice. Nasser had become Premier in Egypt on April 18. Dienbienphu had fallen on May 7. Halfway around the world, Ambassador Peurifoy, recently returned from consultation in Washington, was guiding American policy to aid the refugees under Colonel Castillo Armas in Nicaragua and Honduras. Information with regard to military aid to President Arbenz from European communists had reached our officials; it was clear conditions were moving toward a climax.

It was no surprise, therefore, when it was learned that a shipment of arms from the East German port of Stettin had been unloaded at Puerto Barrios in Guatemala on May 15. The official announcement on May 17 described the event as a "development of gravity." Only a few were following these communist activities with understanding, but the spotlight of public opinion was to be turned on Central America in the last part of May and in June as the United

States faced the threat to its vital interests in the Western Hemisphere.

The preparations of the previous months would have been of little consequence if the leaders in the United States had not decided promptly to accept the risks of action. They saw in the first shipload the beginning of a serious threat. Two thousand tons of rifles, pistols, artillery, ammunition, and light military pieces, manufactured in the Skoda arms factory in Czechoslovakia, had come by a circuitous route and under false papers to the shores of the Caribbean. On May 24, President Eisenhower informed Congressional leaders of measures that were planned.[32]

The later phases of our action were directed squarely to this challenge. They were many-pronged and effective. They can be traced through the actions of our intelligence agencies, our diplomatic consultations and work for unity, and in our military support, of limited nature but timely and encouraging, to the Armas rebels. Both the United Nations and the Organization of American States became active. The outcome demonstrated practical gains for the Americans from their diplomatic maneuvers and the stand they took in the UN.

Meanwhile, Colonel Castillo Armas had been accelerating his CIA-supported training of exiles who planned to overthrow the Arbenz regime. Foreign Minister Toriello, placing emphasis on the interests of the United Fruit Company in Guatemala, sought to persuade the American Ambassador that difficulties could be adjusted; he requested the scheduling of a conference. On May 25, however, Secretary Dulles stated in a news conference that evidence was being accumulated to indicate the justification of invoking the 1947 Rio Defense Pact consultative clauses. He said:

> The important question is whether Guatemala is subject to Communist colonialism, which has already subjected 800 million people to its despotic rule. The extension of Communist colonialism to this hemisphere would, in the words of the Caracas Resolution, endanger the peace of America.[33]

Three facts were cited: Guatemala was the only American state that had not ratified the Rio Pact, the only one to vote against the Caracas Resolution, and the only one to receive massive shipments of arms from behind the Iron Curtain.

From this time on, for several weeks, there were almost daily front-page reports on Guatemalan conditions in the New York *Times*, including frequent quotations from government pronouncements. The world was put on notice that a tense and menacing situation was developing. In Guatemala, there were charges of a plot to kill President Arbenz, and five men fled for their lives to Embassy haven.[34] There were continuous arrests as the drive against the opposition increased. The case was up for consideration at another meeting of the Organization of American States, scheduled for later in June.

The responses of the United States were varied. We announced that we would take measures to prevent communist arms from reaching Guatemala. Military pacts with Honduras and Nicaragua were immediately negotiated, and the flow of arms to both countries was started. The United States' Military Mission in Honduras announced a training program for a new 800-man battalion, and the U. S. Navy patrolled the Caribbean.

"A Small Amount of Support."[35]   After the reported plot on the life of President Arbenz, the drive against the rebellious majority became so intense that a significant number of officers fled the country. On June 9, the New York *Times* reported the suspension of civil liberties. It also disclosed American plans for "airing the Guatemalan case." Dulles was said to favor a hemisphere meeting but to be seeking the views of the other republics on the matter. In speaking of the issues in a news conference on June 8, he said:

> If the United Fruit matter were settled, if they gave a gold piece for every banana, the problem would remain just as it is today as far as the presence of Communist infiltration in Guatemala is concerned. That is the problem, not the United Fruit Company . . . a number of other states which are seriously threatened or would be seriously threatened if Communism, in the words of the Caracas Resolution, gets control of the political machinery of any American State.[36]

He spoke later (June 28) of the protest of the Guatemalan people against being used by a communist dictatorship and the response of "mass arrests, the suppression of constitutional guarantees, the killing of opposition leaders, and other brutal tactics normally employed by Communism to secure the consolidation of its power."[37] Speaking on June 10 in Seattle, he indicated his reliance on the OAS to help ward off communism.[38]

On June 14, the U. S. High Commissioner in Germany announced that six tons of Swiss antiaircraft ammunition destined for Guatemala had been held up in Hamburg at his request.[39] Quarantine measures were in force to halt the flow of arms, but it was recognized that action on the high seas would require at least tacit cooperation of our allies.[40] Anthony Eden issued a statement on June 18 that said, in part, "There is no general power of search on the high seas in peacetime. The British government, however, has certain powers under defense regulations and otherwise to detain or requisition under certain circumstances."[41] He indicated that the Commander-in-Chief in the West Indies would take appropriate action.

There were at this time "serious uprisings," according to reports in the New York *Times*.[42] On June 20, Ambassador Henry Cabot Lodge, at the United Nations, recommended OAS action. It was held that the situation did not suggest aggression, but a revolt of Guatemalans against Guatemalans.[43] Since it was becoming increasingly plain that the situation in Guatemala was a civil and not an international war, it was not appropriate for the Security Council to intervene.[44]

On June 18, attacks were launched by Castillo against the port of San José and other strongholds. The long-awaited civil war had begun.[45] By this time, the OAS had agreed to a meeting in a nearly unanimous decision that was described as "a triumph of U.S. diplomacy."[46] It was tentatively scheduled for the first week in July.

But Colonel Castillo Armas could not wait. In a battered station wagon he led his small group of followers down the road, to be joined just across the national border by some 1500 sympathizers. His planes had dropped bombs on the capital city. The rebels were driving forward in Guatemala. Hundreds joined the ranks. (This was his second attempt to overthrow the dictatorship. The first, in 1949, had failed.) President Arbenz protested to the United Nations Security Council.

An emergency meeting of the Council was called for Sunday, the 20th. A resolution by Brazil, Colombia, and France proposed the referral of the question to the Inter-American Peace Committee of the Organization of American States. Ten of the 11 nations voted for it, but it was vetoed by the Russians. In spite of this expression of views, the Arbenz regime again sought United Nations support, withdrawing its request for OAS intervention. Thus, reliance was placed on Soviet good offices. The headlines in the New York *Times* on June 21 were: "UN VOTES CEASE-FIRE—SOVIET VETOES HEMI-SPHERE ACTION; U.S. WARNS RUSSIA TO KEEP HANDS OFF." The editorial that day said that most of the states would accept a modern exten-sion of the Monroe Doctrine and consider it " 'dangerous to their peace and safety' that Russian imperialism, in any guise, should gain a foothold in this hemisphere." On the 23rd, under the heading "Shadow and Substance," the *Times* said editorially, "we cannot use unilateral action, but we must use our leadership" and pointed to the need for U.S. help. Lyndon B. Johnson, Democratic leader, told Congress on the 23rd that "the Reds seek a hemisphere beach-head."

The fact that there appeared to be diplomatic support and a degree of United States help, combined with evidence that the bombings were shaking the foundations of the Arbenz regime, had led Castillo Armas to speed up his plans. Even those who favored his action were surprised by the speed with which he gathered ad-ditional recruits and progressed toward the capital.[47] The unfolding of events, as the British Minister reported to his government, proved that the movement was a popular one. The moment of danger, how-ever, came a few days after he started his march. Two of his air-planes were shot down, and the lack of air support meant that the whole enterprise was threatened with failure.

It was on June 22, according to President Eisenhower's account of the affair, that he was told by his advisers of the critical need for the United States' help. In the course of the deliberations in Wash-ington, he was particularly anxious to know what the probabilities of success were estimated to be. There was controversy as to whether or not it would be wise for the U.S. to become further involved in this unusual operation. Now was the moment for the United States to determine the extent of its commitment and the nature of the risks that it would assume.

"What do you think Castillo's chances would be," I asked Allen Dulles, "without the aircraft?" His answer was unequivocal: "About zero!" "Suppose we supply the aircraft? What would the chances be then?" Again, the CIA chief did not hesitate: "About twenty per-cent." I considered the matter carefully. I realized full well that the United States' intervention in Central America and Caribbean affairs earlier in the century had greatly injured our standing in Latin America. On the other hand, it seemed to me that to refuse to cooperate in providing indirect support to a strictly anti-Communist faction in this struggle would be contrary to the letter and spirit of the Caracas resolution. I had faith in the strength of the inter-American resolve therein set forth. On the actual value of a shipment of planes, I knew from experience the important psychological impact of even a small amount of support. In any event, our proper course of action—indeed my duty—was clear to me. We would replace the airplanes.

The air support . . . gave the regular armed forces an excuse to take action in their own hands to throw out Arbenz. The rest of Latin America was not in the least displeased.[48]

The selection of particular events as critical to the outcome of foreign policy in action is always subject to varying judgments. It is not possible to prove that the decision to send planes was the key element in the situation. It is clear, however, that this choice represented the culmination of American policy toward Guatemala up to that time. It was the act that was judged to be just enough to turn the tide. Such risk-taking and "casting of the die" are the highest type of policy formation. Those who have reviewed the course of events are inclined to agree with the appraisal of President Eisenhower that the decision of June 22 was crucial.

President Arbenz resigned on June 27. The opportunities and dangers at the time of Arbenz' disappearance from the scene would have been entirely different without the decision to use U.S. planes. This had brought quick success to Colonel Castillo Armas' first strike into Guatemala, but it had not assured the definitive take-over of the government.

Time magazine, which gave good coverage to the entire rebel action, referred to the "double-cross" by Arbenz. The President had stepped down in favor of Colonel Carlos Enrique Diaz, one of his close aides. "But Castillo Armas, evidently convinced that Diaz was just a front for Arbenz, continued his war, notably by bombing Guatemala City's Matamoros Fort."[49] The bombing was said to have knocked the fight out of Diaz. Meanwhile, Peurifoy had got in touch with Colonel Monzon, who was known as an outspoken anticommunist.

Mrs. Peurifoy described the events in this momentous week:

June 27, the tenth day of the war, events happened so rapidly that they defy chronicling. First, Toriello, the Foreign Minister, in conference with the American ambassador, offered to resign if his resignation *would bring an end to hostilities. He asked my husband to use American influence and prestige in Guatemala to end the war. My husband replied that, unfortunately, the Arbenz government had used every means to sink Latin American prestige in Guatemala to the lowest ebb. Later in the afternoon, a radio announcement told us that President Arbenz would make a nationwide address at nine o'clock. We hopefully suspected that Arbenz, himself, had mounted the trading block. Just before nine o'clock, Mrs. Parinello, wife of the chief of the armed forces, appeared with her two small children at the back door. Not a word was exchanged, but obviously she had come seeking safety, and obviously, I was going to see that she got it. After all, her little girl, age four, was an American citizen, having been born in Fort Sill, Oklahoma. They had come through the machine-gun fire from the center of the city to the Residence. It was dreadful to see children looking like scared rabbits. So when Arbenz gave his farewell address, Mrs. Parinello was here to translate it for us in her modest English. Even if she had been fluent, she could hardly have repeated to us exactly what the President said, but none of us needed an interpreter to make us understand that the speech was defamatory to the United States. No one could miss his angry references to Norte Americanos and the United Fruit Company. If Arbenz had honestly wanted peace he would never have made that unconciliatory speech. There was no promise of peace, no change of government, but merely a changing of hats. Colonel Diaz inherited the Arbenz mantle. . . .*

Mrs. Peurifoy continued her account:

From then on the events are well known. At 4:00 A.M. my husband was called to witness the formation of a junta, a triumvirate composed of Colonels Diaz, Sanchez, and Monzon. As one of the conditions of peace, they promised to round up the Communists, and they did. The Communists were jailed, but someone failed to lock the back door, and by morning, the two most outstanding Communists had escaped. This policy was not one to soothe the anti-Communist rebels, and their planes continued to pound the fighting front.[50]

She described the rush of refugees seeking asylum in the various embassies. In the Mexican Embassy the guest list consisted of about 500 communists. Two thousand communists are said to have taken refuge, "but not one Communist turned up at the Bolivian Embassy," whose stalwart Ambassador moved to a downtown hotel, taking his country's flag with him, to avoid supporting the communists.

Diaz, fearful not only for his position, but also for his life, again asked the American Ambassador to come to his house in the middle of the night. So, as *Time* reported it, "With a .38 Colt in his shoulder holster, Peurifoy drove through the empty, fear-haunted streets to the armed forces headquarters, where Diaz was staying."[51] Diaz proposed peace talks with Castillo Armas in El Salvador. In the next room, the angry talk of anti-Diaz men could be heard. Peurifoy waited, thoughtfully checking his pistol. Mrs. Peurifoy wrote:

> While my husband was conferring with two members of the junta, Diaz and Sanchez, our Embassy Air Attaché, Colonel Martin, appeared in the door with an important message for the Ambassador. In private the attaché told my husband that Monzon, the third member of the junta, was coming with a group of armed soldiers to force the resignation of the other two members. There was an unhealthy possibility that the American Ambassador would be caught in the cross-fire of the two forces. Hardly had my husband returned to the room, when Diaz and Sanchez announced their resignation. They too had been warned by someone. At that moment the Monzon party invaded the house, and it is more than likely that the unexpected presence of the American Ambassador saved the lives of Colonels Diaz and Sanchez.[52]

The Monzon group thus forced the issue. When Diaz found a gun at his ribs, Monzon was able to announce, "Our colleague decided to resign."[53]

This dramatic incident ended in the formation of a new junta, the fourth government in 36 hours. "At six A.M. a weary American Ambassador went home to sleep fast before the 8:00 call from Washington," Mrs. Peurifoy added.

But his work was not over. The instability of the new arrangement was obvious. The new junta requested the services of the Americans again. Peurifoy had arranged talks between Monzon and Castillo Armas in San Salvador, but the talks appeared likely to break down, and he had to fly to El Salvador to participate. After two days of conversations, Monzon and Castillo flew back to Guatemala City. There a hero's welcome awaited them. Elections were to take place, 15 days later, but it was already clear that in the eyes of the people the "little colonel," Castillo Armas, was the *Libertador*. The journalists said that in looking back it was apparent that the United States' Central Intelligence Agency had correctly appraised the situation:

*Arbenz' fundamental unpopularity and brutality, his army's unwilling-
ness to stand up for him or for his communist advisers, and Castillo
Armas' capabilities . . . Students demonstrated against the United
States in Panama, Uruguay, Chile, Peru, Cuba, Argentina, and Honduras: a U.S. flag was burned in Chile. But in Guatemala itself,
the role of the U.S. was understood and deeply appreciated.*[54]

Mrs. Peurifoy, writing a letter to relatives at home about Castillo
Armas' return, said:

*A more spontaneous and unorganized demonstration of mob ex-
citement I never expect to survive. By order of the Archbishop bells
clanged in every steeple in Guatemala, native flags flew from every
window, shops closed and thousands swarmed to the airport. The
crowd was enough to make even an Oklahoma girl quiver. The
air was alive with excitement and firecrackers, an explosive reminder
of the recent machine-gun fire. I hoped the crowds understood why
they were celebrating, and I hoped that soon my husband could steal
six consecutive hours of sleep. However, for some men the real work
begins when the fighting ends. The arts of peace can be more insidious
than the arts of war.*

*The next day was the Fourth of July, and this year it was doubly
celebrated by both Guatemalans and Americans. For the first time in
history a communist-dominated country had ousted its government
and sent the Communists packing.*[55]

The end of Arbenz' oppressive regime had come. The surviving
political prisoners were free. As Secretary Dulles said, the fate
of Guatemala now rested with the citizens of the country.[56]

Ten days of civil war saw a complete change in conditions in
Guatemala. The ousting of the communist regime was a complete
take-over. The influence of the Kremlin was eliminated. Efforts to
bring the issue into the United Nations in a manner which would
have given the Soviets the opportunity for prolonged debate, had
been attempted and then frustrated; this kept the problem in the
area of regional disturbances. The OAS, which had been scheduled
to meet in Mexico on July 7, never met. On the day that Arbenz
capitulated, the fact-finding commission of the Inter-American Peace
Committee had planned to leave for the Central American countries
that had been nearly involved. The new government withdrew the
request for investigation, which had been lodged by Arbenz.

The 10 years of communist control over the government had
ended. A time of peace had come. The people and the army had

backed Colonel Castillo Armas in his efforts to free the nation. The role of the United States, crucial at times during the days of shifting emergencies and unpredictable happenings, was ended. Our diplomacy had taken on a new vigor in dealing with the old and new leaders. It was then to return to normal. Many aspects of the critical drama were forgotten. Dulles said, as the episode of the revolution was closed, "At least one grave danger to the hemisphere has been averted."[57]

World Opinion. Public opinion is something that is superimposed on private appraisals and evaluations. There were a number of groups that voiced objections to the action taken by the United States. They were against operations half known to them and half hidden by the need for security measures. No convincing voice, however, was raised against the support given to Castillo Armas. Indeed, there was an almost audible sigh of relief as the danger was realized and the solution welcomed. There were, to be sure, a number of protests by students in half a dozen countries in Latin America. But there were none in Guatemala, "where the U.S. role was understood and deeply appreciated."[58]

Some of the more subtle comments came a little later, as the whole story was reviewed. There were critics, including Daniel James, who raised the issue that the United States' having taken part in these events would do more to contribute to Guatemala's future welfare than its immediate stability. They went beyond their appraisal of the particular events of June to the longer range of responsibilities of this government in assisting the nations to the south.

There also were, of course, writers who condemned the use of our power and prestige to influence events beyond our borders. A few of them railed at the United States' action, apparently following the communist line that reforms had been fought tooth and nail by the United States Embassy. Demonstrators in several countries raised the cry of imperialism. In Chile, the American flag was burned. The offices of two Chilean newspapers favorable to the United States were stoned. James, in his well-balanced book, concludes that the protests were to a significant degree spontaneous and not purely the work of communists. He states that the lesson of Guatemala was not communism alone, but the danger of an alliance between communism, "which was not yet a major force," and native nationalism, which was rampant.[59]

There were various ways of looking at the Guatemalan extension of the Monroe Doctrine. Few objected to its use, and the manner in which the Organization of American States dropped the issue and tried to gloss over any lingering doubts indicates the superficial nature of the short-lived protests. In fact, the whole episode was forgotten in a few weeks, except in communist supernationalist quarters and by historians.

One of the most interesting and least biased views of what took place was that of the British Minister, Richard Allen. In a report later published by his government, he reviewed the issues, and by stressing the fact that the people had been subjugated, rather than won over, by the communist leaders and Moscow techniques, he explained both the growing danger of the communists and the success of the Castillo Armas movement, which was a popular one. Allen stated:

> The communist-dominated regime . . . [was] overthrown with far greater ease and speed than seemed possible before the invasion of the country by some two hundred armed volunteers from Honduras . . . the movement was a popular one . . . not in any sense a triumph of alien aggression.[60]

The fact that a few hundred people were able in 10 days to turn out a seemingly entrenched government with strong support from the left demonstrated the miscalculations of the communists. Taking Allen's statement at face value and noting his treatment of the American intervention, one can clearly conclude that success breeds its own public opinion.

The United States had been aware of the floodlight of opinion that might be turned on their action. In order to do anything, there had to be a willingness to face criticism. Though the details of the operation could be concealed from the press—and have been kept secret to this day—there inevitably was considerable knowledge of them in the Latin American countries. It was the possibility of widespread condemnation, particularly if our assistance was inept, that emphasized the political aspects of risk-taking. These had been considered in the preparation during the previous months. Thus, the Caracas meeting, with its gratifying consensus, had indicated where we stood, lessening the element of surprise and increasing serious support among those who might have been critical. In any case, partly because of the speed of the operation and partly because of critical happenings elsewhere, the episode soon faded from public concern.

Throughout this period, the crucial element was the ability of the United States to exert leadership in such a way as to strengthen cooperation in Latin America. Though the unusual course of inter-vention was forced by the growing menace to the freedom of the area, it was intervention in the context of a popular desire for independence. The situation was in some ways unique. Measures like those attempted in Greece in 1947, or those used in Czechoslovakia in 1948, were frustrated. (The infiltration in the early 1960s in Cuba also was to present different problems.) The United States, slow to recognize the difficulties lying ahead, finally roused itself to action on the international and local fronts. The striking characteristic of the case is that the aid, though never large in amount, was adequate to help turn the tide. There was, moreover, no embarrassing overtness about the support; thus it did not need to be acknowledged and could be handled in a discreet and nonprovocative manner.

Here, as in Korea, information had been partially underevaluated. The issue of vitally needed reform had obscured some of the fundamental relationships. Then, when the United States determined that the threat must be met, intelligence, covert action, diplomacy, and negotiation were all combined in an effective combination for the moment when "a small amount of support" could be crucial. Minister Richard Allen, reporting to London, referred to "a few planes of the American type"[61] participating in Castillo Armas' successful rebellion. His implication was that this contribution, though it was small, had a special significance. The fact that the decision made in June was followed by complete success—insofar as action in the shifting world of international affairs can ever be successful—caused the incident to be absorbed into the general history of this period. The fact also that it was given little notice except by those closely involved is proof of the astuteness of those who played the crucial roles.

This willingness to follow the course which had been decided on in previous weeks, even in the face of possible failure, gave the hard-pressed Guatemalans the chance to expel communism. This move had to be bold and firmly grounded in our continuing and clearly enunciated hemispheric policy.

We Say "No Farther." The meaning of this stand had broader significance than the welfare of one small state. It was undoubtedly a factor in influencing communist attitudes over a much wider range of problems. It tended to round out the program of cooperation and containment. It was even an instance of "roll-back." The calculations as to what kind of intervention we could make and the response to requests for help in Latin America all combined to give a conclusive meaning to our action.

Several writers have said that the United States had taken insufficient notice of the earlier efforts of the Soviets to indoctrinate leaders and infiltrate the political leadership in Guatemala, but the final phases of our policy were many-pronged and effective. The groundwork laid in the Caracas meeting and the attitude of the United Nations were impressive and brought about support in Latin America, which was important in the later weeks of cleaning up the situation.

The involvement of the Central Intelligence Agency and the Department of State in the plans of the exiles in Honduras and El Salvador was so smoothly conducted that, even now, little is known about it. Accounts of the operation recently printed make interesting reading, but no one seems to find it necessary to authenticate or deny the statements made.

The prompt and vigorous actions of Ambassador Peurifoy in his dealings in Central America, and also in his reporting to Washington, have been heralded for the part they played both in influencing local events and in guiding Washington policy. The way in which he carried out his mission illustrates the contention of Ambassador Ellis Briggs that an ambassador who cannot make policy should not be an ambassador. The part Peurifoy played was most conspicuous in the last week in June, though his contribution to the Washington decision was also crucial in the preceding weeks. He undoubtedly was aware of some of the less conventional aspects of the situation, but he was sufficiently confident of the manner in which operations were conducted and of the solid backing of the

Castillo Armas rebellion among the people to give a summary that coincided with the open and generally acknowledged facts. Even some of those who condemned the United States for its participation in the earlier as well as the later phases of the episode were convinced by the success of the return of the exiles and the elimination of the communist government that the strength and freedom of government in Latin America had been significantly enhanced.

The Soviets and other anti-American propagandists had not been able to convince the world that the United States was acting mainly in the interests of the United Fruit Company, and subsequent anti-trust action against United Fruit in the courts of the United States bore out the contention of the State Department that they were only showing the normal responsibility toward American business when they protested the seizure of large land holdings by the Arbenz government.

The anti-Yankee campaign had been designed to deter Washington from any action against the communist infiltration and also to distract the Guatemalans and those in neighboring countries from their troubles. But the Arbenz regime of terror had made too deep an impression for these efforts to succeed, and Washington was finally convinced of the need for firm action. As in other critical situations, events served to narrow the choice from many possible options to a few—in this case, support of an inconspicuous nature or abandonment of the rebels. Though several courses of diplomatic and international action, particularly through the OAS, had been pursued in the early months of the year and though there had been efforts to educate public opinion and attempts to persuade Arbenz to abandon his heavy reliance on the communists, one by one we had had to turn from these considerations to the one line of effective operation—helping Colonel Castillo Armas. In this, for a few brief days, we stood alone, and the pivotal decision was made by the President. None of these efforts would have been significant if it had not been concluded by those who were in high positions that the taking over of Guatemala by international communism would seriously damage our national interest. Nor would our position have been vigorously pursued if there had not been close and understanding collaboration among the Department of State, the Central Intelligence Agency, and our Embassy in Guatemala.

It had been necessary, as well as traditional, in the preceding six months to seek to the greatest extent possible the cooperation of England, West Germany, and other friendly nations in this hemisphere and elsewhere. Nevertheless, time pressures after the landing of the Czech arms and the growing impatience of the rebels in exile made more definite joint actions impractical at the final moment. So in June the die was cast. Our replacement of the destroyed airplanes was an open action that could not be concealed, whether there was success or failure. It meant that we were willing to face criticism, but that we had decided the psychological risks were justified by our intent to impress the Soviets with the fact that we would not tolerate subversion of our neighbors. Our action was an extension and reshaping of the Monroe Doctrine in that the OAS had been made a partner in our efforts by means of the Caracas Resolution. Along with the parallel actions taken, it underscored the principle of regionalism in this hemisphere, as contrasted with the principle of universalism, which might have been applicable if there had been an alien invasion. Thus, in the moment of decision much information had been gathered, and there was a record of warnings to the communists and negotiations with the OAS. Furthermore, there were active plans for helping the rebels in their undertaking.

In spite of all this, there was danger to be faced (as there is in most important foreign policy decisions). The odds had to be calculated, and the way in which this policy would be displayed to the world had to be considered. In the final analysis, strength and courage, as well as a shrewd sense of "the adequate," were displayed. If the early awareness of the nature of the developing threat was inadequate, the later phase of preparation, intelligence, policy formation, planning, and financial and military support justified the best tradition. The results were of vital importance in holding back—in pressing back—communism in this hemisphere.

Intervention in the affairs of other nations always involves hazards. Success in such an action calls for an astute appraisal of both the risks and the chance of gains when the final outcome brings a new situation. Many have stressed the narrow margin between an acceptable course in support of a genuine movement to overthrow a tyrannical regime and unjustified participation in an internal struggle for power. The verdict as to the propriety of American action in the crisis of 1954 is found in the calm way in which the events were viewed in most capitals and in the failure of the Soviets to capitalize effectively on any aspects of the incident. The criticism, which was to be expected, was partly for the record and soon died down. Those who understood the issues were encouraged by the fact that enough and not too much, had been done at the moment of greatest opportunity. Among those who were alert to the motives and methods of the United States were the policy-makers in the Kremlin. They did not repeat their attempt to gain a beachhead until eight years had passed.

The determination that there was a threat to a vital interest, here, as in other cases, lies at the heart of statesmanship. When this occurs, decision and action must be so swift that an appeal for public approval is not always feasible. The responsibility cannot be shifted. It rests on a few people in the State Department, the Defense Department, the White House, and at one or two other points. Congressional leaders are involved to a greater or lesser degree, depending on the time factors in each case. Without the continuing confidence of the public in their leaders—making possible such swift and decisive actions—foreign policy would be virtually paralyzed in time of emergency. Often, only after the dust has settled is it possible to explain some of the happenings. Even when a crisis is over, it is not wise to reveal all aspects of intelligence gathering, delicate planning, negotiations, and financial and military maneuvers.

How much the average citizen needs to know and what his part can be in crucial decisions varies according to the nature of the threat to our aims and the extent to which he is asked to sacrifice through financial outlays and risks to individual security. If the government can exert its influence soon and in a restrained and limited manner, the outsider is willing to leave the details to the experts. If the costs are considerable, there is a continuing pressure for more information. The case of Guatemala demonstrates that the more skillful the operation and the smoother the handling of the external participation and relations with responsible agencies at home, the sooner the crisis is forgotten. (Cuba, later, because of its threat to the peace of the world, was a special case.) Fortunately, the United States performed in such a way with respect to Guatemala that the international communists were warned—and the nation gained time for consolidation and constructive planning. The Latin American countries no longer offered the green pastures which the communists had found in Latin America in the decade just past.

THE CHALLENGE OF LEBANON: 1958

Below the high snow peaks of Lebanon lies the busy seaport town of Beirut. On its beaches and in its crowded streets an unusual drama in the conduct of American foreign policy was enacted in July, 1958. Here was demonstrated the meaning of decisive and effective response in a time of crisis. Rarely have the capabilities of a great power been brought to bear on a critical situation so fast and so appropriately as in the landing of Marines in 1958.

The basic problems and the long sequence of events leading to this decision were complex, as complex as the history of this region. Varied civilizations have developed, flourished, and disappeared in Lebanon. They have left the ancient ruins of Tyre and Sidon, the gaunt castles of the Crusaders on the headlands, traces of Roman legions and Turkish armies. Warring nations have clashed, conquered, and vanished here. Arabs, Christians, Moslems—nomads and traders—crossed the deserts and followed rough mountain trails to the sea for gain or conquest. The conflicts of religion, race, and tradition stirred constant ferment. All sought oil from the peaceful, silvery green olive groves, but there was little tranquillity. The land seemed to lie open to intrusion, which was the more menacing as neighboring nations gained strength and tried to propagate their religious or political doctrines. Communists were not the first—nor will they be the last—to infiltrate the Middle East through this open gateway. Because of its location in relation to trade and the oil-rich nations for which it is a focal point of communication and economic support, the seacoast of Lebanon has been a prize of interest not only to the immediate area but also to nations far away.

After the weakening of French and British influence following the Second World War, the United States had come to recognize special responsibilities in the Middle East. The Truman Doctrine was the first and most crucial expression of this new interest. The Eisenhower Doctrine was a further extension and reiteration of the significance of this part of the world to the Western powers. Not only the active commercial life of Beirut, but also the traditional friendly relations of the United States with the country, half Moslem and half Christian, gave the city a special importance both for America and for the foes of American influence. The Soviet communists were not indifferent to these facts. The postwar years were disturbed by rumors, border conflicts, and active subversion on the frontiers and in the city bazaars. There was no stable peace.

The Background of Conflict.   Lebanon had been situated in the path of warring armies for centuries: Alexander had crossed mountains and deserts to expand his empire; Crusaders from Europe had landed to hold fortified positions along the coast; for centuries after the incursions of the Greeks and Romans, the powerful Ottoman Empire ruled the subjugated tribes. Then, after World War I, the French were given a mandate over the territories bordering on the Mediterranean. In the period between 1926 and 1936, in spite of the economic and intellectual capabilities of the region, there was little apparent progress toward independence. Only near the end of World War II was a treaty negotiated; it became effective on January 1, 1945. Independence was granted as a part of the strategic maneuvers of the Western powers; Lebanon was, therefore, able to become a charter member of the United Nations when it was established in that year.

Thus this little country of 3 million people, in a key location but with no significant military strength, emerged from a troubled past with the hope of sharing international peace through mutual security with the great democracies. It was aware of its increasing economic importance to both oil-producing and oil-consuming nations, but it recognized that the preservation of its identity and its future development required the continuing support of stronger nations. Its heritage made it the natural victim of internal racial and religious dissension. During the Cold War period it has been the inevitable object of the ambitions of the Egyptians, as well as of the communists seeking warm-water outlets and influence over oil-rich countries.* Feuding Arab states on its borders and unsettled political conditions within made it vulnerable to all these pressures. Efforts to

---

*Lebanon's wealth came from businessmen and from the use of the pipe lines bringing oil from lands farther to the east.

establish a Western-style democracy were precariously near failure in 1957 and 1958.

The United States could well have left these problems alone if the British and French had been willing and able to continue their active interest in Lebanon; their capacity to do so, however, had greatly diminished after the Second World War, and their policy was to withdraw from many of their overseas commitments. The British had declared this new position in February, 1947; the French, distraught by the unsettled conflict in Algeria and crushed psychologically by their defeat in Indochina, were clearly unable to show more than a token interest in the Middle East.

One nongovernmental tie with Lebanon was represented by American support of the University in Beirut, founded in 1866. Archeologists had used this as a center, as had missionaries. The Lebanese thus found it easy to turn to America for sympathy and support.

The Suez crisis of 1956 greatly increased American responsibilities in the region. It was imperative that the misunderstandings following the condemnation of the British, French, and Israelis, as well as the deep significance of that action in the United Nations, should be clarified. While we had to demonstrate that we could not tolerate the attack on the Egyptians, we had no intention of permitting a communist take-over as the result of the increasing vigor of the Nasser regime and the apparent coincidence of our interests with those of Moscow. The danger of a weakening of Western support and the uncertainty in some quarters as to American aims called for positive action.

The Eisenhower Doctrine.   Thus in late 1956 and early 1957, the Eisenhower-Dulles decision to assume a more active role in the area took the form of a resolution put before Congress; it was vigorously debated both by those who thought the President had sufficient latitude without special action and by those who felt our undertakings already represented an overextension of our commitments. The uneasiness following Suez was, however, a persuasive argument for indicating our determination to come to the assistance of small Middle Eastern countries; the Truman Doctrine had embodied similar principles (see pages 111–112). The resolution, introduced on January 5, 1957, was adopted by Congress in early March and became effective as of March 9. It was the basis for action some 15 months later.

The purpose of the resolution, which declared that the United States would come to the aid of countries affirming that they were subject to indirect aggression, was, as Dulles said, to add "the extra wallop" to existing policy by giving a widely based support to the intentions of the Executive branch. It also authorized the use of funds "not to exceed $200 million from the Mutual Security Act" for the needs envisioned. The hope was to increase economic strength in the area and to deter further infiltration and aggression.

At this time President Eisenhower appointed James P. Richards as Ambassador and sent him on a mission of explanation and friendship to the Middle East. He was to make clear our support and the nature of our interest in their welfare. We were aware of the explosive conditions and the high sensitivity of our allies as well as of the Arab countries, which were inclined to look on our actions with suspicion. We were actively considering conditions and how we could best offer support. We were determined as soon as possible to heal the wounds of 1956 and to improve the stability and independence of the small nations in this strategic location. We wished to demonstrate, in advance of further trouble, that any efforts on the part of leaders in Moscow to increase their influence would be countered without delay.

Thus preparation was made for a larger American influence and the acceptance of responsibility for peace and democracy in areas that had not known a great deal of either.

Two years earlier, in 1955, the Baghdad Pact had been set up as a defensive alliance on the initiative of the United States. Iran, Iraq, Pakistan, Turkey, and Great Britain were members. The United States, partly to avoid accentuating the tensions and rivalries between Arab states, did not join but associated itself with the treaty states as an observer at the meetings and by participating in some of the committee work. After the revolution in 1958, Iraq resigned and the name of the organization was changed to the Central Treaty Organization (CENTO). The purpose of the defensive alliance was to deter Russian action in the Middle East and to warn against efforts to foster communism there. There had even been hopes, in 1955, that a basis could be found for accommodation with Nasser.

Gamal Abdel Nasser was, however, playing for high stakes and wide power over all Arab states. He capitalized on the Russian anger over the Baghdad Pact to obtain arms from Czechoslovakia and proceeded with his efforts to extend his influence. One expression of this was found in the creation of the United Arab Republic, a union of Egypt and Syria, a combination that flanked Lebanon to the north and south. This extension of Nasser's authority was, ironically, facilitated by Syria's fear of growing communist subversion. In October, 1957, Nikita Khrushchev threatened to act if Turkey, persuaded by the West, should attack Syria. Gromyko shortly thereafter stated that Russia would aid Syria if there were military aggression. Many signs pointed to the aspirations of the U.S.S.R. in exploiting conflicts in the area.

Tension increased again in 1957 as the communist-dominated government of Syria charged the American Embassy with plotting against it. A Soviet request in the United Nations for a commission of investigation was not put to a vote, but the threat to stability continued as Syria and Egypt schemed to subvert the pro-Western governments in Iraq, Jordan, and Lebanon. President Camille Chamoun of Lebanon was planning to change the constitution so that he could have a further term in office. This intention aggravated the internal conflict. Meanwhile, propaganda from Egypt incited the more rebellious elements, and hundreds of politically indoctrinated teachers were sent to exert an influence on the borders of Lebanon.

In March, a general strike was called in Tripoli. A critical moment came in May, when Nassib el Metni, the prominent publisher of the *Telegraph*, was assassinated, and Lebanese factions were torn by dissension. A revolt broke out in Beirut on May 9, and shortly thereafter a rebel government was formed in the south.

United Nations Concern. Both the Arab League and the Soviet Union endeavored to intervene at this point. Moscow, in a maneuver to enhance its prestige in the area, asked for a five-power summit meeting with the United States, the United Kingdom, France, and India to consider the problem. Charles Malik, the Lebanese Foreign Minister, flew to New York with a sense of great urgency to put the matter before the United Nations. As a result of these requests, the United Nations took the question formally to the Security Council, and they agreed to send an Observation Group. The group was to gather information and report to the Council on conditions in the country, with a view to the prevention of "illegal infiltration of personnel or the supply of arms across the Lebanese borders."

The group was sent in under a Swedish peace resolution adopted on June 11. Its members were greatly handicapped by their inability to obtain access to those parts of the country where the infiltration was said to be taking place and by the fact that they did not carry on their search at night. Moreover, they drove in plainly marked white jeeps that could easily be spotted by those carrying on illegal activities by day or by night. Their reports that they had found little hard evidence of improper intrusion or infiltration were unconvincing to those who had been watching the subversion over a considerable period of time. They did little to dispel the fears of those who had been facing the problem for many months. In other words, the nerves of the disturbed political leaders were not calmed.

Ninety-four officers from 11 countries had served as military observers in the UN group, and because of the continuing apprehension over the possible outbreak of serious hostilities, Secretary General Dag Hammarskjöld himself went out to consult with these investigators. The final report emphasized the difficulty of their task, the lack of roads, the rough terrain. It referred to the traditional ease with which Syrians and Lebanese crossed the border. They said they had not been given permission to enter the more disturbed areas and had not patrolled the frontiers. Some portions of the cities were behind barricades and an attempt to make a complete survey would have held considerable danger.

Hammarskjöld lunched with Secretary Dulles on July 7, immediately after his return. He gave an optimistic report, concluding that the demonstration of the United Nations' interest and a slight internal improvement of stability gave promise of better conditions. No special action was required for the moment. This was still the state of affairs on July 13.

The Precipitation of Crisis. The blow fell in neighboring Iraq on the night of July 13–14. At about midnight King Faisal and the royal family were roused from sleep and dragged from their beds to the Palace steps. A group of Arab nationalist officers led by Brigadier General Abdul el-Kassim surrounded the Palace and shot the King and his wife and children. Prime Minister Nuri as-Said fled to the house of a friend but was later found and killed in the streets of Baghdad. Kassim took over the government, as rioting, arson, and murder spread through the city. These events caused panic in Lebanon and Jordan. Chamoun in terror appealed for immediate help from America. King Hussein in Jordan also asked for aid. The explosive effects in the two countries indicated that prompt action was required.

For the United States, a quick appraisal of the risks and capabilities for action was necessary. Our judgment of the importance of the area, widely evident at the time of the Suez crisis, had been made explicitly part of our policy in early 1957. The question to be faced was not whether to act but when and how. Our commitment to come to the aid of a nation subject to direct or indirect aggression when requested had already become a declared part of our foreign responsibilities. The judgment in this case called for an appraisal of the nature of the need, the capabilities we could use, and the way in which to bring our aid to bear on the situation. The *narrowing triangle of choice* had brought the problem quickly into focus. A purely negative response had been ruled out by the Eisenhower Doctrine. Lebanon had been the only country to take formal action in acceptance of the Doctrine. Time-consuming joint arrangements and diplomatic negotiations were excluded by the desperate appeal from Chamoun. Only a few options remained to be considered after the night of July 13.

Washington Faces the Crisis. Shortly after midnight, in the early hours of Monday, July 14, the urgent cables from Iraq and Lebanon began coming through. The watch officer at the State Department, scanning the decoded messages as they were handed to him, noting NIACT (night action) and URGENT on them, looked up the names of the desk officers most concerned. Several of these men, wakened by his summons, came to the Department immediately. They identified themselves at the window on the fifth floor and were admitted to the small anteroom where the first printing of the incoming cables could be read. (The routine then, before the establishment of the Operations Center, was somewhat inconvenient, but the essentials were provided for.) The first messages were confused but alarming. Rumors were followed by eyewitness reports. It was only toward morning that firm information on the murders and rioting in Baghdad and the panic among the leaders in Lebanon and Jordan was available.

The desk officers assembled the policy statements and position papers on action in the Middle East without delay. They wrote brief summaries of the incoming reports, pointing to the assessments from the Embassies. Before the beginning of the normal working day they had a reasonably clear picture to put before the Secretary. They had talked with each other and had conferred with the Pentagon and with the Central Intelligence Agency on the events of the night and so had a coordinated opinion on the situation.

By the time the Secretary was awakened by an urgent call from the Department, the outlines of a serious crisis were clear. A cable from Ambassador McClintock in Beirut had transmitted President Chamoun's appeal for help within 48 hours, predicting revolution if such support did not materialize quickly. His government could not last any longer, he said. The Ambassador concurred in his view of the desperate need.

During Monday morning, those officers directly or indirectly concerned with these matters were entirely at the disposal of the Secretary. The intelligence briefing and the early staff meeting gave cursory attention to problems in other areas and then focused on the questions growing out of the murders in Baghdad. Out of these first meetings developed a series of others that fed material into the head office. The record shows that the Secretary spoke with more than 70 high-level officers and small groups of experts during the next five hours. During this period he was in frequent touch with the President, keeping him informed of facts and conclusions as these unfolded. He talked not only with other Cabinet members and American officials but also with the Ambassadors from Lebanon, the United Kingdom, and France. A wide variety of people were consulted (some by telephone) in brief conversations designed to sharpen the issues and prepare for decision.

The possibilities for action were closely related to the position and capabilities of the Sixth Fleet, already deployed in the eastern end of the Mediterranean. An appraisal of the risks included an opinion as to the attitude of the Lebanese General Chehab in his influence over divided factions among his troops. The probable reaction of the disturbed elements in the cities to American action was also of great significance. In balancing opportunities and dangers, the Secretary kept in close contact with the Joint Chiefs of Staff, the Central Intelligence Agency, the United Nations, and the White House. Other officers conferred with their opposite numbers in various ad hoc committees. Congressional leaders had been alerted.

The machinery of consultation worked smoothly, as the gaps in the early information were filled and a consensus began to develop. In this case, there were few dissenters to throw doubt on the need for action—action for which preparation had begun 18 months earlier. Hundreds of persons were involved in the plan that was emerging. There was no confusion, as the system responded to the urgency of arriving at a momentous conclusion.

Although some possibilities were ruled out by events, a number of alternatives had to be given at least passing consideration. It was, of course, possible to wait for further developments. It was also possible to try to cast the major responsibility on the United Nations. Presumably, some suggested the development of diplomatic efforts, including some type of international meeting. Attention had to be given to the role of economic measures. During the discussions, the trend toward bold and immediate support of the Lebanese government became increasingly clear. The proposal the Secretary was to make was in line with this affirmative decision and was characteristic of his style of seeking decisive and unmistakable positions that would fend off further aggression. It was also in accord with the guidelines laid down in position papers prepared months before. By early afternoon, the choices had been narrowed to one major recommendation, with lesser alternatives. These were to be presented to the President.

Monday's Decisions.   A crucial meeting was set for mid-morning in the White House. At 10:30, Foster Dulles and a few of his close aides—Under Secretaries Robert Murphy and Loy Henderson, the head of Policy Planning, Gerard Smith, and a few others—drove from the Department to 1600 Pennsylvania Avenue.

Allen Dulles and one or two others from the Central Intelligence Agency and several officers from the Pentagon joined the group. Brigadier General Andrew Goodpaster and Press Secretary James Hagerty sat in as presidential aides. The President asked for the report of Secretary Dulles.

Dulles explained the recent events and the resulting crisis, stressing its significance for the entire Middle East. His statement was stripped down to the essentials, but it emphasized the growing panic in Lebanon, Jordan, and elsewhere. He also outlined American capabilities and the risks that would accompany any action. Either action or failure to act would have worldwide implications, he said. There was a moment of silence after this analysis; then Eisenhower asked for Dulles' recommendation. Without hesitation, the answer came. The United States forces on ships already near the Lebanese coast should be sent in to support the government on the basis of the Eisenhower Doctrine.

The President took over the discussion. He said that from the first few sentences of Dulles' statement he had known "what Foster would recommend." He agreed that immediate instructions should be sent to the Sixth Fleet. The Marines should land as soon as possible. The presidential order was to be issued at once. As he said later in *Waging Peace*, "the decision to send troops to Lebanon was not taken lightly"; there was risk of general war with the Soviet Union.[62]

That Monday there were further meetings at the White House, but the first group scattered to carry out their appointed tasks. There was much further work to be done. Congressional leaders had been consulted; Eisenhower reports there was little enthusiasm but no definite objection. A special message to Congress had to be written explaining the basis and the need for going in. Television and radio statements had to be written for the President. The press officers in the White House and in the State Department coordinated their releases.

One phase of the preparation was to inform both the Ambassadors immediately concerned and others more remotely interested of what was taking place. Some were called into the Department for briefing. Thought had to be given to the sensitivity of various nations and the reaction of scores of capitals to the plan adopted. There were consultations with Ambassador Lodge in New York to assist in the drafting of several statements to the General Assembly of the United Nations. In these he declared that American action was required "to support the integrity and independence of a nation attacked from the inside by subversion and erosion." Help not available from any other quarter, in this emergency, had to be given. Meanwhile, the coordination with British action in Jordan was accomplished. As a routine matter, a notice was prepared in the Department advising against "travel in and through Lebanon and Iraq except for imperative reasons."

The British Chargé d'affaires, Lord Hood, had, in the absence of the Ambassador, been in the Department for consultation before noon. He recognized the importance of British participation because of both the diplomatic and military aspects of the crisis. Their special responsibility had been Jordan, now profoundly shaken by events in Iraq. He was proposing to his government steps to accomplish a coordinated action. Paratroopers from nearby Cyprus could be sent in promptly—in fact, they landed on July 17. The French Ambassador, Hervé Alphand, and his minister, Henri Lucet, came early to discuss the part France could play. They knew well the importance of regaining stability in the troubled area. Hard-pressed as they were in Algeria, they concluded they could give only token support. They would send the warship *De Grasse* to stand off the coast of Lebanon. Ambassador McClintock in Beirut was informed of all these arrangements.

Dulles continued the long succession of meetings. He was convinced that all the important angles had been considered. Nevertheless, he was full of apprehension, which he admitted to those close to him. As he said later to newsmen, "Don't think I wasn't scared." His last session that night was at his home, where Lord Hood called at 10:30 P.M. He went to bed, weary, but convinced that the Soviet leaders would know that the United States would fight if necessary. The die had been cast.

Operation BLUEBAT. The sun was bright on the sandy beaches near the Khadle Airport, six miles from Beirut, on July 16, 1958. Hundreds of people were picnicking, playing volleyball, and swimming. Vendors were hawking their soft drinks. Only a few in the holiday crowd knew the importance of the tragedy in Baghdad and the meaning of the rumors circulating in the bazaars. Panic was spreading in their country, but they were seizing a day of enjoyment. They looked seaward with surprise as they saw ships heading for the beach.

Many of those concerned with affairs in the Middle East had thought that the Sixth Fleet was cruising near Spain. Actually, Vice Admiral James Holloway, Jr., and his seven ships were not far from the Lebanon coast, having been ordered there with a view to possible trouble. By noon (Lebanese time), the Marines were in battle dress, strapping on their equipment, receiving final instructions and live ammunition. They had been in many practice landings; now they were told: "This is it." They were crowded onto the landing barges to face unknown dangers.

Exactly at 3:00 P.M., the first of the snub-nosed landing craft touched shore, and the Marines waded through the water to dry land. Operation BLUEBAT, decided on in Washington some 12 hours before, had been carried out in perfect precision only 26 hours after the receipt of Chamoun's appeal.

The first men ashore were met by eager sellers of pop and ice cream. There was little awareness of the meaning of the unexpected visit. The men took battle positions, ready to shoot, if necessary; they prepared to bivouac if so ordered. They were 6000 strong, with supporting jeeps and tanks.

Admiral Holloway had been warned of subversion among the Lebanese military. There was for a time, however, a breakdown of communications between the naval contingents and the Embassy. Ambassador McClintock feared a bloody clash between the American and Lebanese troops in spite of the fact that the Americans had been invited to come by President Chamoun. He sought to delay the march into Beirut. The Ambassador, who was seeking facts and sifting rumors and reports, learned that troops garrisoned in the neighborhood were deployed along the road to the airport, under orders from insubordinate junior officers. They had taken up positions with artillery where they could fire on advancing columns of Marines.

General Chehab had held himself somewhat aloof from the conflicting factions. The men close to him were not committed to either side. With some difficulty, McClintock got him to come to the Embassy and persuaded him to drive in the Embassy car to the point on the Beirut-airport road where the soldiers were approaching each other. There had been a short delay in the American advance at the Ambassador's request; then they continued their march. The Ambassador, with Chehab in the car beside him, joined the forward units. The two men, at the front of the column, with the American flag flying on the car, moved toward the Lebanese soldiers, who were hesitating as to what action to take. They saw the six battalions, with six tanks and 12 amphibious personnel carriers, moving down the road under the command of Lieutenant Colonel Hadd. The army, though reluctant and divided, had been prepared to fight, but when they saw their General in the American car in front of the American troops, they offered no resistance. Not a shot was fired.

It was not without difficulty that Chehab had been persuaded to agree with the Ambassador and had then persuaded his staff to call off the resistance. Admiral Holloway, who had joined the convoy before it moved ahead, had agreed to break up his column into segments and to place Lebanese jeeps in the intervals. The entry into the city was peaceful. It was followed by arrangements for joint patrols of the more disturbed areas. The most critical moment after the Washington decision had been passed without incident.

The troops were to remain in Lebanon for about three months. The total strength of the forces landed reached its peak on August 8, when there were slightly more than 14,000 American troops in Beirut. The people knew that this was not an invasion and was not an unwelcome intervention. It was a well-coordinated response to the government's request for aid. There were no armed clashes in the city; the cooperative action did not lead to bloodshed. Peace and calm were restored.

Consequences of the Landings. The major political result in the country was the agreement to hold elections and the withdrawal of Chamoun from the Presidency. Thus the constitutional prohibition of a second term was preserved. In order to grant assistance in the projected election, Under Secretary Robert Murphy was sent from Washington. On September 23, General Chehab was elected President.

The Baghdad Pact had been shaken by the crisis. The leaders of member countries, meeting in London in July, were particularly anxious to know what support they could expect from the major powers. The Secretary of State discussed the situation in Lebanon, Iran, Iraq, and Jordan at some length. He indicated that the United States would take a larger role on the defense committee. It also would enter into bilateral pacts with the member countries. It still did not join the Central Treaty Organization, or CENTO, as it was now called.

The determination to support the small nations in their fight for independence had a noticeable effect in deterring subversion both within and from outside. The leaders in Moscow and elsewhere refrained from the provocative acts that had characterized the period from November, 1956, to July, 1958. From then on there was relative quiet in the Middle East. On October 25, after the new President took over, the United States troops withdrew.

Operation BLUEBAT was an instance of that anomalous occurrence—a limited war for political objectives. Internal insurrection was suppressed without casualties; external threats of aggression were halted before they were well underway.

The international diplomatic repercussions of the Lebanese crisis were reflected to a considerable extent in the debates in the United Nations in the following weeks. Ambassador Lodge had reported in detail the nature and reasons for the American action—he had indicated that no one else had been ready or willing to prevent the outside interference in the internal uprising which was threatening the peace of the area. He did not refer directly to the inconclusive findings of the United Nations Observation Group. He stated, however, that we would be glad to turn over responsibility as soon as the United Nations was willing to take it on.

Moscow apparently wished to prevent such a move. On July 18, the Soviet delegate cast the one unfavorable vote in the Security Council against a resolution to have the United Nations take measures to halt the infiltration of Lebanon. This veto was followed by another to block a resolution by Japan requesting that steps be taken to stabilize the situation. This was also intended to prepare for the United States' withdrawal. A Russian proposal calling for an immediate end to the presence of American troops in Lebanon and British soldiers in Jordan attracted only one favorable vote. In the face of these frustrating maneuvers, Lodge called for an emergency session of the General Assembly. Khrushchev, who earlier had sought a summit meeting to deal with the issue, concluded that he had Afro-Asian support and modified his line at this point.

By the time the Assembly was convened on August 8, the tensions in the Middle East had substantially lessened. The United States had recognized the Kassim regime in Iraq. There had been no bloodshed in Lebanon. The general acceptability of General Chehab as President had reduced the conflict between factions in the nation. The Arab League indicated that it would abstain from action likely to upset established governments. It requested the Secretary General of the United Nations to take steps in support of the Charter in Lebanon and Jordan, with a view to the early withdrawal of foreign troops. The departure of the American contingents in October was followed on November 2 by the British withdrawal from Jordan. The United Nations Observation Group was disbanded on December 10.

Thus the crisis precipitated in July came to an end. The action that served the immediate purpose could not solve the underlying problems or bring a halt to conflict between hostile interests. The Arab-Israeli conflict, the Western-communist struggle, the inter-Arab differences remained. The region was subject to ambitions and threats growing out of social, religious, and economic factors that were causing unrest. Riches invited greed; poverty stirred rebellion. The Middle East could not be pacified by any simple formula and swift action or by any new imperialism. Trouble was bound to recur.

The Significance of the Landings. The landings of the Marines in Lebanon were the deeds that gave significance to the words of the American leaders. They gave reality to the Congressional resolution, and they showed the seriousness of the commitment to offer support to the nations struggling to maintain their independence in the Middle East. The problem of survival in freedom had been formally recognized in 1957, and the preparation for action had been made. Moreover, the military capabilities had been readied in such a way as to permit prompt action. The general situation was well understood and intelligence coming in was adequate, but the specific precipitating event could not have been forecast. The value judgment had been made late in 1956 after the Suez crisis and had been expressed in the open debate of the President and Secretary in support of the new resolution. The choices between feasible types of action—or inaction—could be quickly outlined in the urgent discussions of July 14 that made possible a decision momentous and full of risk. The decision was straightforward in its response to the developing danger, and it was made a few hours after the events were known in Washington. Operation BLUEBAT was executed in almost flawless precision, though it passed through precarious moments and hazardous conditions.

The patent ineffectiveness of the Security Council to bring coordinated international influences to bear on the situation was disturbing. The inconclusive explorations carried out by the UN observer team were also a demonstration of the slow progress toward cooperative security action which characterized the postwar decade. Joint response to danger was still a matter of courageous leadership by the few. The majority of nations could not be counted on to assume useful responsibility in sudden emergencies. Much work must be done before the motives and machinery of group action could be adequately prepared. Coordination with the British and French came with the unilateral decision in the White House and was little influenced by the debate in the United Nations in New York.

There were critics of the measures taken, as always when bold and unprecedented steps are taken. It is almost impossible to avoid opposition. Neutrals and enemies are required by political necessities to condemn a positive policy. No performance meets the standards of the idealists. Clearly, it would have been preferable to avoid sending troops to foreign soil, if other effective measures had been available. While the contest between those who hold different political doctrines continues, while some still entertain the ambition to extend their areas of control beyond the accepted limits, the struggle between nations takes on forms that are often dangerous and brutal. The objectives of the United States in this instance, to end aggression, to halt panic, and to preserve political stability and freedom for Lebanon and Jordan, were met. The cost of this accomplishment was slight in comparison with the ends achieved.

THE CHALLENGE OF BERLIN
AND GERMANY: 1958

Giving Thanks for Peace and Plenty.   Foster Dulles was getting ready for the diplomatic Mass to be held in Washington on Thanksgiving Day, November 27, 1958. Allen Dulles, Director of the CIA, was talking to his aides by telephone from his house on Q Street. Senior officers, members of the German Office, were reading the incoming cables in the Department. Different posts in the capital were on the alert. It was on this chill but bright morning that the word came from Ambassador Thompson in Moscow that Khrushchev's long note on Berlin had come in to the Embassy and was being translated for transmittal in several sections. Our position in Berlin was being challenged.

Only the broad outlines of the Soviet demands were transmitted in the early summary telegram. Three or four members of the German Office met with Assistant Secretary Livingston Merchant in his office. They sent word to Secretary Dulles that the full text would not be ready until afternoon. He spoke with Allen Dulles on the telephone. The brothers agreed to meet as planned at the McLean home of Eleanor Dulles, their sister. She had been asked to take a brief memorandum to them from the Department before the family dinner. The general nature of the move in Moscow was not unexpected; however, the exact nature of the proposal would need to be carefully studied. The questions were: How far did it go beyond the Khrushchev speech on November 10 in Poland? Did it suggest anything new? Several hours of study would be required before the intent of the message could safely be interpreted.

Foster Dulles changed after the Mass from a formal suit to greenish tweeds before driving to McLean. The family were 14 gathered around the table laden with turkey, sweet potatoes, cranberries, pies, ice cream—all the traditional foods of a typical American Thanksgiving dinner. The telephone rang several times. The Assistant Secretary for Public Affairs, the Soviet desk officer, and others in the Department asked whether there was to be a meeting. President Eisenhower, vacationing in Augusta, Georgia, was well versed in the Berlin problem. A call to him would bring an immediate response in line with Department thinking.

The meal was lively with casual talk, the children asking whether there was any real excitement in the Department. It was too cold to swim, but there was a little conversation about the recognized duty to go in the water when the temperature was above freezing. At 2:30, the Dulles brothers got ready to leave. It was agreed that there should be an afternoon meeting to review the message, which was now in the hands of the Department. The relaxation was over; the work began. On Thanksgiving Day, 1958, Berlin was again on the firing line, and an early Western response was urgently needed.

Berlin Becomes a Symbol and a Key Issue: 1948. In the early years, there was doubt as to the future of Berlin. The importance of the city had grown from 1945 to 1958, with the mounting pressure of the communists to gain control over Germany. Its position had not been deliberately planned. In fact, it was mainly the lack of adequate early planning that had created a situation full of peril and causing difficulty over more than 20 years.

The original concept was that there would be a peace treaty for a united Germany a year, or at the most two years, after the end of the war. In this treaty there would be provision, perhaps through a loosely federated political system, to control and keep Germany from threatening the peace. The four Allies would work on this new arrangement together, assuring a cooperative effort to protect Europe from aggression.

Only after the Potsdam meeting of July, 1945, and after difficulties in Austria as well as in Germany, was it gradually recognized that the Soviets had a different conception and plan. By 1947, the unwillingness of the U.S.S.R. to work toward a united economy, the continued removals and repressions in the Eastern occupied zone, and the difficulties with the Soviets in the United Nations and elsewhere revealed the inadequacy of the agreements on the city of Berlin. It was not until after the blockade in 1948 (see pages 116–119) that the full danger of the position of the city became evident. Then it was widely realized that the narrow access routes and the three air corridors represented the essential lifelines to the city of almost 5 million (in all sectors) and that the Soviets if they wished could bring almost intolerable pressure to bear.

Then the decision had to be made as to whether the Western Allies would allow themselves to be pushed out of the city. The consequences of a Soviet victory here were evident. By gaining the upper hand and wringing concessions from the Allies, the Soviets would not only consolidate their hold on territory of immense value, reaching almost to the Rhine River, but they would also demonstrate their capacity to do what they wished with the Germans. The will to resist in the zone of occupation would diminish; the feeling of dependence and gratitude to the Western powers would dissipate. In fact, the likelihood of losing all Germany to the communists would be menacing. The decision to become more firm in 1948, made manifest in the airlift, was soon to become a central policy for the Western world.

The United States declared in 1948, 1949, and 1954, as well as on dozens of other occasions, that the security and welfare of Berlin were essential to the peace of the free world. We stated that we would not abandon Berlin. The city, rebuilt in part with American money, showing courage and fortitude through many crises, stanchly anticommunist—pro-Western in culture and inclination—became a symbol of strength and resistance to Soviet aggression. It was considered to be a key element in the German problem and thus basic to NATO and the defense of Europe. It could not be abandoned, after the nature of the Soviet intent was clear, without shattering the confidence of all small nations, of all border lands, and of those who put their trust in American support.

Story of Success and Failure. There have rarely been cases in history that have shown such a strange mixture of error and insight as the case of Berlin. The city had become the center of Nazi aggression against the peace of Europe. Some of the most dangerous political leaders of the 1930s and 1940s had lived and worked there. It had been flattened by a massive Soviet bombardment in 1945, following on air raids of previous months. Thousands fled the smoking rubble; others lay dead in the ruins. Only slowly did the city come to life. There was no enthusiasm among the Allies over the rebuilding, and little thought as to its future. The talk of Germany at Yalta in February, 1945, had not focused on Berlin. Because there was considerable desire for a decentralized Germany, the former capital did not seem of prime importance. Similarly, at Potsdam, the arrangements for the four-power occupation were made along the lines laid down in the document signed in Berlin on June 5, 1945, by Eisenhower, Zhukov, Montgomery, and De Lattre de Tassigny. The four-power plan set up the Allied Control Council and a *Kommandatura* to administer "Greater Berlin."[63] There was no special provision for "access." The "access" concept and problem came later.

The map attached to the agreement shows Berlin as an island in the midst of the Soviet zone, with no access routes. The statements on zones of occupation and on control machinery provided that the decisions should be unanimous and that the basic requirements should be carried out jointly. These agreements were made before the events in Austria, which guided the administrators along a different and more effective path. There was no veto power in the hands of any one power in Austria. The Central Government had some independent power there from the initial period in 1945.

The difficulties over Berlin came not so much from oversight as from the different concepts for the future of Germany at the close of the war and the failure to anticipate the harder line we were soon to develop toward Russia, a government more anxious to crush than to rebuild for the future. In any case, the mistakes made in 1945 were to be a hazard which the United States would have to face for several decades.

Efforts on the part of our government to reverse our policy came in 1946. The Morgenthau Plan was a "Program to Prevent Germany from Starting a World War III."[64] It had been taken to Quebec in August, 1943, after having been discussed in the Department of State six months earlier. It was never adopted as the policy of the United States, but it influenced many of the directives drafted by experts who felt it was implicit in top-level government thinking. It did set the tone of our policy until the Stuttgart speech of Secretary James Byrnes in September, 1946.

The Morgenthau Plan called for the removal or destruction of key industries. It suggested the dismemberment of Germany, parts going to the U.S.S.R. and to France and the remainder being divided north and south into "two autonomous, independent states." The Ruhr, "the heart of German industrial power," was to be "so weakened and controlled that it cannot in the foreseeable future become an industrial area." The policing and administration of Germany should be "assumed by the military forces of Germany's continental neighbors." Specifically, these should include Russian, French, Polish, Czech, Greek, Yugoslav, Norwegian, Dutch, and Belgian soldiers. Under this program, although America would be represented on the appropriate commissions, "United States troops could be withdrawn within a relatively short time."[65]

It may be difficult to imagine the contemporary point of view which could give serious status to ideas of this type. The document, though never official, was clearly influential. It was based on the hope of cooperation; its abandonment is evidence of the complete change in point of view after the Soviet take-over of Czechoslovakia, the difficulties over the Austrian treaty, the blockade of Berlin, and the recognition of Soviet aggressive intentions. The continued presence of American troops, the development of NATO, the billions spent on the rebuilding of Europe, including Germany, were to be the material evidence of the complete change in policy which soon began after the beginning of the occupation of Germany.

The Byrnes speech referred to stated emphatically, on the basis of earlier European experience, that there must be no vacuum in the heart of Europe. It favored a provisional German government, a new constitution, and economic unification, with a recognition of the need in Germany for more food, coal, and steel, and of the importance to Europe of the production in the Ruhr. There should be economic opportunity to achieve a reasonable standard of living and an export potential, with proper safeguards. Moreover, as to American forces, Byrnes stated emphatically: "We are not withdrawing. We are staying here." Rarely has a government issued a more clear-cut statement of policy and done so in contradiction to what had been assumed to be accepted policy a year before. The truth of the matter lying behind the change was that the Morgenthau Plan had never represented a consensus. It had been the idea of a considerable minority who impressed the President in 1943. Postwar events, which came in quick succession—the difficulties with the communists in all of Europe, the need for reconstruction of the economies of the war-devastated lands, the recognition of the profound effect of war disasters, and the rejection of Naziism in Germany—made it possible for the other school of thought in the Department, which had been against a "Carthaginian peace," to reassert their views. The time when the peace treaty should have been well underway found the Soviets digging in their heels and ignoring the economic, psychological, and political facts of the Europe of 1946. Public opinion in America undoubtedly still distrusted the Germans, but those working in the occupation programs found a desire to cooperate and to establish a true democracy.

The conditions that were to set the stage for the battle of Berlin were not, even in 1946, evident to Washington, Paris, and London. This unique problem became evident only with the development of the currency reform and with refusal of the Soviet occupying generals to participate in this measure, essential to restoring viability to the area; the lack of production was draining funds and supplies from the United States in these years of desperate want and misery.

In December, 1946, a concrete step along the lines of the declaration of Secretary Byrnes was taken in London.[66] An agreement for bizonal fusion was signed by the British and the Americans. It stated that the two powers were ready at any time to talk with the other occupying powers with regard to their adhering to this agreement to fuse their respective zones as one. The French responded in April, 1949. The Soviets, on the contrary, increased their formalities and their barriers to economic interchange.

The planning that continued through 1947 was designed to lay a sound basis for industrial recovery and the elimination of the black market that was paralyzing serious economic activity; this planning was carried on with the full cooperation of the Germans, notably that of Professor Ludwig Erhard, who was to become Chancellor some 15 years later. The communists were faced with a real problem. They could participate in the monetary conversion which was projected or, if they did not, they would find goods and labor drained out of their zone into the newly activated economic life that was certain to develop in the West alongside their zone. Though the nature of this dilemma was not a major factor in the Allied plans, there is no doubt that they saw the prospects and that some, at least, counted on the possibility of progress toward economic unity in the four zones.

It was not until after the coup in Czechoslovakia in February, 1948, and after the full effects of the Austrian currency reform of two years earlier were widely understood, that the more disturbing prospects of Soviet refusal became evident. In March, 1948, the occupying authorities in the East zone began to harass traffic and to threaten the use of the roads which had been administratively assigned to the Western powers for use in supplying their garrisons.[67] The fear of more serious trouble grew, until in June the menace to the maintenance of our position in the city was evident. The failure of the Moscow Conference a year earlier had indicated that a reasonable solution to the problems of occupation was far distant.

In fact, the creeping blockade of Berlin began early in 1948. The Soviets had tried to capture the Berlin parties. They began to see in the firm resistance of Ernst Reuter, Louisa Schroeder, Franz Neumann, and other stanch Berliners, who had what they thought were socialist leanings, the danger of anticommunism, which would make difficulties for them in Berlin—the city that was crucial to their control of a future Germany. Marshal Sokolovsky early in 1948 declared that Berlin was a part of the Soviet zone and prevented British representatives from attending a political meeting in their sector of the city. The Soviets attacked the Allied Control Council on March 10. They walked out on March 20.

They had spread rumors in their controlled press that the Western powers were about to leave the city. Meanwhile, interference with traffic into and out of the city became more frequent. There were a number of new restrictions that delayed the Allied military trains: the Soviets claimed the right to board the trains and examine baggage. The Allies refused to allow Russian soldiers on the trains. During May and June, there were new regulations that tended to choke off trade with the city. Interference with freight was said to be justified by "technical reasons." One of the first air incidents occurred on April 5. There was a crash between a Soviet plane which was maneuvering over Berlin and a British transport aircraft. The Soviet pilot and 14 British passengers were killed over Gatow airfield in the British sector.

Along with the pressure to cut off air and surface travel, another harassment took the form of cutting off the major source of electric power, to deny the Western sector. The directors of the Berlin Electric Company (BEWAG) were ordered to stay off the premises.[68] The Soviets issued a number of unilateral orders to the members of the city's Assembly. These the Berliners refused to honor.

The Blockade and Airlift. In the case of Berlin, as in several other areas, there was a series of crises. It is not possible to say which was more definitive. All affected American policy and impressed the world as to our position. Certainly, the decision of General Clay in 1948 to mount the airlift, which continued for almost a year, was one of the early important manifestations of the extent of our commitment in Europe. It was in 1948 also that the Truman Doctrine of 1947 was followed by the Marshall Plan. The support of Berlin, with its military aspects under the occupation committing money and lives on the theory that Germany would be a true and trusted ally, was impressive. Like other major efforts in foreign policy, it was a risk. The uncertainty we faced was the greater because of the fluctuating behavior of the Soviets in previous months. The attempts to restrict rail travel and freight in March had been relaxed after 10 days. The trains, halted by the Allies, who did not wish to conform to the proposed new rules, ran again. The occasional buzzing of Allied aircraft in the corridors had not been sufficiently disturbing to alter flights. The Berlin Air Safety Center (BASC), one of the few vestiges of four-power arrangements to persist in Berlin in 1967, still functioned, apparently unaffected by the general policy of Soviet harassment.

The atmosphere of danger which was recognized at this time is reflected in the cable of General Lucius D. Clay on March 5, 1948:

> *For many months, based on logical analysis, I have felt and held that war was unlikely for at least ten years. Within the last few weeks, I have felt a subtle change in the Soviet attitude which I cannot define but which now gives me a feeling that it may come with dramatic suddenness . . . a feeling of a new tenseness in every Soviet individual with whom we have official relations. . . .*[69]

While Washington was in general prepared to support General Clay in his measures to prevent Soviet interference with the trains, there was some fear that he would encounter difficulty, so an inquiry was made to Berlin as to the advisability of shipping the dependents of the military out of the city. This suggestion was opposed by General Clay. The rumors about Allied withdrawal, shortages of food, the removal of scrap metal, and economic discrimination against the workers in West Berlin caused uneasiness. Interference with the city government increased. While there were some grounds for the Soviets to conclude, on the basis of earlier statements, that United States policy with respect to remaining in Europe was not entirely clear, they had some doubts which had not been resolved by our actions in 1947. Secretary of Defense Forrestal noted in his diary that Alexander S. Panyushkin of the Soviet Embassy asked Charles Bohlen and Llewellyn Thompson of the State Department "whether the United States really intended to stay in Europe."[70] The answer given at the time must have been construed as not entirely convincing, or perhaps it was not transmitted to the leaders in Moscow. In any case, the pressure was increasing even more in June.

The result of the Six-Power London Conference was announced in the first week in June—the plan for an International Ruhr Authority. As scheduled, the currency reform was put into effect on June 18. This was to apply to West Germany and, as a temporary compromise, not to the city of Berlin. On June 11 and 12 there was interference, again, with road and rail traffic. On June 16, the Soviets walked out of the Berlin *Kommandatura*. On June 24, they imposed a "full land blockade" on the city. Because of the many variations in interferences with communications with the West and because of the changing pretexts for stopping transportation, the more drastic action came as a surprise.

There had been more doubts than firm predictions during these months. The uncertainties included differing estimates as to Soviet willingness to bring hardship to the people, the question as to whether they would endanger their psychological position by an aggressive act, doubt as to whether civilian opinion in the West would support strong and even hazardous action to remain in Berlin, and uncertainty as to the reaction of the populace once the pressure became severe. These and other questions had prevented a clear look ahead by our authorities. Moreover, the military capabilities of the United States were then at a low ebb.

General Clay knew he could count on the leaders in the city, but the point of view of the masses had not yet been made entirely clear. Political events in recent months had been confused, although the indifference of the people to political concerns seemed to be giving way to a firmer will to resist communism, as the pressures on the labor movement and the threat of absorption by the so-called unity party (SED) by the communists became more evident. The importance of the issue for the free world was beginning to emerge in these weeks for the first time. To General Clay, the strongest action seemed the best action. He found Washington hesitant, however. There was no instruction that would have permitted driving tanks through on the ground. There were, moreover, technical difficulties in getting through hostile territory and crossing rivers and fields without prior planning for such an operation. Whether it could have been done without a fiasco is not entirely certain even now, on looking back.

This was a time of great confusion. The Soviets attempted to institute an Eastern currency reform for all Berlin. They issued new orders. There were protests and demonstrations. On the night of Wednesday, the 23rd, the members of the Assembly, fearing arrest, escaped from City Hall in the Eastern sector and took refuge in the Western part of the city. On the morning of the 24th, they learned of the stoppage of freight moving into the city. Water and electricity shortages were feared; food and raw material shortages were threatened. There was considerable indecision in Allied quarters as to the seriousness of the Soviets' intentions, the capabilities of the Allies, and the desirability of various courses of action. A precise account of what alternatives were considered and how the choices were made is not now available, although there are several unofficial accounts. The various reports, based mainly on memory rather than on documentary evidence, differ widely. There is reason to think that the men in Washington, farther from the scene and having fewer data, were more indecisive in these critical days than those in Germany. There are indications that General Clay consistently favored a strong position. Even so, he could not foresee the scope of the airlift and the extent to which it would serve not only the occupying troops but the people and the industry of Berlin. This doubt is understandable; nevertheless, it was only a matter of hours before he put the planes in the air (see pages 116–118). By June 26 the schedule called for approximately 500–700 tons of supplies a day. With careful husbanding of all resources, it was thought the city could survive for a few months, perhaps into the winter.

The story of the next eleven months showed the stamina, ingenuity, and courage of the Berliners, of the Allied pilots, and of all the others involved in keeping the city alive. If the challenge was not met on the ground, as some think it should have been, the airlift was nonetheless impressive. From this time on, the doubts about the determination of the citizens and the policy of the United States and the gravity of the issue would not be seriously urged. Yet, in spite of evidence, Premier Khrushchev was to entertain hopes of a reversal of Allied and German policy when he came to control the Kremlin in 1958.

In Berlin, after a few months the Soviets concluded the blockade was unavailing. It even strengthened the will to resist their aggression. The blockade ended in May, 1949; the long ordeal seemed to be over; the city returned to its task of rebuilding and restoring economic life to a reasonable standard of production and well-being.

Recovery Increases the Political Stakes.   From 1949 to 1958 there was a period of relative calm in Berlin. In the 10 years or so, between major crises there were times when the Communist strategists took the temperature and tried the will power of the occupying powers and of the citizens of Berlin. They occasionally gained some ground in their dealings with specific problems, but they uncovered no major weakness. In spite of the annoyance from the stoppage of barge traffic, the exacting of road tolls, threats in the air corridors, and occasional kidnappings and contrived riots to disturb the peace, the city flourished. The American programs, worked out in careful detail with the Berlin authorities and concurred in by the Bonn officials, cut unemployment from over 30 percent of the labor force to a negligible amount by 1958. (Actually, in 1965 there was a labor shortage, as industry flourished.) Impressive new structures bore witness to the long-term plans of Germans and Americans. The volume of production rose and the standard of living improved, more or less in line with that in West Germany.

There were in these years repeated diplomatic efforts to settle the German question and to provide for the continuance of a free and democratic Berlin. The Soviet efforts to have a summit conference, first in 1953 and then in 1954, led to the Eisenhower-Bulganin-Eden-Faure conference in Geneva in 1955.

The Berlin conference, an interesting test of skill in diplomacy (see Chapter II), had brought no concrete results. It was evident that the Soviets had not come to the point where the control of Germany seemed to them to have escaped their grasp. They would not consider a solution including the protection of the rights of Berlin. The fact that the recovery of the city was outdistancing all expectations actually led to more efforts to choke it off. The economic, political, and cultural life in West Berlin, in sharp contrast to that in the Soviet zone, made it a beacon and a showplace. The constant stream of refugees leaving the "Workers' Paradise" in order to find a better and freer life in the West was both a loss to important East German factories, as manpower became scarce, and a cause of unrest among those who stayed and those who considered leaving. It was not easy to consolidate the communist regime when those in the Eastern zone could visit the Western zone so easily. The contrast caused unrest. The problem of interzonal relations was of some urgency for the Soviets. It is difficult to interpret some of their actions in those years, but apparently they were seeking, by inducements, threats, and novel proposals, to drive a wedge between the Allies.

Meanwhile, the Germans had been brought into NATO in 1954.

The elections in 1957 returned Konrad Adenauer as Chancellor, and the rapprochement with the French was evidenced by the agreement, in the ministerial meeting in Paris in May, 1956, on uniting the Saar with the Federal Republic of Germany. In the light of these many-sided developments, the four-power statement in Geneva calling for the unification of Germany by free elections casts a strange light on the Soviets' underlying intentions and estimates. The Western position would appear by this time to have been visible and constant in the support of Berlin.[71]

The many minor incidents called for a series of protests by the Allies, but countermeasures or effective steps to penalize those who caused trouble were not easy to invoke. Those who had been through the desperate postwar years—the blockade, the revolt of 1953, and the alternating pressures and relaxations—found some of the incidents trying, expensive, even frightening, but not of such a nature as to change their political orientation or to make them want to leave the city. The Free University was crowded. Many students came from the Eastern zone, as well as from the West. Travel back and forth was easy and relatively safe. The border-crossers moving both ways in the city numbered between 30,000 and 40,000. They lived in one half of the city and worked in the other. There was a sense of fatalism, and there was little hope of an early alteration of the unusual conditions. Reunification was regarded as important—almost everyone had close relatives among the 17 million in the Eastern zone—but it was not considered imminent. It was included in every political platform, but there was little or nothing that could be done to bring it about.

Opinions differed as to the extent of interzonal trade to be permitted. Many felt that it was a patriotic duty to keep effective contacts with business within the zone. Others looked to short-term profits and thought that the gain from interzonal trade was justified. Meanwhile, the "All-German Ministry" endeavored to reach out a helping hand to those behind the Iron Curtain and to keep alive the hopes of ultimate restoration of the Eastern provinces to the Federal Republic.

Premier Khrushchev was reported to have termed the continued existence of a flourishing Berlin in the zone of Soviet occupation a "bone in his throat." When he gained what he considered to be a position of power in the Kremlin and in the party, he fixed his mind on extending his areas of control, in the Middle East, in the Far East, and in Germany. His ambitions were to lead him into dangerous territory, where the West did not hesitate to meet the challenge in spite of the possible cost. Though he had been watching the signs, they had failed to convince him of the determination of the men in Washington and in NATO. Strangely enough, this was the explanation of his action in 1958. A new crisis was to cause temporary consternation in the beleaguered city.

The Pressure Is On: 1958. The Thanksgiving Day demands of Premier Khrushchev had been heralded by the statements in Khrushchev's November 10 speech at the Polish Embassy in Moscow. This was the beginning of a serious attack on the status of Berlin. He had spoken with vehemence as he assailed Western militarism. In a press conference on the day before Thanksgiving, Dulles replied to a question on the violent charges in Moscow against the occupying power. The Secretary said he was not surprised—he referred to the periodic attempts to catch the free world off balance. There had been a delay in following up the November 10 attack, with its statement that the Potsdam Conference agreement had been broken, thus relieving the Soviets of their obligations. Secretary Dulles suggested that in the days since that statement, perhaps Khrushchev had consulted his lawyers and that he had been cautioned as to the invalidity of his statement.

The later Soviet demands—contained in the note presented to the United States Embassy in Moscow—were more formal and explicit than the previous attempts to force the Western powers out. The note was more insistent than the earlier attacks on the position of the Western powers, and for the first time it contained an ultimatum. It stated that if no agreement along the lines suggested had been reached by the end of six months, the Soviets would sign a separate peace treaty with the Germans in their zone of occupation.

The note said that "present procedures of military traffic" would be altered and "all contacts between the representatives of the armed forces and the officials of the armed forces of the United States of America, Great Britain, and France would terminate." This would have left the Berlin occupying forces under the control of the officers of the German Democratic Republic (GDR), the unrecognized and communist-ridden regime acting for the Soviets but with no genuine representative power. This would have made the Western powers the prey to arbitrary acts of interference and with no competent government with which to deal.

Another new aspect of the situation was the concept of a "free city." This would have given the Soviets unlimited possibility of pressure from the surrounding areas, with the capacity for blackmail, kidnapping, and economic pressures, and the ability to disturb the peace; and there would have been no counterforce. Once the occupying forces withdrew, the legal chain of rights and responsibilities would be broken, and the isolated city could be choked, gradually, perhaps, or with a swift coup. The NATO powers would have no possibility of effective action, short of a major attack against the enemy. The victory in Germany would be partially wiped out, and our commitments would be impossible to maintain.

All aspects of the situation and the spurious nature of the "free city" proposal were immediately understood by the Berliners, by the Germans in Bonn, and by the Allied experts and statesmen, many of whom had been working on the German question for 20 years. To meet this contingency, a series of declarations and contingency plans had been made. The involvement of the United States in the continued protection of Berlin was a major element in policy. The last moment of conceivable choice to leave the city had been made in 1948. By maintaining the airlift the decision to stay had been made firm. It was a cornerstone of our defense of Europe. There could be no question in 1958 as to our reaction. In fact, there was no hesitation.

In the afternoon of November 27, Thanksgiving, Foster Dulles returned to work. In a meeting with several of his staff, he drafted a brief press release. Its tone was firm:

> The United States, along with Britain and France, is solemnly committed to the security of the Western sectors of Berlin. Two and a quarter million West Berliners in reliance thereon, have convincingly and courageously demonstrated the good fruits of freedom . . . the United States will not acquiesce in a unilateral repudiation by the Soviet Union of its obligations and responsibilities.[72]

This statement was made within a few hours of the reading of the note from Moscow.

The phrase "free city" had seemed to the Soviets perhaps a bait to lure the unsuspecting to give the proposal favorable consideration. There might have been some attraction in the idea if it had not been limited to the Western half of the city. The artificial division which Khrushchev proposed would have retained the Eastern part under communist control; the Western part, preserving "the present way of life, based on private capitalistic ownership, would be an independent political unit, without any state 'interfering in its life.'" "There would be no objection," Khrushchev said, "to the United Nations sharing in one way or another in observing the free-city status of West Berlin."

Khrushchev demanded that the armed forces depart, that the city be demilitarized, and that arrangements be made with the GDR for the movement of freight and communications between the city and the outside world. He spoke of their "desire to normalize the situation" and "to contribute to the stability and prosperity of the city's economy to raise their standard of living."[73] The threat to throw over the control of access to the communist GDR came at the very end. The message offered no concessions to the Western powers in return for their withdrawal.

The publication of the Moscow note caused a short period of consternation in Berlin. There were large transfers of funds to the Federal Republic, and some talk of moving to the West. The air of panic prevailed for a matter of hours. In the meantime, the Washington press release of November 27 was examined by the Germans and others. It was followed three days later by the reaffirmation of our continuing support of the city from the temporary White House in Georgia. Calm was restored to a stout-hearted public in Berlin. The more formal reply was held until the four powers could coordinate their draft in the course of the December NATO meeting. The President had been kept informed in Georgia, and when the Secretary visited him on November 30, he authorized a further statement saying that it was our "firm purpose that the United States would not enter into any arrangements which would abandon the responsibilities . . . for the freedom and security of West Berlin."[74]

The crisis over Berlin was, in fact, of short duration. The action of the Soviets was not unexpected, though it had some new angles. Our policy and plans were so deeply embedded in 10 years of diplomatic activity and economic and political history that there was no element of doubt. The procedures in dealing with the British, French, and Germans were almost automatic, having been used on many occasions. There was no gap in thinking and intentions between the staffs in the State Department, in Bonn, and in Berlin, and those who had the final word in Washington, the President and the Secretary of State. The brief conference between Dulles and Eisenhower, on November 30 was concerned merely with considering whether or not there was any significance to the new wording and the change in approach implied by the ultimatum. Drafts prepared by the staff circulated among the Embassies in Washington and abroad; they had to do with minor matters of wording, not with the continuing policy. Consideration was given to the possible need to strengthen morale in Berlin. Those concerned with the psychological and financial aspects of the conditions in the city addressed themselves to the plans for additional aid and to exploring any points of doubt or weakness.

The rebound of the confidence of the citizens was demonstrated not only by the return of funds to the Berlin savings banks, but also by the December 7 elections in which the voters cut back the small communist vote from almost 4 percent to less than 2 percent. It was the largest turnout in free elections in German history.[75] The statements made in Washington thus had an immediate echo in Germany.

We Reaffirm Our Position. In order to evaluate the Soviet note and the Allied response, it is necessary to recall the pressure of the Soviets over the previous 12 months for a summit conference. In agreeing to preparatory discussions, the Western Allies had reaffirmed, on several occasions, the need for inclusion of reunification along lines agreed on in Paris in 1949 and Geneva in 1955. Meanwhile, the Germans had officially requested on September 9, 1958, that the four responsible powers establish a working group to prepare joint proposals "for a solution to the German problem."[76]

In the reply of September 30 to this note, as well as in Secretary Dulles' news conferences of November 7 and November 26, there had been emphatic restatements of the unvarying determination of the United States to hold to a solution which would guarantee the freedom and the democratic choice of the German people. There was not the slightest indication that the policy toward Berlin had weakened. The Soviets in their reply to the request of the Federal

Republic of Germany stated that the GDR (German Democratic Republic) was disquieted by the long delay in the preparation of a treaty, and that they (the Soviets) therefore proposed a commission to work out a treaty in which the GDR and the FRG would be included. Such a proposal, which would appear to put the communist puppet officials in a position of international bargaining with free governments, was unacceptable, and immediately repudiated by the FRG, as it woulld rule out a democratic solution. In this exchange, however, it was apparent both that the U.S.S.R. wished to use the German question as a road to the summit and that the Soviets thought that the threat of a treaty for the GDR would be efficacious in making the Western Allies modify their position in Berlin.

Because of the constant repetition of our stand on Berlin and the recurrent explanation of the relation of Berlin to Germany and to all Europe in the defense of freedom, we encountered a minor difficulty in successive declarations. It was almost impossible for the President and the Secretary to make a statement that was not repetitious. They had to consider carefully the possible misconstruction of any variation in wording as grounds for the conclusion that we would relinquish our support or that there were differences of policy among the Allies.

The hypersensitivity of all Germans to the accepted words referring to the methods to be used in attaining reunification and dealings with the East Germans required special attention. The reaction to speculation by the Secretary which was wrongly construed as constituting a change in Washington's position required painstaking explanations to clarify the hastily reported dialogue at a press conference; this was an illustration of this delicately balanced situation. Dulles in speculating about the various ways in which political fusion had been possible in a number of historical instances had thrown out the the suggestion that elections could theoretically follow other acts to bring about union. Similarly, he had explored, in an abstract manner, the use of *agents* to act for their principals. The flare-up of a nervous German public opinion at the thought of changes in the time-honored formulas was evidence of their dependence on the three Western occupying powers for their continued existence.

It was for these well-recognized reasons that the Washington experts, working on the precise wording of the formal reply, had to coordinate every phrase with each other and with those in Paris and London, as well as in Bonn. There was no question as to the determination to stand firm, and after the first few hours, this was realized in Berlin and also in Moscow.

Premier Khrushchev, during a reception at the Albanian Embassy in Moscow on November 29, was reported to have backed away from his ultimatum.[77] At about the same time, it was said that the "Soviet Union might delay the transfer of its Berlin responsibilities to the East German Government." This was the word of a "Soviet Embassy official in East Berlin." Apparently, the Western reaction, both officially stated and transmitted by the "grapevine," had gotten through to the Kremlin.

General Henry I. Hodes, Commander-in-Chief of the United States Army in Europe, made a visit to Berlin on November 30. By the time the NATO communiqué was issued on December 16, calm had been restored. American Major General Barksdale Hamlett, meeting with the other generals, reviewed the situation and increased the preparations to counter a possible coup by the East German communists. The formal Allied reply was transmitted on December 31. Berlin had again served as a barometer of tension in the conflict between the communists and the free world. Another crisis had been weathered. The Berliners went about their business with a shrug of the shoulders.[78]

Hidden Dangers.   For the Western powers, however, there were a number of considerations that had to be taken into account. Although the crisis as it came to its apex at the end of November did not seem to hold serious risks for most Americans, accustomed to the ups and downs of the Berlin question, for those who were working with the various specific aspects of the problem, it was troubling and necessitated intensive work. It was agreed that some visible signs of U.S. support in the city should be planned and publicized at this time. A new U.S.-financed political science building at the Free University was approved, and construction began within a few months. Special attention was directed to maintaining confidence in Berlin production; insurance measures were instituted and new branches of American firms (including a new building for the International Business Machines Corporation) were promised in the center of the city. Production expanded under these encouragements, orders from outside increased, and unemployment declined still further.

The steady flow of refugees from the East continued, but at an accustomed level. The situation that Khrushchev had called "abnormal" continued to be the norm.

On the diplomatic front, further activity was required by the fact that the note to the Soviets had said:

> The Government of the United States is ready at any time to enter into discussions with the Soviet Government on the basis of these proposals [i.e., the Western proposals for free all-German elections and free decisions for an all-German Government], or of any other proposals, genuinely designed to insure the reunification of Germany in freedom, or in any appropriate forum.
>
> On this basis, the United States Government would be interested to learn whether the Soviet Government is ready to enter into discussions. . . .[79]

There was a consensus that a meeting must be held to explore the Soviet intentions further and to test whether there could be a new approach to the German question which would not destroy the accepted policy and which would maintain the position of NATO, with a strong and democratic Germany contributing to the defense of Europe. This meeting was scheduled for April 1. Dulles, to assure the unity of the Allies, made what was to be his last trip to Europe, in February, 1959.

The experts were studying all conceivable aspects of the support of Berlin and the meaning of any changes in the control of access and whether or not they were the result of any modification in the Soviets' relations with the East Germans. It was recognized, for instance, that subtle changes in the handling of the papers of troops going in and out of the city might prejudice, by a process of erosion, the rights for which we had held the U.S.S.R. responsible over a period of more than a decade. Only those who dealt with this question on a day-to-day basis and, of course, the Germans, who referred to these acts by the Soviets as "salami tactics," realized the dangers implicit in small details.

Here, as elsewhere in the strange maneuvering of the Cold War, the inability to use nuclear strength or even to throw the weight of considerable conventional forces against an enemy ready to destroy not only a nation, but perhaps a world, was evident. To provocative harassment we answered with protests. To threats we replied with efforts to negotiate. Here, we could not use our military potential without risking a very serious incident. This fact led to continuing frustration—but Berlin prospered.

The Aftermath of Crisis—Opinion Not Shaken. The Soviet note of January 10, 1959, and subsequent exchanges led to a meeting of the Foreign Ministers in Geneva from April into mid-summer. This was a consultation that was expected to prepare for the summit meeting, later set for May, 1960. That was a meeting never to be carried through, because of Khrushchev's sudden angry departure from Paris after the U-2 incident (see page 181). Thus the aftermath of the November crisis dragged on for many months. There was no significant change in the situation in Berlin. Economic conditions continued to improve. Politically, there was no noticeable anxiety. Conditions were not significantly altered until the Wall was built in 1961.

Opinion in outside official circles was not greatly stirred by the crisis of 1958. In world capitals, some thought there had been a loss, because there had been no Western gain, but it is probable that few realized the seriousness of the Soviet proposal or the manner in which a change in the status of Berlin would have demoralized the German public and their position in NATO. Since the reaction of the Western powers left no room for doubt, many thought that, however unsatisfactory it might be to postpone the settlement of the German question, it was still a situation that could be tolerated. The reasons why a separate peace treaty between the Soviets and the East Germans would disturb the Western alliance were not always clear to the uninitiated, but the idea was accepted as policy, along with others of the more specialized aspects of European relations—part of the new efforts to defend the free world.

Berlin was becoming a watchword and a beacon for many; for others, it was a mystery and a typical diplomatic conundrum. The realities of life in the isolated city, though often featured in news stories and television documentaries, were still hard to grasp. There was a measure of incredulity about the extent of our commitment. It was not generally realized that a war, involving many nations, might result from an incident in the corridors of access by which the Allied soldiers entered and left the city. The proportion which reasonable people seek, in their estimates of risks and results, did not seem to be achieved in this case. Thus the grave challenge, quickly met, had caused little anxiety in Washington, New York, Chicago, and other cities which were *real* and which fitted into a familiar pattern. The diplomats could struggle over the former German capital, but somehow the danger would continue to be remote for most Americans.

The stress and strain of the end of the year and the attacks on our firmly held policy and on our strongholds that followed; those launched in the Middle East and countered in July in Lebanon; another in the Far East that was thwarted in October, when the shelling of Quemoy and Matsu ended—the meaning of these was clear. They were attempts to induce us to break our time-honored commitments. These had become a part of the structure of the European alliance, stemming from before the blockade and made more vital during the airlift, which had been supported in the United States by all the postwar administrations. In the case of Berlin, there had been no significant change in policy for more than 10 years.

The Framework of Crisis.   Setting the crisis of November, 1958, in the framework in which the other crises have been analyzed, we find that (1) the fundamental policy had been clearly articulated; (2) plans for various contingencies had been developed, with variations to provide for a number of possible modifications of the manner in which the communists would apply pressure; (3) information as to conditions and possible changes in the situation was adequate. When it came to the phase where (4) recommendations were to be made, (5) decisions were almost instantaneous, since the alternatives to rejecting the Soviet plan were agreed in advance to be unacceptable.

Thus phases were telescoped in the handling of the emergency, and the decision had been predetermined. There could be no response except a flat negative to the Soviet proposal. They offered no substance in return for the concession to be made by the occupying powers. There was not even a plausible advantage that could have furnished grounds for negotiation, or hesitation. The suggestion, while using phrases such as "peace," "relaxation of tensions," "improved standards of living," and "free city," had no content that justified the words. The choice was spurious, the decision was inevitable, and the explanation was developed as a matter of course.

For the general public, the crisis almost immediately became unreal. For those directly concerned, many problems were posed. They were the ones called on to live with a new danger.

THE CHALLENGE OF THE CONGO: 1960

Independence and Revolt. The problem that confronted the world as the Congo broke into revolution in 1960 was a violent transition from colonialism to independence. No nation had anticipated the type or extent of the trouble with the Congolese army that developed. Most expected the Belgians to remain as advisers. The government in Leopoldville and the leaders in the various provinces were completely without administrative and material resources to meet the emergency that faced them. Excitement gave way to chaos, and violence threatened to annihilate the forces of law and order.

The United States was deeply concerned about the turn of events and wished to assure the continued existence of the new government and its power to dominate tribal conflicts and build up a viable political system. It had sent a number of "old African hands" to staff the new Embassy. Its capacity to act in 1960 was, however, limited by the fact that direct intervention would be considered an objectionable imposition of white imperialism. Great skill had to be exercised in the efforts to reach a solution. The manner in which the United States faced the difficulties and decided on a course of action through the United Nations at this early stage of African independence was therefore of great importance during the years of increasing national autonomy for Africa. The account of these events and actions constitutes an important phase in recent foreign policy developments.

The United Nations' performance in the Congo has been called the largest and most difficult operation ever administered by an international organization. The need to act was spurred on by the complex issues associated with the struggle of the U.S.S.R. to exploit opportunities for communist dominance among the new nations. This was a major foreign policy problem for all the great powers.

It reflected many misconceptions, false estimates, and disillusionments. It demonstrated that the hopes of the emerging nations could not be easily and quickly fulfilled.

In the Congo we see a new type of responsibility and initiative taken by the United States. Our action in advising the leaders in Leopoldville and guiding them in their appeal for international support is evidence of the diplomatic importance of the indirect use of power. Yet, in spite of prompt and well-devised action—our response to the difficulties between the first rapid increase in disorder and the entrance of United Nations Forces two weeks later—our handling of the Congo crisis cannot be considered a complete success. Nevertheless, it must be viewed against the background of the desperate situation that existed and the major disaster that would have occurred if our policy had not been adopted. The significance of the events in the Congo is related to many complex requirements that must be met to help the newly independent nations along the road to maturity.

Many aspects of the Congo situation are typical, but some are exceptional, in the progress from colonialism to freedom. The legacy of Belgian control takes on more significance when compared with the handling during the past decade of transitions from British, French, Spanish, Italian, and Portuguese rule to national independence. The need for outside support to improve health, literacy, currency, investments, law, and administration was typical. The combination of wealth and poverty in the Congo was exceptional. The opportunities for subversion were probably greater in the Congo in 1960 than in some other countries. The case merits careful study.

Glass Houses Are Vulnerable: July 8, 1960. There were terror and violence in Leopoldville on July 8, 1960. On that Friday a circling jeep with three Congolese soldiers in it finally stopped in front of the U. S. Embassy. These men represented the people who had just been granted release from colonialism. They now had independence, and to them it was *Uhuru*—freedom, prosperity, and hope—a future that would magically bring all good things. At least one enterprising man sold shoe boxes done up in brown paper and labeled "Independence"—when opened, they were found to contain nothing but dirt.

At this time of change, many went wild with enthusiasm. The

soldiers were becoming colonels and generals overnight. Everyone asked for more pay. Restraint was gone. Excitement reigned. After two days of gay celebration on June 30 and July 1, disorder among the soldiers broke out on a serious scale. The first trouble was followed swiftly by widespread mutiny in the army, and fear spread through both the white and the black communities. The jeep that came to the Embassy was patrolling the streets, which were temporarily empty as the soldiers moved to other parts of the city. The men in the jeep were armed.

The newly constructed American Embassy was walled with glass. More than a hundred visitors—tourists and businessmen—were crowded in the lobby, a showcase in which every person waiting on the first floor or climbing the stairs to the offices above could be seen from outside. The anxious Americans there had sought shelter from roving soldiers running wild and assaulting white people, Belgians, or those who might be Belgians, and even Congolese. They had been in the Embassy many hours. Even escape across the Congo River to Brazzaville had been cut off for a time.

When the jeep stopped, there was an angry demonstration in front of the Embassy. Ambassador Clare Timberlake went to the door. He was responsible for those seeking refuge. Rather than have the glass shattered, he opened the door and faced the soldiers. "Take away the cameras," they demanded. Through an interpreter, he tried to reason with them. "There are no cameras," he said. "We are not taking pictures."

At that moment, a heedless tourist inside pushed forward a camera and photographed the soldiers. They jumped back, aiming their rifle butts at the large glass panes. Timberlake interposed himself between the men and the windows. Unruffled by their menacing pose, he pulled out his cigarette case. *"Prenez,"* he said. The three Congolese, taken by surprise, hesitated. Then they rested their guns, and each took a cigarette. A moment later, awed and abashed, they turned back to their jeep, got in, and drove away. Clearly, this man Timberlake was in control. The frightened spectators inside the Embassy breathed a sigh of relief. Here, at least, they were safe.

The Heart of Africa: From Stanley to Lumumba.   The Congo, more than 900,000 square miles in the center of Africa, drained by mighty rivers and bordered by large lakes, has represented, for many, the best and the worst of colonialism. Here the people responded with frantic enthusiasm to Patrice Lumumba, the new Prime Minister, when he spoke of the "struggles of tears, fire, and blood" and now "an end to the humiliating bondage imposed on us by force." Here the quick change of pace from slow development to sudden and unaccustomed responsibility was to show the disrupting force of passion and disunity in lands that had little preparation for the new power thrust into their hands or seized from the representatives of their former rulers.

The thick forests that Henry Stanley penetrated in 1876 on his original journey down the Congo still choke the rivers and separate the villages of the tropical land in the center of the "dark continent." The horrors of Stanley's explorations—the loss of hundreds of men in the lethal jungle, which brought sickness, starvation, and calamitous accidents—still dog the footsteps of soldier or businessman, tourist or politician who try to learn the nature and master the forces of the large territory. Still they find themselves in the gloom of the almost impenetrable forest, navigating rivers where swimmers are attacked by crocodiles, and ants swarm over the carcasses of dead beasts. Tribal groups appear suddenly in hostile guise, and primitive villages offer scant shelter. A few miles from the business district of Leopoldville, one has gone back centuries in time. Although frequently one hears an airplane overhead, the landing fields are rare and far between. Thus a true understanding calls for some appreciation of these continuing natural obstacles to development.

For 75 years the Belgians ruled this land with a heavy hand. The contrast between the works they developed and the manner in which they carried out their colonization supplies much of the reason for the trouble which was the heritage of the leaders for independence.

The 1885 conference of Berlin, called together by the Turks and the Americans, was attended by delegates from 13 other nations. Ostensibly, it was to regulate trade and navigation on the Congo and Niger rivers. It went much beyond the original idea and resulted in territorial arrangements of considerable importance. Leopold II, King of the Belgians, was accorded recognition of his claim to the International Congo Association as a sovereign power and was thus enabled to organize the "Congo Free State" as a legal entity separate from Belgium, with the monarch for squire. The area was large and formed a prosperous investment; it had rubber and copper and other rich resources. These were exploited, with considerable profit and notable brutality, for many years. As a result, a Reform Association was established to consider the alleged scandals involving forced labor and deaths. In 1904, the King instituted an official inquiry. The result was a change in status which made the Free State a Belgian colony in 1908.

The United States had not signed the treaty of Berlin, holding the position that it should not be a party to the territorial adjustments involved. It was not until the late 1950s that we felt impelled by circumstances to take cognizance of the results of the decades of exploitation and colonial activities.

Some of the work of the colonial powers was good. It varied in style from case to case. In the Belgian Congo, in spite of some opinion to the contrary, there was a large effort in public health and education, particularly in the establishment of primary schools. It is reported that in the time just before liberation a considerable number of children of primary school age were in classes (the total was probably more than 1,400,000). As a result, the literacy rate—though measured in very general terms—was higher than in some other parts of Africa. There were many hospitals, close to or even exceeding the need, and considerable medical care. Welfare of a sort was administered, but all was on a completely paternalistic basis. In the army, as in the civil administration, the officers were all white. No responsibility devolved on the blacks. Though two universities had been built, they were just beginning to turn out graduates at the time of independence. Louvanium, a large and handsome structure near Leopoldville, had several hundred students at the time of freedom. Only five or six were studying law. Some were studying medicine, but there were no graduate doctors in 1960.

Since few had been allowed to leave the country, only a handful had attended foreign universities. In contrast, more than 200 had gone abroad from Nigeria to study, and significant numbers had gone from the French colonies. Approximately 100,000 white businessmen, officers, and missionaries ran the Congo. (A few Congolese were added to the administration of the provinces in the 1950s.)

For many years, the paternalism of the government seemed to work. A considerable part of the profits was plowed back into the economy to raise the standard of living. As a matter of fact, the level of living was higher than that of the neighboring countries. A 10-year program that began in 1950 devoted approximately $900 million to housing, education, sewage systems, water purification, medical centers, and similar programs. The Belgians had planned a "methodical pyramid-shaped development scheme which visualized another 50 years of peaceful colonial rule."[80] Unfortunately, there was not to be sufficient time for the plan to develop. Thus the sudden rush of events left the country with only the base of the pyramid and no upper structure to provide leadership and discipline.

Racial discrimination against Africans was lessened by a number of legislative acts and ordinances in the decade of the 1950s. The theory of the *évolués*, which had its counterpart in Angola and Mozambique, led to a procedure for selecting the elite and binding them to the Belgian government in a special feeling of loyalty. This provision was carried further by a decree in 1952 establishing registries for the "immatriculation" of the "civilized Congolese population." These artificial measures brought into special situations less than one-tenth of 1 percent of the population. They were therefore of little significance and failed to halt the drive for genuine independence which was swelling in the Congo, stimulated by similar drives in neighboring countries.

In this rapidly changing situation, the economic resources of the Katanga mines were a source of both strength and weakness for the nation. Without them there would have been much less incentive for holding onto power in this tropical country. As it was, the *Union Minière du Haut Katanga*, incorporated in 1906, was a major factor in the political, as well as economic, life. From this source came about one-third of the revenue which flowed into the public treasury. The rich deposits included copper, uranium,* tin, manganese, zinc, and industrial diamonds. The production of cobalt was half the world's supply. The ownership and corporate structure of the *Union Minière* (UMK) had become so complicated that negotiation between the government of Belgium and the Congo on financial distributions is still proceeding. There is no question that the potential is so great as to induce continued interest on the part of many Belgian nationals in the fate of the nation. It is reported that foreign interests derived $47 million in 1960 in net mining profit in the Congo.

---

* The uranium had become less important.

Because of the fact that a large segment of the population is mainly concerned with subsistence farming and hunting and fishing, a plan was put into effect by the government to rotate the workers between rural and industrial occupations, in an attempt to spread the benefits of the richer sector of the economy. This plan was expected to improve the tone of political life and somewhat equalize economic opportunities. Production of the *Union Minière* was sustained to a remarkable extent through the years of civil disturbance and war. In addition to mineral wealth, the country had large hydroelectric power resources, mostly located in the province of Katanga.

In the time of strife, Katanga was vitally important to Moise Tshombe, the ambitious leader of antigovernment forces; the importance of the area, though related to the economic significance of the nation, was essentially political. Nevertheless, the existence of the economic resources, as well as the presence of Belgian administrators there, affected Tshombe's point of view. It also created bitter opposition to his activities.

The Rush Toward Independence: January–June, 1960. Events in the last six months of the Belgian colony were to cascade in quick, confusing succession. The colonial administrators at first tried to stem the tide by concessions and then reversed themselves in panic as they recognized the impetuous will of the Congolese leaders for freedom—a will echoed by world public opinion. The "Round Table" held in Brussels in January, 1960, was the last major phase in the struggle for gradualism. Representatives of 19 tribes and 20 parties were present—a total of 62 Congolese leaders, including Lumumba. He had been flown there from prison, where he had been held since the October riots in Stanleyville; the unhealed wounds from his handcuffs were still visible. Kasavubu, who also was there, lost his leading position when he walked out after his demand for the immediate formation of a national government had been rejected. He favored a loose federal structure; this plan left the way open for separatist tendencies which, after independence, were to plague the new government, while Moise Tshombe rose to power in Katanga. At the time, however, some, including Tshombe, thought only that the meeting would end excessive centralization.

The Belgians gave in to the demands for early independence, which was scheduled for June 30. Many resolutions were passed;

they called for elections and the formation of a central government before independence. They also provided for Congolese participation in government before independence. A constitution, or *Loi Fondamentale*, was enacted in May by the Belgian Parliament. In that month, the six provincial Assemblies and 137 members of the National Chamber of Deputies were elected. Lumumba's wing led the other parties, with 41 of the 137 seats. He was thought by some to be a truly outstanding politician, with a flair for the dramatic. He favored a strongly centralized government. Actually, however, the government formed in May was a compromise between Lumumba and Kasavubu, neither of whom was able to form a government alone. At the end of May, a Belgo-Congolese Treaty of Friendship was signed. The atmosphere was one of repressed resentment.

There had been an economic round table in April and May. The Belgians had agreed to a loan of almost $80 million to meet the expected deficit of the new government. Although everyone, including experts in the United States, realized that there would be economic troubles during the time of transition, everyone underestimated the coming difficulties.

On Thursday, June 30, at ceremonies attended by many foreign dignitaries, King Baudouin proclaimed the independence of the Congo. Ambassador Robert Murphy was sent to represent the United States. There were two days of peaceful celebration, then chaos.

The United States' Concern. The United States, though it recognized the importance of the new Congo, was not anxious to assume large burdens in Africa. Watching with anxiety events in Cuba, in Vietnam, in Algeria, and elsewhere, Washington had nonetheless turned its attention to the new nation. There had been promises of scholarships and consideration of economic problems while Murphy was in Leopoldville for the festival. The small Embassy staff was familiar with African problems and was destined to show both ingenuity and courage in the trying months to come. To those who know the stresses and strains to which they were subjected, many of these Americans are among the heroes in the long annals of diplomatic history.

In this time of political transition, it was natural for the troops to expect some relaxation of discipline and to feel a deep sense of injustice when told that they must not take personal advantage of independence. They had anticipated the throwing off of restraints. Thus, the soldiers began to run amuck. Privates became officers overnight. They had not been accustomed to responsibility; they understood discipline to be synonymous only with oppression. The great misconception about freedom was bringing unbelievable horrors. The land had not become a paradise. The economic problems of an undeveloped country remained and were, in fact, accentuated by the throwing off of the old system. The wild days to come were the result of this frustration and confusion. There was no experience to serve as a basis for control by the local leaders.

Several tribal clashes were reported on July 2 and 3. Before the outside world realized what was happening, the main source of strength, the *Force Publique*, mutinied on the 5th. By July 8, the country was swept by panic in all the main cities and in many of the rural areas. The whites everywhere were fleeing across the borders or to foreign embassies. Some gathered in urban centers where they hoped to find refuge. Reports in Leopoldville of troubles elsewhere indicated that hundreds of armed Congolese troops were roaming the towns in unbridled excitement. As fear mounted, on July 8 the Belgian residents who had not already fled rushed in a mass to the Belgian Embassy, asking for protection. This news was flashed all over the country. In Elisabethville, in particular, as the Belgians brought their wives and children in from their scattered homes, the Congolese misunderstood their intentions. Each group thought the other was preparing to attack.

By this time, about three-fourths of the white population had taken flight. Those who had charge of administrative, technical, and health facilities and services were gone, and a complete breakdown of the social and economic organization was threatened.

Those who were endeavoring to appraise the situation outside the country were somewhat misled by the fact that the early Belgian newspaper reports, endeavoring to scale down apprehension, spoke of the events as being caused by "effervescence." The New York *Times* picked up the word on July 2 and added: "Perhaps it was a correct word for the sudden bubbling of the spirit of independence among the troops without any truly violent manifestation." On July 4, the *Times* had said in its first reports of manifestations: "Despite these clashes, there has been nothing like the violence that had been predicted to follow independence."

A few days later, the true nature of the situation became apparent. The early mutinies, which had subsided temporarily, broke out with new violence. Though the expressed demands of the soldiers were for more pay and the immediate replacement of the Belgian officers by Congolese, actually, they resented what they considered the unfair restraint that came with efforts to maintain discipline at the moment of liberation. A reporter in Leopoldville described the situation as he watched the throngs from the outlying districts streaming into the city, telling of terrorism and rape. "Weeping women, some in nightgowns, ran to the Belgian Embassy compound. Many carried infants in their arms." The continuing flight angered the mutineers, who found another evidence of racial hostility in the fear that lay behind it. On July 11, the New York *Times* reported a British diplomat as saying: "The Congo is falling apart. This has become a country which is a body without a head. Everything is crippled. All is chaos. Law and order are rapidly disintegrating!" A State Department release announced on the same day: "The 10-day-old government of the Congo has been out of effective office for the last 24 hours, and the Belgian troops are taking control."

The United States' Policy.   During the first week in July, American policy in the Congo seemed to the outsider to be on a "wait-and-see" basis. The Embassy staff were busy arranging for the safety of individuals and trying to discover the nature of a crisis that was without clear pattern. It was their job to keep Washington informed in a manner which would lay the basis for whatever assistance the United States could give, whether military, economic, diplomatic, or, perhaps, only advice and support to the men who could bring a new order to the chaotic situation. To those on the spot, aware of the weak position of the men who were at the head of government, the wild reports warned of worse conditions to come. They saw how panic among the whites, and particularly among the Belgians, had infuriated the Congolese. Reports from the refugees pouring into Leopoldville indicated the possibility of tribal conflicts.

The Americans were aware of the attempts by the Belgian government to persuade Lumumba to invoke the Treaty of Friendship between Belgium and the Congo. This would have given a basis for the former colonials to endeavor to restore order. Lumumba, however, insisted that his government could bring the situation under control. Subsequent events demonstrated that this hope would never be realized. Ralph Bunche, the special representative of the UN Secretary General, who had remained for a few days in the Congo, warned the Belgian ambassador in Leopoldville that unrequested intervention would bring serious consequences.

Lumumba and Kasavubu went to the interior to try to get the army calmed down. In the state of passion of the soldiers and the tribal leaders, such efforts made only a temporary impression.

The U.S. mission was disturbed by the increasing pressure on the Belgians to intervene. On July 8, undisciplined, armed troops triggered a new wave of panic in the capital. The troops drove out their European officers and rampaged through the city and the outlying districts. Crowds of Belgians left their homes and sought refuge in their Embassy. In front of the Embassy, which was near the ferry landing, the former Mayor, Robert Van Eyck, walked among the women and children, shouting, "Ferryboats leaving for Brazzaville" (in the French Congo). Word from Elisabethville on July 9 indicated that the American and British consuls were urging their nationals to leave Katanga as quickly as possible and had asked the help of the Belgians in maintaining law and order. The United States arranged to fly 170 Americans out of the Congo.

A correspondent for the UPI, George Sibers, wrote:

> I saw an army of moaning, shrieking, angry—and, above all, frightened—whites jammed on the ferry dockside at Leopoldville through the night, pressing and pushing for a place on the tired old steamboat that could take them across the four-mile-wide Congo River to safety in Brazzaville.
>
> The word "rape" echoed through the European section of Leopoldville. White men, women and children burst from their homes in the middle of the night seeking escape. . . .
>
> Loyal Congo Army troops who had taken no part in the Wednesday's mutiny went out to help the fleeing whites.

This report, on July 9, gave the erroneous impression that the troops were disloyal, whereas they were simply behaving with wild abandon. It was rumored at this time that Belgium was sending soldiers and that the government was in complete collapse. The French and Italian consuls joined the Britsh and Americans in appealing for help in Elisabethville. The government in Washington denied that it had asked Belgium to send troops. Nevertheless, some action by the Belgians was almost inevitable, and reports of local action by Belgian troops increased.

After the mutiny of July 5, the Belgian authorities had tried to persuade Lumumba to permit the Belgian troops stationed in the country to restore order. (These metropolitan troops, not a part of the *Force Publique*, were confined to two large bases, one at Kitona on the Atlantic coast and one at Kamina in Katanga. They were there under the Treaty of Friendship signed on the eve of independence.) Lumumba refused, and, in the opinion of some, thus prevented the restraint of violence. The United States was concerned by the report that the considerable number of communist-bloc agents who had infiltrated the country were playing a part in inciting the soldiers to rebel. As the terror increased, the pressure on the former colonial power was built up locally among the white residents and also among the Congolese, frightened by the departure of the Belgian experts. At the same time, refugees arriving in Brussels by air exerted their influence to secure action to prevent further deterioration in the new nation.

On July 8, the Belgian government announced the dispatch of 600 new troops to join the two or three thousand already stationed at its bases. Ernest W. Lefever sums up the situation in his *Crisis in the Congo:*

> After five days of fruitless efforts, Belgian patience wore thin. And on July 9, against the wishes of the Congo government, Brussels flew in an additional two and one-half companies of paratroopers from Belgium to reinforce the two bases. This reinforcement in itself was probably not a violation of the treaty, but the subsequent deployment of Belgian troops outside the bases to restore order and protect Belgian lives, without the permission of Leopoldville, clearly was.[81]

The soldiers left their bases after the mutinies spread and intervened in Elisabethville, Jadotville, Kamina, and elsewhere on July 10. (The nature and location of Belgian armed intervention were not evident to the Americans until later, when reports of several paratroop drops in widely scattered areas on or about July 11 were received.)

Even now, it is not easy to give a balanced appraisal of the Belgian position. If there could have been a meeting of minds between Kasavubu, Lumumba, and the other leaders, who were sharply divided on policy and inexperienced as to the methods to use in this time of hostility and conflict, discipline might have been achieved. As it was, the ousting of the white officers from the *Force Publique*, on July 9, took priority over the questions related to internal unity. The leaders of the new government were completely at a loss in their dealings with the problems of unrestrained violence and breakdown of the economic life and police control.

There are times when the United States has used Marines, in circumstances not unlike those prevailing in the Congo, with no desire to extend our sovereignty. It is certain that the Belgians, in spite of their lack of wisdom in the previous months in preparing for the independence of the country, were, in this instance, deeply concerned with the safety of their nationals and wished only to re-establish law and order. In this case, unfortunately, as some see it, the weight of public opinion was against the former colonial power. Communist propaganda was already accusing Brussels of intending to recover lost command over the emerging nation. The position of the Belgians in the United Nations and in the court of opinion everywhere was impossible to defend, even in the light of the break-down of civilian control. The New York *Times*, under the heading "The Snatched Sword," said on July 11:

> It is to be hoped the difficulties do not become so acute as to force Belgium to use, even temporarily, measures that would be interpreted by critics of the West as a return to imperialism.

The Congo was to become a hot issue in the Cold War, involving intervention, racism, Hammarskjöld's position, the Russian "Troika" proposal, and the future of the UN. All these issues have been discussed elsewhere. They were to limit and complicate United States action everywhere.

The Need for Decision.   It is difficult for those not intimately concerned in the day-to-day events to reconstruct the story of the tragic outbreak between July 5 and July 9, when the situation fell into a new pattern. It is probably impossible to appreciate the stress and strain of the conflict and the confusion of terrifying rumors. By Friday, the 8th, it was evident that the *Armée Nationale Congolaise* (ANC), which was the new form of the *Force Publique*, was far from being "a cohesive and disciplined army." President Kasavubu and Prime Minister Lumumba had set up a new command, promoting Victor Lundula to Major General in Command and making Joseph Mobutu his Chief of Staff. This was a desperate but unsuccessful effort to restore discipline. Meanwhile, Moise Tshombe in Katanga had appealed to the Belgian military.

There had been various indications (reported in the New York *Times* and elsewhere) from the day of independence that the Congo was being "wooed by Soviets." They were trying to capitalize on the heritage of bitterness felt by African nationalists against their former Western colonizers—a feeling with which Lumumba sympathized. In fact, he had hinted in his speech on June 30 that he was susceptible to this appeal. The Soviet newspapers indicated their interest in a friendship designed to win votes for their bloc in the United Nations and secure a warm reception for their agents in the Congo. The Communist Chinese had also shown their awareness of new opportunities; they had recognized the Congo two days before the independence ceremonies. The Americans in the Consulate in Elisabethville, as well as in the Embassy in Leopoldville, were watching these signs, alert to discover local evidence of communist infiltration.

The pressure for constructive action increased, as the inability of the Congolese leaders to put down the disorder increased each day. The American Embassy was urgently preparing its recommendations.

Advice at the Airport.   On Sunday, July 10, with no time to lose to catch the leaders at an opportune moment, Clare Timberlake and a staff aide rushed out to the airport to talk to Kasavubu and Lumumba, who were due to return from the interior. When Timberlake saw that they were planning to get off their plane at the maintenance hangar, without coming to the administration building, he hailed a bakery truck and drove across the field. The truck drew up at the hangar as Kasavubu and Lumumba were alighting from the plane. The men conferred in the operations room. The two leaders said their efforts to rally support in the provinces had not been effective. They did not see any hope, but they feared Belgian troop intervention.

It was during this consultation that the United States Ambassador took the initiative and suggested they ask the United Nations for help in restoring order. The Congolese leaders were at first surprised and puzzled. Only after some explanation of the possible international action, did they grasp the idea. Timberlake suggested that they explore the possibility with Ralph Bunche, who had come to the Congo as UN representative at the independence ceremonies. Kasavubu and Lumumba then did make an oral request of Bunche for United Nations aid. Two days later, July 12, they telegraphed their proposal to the Secretary General of the UN, Dag Hammarskjöld, who had asked for a formal written request from the Congolese leaders. Meanwhile, the Embassy wired an urgent report of the conversations to Washington. The new phase of handling the consequences of the Congo's independence had begun.

Thus the methods used by the Americans in Leopoldville to meet the crisis took the form of diplomatic action, as the first days of terror and disorder were followed by a clear appraisal of the speed of social, political, and economic deterioration throughout the nation. The messages to Washington had indicated that the need was urgent not because of political revolution but because of the complete collapse of authority. They had pointed out that the rioting troops had no unified command and no specific objective. In the week of crisis the situation had degenerated to a point where quick action was needed to prevent irreparable damage to the people and the nation.

It was at this critical stage, after the request for UN help, that Deputy Prime Minister Gizenga made his plea for American soldiers. Gizenga called Timberlake to a cabinet meeting on July 12, while Lumumba was out of Leopoldville, and asked for direct American help. The Ambassador referred to the fact that the Congo issue was already before the UN and that the United States was unlikely to act unilaterally. He said that he would of course forward the request if the cabinet insisted. Gizenga asked why they had not yet received an answer to the request for United Nations action. The leaders had thought that a few hours would suffice to bring a favorable response. Miracles were still expected.

Actually, the decision in the United Nations stands as one of its quickest and in some ways most momentous acts. The outstanding fact was the American initiative, which led to the immediate coordinated effort of the White House and the State Department, on recommendation from the field, supported by the American mission in New York. The effective performance of these representatives of our government has merited general appreciation.

There was no delay in shaping the firm policy behind UN action once the request that the United Nations should act to save the

Congo had come. There were alternative courses, but they were not given serious consideration after the explicit recommendation from the Embassy. Although the Embassy staff was not entirely prepared for the degree of financial and diplomatic involvement, they were not frustrated in this initial phase of the rescue operation.

Because it was not immediately clear to the Department how the issue would be resolved in New York, inquiry was made of the Command in Germany as to the feasibility of sending American troops from Frankfurt to Leopoldville. Though the reply was that suitable arrangements could be made, it was agreed in Washington that military assistance for the Congo should not come from the United States, nor from any other large Western nation. Secretary Herter expanded on the statements, made from the White House, that the UN had before it an appeal for assistance and that help should come from the UN and not unilaterally from any single nation. Thus, by the night of the 13th, the interest of all UN member nations was focused on the meeting in New York.

The White House and the Department had been receiving complete reports from Leopoldville. When the advice from Timberlake on July 9 and 10 became specific, Washington responded with definite approval of the action that was recommended. Thus Washington was in tune with the Embassy, and the course of action came swiftly in support of the Secretary General's advice. The decision that had been made in the President's study in response to the Embassy's advice was not questioned.

"Let Dag Do It." The days between July 10 and July 14 were times of quite active diplomacy for the United States. The spur-of-the-moment conference at the Leopoldville airport laid the basis for the policy executed through the United Nations. The Security Council earlier had considered some of the problems briefly: on July 7 it had acted to "extend the hand of friendship [to the Congo] and to endorse its application for membership in the United Nations." Ambassador Henry Cabot Lodge recalled this prompt action when on the night of July 13 and the morning of the next day he spoke of "the unfortunate sequence of events in the Congo which makes the speediest possible United Nations assistance imperative. . . ."

From the moment the proposal was made, the great powers were willing to have the United Nations assume responsibility and prevent the kind of involvement which might have endangered world peace. At this time, there was solid backing from the new African states. The initiative and planning of the Secretary General seemed to promise a reasonable solution. The Soviet Union, which had hoped to find this occasion a ready-made chance to champion the rights of colonial peoples, had been thwarted by the West. The United Nations had to steer a skillful course between the potential cross fire of criticism of the West, the demands of the Africans, and the desire of Belgium to protect its citizens and property in danger.

Before the resolution was passed, the Belgian representative, Walter Loridan, made a statement:

> When the United Nations forces have . . . moved into position and are able to ensure effective maintenance of order and security of persons in the Congo, my Government will proceed to withdraw its intervening metropolitan forces.

The first proposal for UN action had come from the Ambassador in Leopoldville; it was followed almost at once by the message from President Kasavubu and Prime Minister Lumumba, urgently requesting the dispatch of troops by the United Nations. Although the first oral request had been made on July 10 to Ralph Bunche, it was essential for Hammarskjöld to have a piece of paper to put before the Security Council. He indicated this need, and on July 12 a cable signed by Kasavubu and Lumumba was received and submitted to the Security Council. A second message from them amplified the request, referring to the need for protection from an "act of aggression" posed by Belgian metropolitan forces and stipulating that the petition was for "military personnel of neutral countries and not of the United States as reported by certain radio stations." Belgian troops had actually come in on July 9, and some left their bases on the 10th.

The first resolution on the Congo request was introduced by the Tunisian representative in response to Secretary General Hammarskjöld's invitation that the Security Council act with the utmost speed. It was passed in the early morning of the 14th by a vote of 8 to 0. There were three abstentions—the Republic of China, France, and the United Kingdom. It authorized the necessary steps to furnish military assistance until "with the technical assistance of the United Nations, the national security forces may be able, in the opinion of the Government, to meet fully their tasks."

Within 24 hours, General Alexander, military adviser to Nkrumah, had flown to the Congo, and by July 15 UN troops from Ghana had begun to arrive in U. S. Air Force planes. The first report of the Secretary General describing the measures carried out was rendered on July 18. By the 31st, United Nations troops in the Congo had arrived from Ethiopia, Ghana, Guinea, Ireland, Liberia, Morocco, Sweden, and Tunisia—a total of 11,155 men. The problems they faced were more difficult than anticipated, and the situation had become more complicated because Moise Tshombe on July 11 had declared the independence of Katanga. This was a further serious aspect of disunity with which the central government and the UN had to contend for many months.

Although there was general agreement that the Congo situation was a serious threat to world peace, Lumumba was not pleased with the turn of events. When he and Kasavubu returned to Leopoldville from Luluabourg, he learned that the appeal to the United States had been made by the cabinet in his absence. On July 13, he sent a message to the United Nations disavowing that appeal; he followed it the next day with a cable to Nikita Khrushchev in which he referred to the continuing occupation of the country by Belgian troops and begged the Soviet Union to "watch hourly over the situation." There were several other friendly exchanges with the Soviets. Eventually, the U.S.S.R. furnished some unilateral military aid—trucks and planes—and a considerable number of technicians, who engaged in propaganda.

These two factors, the Katanga secession and the Soviet intervention, together with the widespread unrest and frequent violence, resulted in restraints being put on the UN forces in the Congo that materially limited their effectiveness. Dag Hammarskjöld interpreted the mandate to mean that he was not to intervene in the internal affairs of the Congo. This concept, by limiting the actions of the UN troops, made it virtually impossible to create the confidence essential to bringing peace and economic stability in the following months. The length of time needed to accomplish a degree of tranquillity thus became years, instead of months.

The UN command included, at its peak, slightly more than 20,000 men in the blue beret in June, 1964. There also were specialized personnel from 35 states. In the course of rotation, some 93,000 different persons served in the UNF. The Congo mission had established new procedural and legal precedents which affected the UN's long-range potential and posed some difficulties for the General Assembly, as well as the Security Council. The Soviet "Troika" proposal (see page 191) and the disputes over financing were unanticipated outgrowths of this action.

An examination of the peace-keeping operation by the United Nations from July, 1960, into 1964 would necessarily extend beyond the time limits set for this study of the July crisis. It would call for detailed discussions of the subsequent emergencies and conflicts in the provinces and in the cities—the later riots, murders, and dark episodes in the struggle for unity. As Assistant Secretary of State G. Mennen Williams said on April 25, 1965, the Congo problem provides material "not simply for a speech or even a book, but for a library." The end of the story has not yet been written.

In the case here considered, the focus is on the action between July 8 and 16, the period when, after complete chaos, the capital and some of the provincial areas emerged from their nightmare, and a semblance of law and order was restored. The United Nations assistance was carried out under Chapters VI and VII of the Charter, which permit military operations and appropriate procedures in the interests of pacific settlement. Walter Lippmann referred to it as "the most advanced and sophisticated experiment in international cooperation ever attempted."[82] It was remarkable not only for the speed of decision and swiftness of execution, but also for the complexity of the logistic and command aspects.

The reasons for intervention, which was considered by our Embassy to be the most promising and probably the quickest way to restore discipline to the army, were largely expressed in the request at a time of great uncertainty. The interchange of messages suggested the dangers of several more perilous courses of action. The fact that the United States was not only behind the original suggestion, but backed it fully as it developed was crucial to the discussions that ended in the resolution in New York at 3:00 A.M. on July 14. A major consideration both in the decision and in its early implementation was the fact that the Soviet Union agreed initially with the United States that the peace-keeping force should be sent. The Soviets could not oppose a rescue operation backed by most of the new African nations, as well as by Europe and the United States.

Choices and Decisions. The other theoretical choices open to U.S. policy-makers included a "do nothing" policy, acquiescence in intervention by the Belgians on a large scale, encouraging support from some one or two of the African neighbors, or offering American military support. Soviet intervention was considered by some in the Congo to be a dangerous threat, even though the Soviets had no practical possibility of establishing bases and mounting a force of significant size. The solution through Belgian action was generally unacceptable and unlikely to restore tranquillity even by means of the drastic use of force. No African countries had the capability or the authority to act except with the support of the United Nations. Moreover, the financing, coming mainly from the United States, was an important factor. (The undesirability of sending actual American forces to the Congo had immediately become obvious.)

The logic and the diplomatic validity of Clare Timberlake's proposal on July 10 thus make it stand out as one of those American policy decisions which has not been challenged. The proposal, though it did not bring a lasting solution, won for the world a breathing space and put a firm rock under the shaky structure of the new African nation.

The resulting United Nations mandate was under six headings:

1. Restore and maintain law and order.
2. Protect life and property throughout the country.
3. Transform the Congolese army into a reliable instrument of internal security.
4. Prevent civil war and pacify tribal conflict.
5. Protect the Congo from external interference in its affairs, particularly from foreign military personnel.
6. Restore and maintain territorial integrity in the Congo.

It is obvious in the light of later events that the hopes of many of the sponsors of the operation far exceeded its accomplishments. Nevertheless, it is agreed by impartial analysts that both Dag Hammarskjöld and U Thant kept to the broad objectives. The criticism which was to come a few weeks after the initiation of the effort was that the men were restrained from effective action in conditions which called for a reasonable show of force. Thus, the men could not in most circumstances support the local authorities or defend private individuals from attack. This lessened the overall effectiveness of the military contingents and limited their duties at a time when more authority was needed to create a sense of determination. It was because of this restraint that they could not exert a highly effective influence in strengthening the Congolese army (ANC).

The main result of the UN presence in the Congo, in addition to saving lives, was to make Belgian military intervention no longer necessary and to bring a moment of relaxation of tensions. (Though Russia hastened to send a limited amount of unilateral military aid to Lumumba, this aid was contrary to UN policy and did not flow through UN channels.) The Congolese leaders, Lumumba and Kasavubu, were destined soon to become bitter enemies, but they had a brief glimmer of hope, and the capital was restored to a degree of calm. It is likely that a continuation of the wild disorders, with intervention from one or another of the powers confronting each other in the battle for the newly emerging countries, might have brought war to several of the major powers.

World Opinion on New Phases of the Colonial Problem. Opinion on the decisions made in the second week of July has for the most part recognized the desirability of the policy adopted first by the United States and then by the UN Security Council. What is not generally realized is that the Belgians did not wish to intervene but thought it might be necessary. The criticism of the UN operation which came later was directed more against the weakness or inefficiency of the operation than against the general concept or the purposes which had been adopted to guide the UN in the Congo. Even if it had been possible to estimate the extent of the difficulties and to anticipate the magnitude of the dangers that lay ahead, a more forceful effort still might not have been possible under international auspices. In the summer of 1960, public opinion would not have stood behind a greater militancy for the purpose of peace-keeping.

A few have criticized the whole effort to keep the Congo together as a unit. It is a large country; it lacks the normal structures of local administration; it was governed by inexperienced leaders and torn by tribal conflict. While this point has been urged, no clear alternatives have been put forward. There was an unusal amount of consensus in the Security Council and also in the General Assembly.

With a few exceptions, serious students of the initial crisis and its aftermath approve the course adopted—at least the measures taken during the critical week in July.

Smith Hempstone, in his book *Rebels, Mercenaries, and Dividends*, sharply criticized both the U.S. and the UN roles in the crisis.[83] He called the policy shortsighted and unethical. He claimed that "restoring territorial integrity" was actually a clear case of intervention. He attacked what he called the myth of Katanga's vital importance to the Congo's survival. Few of the other studies take this view.

The newspaper reactions reflected a temporary feeling of relief that constructive action was being taken. As the Washington *Post* said, "Almost everyone who understands what is happening in the strife-torn Congo is expressing profound thanks to the UN."[84] The New York *Times*, on July 24, presented a summary of world opinion as expressed editorially in a number of dailies. There was recognition of the vast scope of the effort of the UN, of the difficulty of organizing a really effective administration, of the complex political issues, and of the fact that false propaganda was being issued by Moscow.

In the early phase of action, Dag Hammarskjöld issued an assessment of African opinion. He concluded that the operation had the solid backing of the African states. He said his previous African trip had impressed him with the unity of the approach to international problems. He was to return to the Congo on a last fateful mission, to die in a plane crash on September 13, 1961.

Criticism was voiced in some quarters, however. The U.A.R., Yugoslavia, India, Ghana, Guinea, Mali, and Senegal supported Lumumba, who increasingly diverged from the government in Leopoldville in its cooperation with the UNF. The Soviet view was expressed in a constant flow of criticism of "the new efforts of the imperialists."

Secretary Williams concluded: "Our generally good image in Africa reached a remarkable apogee when we fully supported the UN in ending the secessionist movement in Katanga."[85] The official view, though more optimistic than outside opinion, was reflected in, and based upon, general attitudes toward the termination of colonialism. These views are oversimplifications of long-continuing problems, but they are not without strong influence.

The Long Road to Nationhood. Few imagined in 1960, in the enthusiasm of the dawn of independence, that the difficulties would be so grave or long continued. Now, more than seven years after the proclamation of the Congo State, this country and others in Africa are attempting to nourish and consolidate a nationalism which did not come automatically and which required long months and years of struggle before the cornerstones of education, communication, and administration could bear the full weight of a complex democracy.

Perhaps the most important lesson learned is the long time required to build a nation. The United States in supporting international action in the early Congo crisis was responding to the strong impact of the events that revealed, almost in a lightning flash, the deep troubles that beset the new leaders. It was clear to the Embassy in Leopoldville that ordinary measures would not suffice. The need to turn to an international instrument to prevent communist intervention and to lessen Cold War pressures—*if* possible —*when* possible—was recognized. The United States, while not anticipating the complete breakdown of military discipline, was quick to correct the earlier estimates. In this case, decision in the field was quickly accepted in Washington and in New York. The recognition of our limited but essential role taught us new aspects of our foreign relations and developed for us in the Congo a fund of good will.

THE CHALLENGE OF THE
DOMINICAN REPUBLIC: 1965

The Problem. The questions raised by the American action at the time of the 1965 Dominican revolt basically concern our rights, responsibilities, and limitations in the Caribbean area. The decision of the United States to send in, first, Marines and then additional troops in cooperation with the OAS has raised controversial issues and is the subject of many conflicting views.

Our problem was to meet our responsibilities without offending our international partners and neighbors in the hemisphere. The extreme opinions hold, on the one hand, that we should have gone in sooner and acted with more force, and, on the other hand, that we should have done nothing—with the idea that local factions would have worked out an accommodation, more to our advantage if we had not intervened. Between these extremes are ranged those who approve our action, but with varying appraisals. There are a number of semantic and legal questions which cloud their opinions. These, however, can be clarified by a careful look at the events.

The Background. The political, economic, and social life of the Dominican Republic was under an ironclad and corrupt dictatorship from 1930 to 1961. All the major institutions were oppressive, and government was carried out in a brutal manner. After the assassination of Rafael Trujillo Molina on May 30, 1961, there was a period of dissatisfaction and unrest, while various regimes ran the country in turn. Juan Bosch, elected President in December, 1962, was ousted in a bloodless coup on September 25, 1963. After Bosch, Donald Reid Cabral, who was the leading figure in a triumvirate, took power. He planned to bring about reforms, but in acting to curtail the traditional rights of the military and the power of the left wingers, he only aroused dissatisfaction on all sides, while failing to achieve any substantial reforms. Thus the imminence of an overthrow became apparent to the government in Washington and to others. The main question was: when and how?

The growing influence of the communists, many of whom were Cuban-trained and a number of whom had been to Moscow, Peking, and elsewhere behind the Iron Curtain, disturbed observers. Their efforts were known to the Central Intelligence Agency and also to the Federal Bureau of Investigation, which was directed by President Johnson to take over some of the functions usually carried out by the CIA. Ambassador W. Tapley Bennett, Jr., reported the facts to Washington and informed the State Department that in the view of Reid Cabral and others, the revolt, which was bound to come soon, would take place in early June of 1965. This prediction caused Washington to instruct Bennett to return for consultation. He left for home on April 22.

Meanwhile, Reid had learned from his lieutenants that the plans for a revolt were crystallizing and might call for an uprising as early as April 26. He concluded that preventive action should be taken; therefore, he sent the Army Chief of Staff, General Marcos Antonio Rivera Cuesta, to the camp where the officers who were the ringleaders were, in order to strip them of their commissions. Through ineptitude and a misunderstanding, Rivera Cuesta went alone. When he informed the conspirators that they were to be deprived of their rank, the three main officers arrested and held him.

Saturday, April 24. This act in the late morning of Saturday, April 24, was not reported to Reid immediately, but by 2:30 P.M. he knew that the revolt had begun. Shortly thereafter, the loyal government radio stations were captured and then began broadcasting incitement to rebellion. Small groups roamed the streets, and sound trucks and left-wing party leaders began to shout: "Down with the Reid government!" and "Bring back Juan Bosch!"

Bosch, who was then in Puerto Rico, took no direct part in the action at this time—even his enemies concede that he has never been a communist; it is not clear that he wanted to return to the Dominican Republic.

Apparently, the communists were caught off guard by the premature action of Saturday. They were not prepared for action then, but by Sunday they had gained their momentum and adjusted their plans, and they began to appear on the streets. Well-recognized leaders, using Castro-type slogans, tried to arouse the people; they distributed arms and Molotov cocktails to crowds estimated in the thousands. By midday on the 25th, mobs were roaming the streets, sniping at the police and looting and burning. The political groups were joined by the *"Tigres,"* young hoodlums looking for excitement but without party discipline.

The American Embassy reported this disorder to Washington, but said on Sunday afternoon that although the communists had appeared on the streets in an active role, the Embassy did not think that intervention by the U.S. military was desirable at this time. Reid had resigned at noon on Sunday, and temporary government under Molina Urena, as an agent for Bosch, had begun. The radio had been recaptured. There seemed to be a moment of calm, and the military under Wessin y Wessin, as well as the rebels, seemed uncertain of the outcome and unwilling to take further drastic measures. Though there had been talk among the military of American armed intervention, it was not recommended on Sunday, the 25th, or Monday, the 26th.

On Monday there was again a rise in public action. The more

disciplined of the leftist political leaders, among whom there was a core of trained communist agitators, were thought to be running the revolt. The shooting became widespread. The Americans and various friendly nationals began to assemble in the Embajador Hotel. A few gathered in the Embassy, which was in a state of confusion because of outsiders crowding in, pleading for protection and evacuation. On Monday there were about nine Marines, the Embassy guard, in the capital city. A few persons were evacuated to the port of Haina.

The USS *Boxer* had been ordered by CINCLANTFLT, headquarted in Norfolk, to proceed from the Puerto Rico area toward the Dominican Republic and to remain below the horizon but be ready, if need be, for evacuation operations. Ambassador Bennett, who had been in Washington on Saturday and Sunday, was ordered back to his post. He arrived before noon on the 27th.

Wednesday, April 28.   Bennett reviewed the growing revolt and the chaos in the city. The rebels went on fighting, and many were killed. The military brought some tanks and guns to the bridge and to the river close to the rebel positions, but they did not proceed into the disputed area. The uncertainty of the action by the main factions made the problem before the Embassy country team difficult to assess. The Ambassador sent several cables and talked by telephone with Washington. In his first messages he said that the deteriorating situation, with no effective police action, might require intervention, but that the conditions were not such that he felt we should intervene on Wednesday, although preparation for possible future action should be made. He added that no steps should be initiated for the time being other than Marine landings to save American and other friendly lives. Though the number demanding evacuation had at first been estimated at 1500 or less, during the 27th and 28th the number grew to more than 3000. Most of these persons gathered in the Embajador Hotel, and some proceeded to the polo grounds, which was being used as a landing field by the helicopters.

By the afternoon of the 28th, the United States had ordered the *Boxer* and other ships to move in and carry out emergency evacuation procedures. Meanwhile, increasing violence, the inability of Colonel Benoit (chief of the military junta at the San Isidro base outside the city) or his associates to establish order, the making and breaking of several cease-fires, and the relative impotence of the military based on San Isidro to gain and hold any substantial positions led the Embassy to modify its appraisal. The more moderate leaders of the revolt had gone into asylum in various embassies or were hiding out. The extremists continued to incite an uncontrollable mob. The Embassy reviewed its earlier assessment of the situation.

Choices of Action.   The first cable asking for specific action was received in Washington at 5:16 P.M. on Wednesday, the 28th. It described the increasing disorder and the inadequacy of the handful of men on the spot to give protection. This led to President Johnson's decision to order in the Marines. In the evening, 526 of them were landed, and the protection of the civilians had begun. Meanwhile, the breakdown of law and order had become complete.

The choice which the President had before him on the 28th was difficult to make. No one wished to see the United States using its armed forces on foreign soil, and yet no one wished to be responsible for increasing loss or life, whether American or Dominican. The President could have pursued a waiting policy, hoping that the loyal forces and the rebels would resolve their differences with only a moderate loss of life, considering that the risk to United States citizens was a small price to pay for nonintervention. He might have sent in moderate forces, recognizing that this action would be subject to criticism but that his responsibilities were overriding. He might have sent in large forces and wiped out the rebel strongholds, establishing an American-imposed truce and an occupation government. He might have waited for official OAS action, without exerting any separate initiative. These four options were open to him on the 28th—if he had waited 12 hours, it is likely that his possibilities would have been narrowed to the need for drastic action. Though this would have been more widely understood than the course actually taken, it would probably not have fulfilled in a proper manner the responsibilities which he carried out.

The Hour of Decision.   The crucial cable was received by President Johnson shortly after it was clocked in at 5:16 P.M. He and Secretaries Rusk and McNamara were holding a meeting on another subject. They turned to the staff officers and called in related cables and a number of advisers. The Operations Center in the State Department went into action. The decisions as to the urgent need for action and the particular nature of the response were made about an hour and a half later. Arrangements for a television announcement were then made at once.

The President's announcement to the American people came in the next two hours—beginning at 8:51 P.M. In this statement he failed to differentiate between the type of action which was then being undertaken and the further measure about to be considered. He emphasized, as had Bennett, the peril to American lives and gave an impression to some listeners of panic among Americans in Santo Domingo. This impression had not been intended by the Ambassador and had not been reported in the cables from the Embassy. In explaining the emergency, the President made sweeping and dramatic statements which, while reflecting the terror in the streets, omitted analysis of the action and its justification and passed over many of the nuances of the political situation. The announcement seemed to ignore the causes of the revolt, the genuine social unrest, and the problems connected with the position of Bosch, the duly elected President then in exile. Johnson's statements were to have a wider resonance than the story of the actual events, which never adequately caught up with some of the announcements of that evening.

By the time the President appeared before the American people to report the landings, the men were already coming into the polo grounds and landing at the port of Haina near Santo Domingo. The evacuation had begun.

Unfortunately, no American reporters had yet arrived on the scene. There were several of them in San Juan, Puerto Rico, where they were trying to piece together rumors and facts coming by telephone or otherwise, since the airport in the Dominican Republic was out of commission. Thus, these writers had neither the Washington story nor the Dominican facts. They managed to get to the island on the afternoon of the 29th, as action was in its second phase and approaching the third phase.

American Action—Three Stages. In order to understand the response of the United States, it is essential to review the changing situation and to see the decisions in their three stages—as outlined later by Under Secretary Thomas C. Mann. The first stage was the landing of the 526 American Marines on April 28 to protect the Embassy, then under fire, and to assist the hundreds of people at the hotel to get to the evacuation area. The second was the sending of reinforcements, as it became evident on the 29th that the first 500 troops could not grant sufficient protection in the mounting conflict. The rebels and the military had informed the Embassy that though they would not hinder evacuation, they could not control the mobs. The police had been shot down or had disappeared. The third stage, which came after violence had increased, was undertaken after requests by the OAS for the establishment of an international safety zone to separate the warring factions. This stage, on April 30, involved the landing of still more troops and fanning out the Marines until eventually they occupied nine square miles of the city and had established the international safety zone. This third stage merged with the joint U.S.-OAS action, with the combined military under Brazilian command.

The Embassy reporting had also been in stages. First, there were tentative indications of the need for outside help to protect Americans; second, because of the intensification of the danger to the lives of Americans and other friendly nationals, there was an urgent request for further aid; third, there was the recommendation that there should be intervention *beyond* action to protect lives by the American forces, to stop the bloodshed and to prevent mounting destruction.

It was thought in Santo Domingo and in Washington that the revolt would almost certainly result in a communist take-over, with controls from Cuba, Moscow, and Peking guiding the future political situation.

The Controversy. There continues to be acrid debate about the motives and methods of U.S. action. Moreover, there is controversy about the facts. These were not known to the public at the time, and many have not been made clear since then. What is known may be outlined as follows: (1) the extent of the rebellion; (2) the danger to Americans; (3) the amount of help needed; (4) the possibilities of acting more speedily through the OAS; (5) the extent of communist control.

1. The first question concerns the possibility that the rebels and

the military could have agreed or that one or the other could have restored peace and cut down the bloodshed. These facts are relevant: the estimated loss of life was about 2500 (according to the International Red Cross), the utilities were closed down, looting was widespread, arson was steadily increasing, and panic had spread to all segments of civilian life, as well as to many military contingents. The shooting around the Embassy was not systematic, but it was intermittent and disturbing. Some of the diplomatic premises were invaded, and the Military Advisory and Assistance Group (MAAG) offices of the United States were sacked and looted. The estimates of future destruction, though problematical and varied, were alarming.

2. Since no Americans *were* killed, except for 22 of the troops, it is contended by some that none would have been killed. The argument is not persuasive, though it cannot be categorically denied.

3. There is considerable argument as to whether the United States sent in too many troops. No complete answer can be given to this question. The first landings were, however, considered inadequate by those on the spot—the 526 Marines were not enough to protect and move the growing number of evacuees. The port of embarkation at Haina was under fire, and it was several miles to Haina from the polo grounds. There was near panic among the civilians seeking help. The second landings were immediately required to complete the agreed-on operation.

The third series of landings, mainly paratroopers from Fort Bragg, later joined by contingents from Brazil, Costa Rica, Honduras, Nicaragua, and Paraguay, exceeded 20,000 troops. It is difficult to say whether 18,000 or 16,000 would have been enough. An exact calculation was impossible then and cannot be made now. It is logical to assume that there would have been some ideal number, just enough and not too many. Some say once you implement such plans and start the men moving, it is difficult to call a halt. If there *were* too many, there are grounds to criticize the error as disturbing to the other Latin American nations. If there had been too few, the criticism would have been even more serious and the results disastrous to the undertaking, without saving the United States from the political criticism it received; in fact, the criticism would have had an even more bitter tone.

4. There is even greater controversy as to whether the United

States could have acted only through the OAS. Here opinions are likely to remain divided. The consultations with representatives of other Latin American governments began informally on Monday. Could they have begun on Sunday or even on Saturday? The opinions of those close to the action are negative; some of those who look at the questions from a greater distance answer in the affirmative. What is not known by most people is that the Inter-American Peace Committee was convened on American initiative on Tuesday, the 27th, and that the representatives met as a Council on the morning of April 28. The resolutions that were passed the following day (during the night meeting of the 29th and the morning of the 30th) called for cooperative action and the establishment of an international safety zone. These did in fact restore basic law and order and end most of the fighting.

The report of the staff of the Center for Strategic Studies presents seven conclusions. One is that there could have been fuller and earlier use of the machinery of the OAS; but it recognizes that consultations began early, perhaps as early as there were, at the time, clear indications of the extent of the uprising.

5. Controversy also surrounds the question of the extent of communist control. Certainly there were three active communist groups in the Dominican Republic, and it seems clear that all three were involved in the plans to overthrow the government. Nevertheless, the actual rebellion, when it came, was not instigated by the communists, though they soon assumed leading roles in it. U.S. intelligence sources compiled lists of names of communists who were active in the rebellion; this information presumably was a factor in the decision to escalate U.S. intervention. There are, however, those who say there is no evidence that the communists were seriously threatening to take over the country. Thus, although many have argued about the extent of communist intervention, the facts are sufficiently available to demonstrate the activities of dozens of known and well-trained leaders.

Aims. The United States had four major aims in facing the revolt in the Dominican Republic. First, it wished to fulfill its responsibilities in connection with the protection of American lives. This right is invoked when the constituted authorities lose control and there is no government capable of enforcing law and order.

The second main objective was, and this was the reason for the second stage of action, to stop the bloodshed and reduce the casualties in the Dominican Republic. This was not possible without sending in a considerable number of battle-ready troops. These troops went in on April 30 and were the beginning of the international force established under the resolution of the Council of the Organization of American States.

The third aim was to prevent a communist take-over. This was thought to be a possibility for some months, but it was not imminent until the clash between the military and political forces, with the participation of hoodlums, drove the police from the streets and sent the moderate leaders into hiding. The conditions which brought this threat were evident on April 27 and 28.

The fourth aim was to open the possibility for the Dominican people to choose their leaders in free elections. The assurance of this was not clear until the new year brought the campaign and election of June 1, 1966.

All four objectives of the Dominican action of 1965 were attained.

Aftermath. The crucial decisions and events took place between April 24 and May 4. After the OAS commission took over responsibility and joint military deployment relieved the United States of what was for a time a unilateral action, there was still uncertainty as to the outcome and unrest, with occasional sporadic violence. Since there had never been a grass-roots uprising and since the rioting had been confined to the city, with one minor exception, the main troubles were in the city areas that the rebels held on the fringes of the safety zone. There had been no effort to clean out the crowded buildings and strong points, and many weapons remained in the hands of the extremists. Similarly, the leftist procommunist leaders remained at large. Some of the more conspicuous, as well as some of the moderates, among the rebels went abroad on government posts or on a personal basis. Juan Bosch did not return until September.

The United States, taking cognizance of the destruction and also of the urgent need for social reforms, developed a sizeable relief program and sent a large team to administer the new funds.

In spite of the local success of the American policy, the reaction in Latin American countries was critical of the action taken, and there was little note of the particulars or of the fact that the soldiers holding the two factions apart were under strict discipline and did not shoot unless fired upon. Their behavior, according to the record, was notably restrained.

Public Reaction. For reasons not entirely easy to explain, American public reaction to the landings of Marines has been predominantly unfavorable. The first decision was given to the people in an atmosphere of panic. They were accustomed to thinking of the Dominican Republic as a trouble spot, but they had not been told in detail about the wavering intentions of most of the leaders since Trujillo's assassination, and they had been told almost nothing of the extent to which the communists had been working with political leaders in Havana and elsewhere. The average American was sure that there was need for reform. He arrived quickly at the conclusion that the revolt was likely to bring about much-needed social change. In fact, during the first hours of the revolt it was not sure whether or not a constructive leader, Bosch or another, might emerge from the ranks and take over the new movement.

Only after it became clear that the leaders who might have controlled the unrest and guided it toward true democracy lacked the strength and the will was the disastrous nature of the revolt evident. This revelation came when the bloody street fighting had become dominated by communist-trained guerrillas and young men seeking excitement, unwittingly serving the interest of the extremists. Only then could responsible diplomats and other Dominican experts label the revolt as a communist threat. This development was not clear until April 26. Even then it could be hoped that the wild disorders might run their course and that the loyal military or other key personalities could bring law and order without emergency help. If the police had exerted authority, and if they had not been outnumbered by the armed civilians, a different outcome would have been possible.

It was not easy for observers in the United States and elsewhere to follow the changing tides of fighting or to realize how erratic was the behavior of the Dominican politicians. There was no general knowledge of the nature of the mob, the extent of the violence, and the uncertainty of the heads of both major factions as to the direction in which they should move.

The only thing that stood out in the minds of the public was the landing of Marines—the return to "intervention," the appearance of American armed forces in the streets of a Latin American city. They did not know of the early conversation in the OAS or of the meetings urgently called at the time of even the first landings. Because the newsmen were for the most part reporting from Puerto Rico on the basis of hectic telephone conversations with their contacts in Santo Domingo, who were talking in the midst of riots, the news reports were confused and in some cases misleading.

The puzzle is why the full story has not been told after the event. Probably the reason is that there was a mass of published material which seemed to give the picture—but which was based to a large extent on early erroneous reports and impressions. Furthermore, the government failed to recount the story while the memory of events was still fresh; and spokesmen, including the President, had in some cases given exaggerated accounts of atrocities, under a misconception that citing such episodes would be convincing to the public. These errors of omission and commission led to cynicism and discouraged impartial observers from searching out the facts.

President Johnson on April 28 was faced with an immediate choice. He had to decide whether the danger described to him warranted the landing of American Marines. He reached a judgment and gave the appropriate orders within the hour. Though he was acting to save American lives, there is no doubt that in the back of his mind there was the memory of Cuban communism and the knowledge that the communists had been working in the Dominican Republic. Since there was this additional fear, the public has chosen to ignore the primary and immediate reason for action. The value judgment of the President, considering his responsibility to Americans and also his leadership in protecting the hemisphere from the intrusion of international communism, was essentially complex and could not be arrived at in a vacuum.

Because of the many-sided nature of the problem and the need to follow the first action with further measures, the sincerity of the President and of his advisers has been challenged. The inability of the government to explain its position or to give a clear picture of the rapidly deteriorating conditions in the Dominican Republic was to impair our reputation and give aid and comfort to our enemies. The major journals, the intelligentsia, the Ambassadors abroad, the average man in the street—few were convinced that American action in using troops was necessary.

The final conclusion for the majority as to the intervention and the manner in which it was executed, including the effort to achieve multilateral and cooperative peace-keeping, will come only as the history of the postrevolt conditions in Santo Domingo unfolds.

Lessons of a Crisis. This case history of a crisis illustrates the characteristic speed with which many emergencies develop, producing an imperative need for decisiveness. It also suggests the importance of preparation, not only in the military sense but in relation to public opinion. It reveals the time factors involved in dealing with the Organization of American States—the Council asked for 48 hours for instructions, and the sentiment in the corridors supported action, while the voting in the meetings showed some dissent. It indicates the difficulty of trying to have adequate forces for protection and the restoration of order, without having too many men or giving the appearance of having excessive aims or making an exaggerated show of force.

It suggests the importance of good handling of the press, including the early presence on the scene of responsible newsmen. It underscores the elemental fact that American Ambassadors abroad should be given full and illuminating briefings from the outset.

It was clear from the beginning that a few must make the crucial decisions, but it was also clear that the problem of prompt communication with the many who needed to be informed was not sufficiently considered. There are those who say that though the government succeeded in its four major objectives, it did not succeed in convincing the body of world opinion that the methods it used to achieve them were wise and proper.

NOTES

1. Richard W. Leopold, *The Growth of American Foreign Policy*, Knopf, 1962, p. 222.
2. Winston S. Churchill, *Closing the Ring*, Houghton Mifflin, 1951, p. 328.
3. Senate Committee on Foreign Relations, *A Decade of American Foreign Policy, Basic Documents, 1941–1949*, Document No. 123, 81st Congress, 1950, p. 682.
4. *American Foreign Policy, 1950–1955, Current Documents*, Department of State, 1957, p. 2453.
5. *Ibid.*, p. 2467.

6. *Ibid.*, p. 2553.
7. *Current Documents, 1950–1955, op. cit.*, pp. 2542–2549. See for a discussion of constitutional authority.
8. *Ibid.*, pp. 2550, 2555.
9. *Ibid.*, p. 2564.
10. *Ibid.*, p. 2565.
11. Richard C. Snyder, *An Analysis of Case Materials on the U. S. Decision to Resist Aggression in Korea, in* James N. Rosenau, ed., *International Politics and Foreign Policy*, The Free Press, 1961, pp. 193–208.
12. Eric Goldman, *The Crucial Decade and After: America, 1945–1960*, Random House, 1960, p. 167.
13. Snyder, *op. cit.*, p. 204.
14. *Ibid.* p. 203.
15. Leland M. Goodrich, *Korea, a Study of U. S. Policy in the United Nations*, Council on Foreign Relations, 1956.
16. *Ibid.*, pp. 97–101.
17. Robert Leckie, *Conflict: The History of the Korean War, 1950–1953*, Putnam, 1962, p. 400.
18. William Reitzel, Morton A. Kaplan, and Constance G. Coblenz, *United States Foreign Policy (1945–1955)*, Brookings Institution, 1956, p. 263.
19. *Ibid.*, p. 263.
20. *Ibid.*, pp. 255, 259n.
21. Unpublished letter from Mrs. John E. Peurifoy.
22. David Wise and Thomas B. Ross, *The Invisible Government*, Random House, 1964, pp. 165–183.
23. Dwight D. Eisenhower, *Mandate for Change, 1953–1956*, Doubleday, 1963, pp. 421–427.
24. Daniel James, *Red Design for the Americas*, John Day, 1954, p .38.
25. John D. Martz, *Communist Infiltration in Guatemala*, Vantage Press, 1956, p. 46.
26. James, *op. cit.*, pp. 59–61.
27. *Ibid.*, p. 297.
28. Leopold, *op. cit.*, p. 777.
29. *Current Documents, 1950–1955, op. cit.*, p. 1312.
30. *Time*, December 18, 1953.
31. *Current Documents, 1950–1955, op. cit.*, pp. 1292, 1297, 1298, 1301.
32. Eisenhower, *op. cit.*, p. 424.
33. *Current Documents, 1950–1955, op. cit.*, p. 1309.

34. The New York *Times*, June 1, 1954, p. 1.
35. Eisenhower, *op. cit.*, p. 426.
36. *Current Documents, 1950–1955*, p. 1310.
37. *Ibid.*, p. 1313.
38. The New York *Times*, June 11, 1954, p. 2.
39. James, *op. cit.*, p. 307.
40. Eisenhower, *op. cit.*, p. 425.
41. The New York *Times*, June 19, 1954, p. 1.
42. *Ibid.*, p. 1.
43. The New York *Times*, June 23, 1954, p. 1.
44. *Ibid.*, p. 1.
45. James, *op. cit.*, pp. 280, 281.
46. *Ibid.*, pp. 308–309.
47. Richard Allen, "Report on Events Leading Up to and Arising Out of the Change of Regime in Guatemala, 1954," October, 1954, C.M.D. 9277, p. 1.
48. Eisenhower, *op. cit.*, pp. 425–426.
49. *Time*, July 12, 1954, p. 38.
50. Unpublished letter from Mrs. John E. Peurifoy.
51. *Time*, July 12, 1954, p. 38.
52. Unpublished letter from Mrs. John E. Peurifoy.
53. *Time*, July 12, 1954, p. 38.
54. *Ibid.*, p. 39.
55. Unpublished letter from Mrs. John E. Peurifoy.
56. *Current Documents, 1950–1955, op. cit.*, p. 1315.
57. *Ibid.*, p. 1315.
58. *Time*, July 12, 1954, p. 39.
59. James, *op. cit.*, pp. 30, 31.
60. Allen, *op. cit.*, p. 15.
61. *Ibid.*, p. 15.
62. Dwight D. Eisenhower, *Waging Peace, 1956–1961*, Doubleday, 1963, p. 273.
63. *Basic Documents, 1941–1949, op. cit.*, p. 506.
64. *Ibid.*, p. 502.
65. *Ibid.*, p. 505.
66. *Ibid.*, p. 528.
67. W. Philip Davison, *Berlin Blockade: A Study in Cold War Politics*, Princeton University Press, 1958, p. 74.
68. Jean Edward Smith, *The Defense of Berlin*, Johns Hopkins Press, 1963, p. 103; Davison, *op. cit.*, pp. 63, 64.
69. Davison, *op. cit.*, p. 73.

70. Walter Millis, ed., *The Forrestal Diaries*, Viking Press, 1951, p. 424.
71. *American Foreign Policy, Current Documents, 1958*, Department of State, p. 487.
72. *Ibid.*, p. 597.
73. *Ibid.*, p. 595.
74. *Ibid.*, p. 597.
75. Smith, *op. cit.*, p. 187.
76. *Current Documents, 1958, op. cit.*, p. 584.
77. Smith, *op. cit.*, p. 185.
78. Eleanor Lansing Dulles and Robert D. Crane, eds., *Détente: Cold War Strategies in Transition*, Praeger, 1965, pp. 124–129.
79. *Current Documents, 1958, op. cit.*, p. 619.
80. Ernest W. Lefever, *Crisis in the Congo*, Studies of U. S. Policy and the UN series, Brookings Institution, 1965.
81. *Ibid.*, pp. 6–10.
82. *Washington Post and Times-Herald*, July 21, 1960.
83. Smith Hempstone, *Rebels, Mercenaries and Dividends: The Katanga Story*, Praeger, 1962.
84. *The New York Times*, July 24, 1960 (summary of editorial opinion).
85. G. Mennen Williams, speech in Boston, April 25, 1965.

BIBLIOGRAPHY

GENERAL

Acheson, Dean, *Power and Diplomacy*, Harvard University Press, 1958.

Allen, Robert L., *Soviet Economic Warfare*, Public Affairs Press, 1960.

American Assembly, *The Secretary of State: The 18th Report*, Prentice-Hall, 1960.

Aron, Raymond, *The Century of Total War*, Doubleday, 1954.

Aron, Raymond, *Peace and War: A Theory of International Relations*, Doubleday, 1966.

Asher, Robert E. et al., *Development of the Emerging Countries*, Brookings Institution, 1962.

Atkinson, James D., *The Politics of Struggle: The Communist Front and Political Warfare*, Regnery, 1966.

Bailey, Thomas A., *A Diplomatic History of the American People*, Appleton-Century-Crofts, 1964.

Baldwin, David A., *Foreign Aid and American Foreign Policy, A Documentary Analysis*, Praeger, 1966.

Ball, Margaret, *NATO and the European Union Movement*, Praeger, 1959.

Barnett, A. Doak, *Communist China and Asia: Challenge to American Policy*, Harper & Row, 1960.

Beloff, Max, *The Foreign Policy of Soviet Russia, 1929–1941*, Oxford University Press, 1947 and 1949.

Beloff, Max, *Foreign Policy and the Democratic Process*, Johns Hopkins Press, 1958.

Bemis, Samuel Flagg, *A Diplomatic History of the United States*, 5th ed., Holt, Rinehart & Winston, 1965.

Benoit, Émile, *Europe at Sixes and Sevens*, Columbia University Press, 1961.

Berding, Andrew, *Foreign Affairs and You!*, Doubleday, 1962.

Berle, Adolf A., Jr., *Latin America: Diplomacy and Reality*, Harper & Row (for Council on Foreign Relations), 1962.

Berliner, Joseph S., *Soviet Economic Aid*, Praeger, 1958.

Black, Eugene R., *The Diplomacy of Economic Development*, Harvard University Press, 1960.

343

Blum, Robert, and Doak Barnett, eds., *The United States and China in World Affairs*, McGraw-Hill (for Council on Foreign Relations), 1966.

Bowie, Robert R., *Shaping the Future*, Columbia University Press, 1964.

Brzezinski, Zbigniew W., *The Soviet Bloc: Unity and Conflict*, Harvard University Press, 1960.

Carr, Edward Hallett, *What Is History?*, Knopf, 1962.

Cerf, Jay H., and Walter Pozen, *Strategy for the 60's*, Praeger, 1961.

Chamberlin, Waldo, Thomas Hovet, and Erica Hovet, *A Chronology and Fact Book of the United Nations, 1941–1964*, Oceana, 1964.

Cheng, Chu-Yuan, *Economic Relations Between Peking and Moscow, 1949–1963*, Praeger, 1964.

Coffin, Frank M., *Witness for AID*, Houghton Mifflin, 1964.

Cohen, Bernard C., *The Press and Foreign Policy*, Princeton University Press, 1963.

Curtis, Michael, *Western European Integration*, Harper & Row, 1965.

Davids, Jules, *America and the World of Our Time: United States Diplomacy in the Twentieth Century*, Random House, 1962.

Davids, Jules, ed., *The United States in World Affairs, 1964*, Harper & Row (for Council on Foreign Relations), 1965.

DeConde, Alexander, *A History of American Foreign Policy*, Scribner, 1963.

Diebold, William, Jr., *The Schuman Plan: A Study in Economic Cooperation, 1950–1959*, Praeger, 1959.

Diebold, William, Jr., *Trade and Payments in Western Europe*, Harper & Row, 1952.

Dinerstein, H. S., *War and the Soviet Union*, Praeger, 1959.

Disarmament, Hammarskjöld Forums Series, Association of the Bar of the City of New York, 1964.

Dougherty, James E., *The Prospects for Arms Control*, MacFadden-Bartell, 1965.

Douglas, Paul H., *America in the Market Place: Trade, Tariffs and the Balance of Payments*, Holt, Rinehart & Winston, 1966.

Dozer, Donald M., *Are We Good Neighbors: Three Decades of Inter-American Relations, 1930–1960*, University of Florida Press, 1959.

Dreier, John C., *The Organization of American States and the Hemisphere Crisis*, Harper & Row, 1962.

Dulles, Allen, *The Craft of Intelligence*, Harper & Row, 1963.

Dulles, Eleanor Lansing, and Robert D. Crane, eds., *Détente: Cold War Strategies in Transition*, Praeger, 1965.

Dulles, Foster Rhea, *The United States Since 1865*, University of Michigan Press, 1959.

Dulles, John Foster, *War or Peace*, Macmillan, 1950.

Eichelberger, Clark M., *UN: The First Twenty Years*, Harper & Row, 1965.

Evans, John W., *U. S. Trade Policy*, Harper & Row, 1967.

Fairbank, John K., *Chinese Thought and Institutions*, University of Chicago Press, 1957.

Finletter, Thomas K., *Foreign Policy: The Next Phase: The 1960s*, rev. ed., Harper & Row, 1960.

Frank, Isaiah, *The European Common Market*, Praeger, 1961.

Frankel, Joseph, *International Relations*, Oxford University Press, 1964.

Frankel, Joseph, *The Making of Foreign Policy*, Oxford University Press, 1963.

Friedmann, Wolfgang G., George Kalmanoff, and Robert F. Meagher, *International Financial Aid*, Columbia University Press, 1966.

Furniss, Edgar S., Jr., *France, Troubled Ally: De Gaulle's Heritage and Prospects*, Praeger, 1960.

Garthoff, Raymond L., *Soviet Strategy in the Nuclear Age 1958*, 1962.

Goldman, Eric, *The Crucial Decade and After: America, 1945–1960*, Random House, 1960.

Goodrich, Leland M. and Edward Hambro, *Charter of the United Nations: Commentary and Documents*, 2nd rev. ed., World Peace Foundation, 1949.

Graebner, Norman A., *An Uncertain Tradition: American Secretaries of State in the Twentieth Century*, McGraw-Hill, 1961.

Hagen, Everett E., *On the Theory of Social Change: How Economic Growth Begins*, Dorsey Press, 1962.

Halle, Louis J., *Dream and Reality: Aspects of American Foreign Policy*, Harper & Row, 1959.

Hallstein, Walter, *United Europe: Challenge and Opportunity*, Harvard University Press, 1961.

Harris, Seymour Edwin, *The European Recovery Program*, Harvard University Press, 1948.

Haviland, H. Field, Jr., ed., *The Formulation and Administration of United States Foreign Policy*, Brookings Institution, 1960.

Herring, Hubert, *A History of Latin America*, Knopf, 1961.

Herskovits, Melville J., *The Human Factor in Changing Africa*, Knopf, 1962.

Herz, Martin F., *Beginnings of the Cold War*, Indiana University Press, 1966.

Hill, Norman L., *Mr. Secretary of State*, Random House, 1963.

Hinshaw, Randall, *The European Economic Community and American Trade*, Praeger, 1964.

Hirschman, Albert, *The Strategy of Economic Development*, Yale University Press, 1958.

Hoskins, Halford L., *The Middle East: Problem Area in World Politics*, 1954.

Irish, Marian D., ed., *Continuing Crisis in American Politics*, Prentice-Hall, 1963.

Johnson, E. A. J., *Dimensions of Diplomacy*, Johns Hopkins Press, 1964.

Johnson, Harry G., *The World Economy at the Crossroads*, Clarendon Press, 1965.

Kahn, Herman, *Thinking About the Unthinkable*, Horizon Press, 1962.

Kenen, Peter, *Giant Among Nations*, Rand McNally, 1963.

Kennan, George F., *American Diplomacy, 1900–1950*, University of Chicago Press, 1951.

Kennan, George F., *Realities of American Foreign Policy*, Princeton University Press, 1954.

Kindleberger, Charles P., *International Economics*, Irwin, 1963.

Kissinger, Henry A., *Nuclear Weapons and Foreign Policy*, Harper & Row, 1957.

Kissinger, Henry A., *The Necessity for Choice*, Harper & Row, 1961.

Kitzinger, U. W., *The Politics and Economics of European Integration: Britain, Europe, and the United States*, Praeger, 1963.

Knorr, Klaus, and Thornton Read, *Limited Strategic War*, Praeger, 1962.

Korbel, Josef, *The Communist Subversion of Czechoslovakia*, Princeton University Press, 1959.

Kraft, Joseph, *The Grand Design: From Common Market to Atlantic Partnership*, Harper & Row, 1962.

Krause, Walter, *International Economics*, Houghton Mifflin, 1965.

Langer, William L. and S. E. Gleason, *The Challenge to Isolation*, Harper & Row, 1952.

Lawson, Ruth C., ed., *International Regional Organizations: Constitutional Foundations*, Praeger, 1962.

Leopold, Richard W., *The Growth of American Foreign Policy*, Knopf, 1962.

Lerche, Charles O., and Adul A. Said, *Concepts of International Politics*, Prentice-Hall, 1963.

Lewis, Arthur W., *Development Planning*, Harper & Row, 1966.

Lippmann, Walter, *The Cold War*, Harper & Row, 1947.

Lippmann, Walter, *U. S. Foreign Policy: Shield of the Republic*, Little, Brown, 1943.

London, Kurt, *How Foreign Policy is Made*, Van Nostrand, 1949.

Lukacs, John A., *The Great Powers and Eastern Europe*, 1953.

Lukacs, John A., *A History of the Cold War*, Doubleday, 1961.

Macridis, Roy C., *De Gaulle: Implacable Ally*, Harper & Row, 1966.

Mallory, Walter H., ed., *Political Handbook and Atlas of the World*, Harper & Row (for Council on Foreign Relations), 1964.

Mason, Edward S., *Economic Planning in Underdeveloped Areas*, Fordham University Press, 1958.

McCamy, James L., *Conduct of the New Diplomacy*, Harper & Row, 1964.

McCloy, John J., *The Challenge to American Foreign Policy*, Harvard University Press, 1953.

Millikan, Max F., and Donald L. M. Blackmer, *The Emerging Nations*, Little, Brown, 1961.

Millikan, Max F., and W. W. Rostow, *A Proposal: Key to an Effective Foreign Policy*, Harper & Row, 1957.

Moore, Ben T., *NATO and the Future of Europe: A Critical Examination*, Twentieth Century Fund, 1958.

Morgenthau, Hans J., *Politics Among Nations*, 1960, Knopf, 1967.

Mosely, Philip E., *The Kremlin and World Politics*, Vintage, 1960.

Nettl, J. P., *The Eastern Zone and Soviet Policy in Germany, 1945–1950*, Oxford University Press, 1951.

Neustadt, Richard E., *Presidential Power: The Politics of Leadership*, New American Library, 1964.

Nicolson, Harold, *Diplomacy*, 2nd ed., Oxford University Press, 1952.

Organski, A. F. K., *The Stages of Political Development*, Knopf, 1965.

Orwell, George, *1984*, New American Library, 1961.

Osgood, Robert E., *NATO, The Entangling Alliance*, University of Chicago Press, 1962.

Osgood, Robert E., *Limited War: The Challenge to American Strategy*, University of Chicago Press, 1957.

Overstreet, Harry, and Bonaro Overstreet, *What We Must Know About Communism*, Norton, 1958.

Padelford, Norman J., and George A. Lincoln, *The Dynamics of International Politics*, Macmillan, 1962.

Patterson, Richard S., comp., *The Secretaries of State: Portraits and Biographical Sketches*, Department of State Publication 6402, 1956.

Plischke, Elmer, *Conduct of American Diplomacy*, Van Nostrand, 1961.

Price, Harry Bayard, *The Marshall Plan and Its Meaning*, Cornell University Press, 1955.

Pryce, Roy, *The Political Future of the European Community*, 1962.

Pye, Lucian W., *Politics, Personality, and Nation Building: Burma's Search for Identity*, Yale University Press, 1962.

Pye, Lucian W., ed., *Communications and Political Development*, Princeton University Press, 1963.

Reitzel, William, Morton A. Kaplan, and Constance G. Coblenz, *United States Foreign Policy (1945–1955)*, Brookings Institution, 1956.

Rivkin, Arnold, *Africa and the West*, Praeger, 1962.

Rostow, W. W., *Stages of Economic Growth*, Cambridge University Press, 1960.

Rostow, W. W., *The United States in the World Arena*, Harper & Row, 1960.

Sapin, Burton M., *The Making of United States Foreign Policy*, Praeger, 1966.

Schelling, Thomas C., *Arms and Influence*, Yale University Press, 1966.

Schelling, Thomas C., *International Economics*, Allyn & Bacon, 1958.

Seton-Watson, Hugh, *From Lenin to Khrushchev: The History of World Communism*, Praeger, 1960.

Seton-Watson, Hugh, *Neither War Nor Peace*, Praeger, 1960.

Snyder, Richard C., *An Analysis of Case Materials on the U. S. Decision to Resist Aggression in Korea*, in James N. Rosenau, ed., *International Politics and Foreign Policy*, The Free Press, 1961.

Snyder, Richard C., H. W. Bruck, and Burton Sapin, eds., *Foreign Policy Decision-Making*, Macmillan, 1962.

Spanier, John W., *American Foreign Policy Since World War II*, Praeger, 1965.

Speier, Hans, *The Soviet Threat to Berlin*, Rand Corporation, 1960.

Staley, Eugene, *The Future of Underdeveloped Countries*, Harper & Row, 1961.

Stebbins, Richard P., ed., *Documents on American Foreign Relations, 1963*, Harper & Row (for Council on Foreign Relations), 1964.

Stoessinger, John G., *The United States and the Super Powers*, Random House, 1965.

Stoessinger, John G. and Alan F. Westin, eds., *Power and Order: Six Cases in World Politics*, Harcourt, Brace & World, 1964.

Strausz-Hupé, Robert, *Building the Atlantic World*, Harper & Row, 1963.

Toynbee, Arnold, *The World and the West*, Oxford University Press, 1953.

Urguidi, Victor L., *Free Trade and Economic Integration in Latin America*, University of California Press, 1962.

Wanamaker, Temple, *American Foreign Policy Today*, Bantam Books, 1964.

Westerfield, Bradford, *The Instruments of America's Foreign Policy*, Crowell, 1963.

Wolfers, Arnold, and Lawrence W. Martin, *Discord and Collaboration: Essays on International Relations*, John Hopkins Press, 1962.

Zagoria, Donald S., *The Sino-Soviet Conflict*, Princeton University Press, 1962.

BIOGRAPHICAL AND PERSONAL ACCOUNTS

Adams, Sherman, *Firsthand Report: The Story of the Eisenhower Administration*, Harper & Row, 1961.

Adenauer, Konrad, *Konrad Adenauer Erinnerungen 1945–1953*, Deutsche Verlags-Anstalt, 1965.

Adenauer, Konrad, *Konrad Adenauer Erinnerungen 1953–1955*, Deutsche Verlags-Anstalt, 1965.

Adenauer, Konrad, *Konrad Adenauer Memoirs 1945–1953*, Regnery, 1966.

Beal, John R., *John Foster Dulles: 1888–1959*, rev. ed., Harper & Row, 1957.

Berding, Andrew H., *Dulles on Diplomacy*, Van Nostrand, Princeton, 1965.

Byrnes, James F., *Speaking Frankly*, Harper & Row, 1947.

Churchill, Winston S., *The Second World War* (6 vols.: *The Gathering Storm; Their Finest Hour; The Grand Alliance; The Hinge of Fate; Closing the Ring; Triumph and Tragedy*), Houghton Mifflin, 1948–1953.

Clark, Mark Wayne, *From the Danube to the Yalu*, Harper & Row, 1954.

Clay, Lucius D., *Decision in Germany*, Doubleday, 1950.

De Gaulle, Charles, *War Memoirs: Documents*, Simon & Schuster, 1959, 1960.

Dulles, Eleanor Lansing, *John Foster Dulles: The Last Year*, Harcourt, Brace & World, 1963.

Eden, Anthony, *Full Circle*, Houghton Mifflin, 1960.

Eisenhower, Dwight D., *Mandate for Change, 1953–1956*, Doubleday, 1963.

Eisenhower, Dwight D., *Waging Peace, 1956–1961*, Doubleday, 1965.

Feis, Herbert, *Churchill, Roosevelt, Stalin*, Princeton University Press, 1957.

Goold-Adams, Richard, *John Foster Dulles: A Reappraisal*, Appleton-Century-Crofts, 1962.

Hull, Cordell, *The Memoirs of Cordell Hull*, Macmillan, 1948.

Millis, Walter, ed., *The Forrestal Diaries*, Viking Press, 1951.

Murphy, Robert, *Diplomat Among Warriors*, Doubleday, 1964.

Ridgway, Matthew B., *Soldier: The Memoirs of Matthew B. Ridgway*, Harper & Row, 1956.

Schlesinger, Arthur, Jr., *A Thousand Days: John F. Kennedy in the White House*, Houghton Mifflin, 1965.

Sherwood, Robert E., *Roosevelt and Hopkins: An Intimate History*, Harper & Row, 1948.

Shub, David, *Lenin*, Mentor Books, 1961.

Sorensen, Theodore C., *Decision-Making in the White House*, Columbia University Press, 1963.

Sorensen, Theodore C., *Kennedy*, Harper & Row, 1965.

Thayer, Charles W., *Diplomat*, Harper & Row, 1959.

Truman, Harry S., *Years of Trial and Hope: Memoirs*, vol. 2, Doubleday, 1956.

Welles, Sumner, *Seven Decisions That Shaped History*, Harper & Row, 1951.

CRISES

The bibliographies for recent crises in foreign policy are composed mainly of journal articles and documents. Much of the material in Chapter III is from unpublished sources. However, a few crisis studies are listed below.

Abel, Elie, *The Missile Crisis*, Lippincott, 1966.

Acheson, Dean, *The Problem of Peace in Korea*, Department of State, 1952.

Allen, Richard, "Report on Events Leading Up to and Arising Out of the Change in Regime in Guatemala, 1954," October, 1954, C.M.D. 9277.

Berger, Carl, *The Korea Knot: A Military-Political History*, University of Pennsylvania Press, 1965.

Bradley, Omar M., *Substance of Statement Made at Wake Island Conference on October 15, 1950*, U. S. Government Printing Office, 1950.

Brant, Stefan, *The East German Uprising*, 1957.

Brausch, Georges, *Belgian Administration in the Congo*, Oxford University Press, 1961.

Burns, Arthur Lee, and Nina Heathcote, *Peace-Keeping by U.N. Forces from Suez to the Congo*, Praeger, 1963.

A Case History of Communist Penetration: Guatemala, U. S. Department of State, 1957.

Center for Strategic Studies, *Dominican Action 1965: Intervention or Cooperation*, Special Report Series No. 2, 1966.

Center for Strategic Studies, *Panama Canal Issues and Treaty Talks*, Special Report Series No. 3, 1967.

Davidson, Basil, *The African Awakening*, Macmillan, 1955.

Davison, W. Phillips, *The Berlin Blockade: A Study in Cold War Politics*, Princeton University Press, 1958.

The Dominican Republic Crisis, 1965: Legal Aspects, Hammarskjöld Forums Series, Association of the Bar of the City of New York, 1967.

Dulles, Eleanor Lansing, *Berlin: The Wall Is Not Forever*, University of North Carolina Press, 1967.

Eisenhower, Dwight D., *Message to Congress on United States Military Intervention in Lebanon, July 15, 1958*, U. S. Government Printing Office, 1958.

Galante, Pierre, *The Berlin Wall*, Doubleday, 1965.

Geiger, Theodore, *Communism versus Progress in Guatemala*, for the National Planning Committee on International Policy, 1953.

Goodrich, Leland M., *Korea: A Study of U. S. Policy in the United Nations*, for Council on Foreign Relations, 1956.

Gordon, King, *The United Nations and the Congo: A Quest for Peace*, Carnegie Endowment for International Peace, 1962.

Hempstone, Smith, *Rebels, Mercenaries and Dividends: The Katanga Story*, Praeger, 1962.

Hennessy, Maurice, *The Congo: a Brief History and Appraisal*, Praeger, 1961.

Higgins, Marguerite, *War in Korea*, Doubleday, 1951.

The Inter-American Security System and the Cuban Crisis, Hammarskjöld Forum Series, Association of the Bar of the City of New York, 1964.

Intervention of International Communism in Guatemala, U. S. Department of State, 1954.

The Issues in the Berlin-German Crisis, Hammarskjöld Forum Series, Association of the Bar of the City of New York, 1963.

James, Daniel, *Red Design for the Americas*, John Day, 1954.

Johnson, Haynes, *The Bay of Pigs*, Dell, 1964.

Jones, Joseph Marion, *The Fifteen Weeks (February 21–June 5, 1947)*, Viking Press, 1955.

Kurzman, Dan, *Santo Domingo: Revolt of the Damned*, Putnam, 1965.

Leckie, Robert, *Conflict: The History of the Korean War, 1950–1953*, Putnam, 1962.

Lefever, Ernest W., *Crisis in the Congo*, studies of U. S. Policy and the UN series, Brookings Institution, 1965.

Lyons, Gene Martin, *Military Policy and Economic Aid: The Korean Case*, Ohio State University Press, 1961.

Martin, John B., *Overtaken by Events: The Dominican Crisis from the Fall of Trujillo to the Civil War*, Doubleday, 1966.

Martz, John D., *Communist Infiltration in Guatemala*, Vantage Press, 1956.

The Panama Canal, Hammarskjöld Forums Series, Association of the Bar of the City of New York, 1965.

Penetration of the Political Institutions of Guatemala, U. S. Department of State, 1954.

Qubain, Fahim, *Crisis in Lebanon*, 1961.

Roberts, Chalmers M., "The Day We Didn't Go to War," *The Reporter*, September 14, 1954.

The Role of the United Nations in the Congo, Hammarskjöld Forums Series, Association of the Bar of the City of New York, 1963.

Rosenau, James N., ed., *International Politics and Foreign Policy: A Reader in Research and Theory*, The Free Press, 1961.

Rosenthal, Mario, *Guatemala: The Story of an Emergent Latin-American Democracy*, Twayne, 1962.

Schneider, Ronald, *Communism in Guatemala, 1944–1954*, Praeger, 1958.

Select Committee on Communist Aggression, *Communist Aggression in Latin America*, House of Representatives, 83rd Congress, 1954.

Smith, Beverly, "The White House Story: Why We Went to War in Korea," *Saturday Evening Post*, November 10, 1951, pp. 22 ff.

Smith, Jean Edward, *The Defense of Berlin*, Johns Hopkins Press, 1963.

The Suez Canal Problem, July 26–September 22, 1956, U. S. Department of State, 1956.

Szulc, Tad, *Dominican Diary*, Dell, 1965.

Weintal, Edward, and Charles Bartlett, *Facing the Brink*, 1967.

Wise, David, and Thomas B. Ross, *The Invisible Government*, Random House, 1964.

DOCUMENTS

There is a large number of official sources, including Department of State releases, reports of Congressional hearings and debates, periodic reports of such agencies as the Organization of American States, the International Bank for Reconstruction and Development, the European Economic Community, the Federal Reserve Board, and a host of others.

The publications of the United Nations and its subordinate organizations are too numerous to list. Many institutions, both public and private, have monthly bulletins, as well as annual reports.

The best single official source for the student is the series of volumes beginning with *A Decade of American Foreign Policy, Basic Documents, 1941–1949*, and continuing through *United States Foreign Policy: Current Documents, 1963* (these will soon be current to the previous year). Also of prime importance are the State Department monthly *Bulletins*, which include much official source material.

A few others are noted here:

An Atlas of World Affairs, Praeger, 1964.

Congressional Documents and Records of Debates.

European Economic Community, monthly bulletin.

Federal Reserve, monthly bulletin.

Foreign Agriculture.

Foreign Commerce, weekly.

Jackson, Henry M., *The Secretary of State and the Ambassador*, Jackson Subcommittee Papers on the Conduct of American Foreign Policy, Praeger, 1964. (See also: *Administration of National Security: Staff Reports and Hearings*, U. S. Government Printing Office, 1965.)

Roberts, Henry L., *Foreign Affairs Bibliography; 1952–1962*, U. S. in World Affairs, 1964.

The Series of Foreign Relations of the United States: declassified and unclassified (the lag is approximately 20 years).

Stebbins, Richard P., with Elaine P. Adam, *Documents on American Foreign Relations*, Harper & Row (for Council on Foreign Relation) (yearly).

Treasury Bulletin.

U. S. Congress, House, Committee on Foreign Affairs, *Hearings before the Subcommittee on Europe*, 89th Congress, 1966.

U. S. Congress, House, Select Committee on Communist Aggression, *Communist Aggression in Latin America*, 1954.

U. S. Congress, Senate, Committee on Foreign Relations, *A Decade of American Foreign Policy, Basic Documents, 1941–1949*, 81st Congress, 1950. (Prepared by the Staff of the Committee and the Department of State.)

U. S. Congress, Senate, Committee on Foreign Relations, *United States Foreign Policy: Compilation of Studies*, 87th Congress, 1961.

U. S. Congress, Senate, Committee on Foreign Relations, *U. S. Policy with Respect to Mainland China: Hearings*, 89th Congress, 1966.

U. S. Congress, Senate, Foreign Relations and Armed Services Committee, *The Military Situation in the Far East: Hearings*, 82nd Congress, 1951.

U. S. Congress, Senate, Subcommittee on National Security Staffing and Operations, Committee on Government Operations (Henry M. Jackson Committee), *Administration of National Security*, 88th Congress, 1965.

U. S. Congress, Senate, Committee on Foreign Relations and U. S. House of Representatives, Committee on Foreign Affairs, *Legislation on Foreign Relations with Explanatory Notes*, 88th Congress, 1965.

U. S. Department of State, Cumulative List from October, 1929 to the present.

U. S. Department of State, *Department of State Publication 7530, General Foreign Policy Series 187 (1963)*, Office of Media Services, Public Affairs Bureau.

U. S. Department of State, *Foreign Service List*, Office of Operations, Publication 7635, 1964.

U. S. Department of State, *Manpower Profile*, Office of Personnel, Departmental and Foreign Service, 1963, 1964.

U. S. Department of State, *The Record on Korean Unification, 1943–1960*, Far Eastern Series, No. 1, 1960.

U. S. Department of State, *Treaties in Force*, Treaty Affairs Staff, Office of the Legal Adviser, Publication 8042, 1966.

U. S. Treaties and Agreements with the Republic of Korea: 1945–1953, Government Printing Office, 1954.

United Nations, Year book, documents, index, and many others.

Watt, D. C., ed., *Documents on International Affairs, 1961*, Harper & Row (for Council on Foreign Relations), 1966.

INDEX

Acheson, Dean G., 9, 15, 16, 27, 45, 110, 111, 123, 128, 133, 136, 145, 218, 225, 226, 228, 229, 234

Acheson-Lilienthal Committee (1946), 156

Adenauer, Konrad, 120, 145, 198, 295

Administration of Foreign Aid, 125

Administrative functions, Secretary of State, 15–17

Adoula, Premier Cyrille, of the Congo, 200

Africa, 180, 182, 184, 200, 203, 214

    See also North Africa

Agency for International Development (AID), 15, 20, 39, 46, 47, 48, 49, 50, 190; foreign representation of, 67

Agrarian Reform Law (1952), Guatemalan, 246

Agriculture, Department of, foreign representation of, 67

Alexander, General Harold, 322

Alexander the Great, 269

Algeria, 150, 155, 162, 176, 177, 180, 191, 200, 208

Allen, Richard, 262, 263

Allende, of Chile, 204

Alliance for Progress, 132, 189–190, 200, 204, 208

Allied Control Commission, 118

Allied Control Council, 286, 290

Allied High Commission, 120

Ambassador, 39, 49, 56–75; appointment of, 16; caliber of "political" appointees, 61; career men as, 61; communication, flow of, 59; "country team," 57, 59; delegation of authority by, 68; Deputy Chief of Mission and, 59, 66; duties and responsibilities of, 56–58; executive duties of, 65–66; functions of, 58; inspection system, 72–73; intellectual demands, 64; language requirement, 63, 72; nature of job

68 69 70   7 6 5 4 3 2 1